Evaluation and Experiment

QUANTITATIVE STUDIES IN SOCIAL RELATIONS

Consulting Editor: Peter H. Rossi

UNIVERSITY OF MASSACHUSETTS
AMHERST, MASSACHUSETTS

Evaluation and Experiment

Some Critical Issues in Assessing Social Programs

EDITED BY

Carl A. Bennett

Battelle Human Affairs Research Centers
Seattle, Washington

AND

Arthur A. Lumsdaine

University of Washington
Seattle, Washington

ACADEMIC PRESS, INC.   New York   San Francisco   London

A Subsidiary of Harcourt Brace Jovanovich, Publishers

ACADEMIC PRESS RAPID MANUSCRIPT REPRODUCTION

ACADEMIC PRESS, INC.
111 Fifth Avenue, New York, New York 10003

United Kingdom Edition published by
ACADEMIC PRESS, INC. (LONDON) LTD.
24/28 Oval Road, London NW1

Library of Congress Cataloging in Publication Data

Main entry under title:

Evaluation and experiment.

    (Quantitative studies in social relations)
    "Outgrowth of a symposium held at the Battelle
Seattle Research Center in July, 1973."
    Bibliography: p.
    Includes index.
    1.   Evaluation research (Social action programs)—U-
nited States—Congresses.   I.   Bennett, Carl Allen,
(date)   II.   Lumsdaine, Arthur A.   III.   Battelle
Memorial Institute, Columbus, Ohio.   Seattle Research
Center.
H62.5.U5E87   361   75-33408
ISBN 0-12-088850-5

In accord with that part of the charge of its founder, Gordon Battelle, to assist in the further education of men, it is the commitment of Battelle to encourage the distribution of information. This is done in part by supporting conferences and meetings and by encouraging the publication of reports and proceedings. Towards that objective, this publication, while protected by copyright from plagiarism or unfair infringement, is available for the making of single copies for scholarship and research, or to promote the progress of science and the useful arts.

Contents

CONTENTS

CONTENTS

CONTENTS

7. **Feedback in Social Systems: Operational and Systemic Research on Production, Maintenance, Control and Adaptive Functions**
   Daniel Katz

8. **Assessing Alternative Conceptions of Evaluation**
   Arthur A. Lumsdaine and Carl A. Bennett

Preface

This volume is an outgrowth of a symposium held at The Battelle Seattle Research Center in July, 1973. Preliminary versions of Chapters 2, 3, 4, 6, and 7 and much of the content of Chapter 1 were presented orally and discussed by the attendees, who represented a wide range of diverse background and experience with the evaluation of social programs.

The volume focuses upon some selected aspects of the problems in evaluating the outcomes of socially important programs, such as those dealing with education, health, and economic policy; it does not attempt to provide a complete treatise on all aspects of the increasingly important field of program evaluation. Rather, it concentrates on a few major areas to which one or more papers by the contributors are addressed. A brief overview of the eight chapters of the book is given below to provide orientation and perspective.

Chapter 1 is an introductory discussion by the editors, designed to provide an initial view of the scope and major foci selected for emphasis in the book and in the 1973 Battelle symposium. This chapter attempts to identify major issues in the total area of program evaluation, so that the particular aspects of the field discussed in the chapters that follow can be viewed in a broader perspective.

Chapter 2, by John Gilbert, Richard Light, and Frederick Mosteller, incorporates a survey of the needs and bases for evaluating social innovations. It illustrates the kinds of successes and failures that such innovations seem likely to produce, by surveying about 30 examples of controlled randomized field tests conducted to ascertain the effects of various kinds of innovations in the social, socio-medical, and medical fields. This survey is followed by a supplementary examination of findings from nonrandomized studies and an analysis of the problems of the interpretations to which such studies are prone. Building on this extensive data base, the authors then discuss problems of randomization, feasibility of installing regular program evaluations, and matters of cost, timeliness, and implementation. They conclude with a presentation of a number of major findings or recommendations.

In Chapter 3, Donald Campbell and Robert Boruch deal with the case for randomized assignment of treatments by looking at the alternatives. They consider some six ways in which quasi-experimental evaluation in compensatory education tends to underestimate the true effects of such educational programs. This chapter builds on, and in some respects modifies, conclusions previously reached by Campbell and colleagues in a series of well-known papers. Though the Campbell and Boruch chapter necessarily deals with some critical matters of a technical nature, the main gist of these is presented in a way that should facilitate their understanding by decision makers who are not primarily technical specialists.

In Chapter 4, Glen Cain argues for the usefulness and validity of econometric and related nonexperimental approaches for assessing the effects of social programs. His paper was originally presented as a commentary on the presentation by Campbell at the 1973 symposium. Cain's discussion represents an important and prevalent point of view associated with the econometric tradition. Some of the points made should be read in the light of Campbell's and Boruch's criticisms in Chapter 3.

Chapter 5, by Elizabeth Hilton and Arthur Lumsdaine, complements, with a somewhat different emphasis, the examples of program evaluation presented by Gilbert, Light, and Mosteller. This chapter surveys a number of additional program-evaluation studies, in the particular field of family planning or fertility control, mostly carried out as experiments or quasi-experiments in Asian and Latin American countries. This paper is less concerned than that of Gilbert, Light, and Mosteller with assessing the overall effectiveness of programs in relation to their goals, and considers in somewhat more detail certain aspects of methodology of the studies and some of the features of design and reporting that are encountered. It also illustrates the range of rigorous and less rigorous designs which have been utilized in the population-program area, and the feasibility of conducting rigorously executed, randomized controlled field studies, particularly in developing nations.

Chapter 6, by Ward Edwards and Marcia Guttentag, addresses the total process of evaluation, with particular emphasis on decision processes that involve explicit assessment of the worth or merit of outcomes and employ multivalued utility analysis. Edwards and Guttentag contend that evaluation is done to facilitate decision making, and that evaluation research should be considered a branch of decision analysis. From this point of view, experimentation, if relevant to evaluation, will ordinarily be combined with nonexperimental logical and judgmental procedures to provide the information needed to make a decision.

Chapter 7, by Daniel Katz, deals with questions of context and constraints in the evaluation of social programs organizations. Katz outlines the ways in which evaluative data are useful in providing feedback to program or institutional operations and decisions, placing particular emphasis on the way in which organizational structures and constraints will affect the utilization of such data. He departs from the linear stimulus-response model in viewing action and reaction as a continuing circular process, and contends that more attention is needed in the social sciences to the interacting mechanisms that effect change as well as stability.

In Chapter 8, the editors review and comment on the principal issues raised by the preceding chapters and during the symposium discussions, offering some implications and suggestions with respect to program evaluation in general and the role of experimentation in particular. They also attempt to resolve some of the disagreements expressed by others concerning the role of field experiments, constraints in their utilization, and other factors that enter into a comprehensive conception of program evaluation.

Acknowledgments

The book reflects the work of many contributors to whom the editors would like to acknowledge their indebtedness and thanks.

Chapter authors or co-authors who presented preliminary versions of chapters in the volume at the symposium included

Glen G. Cain, Department of Economics, University of Wisconsin

Donald T. Campbell, Department of Psychology, Northwestern University

Ward Edwards, Social Science Research Institute, University of Southern California

Daniel Katz, Department of Psychology, University of Michigan

Frederick Mosteller, Department of Statistics, Harvard University

Other chapter co-authors participating in the symposium were

Carl A. Bennett, Battelle Human Affairs Research Centers, Seattle, Washington

John P. Gilbert, Harvard Computing Center, Cambridge, Massachusetts

Elizabeth T. Hilton, Battelle Population Study Center, Seattle, Washington

Arthur A. Lumsdaine, Department of Psychology, University of Washington

Chapter co-authors not able to attend the symposium were:

Robert F. Boruch, Department of Psychology, Northwestern University

Marcia Guttentag, Department of Social Relations, Harvard University

Richard J. Light, Department of Education, Harvard University

The symposium also included a presentation by Michael Scriven, which has been published separately (Scriven, 1975). The chapter by Hilton and Lumsdaine was developed concurrently for a separate conference and was not presented at the 1973 summer symposium, although it was discussed informally there with several of the symposium participants. The papers presented by Mosteller, Edwards, and Katz at the symposium were each followed by a prepared commentary given respectively, by the following discussants

Thomas D. Cook, Department of Psychology, Northwestern University

Robyn Dawes, Oregon Research Institute and Department of Psychology, University of Oregon

Peter H. Rossi, Department of Social Relations, Johns Hopkins University

Other symposium participants who contributed to the discussion following one or more of the papers included

John P. Conrad, The Academy for Contemporary Problems, Columbus, Ohio

Herbert L. Costner, Department of Sociology, University of Washington

Herbert C. Kelman, Department of Social Relations, Harvard University

John E. Rasmussen, Battelle Human Affairs Research Centers, Seattle, Washington

Lee B. Sechrest, Department of Psychology, Florida State University

Donald P. Warwick, Department of Sociology and Anthropology, York University

Walter Williams, Graduate School of Public Affairs, University of Washington

Transcripts of the presentations and of the portions of the discussion pertaining to each paper were furnished to the authors for their use in preparing the chapters included in this volume.

In planning the symposium during the Winter and Spring of 1973, the editors of the volume held several meetings with a small consultant group who, after considering a wide range of topics and emphases in the total field of program evaluation, selected the issues to which the symposium and the ensuing volume are mainly addressed. This group included Donald T. Campbell, Michael Scriven, and Marcia Guttentag. Elizabeth T. Hilton also participated in these preconference planning sessions.

We would like to acknowledge the assistance given by several members of the Battelle staff in making the arrangements for the symposium. In particular, we would like to thank John Rasmussen and Everett Irish for arranging the financial support from Battelle Institute; Lee Penhallurick for supervising the physical arrangements; Robert Wilton for tape recording the presentations and discussion; Jill Goodnight for preparing written minutes of the sessions and for transcribing the tapes; and Elizabeth Hilton for her invaluable role in many phases of the symposium planning and arrangement, and for preparing followup summaries of the conference sessions.

We are indebted to Renate Lammermann for secretarial assistance and for the preparation of successive drafts of several of the chapters. In the arrangements for the publication of the volume we are greatly indebted to the editorial staff at Battelle, where the final copy editing was done and camera-ready page copy was prepared. Our thanks go particularly to Carol Watts, Janice Tripp, Kathy Koerber, and other members of Battelle-Seattle's Information/Publication staff.

In addition to the editors' personal gratitude for the contributions mentioned above, acknowledgments for help received are also made by authors of several of the individual chapters of the book.

Evaluation and Experiment

1

Social Program Evaluation:
Definitions and Issues

CARL A. BENNETT and ARTHUR A. LUMSDAINE

I. INTRODUCTION

Evaluation is inherent in the planning or operation of
any program or regimen whether it is a space program, the
provision of remedial education, the furnishing of health
services, or one's personal life. Both individuals and
institutions constantly choose among alternative actions
based on their assessment of the degree to which these
actions meet their needs or assist in achieving their goals.
This assessment may be based on either theoretical or
empirical knowledge of the probable outcome of a given
action. Objectively or subjectively, consciously or sub-
consciously, we must evaluate to operate.

In recent years, societal problems have become a major
concern of federal, state, and local governments. Racism,
crime, poverty, education, health services, and a long list
of other problem areas have occupied headlines and the time
of politicians and administrators. Massive resources have
been utilized in attempts to ameliorate all these social
concerns. Yet the resources are limited and the problems
are large. As a result, those who must determine how
resources are to be employed in support of programs and
institutions to solve social problems need a rationale for
efficient allocation of the resources. Developing such a

rationale necessitates information on the relative effectiveness of alternative solutions in order to plan for the use of scarce resources. These planning efforts have generated increasing awareness of the lack of information or agreement concerning the origins of social problems and the importance of their solution, an uncertainty about the social effectiveness of the solutions proposed, and a subsequent interest in comprehensive and insightful evaluation of attempted solutions.

Complicating the situation is the fact that by and large these social programs have not been conspicuously successful. F. O. R. Hayes (1972) states the problem as follows:

> The many innovations in government programs over the last decade have not produced the results we expected or had hoped for. In my opinion, policy formulation and program development processes did not then and are not now receiving the concentrated effort and the commitment of resources that are required. This is particularly true in many of the difficult problem areas treated by government programs. We are still not doing an adequate job in the whole process of thinking through the problem and filling gaps in key program relationships. This is crucial to program choices and program design.

The frequently noted need for a more systematic approach to social problems and social innovation is the subject of a cogent analysis by Rivlin (1971), and is emphasized in the survey of social innovations by Gilbert, Light, and Mosteller (Chapter 2, this volume).

Evaluation of program impact cannot of itself identify the needs nor establish the priorities for social action, much less create the resources necessary to carry out social programs. However, the importance of such program evaluation to the process of planning and implementing action programs and insuring their success and continuation cannot be underestimated. As stated by Light, Mosteller, and Winokur (1971):

> At a time when 'consumerism' has become a major concern, programs using public funds encounter the demand that they should be carefully monitored to insure that they are in the public interest. Competent evaluation makes an important contribution to answering that demand. By measuring the effectiveness of a program, an evaluation serves the needs of Congress, the program designers, and most important of all, the program's intended beneficiaries and the taxpayers.

It is this need for systematic evaluation and feedback as a foundation for effective development of social programs that has led to the recent emphasis on evaluation designed not only to monitor performance and allocate resources, but also to provide the necessary understanding for judicious program modification and selection. The focus has been on the procedures and methodology necessary to adapt the evaluative process to the difficult task of planning, selecting, implementing, and modifying social action programs.

II. PURPOSES AND FUNCTIONS OF EVALUATION

A. DEFINITIONS AND DISTINCTIONS

Various classification schemes have been offered to structure and/or clarify the functions and components of evaluation. The value of these depends partly on the purpose to be achieved. The attempt at clarification and structuring which follows borrows from some similar previous efforts, such as those of Stufflebaum (1971) and Scriven (1967). Some other previous taxonomies that seem less suitable to the present purpose have been discarded or passed over. Part of our purpose here is to provide a perspective which may help illuminate the differences in purpose and emphasis of the discussions presented in this volume. In addition, we hope our analysis will contribute in some measure to the more general goal of resolving some sources of confusion that keep arising whenever program evaluation is discussed.

One important consideration centers around the question of what is evaluated and, secondarily, in what context and under what aegis. Evaluation can be applied to persons, programs, products, or institutions. We.pass quickly over the evaluation of persons--job or college applicants, political candidates, credit prospects, potential associates, etc.--even though this is one of the most common forms of evaluation. It has a long history in social relations and psychotherapy as well as in personnel classification, selection, and assignment, and in the development and use of psychometric devices to assist in some of these processes. We mention it here only because of its salience and the wealth of literature and effort that has been devoted to person evaluation. By contrast, program evaluation, at least as an object of conscious attention and with respect to study of its methodologies, is a newer arrival on the stage of scientific and public awareness.

An institution or program may have as one of its goals, or even its sole purpose, the turning out of specific products. Often these are material products such as automobiles, pencil sharpeners, bikinis, or books. Alternatively, the product may be a human "product"--a skill, capability or characteristic such as clerical competence, business judgment, honesty, or health. The latter kind of "products" may also be viewed as persons possessing various attributes--educated citizens, trained pilots, cured patients, etc.--in which case "product evaluation" can be seen as a form of person evaluation. The immediate point to be made here is that the evaluation of a program or institution is not coterminous with the evaluation of the products--whether they are material or human products--that it produces. For one thing, a generally effective and viable institution may occasionally turn out an unfortunate product; e.g., an Edsel or Corvair, or the black sheep of a good family or college. Also, perhaps more rarely, a third-rate institution may include some superior components; e.g., a strong department in an otherwise weak college.

Even if a program or institution has a single line of products, evaluation of the product, while a very necessary aspect, is not a sufficient basis for evaluating the institution--a company may fail, despite its turning out a good product, because it produces the product in an inefficient manner or because there is insufficient market for the product. Similarly, evaluation of a social program needs to consider not only its impact in terms of fulfilling its intended social goals, but also, among other things, its cost-efficiency in doing so. To accomplish this latter goal may well require comparative evaluation of alternative programs--that is, programs that have been designed to meet common objectives by alternative methods or procedures. Some examples of such comparative evaluations are given by Hilton and Lumsdaine in Chapter 5, and are included among the innovations discussed in Chapter 2, particularly in the medical area.

We should note both similarities and differences between evaluation of programs and of institutions. Any program designed to achieve given objectives requires some apparatus, organization, facility, or institution to carry it out. This may be either an existing facility, or one set up ad hoc to implement a particular program. Conversely, an existing institution may adopt a new program in addition to other ongoing functions, either to meet its own internal needs or to accomplish program objectives in the service of some agency that retains its services for that purpose. In either case, evaluation of the program per se overlaps but is not synonymous with evaluation of the agency or institution associated with the program. Methods for evaluation of organizations and institutions--e.g., corporations, foundations, universities, laboratories, or research and development centers--frequently differ greatly from those for evaluating programs. The differences may arise because the goals of an institution are usually more general and diverse than those of a limited, specific program; or because programs, being more like procedures than like structural entities, are likely to be more easily terminated, modified, or replicated in new locations; or because programs have specific impacts that can be more clearly isolated and measured. This volume is primarily concerned with programs; however, some of the considerations raised by Edwards and

Guttentag (Chapter 6) and, especially, by Katz (Chapter 7) may apply as much to evaluation of continuing institutions as to assessment of the impact of specific programs.

The single term "program" is commonly used to cover a considerable range of kinds or levels of programs. Within the purview of current parlance, there is a need to distinguish broad, comprehensive, far-flung, continuing, "macro" programs (e.g., the "space program," the "defense program," the "social security program") from narrower, more focused programs of limited scope and duration. The latter represent specific program innovations, treatments or procedures whose outcomes may be assessed in terms of specific impacts or effects. These specific impacts, in contrast to the cumulative and multiple outputs of "macro" programs and of continuing institutions, normally can more readily be gauged empirically over a definite period of time, in more circumscribed locales, and in comparison with the impacts of alternative treatments, including no-treatment control conditions.

B. *EVALUATION AS PART OF THE FEEDBACK PROCESS*

Within program evaluation a useful distinction concerns major phases in the genesis and implementation of specific program innovations to which evaluation may be applied. Let us distinguish five phases:

- Evaluating needs or deficiencies that give rise to the initiation of a program;

- Evaluating plans for the conduct of the program;

- Monitoring actual <u>operations</u> of the program, including interim (or "formative") evaluations useful in tactical, day-to-day or month-to-month decisions about program operations;

- Ascertaining determinable cumulative (or "summative") <u>impact(s)</u> the program has produced by the end of a major phase of operation; and

- Making strategic or policy level <u>decisions</u> concerning program continuation, for which impact determination is a major (but by no means the sole) input.

Both the fourth and fifth steps of this sequence are sometimes referred to as "summative" evaluation; usage in this respect is not highly standardized.

These phases of program genesis and implementation represent a specific adaptation of a more general procedure which, with suitable modification, applies to a much broader class of activity. The determination of need, the development of plans, the monitoring of operations, the measurement of impact, and the making of policy level decisions have been recognized as integral parts of the management process in a wide variety of enterprises. The need for "measurement" or "control" as an integral part of industrial management has been recognized for many years, but recent emphasis on "professional management" has pointed out the key role played by evaluation and measurement in a successful management process. The concept of evaluation as part of the planning-action-evaluation cycle is discussed by Caro (1971), with emphasis on the fact that the cycle may have to be repeated many times before the ultimate objectives of the program are realized. Evaluation in this sense is part of the process of planned change, and the utilization of evaluative findings in decisions with respect to the continuance of or changes in a program becomes the key concern.

In terms of the phases in program development and operation that are given above, three successively broader feedback loops can be distinguished: 1) immediate process monitoring; 2) changes in the planned program, based on measurement of output or impact; and 3) policy-level decisions concerning the continuing need for a program.

1. **Process monitoring.** This is immediate feedback analogous to the production control function of an industrial enterprise. It is concerned primarily with whether the program or process is being carried out as planned. Process specifications or standards of performance are established in advance, and the actual program activities are contrasted to these standards. The focus in this approach is on input, most frequently measured in terms of program activities and services, although this is sometimes expanded to include the input of program clients. In any case, the feedback is relatively immediate and is directed toward increasing the correspondence between operational plans and actual activities, or otherwise trying to improve the ongoing operation of the program.

2. **Feedback based on output measurement.** Caro (1971) distinguishes the present emphasis on "evaluative research" from other forms of evaluation on the basis that it is concerned with the outputs or effects of a program rather than input. Astin and Panos (1971) point out that true evaluation must consider not only inputs and outputs, but also the operational treatment designed to produce change and the extent to which it interacts with the changes which would have taken place in the absence of a program. These

9

approaches reflect consideration of a second and broader feedback loop based on the measurement of the output of a program and on the relationship of this output to the program activities. The important questions are: "What was the impact of the program?" and "How should the activities which constitute the program be changed in order to increase its effectiveness?"

This second feedback loop is analogous to the quality control or product assurance function of the usual industrial enterprise. By determining whether the product is meeting specifications or meeting the intended need, we can change the program or decide how to modify the process to produce the desired product or impact. To use this feedback effectively, we must either theoretically or empirically determine the nature of the modification required to produce the desired improvement in product quality or to change the impact of a program. The importance of an evolutionary approach to evaluative feedback in social programs, similar to Box's conception of adaptive process control or evolutionary operation in industrial processing, is emphasized by Gilbert, Light, and Mosteller in Chapter 2.

3. _Policy-level decisions._ This level of evaluative feedback is concerned with the question of whether a program, production process, or institution should be initiated or continued. It is analogous to the question of whether or not a business is potentially or currently profitable, which involves a larger feedback loop that includes the customer, management, and the finance and engineering departments. Decisions here may involve not only technical problems of production, but engineering problems of design, financial problems as to the cost of raw materials, and problems

involved in producing a product that will satisfy the consumer at a price he is willing to pay.

The nature of feedback systems can be significantly affected by the end product of the program or organization being evaluated; i.e., whether the purpose of the activity (as discussed in the preceding section) is to produce a product, to implement a program, to develop a process, or to test a principle. A product as such can be evaluated independently of the process by which it was produced. The feedback here has to do with the intended utilization of the product, rather than with the means of production. On the other hand, social programs are usually designed to produce change, not uniquely identifiable products for consumption. As mentioned previously, the distinction must clearly be made between determining whether the activities or the program are being carried out as planned, on the one hand, and whether the planned activities have the impact intended, on the other. Ultimately, it is necessary to determine whether the whole process of planning, action, and evaluation is leading to an optimum utilization of resources.

The levels of evaluation considered above would typically involve the research and engineering function of an industrial enterprise as well as its production or quality control functions, since they depend on an ability to determine and implement necessary process modifications and improvements. In physical processes, this information is frequently obtained by recourse to laboratory or pilot plant experimentation. Social programs by and large do not have such access to the laboratory or to a vast store of precise process theory, and are forced into the undesirable position of doing "in-plant" experimentation. This necessity underlies several of the major issues considered in this volume.

Another major issue is raised by the fact that the third level of evaluation requires the "valuation," at least in terms of trade-off, of the impacts produced by different social programs. We are faced, for example, not just with the comparison of different approaches to crime reduction, but the comparative advantages of spending a million dollars to rehabilitate 100 criminals or a million dollars to hire 100 extra teachers in ghetto schools. Causal evaluation based on controlled field experiments can help at the second level, but stops short of research on value structures that is required for evaluating and feeding back social information at the third level (see also Chapter 6).

C. *RELATION OF OUTPUT MEASURES TO THE FEEDBACK PROCESS*

From the point of view of the informational requirements for evaluative feedback, Katz points out (Chapter 7, this volume) that simple measures based on specific targets can be very misleading, and can not only distort the information process but corrupt the functioning of the program or organization. In particular, it is possible for the immediate target to be in conflict with long-range goals. There are instances in large industrial organizations where an immediate year-by-year emphasis on profits has been detrimental to long-term business goals. Systematic information about secondary effects of the operation of an institution is often not only unknown but unwanted. The drug industry may, for example, not be able to anticipate the total long-range effects of developments such as the "pill," which gives an immediate solution to the problem of preventing pregnancy, but may have unanticipated long-range side effects. Obviously, the problem is especially difficult when the unanticipated outcomes are both slow to appear and highly negative in terms of their impact.

The possible outcomes of a program can be classified (or, alternatively, scaled on appropriate axes) as desirable or undesirable; short-range or long-range; and anticipated or unanticipated. It is then obvious that because of either necessity or expediency, much more emphasis will be placed on anticipated, short-range, desirable effects than on unanticipated, long-range, undesirable effects. The problem is an old one; there is always a tendency to act on what can be measured rather than to determine what knowledge is necessary in order to act. Even if this fact is recognized, how can long-range, unanticipated effects be objectively considered if they are by definition unknown or unavailable?

The distinction between research and management, scientist and manager, is amplified by this dilemma. There is an old adage that a manager is concerned with arriving at a decision (good or bad) on the basis of the information available, whereas a scientist is concerned with determining the information necessary to make the decision (which is always more than what he has!). Since evaluation is involved with decision, the basic problem is then to decide whether additional information is required, and how it can be acquired. Katz (Chapter 7, this volume) contends that improvement of the informational content of feedback systems is probably the major way in which social scientists can contribute to the improvement of system functioning.

D. *SOME QUESTIONS ABOUT THE PURPOSE AND UTILIZATION OF EVALUATION*

Against the background of the preceding sections, some recurrent questions which pervade the extensive literature on evaluation can be considered. These include the scope of the evaluation and the role of the evaluator, the possibility of using evaluative procedures and data as a basis for acquiring fundamental knowledge as well as for making decisions, and the utilization of evaluative findings as a basis for planning and intervention. The first and third of these questions are closely tied together, since the role of the evaluator will frequently determine whether intervention is possible and whether plans can be modified based on evaluative results.

1. Role of the Evaluator

One determinant of the evaluator's role is the nature of the intended outcomes and the degree to which the criteria of "success" can be quantified. By and large, products can be relatively easily evaluated in terms of the needs they fulfill or the specifications they must meet. Consumer agencies can evaluate merchandise in terms of the degree to which they meet fixed criteria or fulfill their purpose. Inspectors can determine whether manufactured products meet specifications. Teachers give students grades which indicate their success or failure in a course or examination. But the success of a social program is seldom so easy to measure, since it may involve not only multiple criteria but also different value structures.

Considering evaluation as a feedback process extends its role to include the organizational context in which evaluation takes place and the evaluator's relation to other agents in this context. By and large, the pressure for evaluation in social programs has come from the sponsors and project monitors, not from the program directors. Many, if not most, social program directors are convinced that evaluation is a necessary evil imposed from above which interferes with accomplishing their service or research objectives. Until evaluation becomes a concern at all levels, and is built on a foundation of feedback at the program level, there is likely to be little progress in solving the major problems of resource allocation and sound management at the state or federal level. Program directors will continue to be convinced, not wholly without reason, that objective evaluation can "kill" their program, and will continue to minimize evaluative feedback as a means of improving the operation.

This same attitude has a direct bearing on the utilization of evaluative findings. Carol Weiss (1973) has deplored the fact that, by and large, evaluative reports gather dust on the shelves of the sponsor, and neither affect present operations and future planning nor provide understanding of the social processes involved. One way of solving this problem is to make the program director part of the evaluation process, and to support those managers who realistically appraise their programs or operations and modify them accordingly. Campbell (1971) has pointed out that present day bureaucratic structures do not tend to reward this type of behavior, since political survival is likely to be based on "success" rather than "realism."

2. Evaluation for Understanding As Well As for Decision

The preceding discussion has emphasized the utilization of feedback information for predicting outcomes and making decisions. Obviously, in social program research there is also the possibility of utilizing evaluative information to obtain understanding of the social processes involved. Two types of issues arise here.

The first is conflict between research and service goals, and the possibility that this conflict may interfere with the total collection of data called for by research designs (Caro, 1971). The fact that there are very few "laboratories" for social experimentation means that it is always necessary to gather research data in the field. When the research design calls for action inconsistent with immediate service goals, the research needs are frequently disregarded.

This reaction is not unique to social programs. Few industrial enterprises will run in-plant experiments which involve the risk of production losses. The difference lies in the previously noted fact that these enterprises have recourse to "laboratory" investigations which can be used to solve production problems or improve production processes. Social experimentation, for the most part, must take place in the field. The difficulty of obtaining process understanding and determining causal relationships under these circumstances has been recognized for years. In particular, Wold (1956) discussed the need for statistical methodology to deal with "observational" data. The methodological discussion in Chapters 3 and 4 of this volume addresses various aspects of this problem. To add to the difficulty, there are frequently ethical and political constraints which may deter the proper conduct of controlled field experiments even where they are otherwise feasible. However, Gilbert, Light and Mosteller point out (Chapter 2, this volume) that the alternative to randomized controlled field trials may be even more detrimental.

The second issue involved in the utilization of evaluative information is the extent to which process understanding is necessary to the performance of the evaluative function. More specifically, can evaluative data be properly interpreted and utilized without understanding the basic theory or principles underlying the program or process being evaluated? Can findings based on outcome alone be implemented--i.e., intelligently modified, exported to new locations or situations, or even applied in the changing context of the immediate future--without understanding the causal relationships between program activities and program impact? We must concern ourselves with the degree to which the evaluation processes applied to social programs can or should contribute to derived generalizations which will provide a theory on which to base future program planning.

III. METHODOLOGY IN IMPACT ASSESSMENT

A. *SOME GENERAL CONSIDERATIONS*

The preceding section has emphasized the need for evaluation as an integral part of the selection, planning, and administration of social programs. This need has long been recognized in organizational management, and most managers recognize the fundamental importance both of performance measurement and of feedback of this assessment into the planning process. Much recent methodological research has been directed towards the quantitative measurement of program impact necessary for planning, control, and decision making. Methods for quantifying the decision processes involved have formed a large part of the content of operations research and management science efforts. Emphasis in recent years on cost-benefit analysis as a support to program planning, selection, and modification also reflects this trend toward objective decision processes, such as those discussed by Edwards and Guttentag (Chapter 6, this volume).

All of the methodological problems associated with the evaluation of technical and scientific programs are amplified in the case of societal programs. For example, even when reliable descriptive measures of the outcome of a social program can be formulated, the relative importance or value still varies with the individual and/or the environment, and trade-offs between the effects measured are difficult to formulate. Because of the human factors involved in both treatment and response, true experimentation is difficult. Widely accepted standards of reporting for assuring the credibility of evidence in support of claimed impacts are lacking, and the validity of data put forth in support of cause-and-effect relationships is often difficult to assess from the evidence presented. But the long-term approach required to develop a quantitative basis for decisions comes into competition with the short-term need for action based on the present state of knowledge, however inadequate. Assuming that we make the best decisions possible from the information available is no guarantee that these decisions will be good decisions, as is convincingly demonstrated by the survey and analysis of social innovations by Gilbert, Light, and Mosteller (Chapter 2, this volume). Balance is needed between the necessity for a decision and its quality. It is unfortunate that the decision pressures are frequently greatest in those areas where the least information is available.

Good methodology is crucial if we are to garner sound and useful results, but it is only a means to an end rather than an end in itself. What kinds of methods are best depends on what kind of questions we want to answer. Thus, a methodologist's role is only to assist those who pose the questions or problems for which it is his business, qua methodologist, to help them find answers. Methods that may be useful in program development and evaluation include field experiments, quantitative surveys of various sorts, and qualitative research, such as historical description and informal qualitative observation, including the case study. These three--experimentation, survey research, and qualitative-descriptive observation--illustrate differentiation along a so-called "hard-soft" dimension. Obviously, they differ not only in the techniques used, but also in terms of the purposes best served by each, and, as pointed out by Campbell (Chapter 3, this volume), in terms of the equivocality of the results obtained.

This methodological choice is one aspect of a more general issue, the extremes of which are sometimes characterized by a "cold-objective" vs. a "warm-participatory" approach to evaluation. The concern here is not merely with

the equivocality of the results but also with their interpretation and relevance, and emphasizes the fact that methodology, whether descriptive or inferential, experimental or
nonexperimental, can seldom obtain valid results unless
closely associated with substantive knowledge of the process
being studied. Objective experimental procedures which are
designed to unequivocally answer the wrong question are of
little use. In the context of statistical experimentation
and analysis, this need for continuous interchange between
methodologist and researcher has been explored by A. W.
Kimball (1957). The problem seems to be to combine validity
of the question with validity of the answer; to combine the
ability to determine causal relationships within the system
with valid criteria for determining their relative importance. The issue is not resolved by claiming that "soft,"
subjective evaluation is inherently more sensitive to the
true concerns of the people involved, or more sensitive to
long-range goals and unanticipated outcomes. Rather, it
becomes a question of balancing the measurable against the
unmeasurable; theoretical knowledge against empirical know-
how; and the concerns of the participant against the concerns of the investigator. This choice is closely related
to evaluative purpose (whether summative or formative,
external or internal), and to the level of evaluative feedback involved (process monitoring, program direction and
administration, or program planning and selection).

B. *DATA NEEDS AND ANALYSIS*

There are several ways to classify the kinds of data
and analyses needed for evaluative purposes. One which

closely follows the description of evaluative activities given earlier is as follows:

1. Background data, involving determination of the current status of relevant situations and of behavioral, economic, demographic, and other conditions; and thereby identifying specific needs and, perhaps, gauging the relative urgency of various needs. The primary purpose of gathering this type of information is to determine program needs and baselines. For this purpose, informal observational studies and descriptive analysis often seem to be the best first step in order to clarify the nature of the problems before undertaking more ambitious quantitative studies. Sample survey data usually provide the best way to confirm observed tendencies thus suggested, and to determine magnitudes of problem variables.

2. Exploratory-heuristic qualitative research, including analysis of background and survey data designed to 1) suggest what to look for, identify important variables to be taken into account, and suggest interrelations, causes, or program emphasis; and 2) indicate research needs and priorities.

3. Tentative program outcomes, based on obtaining interim or preliminary evidence on apparent effects of programs. These outcomes serve as the basis for "formative evaluation" of programs or campaigns and constitute the first level of internal feedback.

4. Demonstrated program or treatment outcomes, involving the ascertainment of the actual effects a program produces, or of the comparative effects of alternative treatments or program variables by direct experimental test when possible. Such "summative evaluation" of the program

proper can lead also to feedback of the results into the planning and selection of future programs.

One requirement which is apparent in this classification is the need for analytical techniques ranging from exploratory data analysis to confirmatory experimentation. In particular, there is a need to recognize that in science or evaluation the prelude to true experiments that are designed to confirm a hypothesis or demonstrate program effectiveness must be exploratory analyses that provide a basis for hypothesis formulation or for the identification of apparent effects. Classical statistical methods for hypothesis testing and experimental design have not provided a satisfactory basis for this type of analysis. Much of the use of regression analysis in social research has been directed toward exploration rather than confirmation, and both the use and misuse of this tool is probably a good indication of the need. The development of computer based systems for "ransacking" data is another result of the basic desire to explore data and obtain indications of possible effects and/or relationships. Arguments for the validity of conclusions from nonobservational data are in many respects similar to the arguments made by Scriven (1975) for the validity of evaluative conclusions reached by the "modus operandi" method of analysis. One basic problem is whether or not the model used for analysis is grounded in theory or suggested by the data. This is the essential argument in the empirical, economic approach suggested by Cain (Chapter 4, this volume) as an alternative to true experimentation. The question is whether the model is an established reality or an analytical tool.

Whether we need exploration or experiment frequently depends on whether we want indications or conclusions. This in turn brings us back to the purpose of the inquiry. The basic problem is that of choosing appropriate methods with respect to both the stage of the investigation and the nature of the data. We need to be clear whether the objective is a preliminary hearing or a formal trial; whether we are searching for ideas and hypotheses or confirming theory and determining causal relationships; and whether the data being analyzed are observational (uncontrolled perturbation), quasi-experimental (concomitant serendipitous perturbation), or experimental (deliberate, controlled perturbation).

It is an unfortunate fact that in the behavioral and social sciences we are still largely in a position of dependence on empirical determination of program impacts, rather than being able to make confident, verifiable predictions of impact from available theory. The familiar technological approach of the physical sciences (which proceeds from basic research to applied research to development to pilot plant to full-scale production) is not likely to be successful in the absence of a substantial theory. The inner workings of our social black boxes must generally be inferred, not derived. Gilbert, Light, and Mosteller have noted (Chapter 2, this volume) that innovation is more desirable, and usually more difficult, than evaluation. Similarly, the insight and understanding gained from exploratory data analysis is at least as important as the confirmation of hypotheses and postulated effects obtained through designed experiments. The latter seeks to confirm

that we have the right answer, while the former helps assure
that we have the right problem.

IV. ASSESSMENT AND VALUE JUDGMENTS

A. *VALUES AND EVALUATION*

One of the most important questions philosophy can pose
to those who rule (or vice versa!) is what values in a
society we should seek to maximize. We do not take the
position that this age-old question of values is inherently
and forever an unanswerable one. But behavioral scientists
seldom find a good answer through prevailing methods of
research inquiry; indeed, it is debatable whether the
methods necessary to support a defensible answer with
convincing evidence are at hand. Some progress has been
made in determining methods of description and measurement
of social variables, and in adapting and developing methods
for inferring relationships among such variables. But in
the final analysis, most decisions require not only
measurement and the understanding of causal relationships
between inputs and outputs, but also the development of a
value structure that enables the comparison of outcomes,
trade-offs between them, and the balancing of output value
against input cost.[1]

---

[1]In common usage, the word "evaluation" can have two quite
different (and, in a sense, almost opposed) meanings,
corresponding to the two meanings of the root word, as in

One may regard choosing or weighing measurable outcomes as primarily a substantive rather than a methodological problem. Of course, conceptual issues seldom have methodological solutions; one does not solve the problem of asking the wrong question by devising a better method of answering the question as posed. The importance of exploratory analysis for determining the right questions is reflected in the claim that, in the conduct and evaluation of social programs, substantive ignorance dominates methodological ignorance. A meaningful parallel in the area of educational research is the contrast between research on how to teach something and on what to teach. It profits you little to have a better method of teaching if you are teaching the

---

"numerical value" vs. "value judgment." Some hold that an emphasis on the reporting of program effectiveness in terms of output data often should be primarily descriptive, rather than "evaluative" in the sense of passing judgment on the desirability of different kinds of objectives. In the case of educational programs, the aim of such descriptive data is to provide a clear picture of what a particular program will do--e.g., will teach--under one or more conditions of use, rather than to pass judgment on what the program should accomplish. This leaves it still to be decided whether the kinds of outcomes that demonstrably can be realized are in fact the ones that it is desirable to attain. Even more difficult judgments are involved, of course, in decisions as to whether demonstrated outcomes are commensurate with the cost of attaining them, or in weighing the trade-offs between concurrent desired and undesired outcomes.

wrong things. Whether or not you are, of course, involves a value judgment. However, the question of what to teach need not remain wholly in the realm of opinion, but is to some extent susceptible to experimental inquiry.[1]

B. *CRITERION FORMULATION*

Formal statements of optimization problems recognize three essential parts: 1) the characterization of the system to be optimized, and the variables by which the state of the system can be measured; 2) the functional relationships among the variables, which determine the dynamic nature of system changes; and 3) the determination of the property of the system that is to be optimized, as well as the constraints under which the system must operate. For both decision theorists and operations analysts, the last of these has generally proved the most difficult. Complexities arise rapidly when outputs become incommensurable and/or "success" is not a well-defined function of the measurable

---

[1]For example, suppose you have defined some basic competences that you want to create by education. You can raise the question, in terms of transfer of training, of whether the things now being taught actually lead to the later competences or dispositions that have been agreed to be desirable goals--e.g., the attributes of a technically qualified specialist or of an informed, productive, and useful citizen. Likewise, empirical data may help illuminate other value issues.

characteristics of the system. Roughly speaking, the problems are those of establishing trade-offs between the variables measured, and determining the weights to be attached
in making a value judgment. A basic issue is whether or not
it is the role of the evaluator to attempt to determine and
apply a value structure, or whether comparisons based on
simple measures will suffice. Methods have been developed
for quantifying trade-offs between differently measured
values, through the empirical establishment of scale transformations based on subjective evaluation of selected cases.
But while we can establish mechanisms to objectively analyze
and exhibit subjective judgments, our ultimate recourse is
to substantive knowledge and/or experience. Problems of
this kind are further discussed by Edwards and Guttentag
(Chapter 6, this volume).

Several additional problems arise when the criterion of
success is a weighted function of several outcomes, even if
a common metric is available. For a given program, it may
be more important that certain results eventuate than
others. In terms of a physical analogy, for a particular
purpose the tensile strength of material might be very
important, but the compression strength might be less critical, while its resistance to oxidation at high temperatures
might be unimportant because it is not going to encounter
high temperatures. In educational programs, while it might
be somewhat desirable that people learn certain facts of
history, this may be relatively unimportant as an outcome in
comparison with their acquiring an appreciation of the
importance of a particular concept. In family planning
programs, it might be relatively unimportant which of
several methods of contraception is adopted as long as

people become motivated and take effective action to adopt some method. These examples emphasize the fact that the criterion may not be a simple linear function of outcomes.

A further problem is the common tendency to assess programs in terms of things that are convenient to measure. An important special case is the difficulty of measuring this year the outcomes that are only going to eventuate several years hence (of which one has at best only a very unreliable prediction). We may have quite precise measures of immediate effects, but the longer range effects, which are less well measured if measured at all, may represent the outcomes that are the most important. This can place us in the strange position of having to weight indices of program impact in inverse proportion to the reliability with which they can be measured.

It is, of course, characteristic of social programs that the value structure which relates success to the out-comes of a program will vary from individual to individual. There is seldom any "true" criterion function, but only one which represents some type of average, or consensus, of a group. When individuals' criteria of success differ mark-edly, optimization or evaluation based on a group criterion may be unsatisfactory for several reasons. For one thing, if individuals differ widely in the importance they place on different outcomes, so that there is little consensus, we can end up with a criterion that does not truly represent the important interests of any individual. The situation is similar to the dark horse candidate of the political conven-tion who wins because he is acceptable to everybody without being the first choice of anybody. The group criterion becomes a sort of lowest common denominator. Moreover, a positive group outcome may include a substantial negative impact on a large fraction of the individuals in the group. In either case, it may be better to look for solutions that are acceptable with respect to several criteria, rather than optimal with respect to a single criterion.

Another important question is whether either the goals of a program or the criteria on which they are based should be fixed in advance, and by whom. If the needs to be satisfied are well defined, then the criteria for satisfying these needs and the level of performance required probably can be clearly specified. But this still does not take care of unanticipated outcomes which are not directly related to established goals, nor does it assure that the needs will be fulfilled in any optimum fashion. Some mechanism is necessary, both for modification of the input required to fulfill the need, and for modification of the process in order to take into account impacts on and changes in the program environment. Both blind adherence to a fixed objective and after-the-fact definition of program success are undesirable extremes. In Chapter 7 (this volume), Katz points out some of the problems that arise from the former. The latter approach is an open invitation to random motion.

V. SOME ORGANIZATIONAL AND ETHICAL ISSUES

In Section III, the role of the evaluator was discussed with respect to its impact on methodological requirements, and in the last section the relationship of this role to the establishment of criteria and value structures was touched upon. We have suggested that, ideally, social program evaluation should be an integral part of the planning-action-evaluation cycle; should be concerned with "formative" as well as "summative" evaluation; and should be based on a complete and comprehensive understanding of the purpose of the program and the associated criteria for determining success in terms of recognized impacts. It is important that the evaluator be equipped with the appropriate methodology for measuring outcomes and determining value structures to achieve these ends. It is also necessary that his relationship to the program and his understanding of program goals and objectives be such that these features of comprehensive evaluation can be effectively incorporated.

Too often, the evaluation of social programs takes place after the fact rather than as a planned part of the program. Yet the usual experience is that attempts to decide how a program should be evaluated lead to reorientation, as well as needed elaboration, of the program's purposes. These changes should be incorporated into the process of program planning and development, rather than being tacked on as an after-thought after the program is under way. How to make the concept of continuous evaluation and feedback politically and operationally acceptable during all phases of planning and implementing a program is an open question.

Social programs have been characterized by the frequent inability or unwillingness of program directors and monitors to quantify objectives and goals at higher levels of the planning process. This is in part due to the difficulty, in the absence of established theory, of bridging the gap between intuitive concepts of program success and available, measurable outcomes or impacts. It may also be due in part to unwillingness of either program directors or program sponsors to commit themselves to an a priori definition of success which might not be achieved. In any case, explicit recognition of the criteria by which success or failure of an experimental program will be judged is very important in order to insure the program's contribution to the eventual solution of a social problem.

Program directors should be responsible for seeing that the program is carried out as planned (input evaluation), but they may not be held responsible for the failure of the assumed relationship between input and impact on which the program is based. In the absence of a clear distinction between those parts of the program which are or are not their responsibility or under their control, they will con- tinue to operate defensively. Sacrifice of personal advantage to the common good as a part of an "experimenting society" is still not a generally accepted norm of indi- vidual conduct.

The perennial questions of in-house versus external evaluation and internal versus external criteria are inti- mately tied to the perceived purposes of the program and of the evaluative feedback. By and large, if the expected out- put of the program can be clearly defined in terms of measurable impacts, then there may be little need for the imposition of external criteria or evaluation on the inputs. Conflicts usually arise when the product or desired process impact cannot be clearly defined, so that internal and external evaluative efforts are directed primarily at either inputs or intermediate goals. At best, this situation will lead to multiple responsibility for program direction; at

worst, it will lead to different internal and external criteria of program success. For example, externally imposed
criteria for the evaluation of a mental health program could
be concerned only with the number of patients treated, the
utilization of facilities, and other numerical data concerning program operation, while internal assessment might be
based on clinical evaluation of treatment effectiveness and
on responsiveness to individual patient need--or vice versa.
If none of these criteria can be related unambiguously to
the impact of the program on community mental health, there
can be little agreement as to which evaluation properly
measures the "success" of the program.

An organization can seldom function properly without a
consistent hierarchy of goals and objectives derived from
the overall purpose of the organization. Given the loosely
structured organization of social programs, it is not aston-
ishing that the internal feedback and formative evaluation
necessary to complement external summative evaluation is
frequently lacking, nor that internal and external criteria
are frequently in conflict. Such problems are considered in
some detail by Katz in Chapter 7.

Even if the experimentation required for impact determination and evaluative feedback is technically feasible,
there are still constraints on its effective use. The constraints imposed by the requirements of field as compared
with laboratory experimentation may be formidable, though
they are a matter of degree rather than kind. But all programs involving people are particularly subject to ethical
constraints, and even where these are not present it is
difficult to divorce social programs at the federal, state,

and local level from financial constraints and political considerations.

There are at least two separate problems with respect to the ethical constraints on social and behavioral experiments. The first has to do with the feasibility of "true" experimentation without violating the rights of individuals. Classical experimental procedures require the random assignment of treatments, including nontreatment, to experimental subjects; this will necessarily mean that some people who might benefit from a treatment will not receive it, at least immediately. Gilbert, Light, and Mosteller shed some needed illumination on this problem in Chapter 2 (particularly in Section VI). The situation is, of course, compounded if it is necessary to deceive the individual in order to avoid confounding the selection process with the treatment itself. Present concerns with social experimentation are heavily oriented toward these ethical problems.

The second problem, which may or may not involve experimentation, is the problem of data access. A major stumbling block in setting up information systems to gather evaluative data has been the protection of the confidentiality of information on individuals. This is particularly true in medical and legal programs, where there is a long tradition of confidentiality in the doctor-patient and lawyer-client relationship. But invasion of privacy has also become an issue in other areas, and it is clearly an important problem facing those attempting to evaluate social programs. People are becoming increasingly reluctant to participate in surveys, and the response rate even for reputable organizations in the survey research field is steadily dropping. Given the fact that individual differences in the response to treatment are often the largest source of uncertainty in social program evaluation, this tendency toward prevention of access to individualized data is in direct conflict with the need for better evaluative procedures and the requirements for improved social research and analysis.

VI. CRITICAL ISSUES

The preceding discussion has suggested something of the complexity of social program evaluation and the multiplicity of facets in relation to which the problem of evaluation must be viewed. Various people--among them Edwards and Guttentag in Chapter 6 of this volume--have remarked on what they call "the confusing diversity of current evaluation practice." The very term "evaluation" has, as they and others have noted, a sometimes bewildering variety of meanings and connotations. For example, the notion of assessing short-term program impacts as reliably as possible seems to dominate the thinking of some, while the process of arriving at a decision from complex and often subjective inputs is uppermost in the minds of others. For some, "evaluation" necessarily connotes value judgments and subjectivity; for others, a quest for hard, objective data seems to be of the essence for valid evaluation. Like the proverbial blind men and the elephant, it sometimes seems necessary, if there is to be communication rather than confusion, to specify on each occasion what aspect or conception of the subject one is talking about.

Of the critical issues that seem to us to emerge most clearly from this initial chapter, and from the evidence and arguments presented by our contributing authors in the chapters that follow, we would single out the following four questions as being perhaps most salient:

- What are the methods that seem most reliable, and most fruitful to further develop and apply, for ascertaining the demonstrable impacts of social programs, including both the larger effects and the smaller but still important ones that are potentially cumulative?

- What are the uses both of impact data and of other information as feedback to provide the basis for practical decisions concerning the initiation, operation, continuation, termination or redirection of programs?

- What models and procedures seem best suited for integrating complex informational inputs--including "facts," "judgments" and "values"--in the making of these programmatic (and organizational) decisions?

- How may we seek the best balance between the emphasis on here-and-now decisions, which must always be based on partial information, and the quest for an understanding of social program dynamics, which may provide an improved basis for choices among alternatives in the planning of future programs?

The first question is a major concern of Gilbert, Light, and Mosteller in Chapter 2, and is the main concern of Campbell and Boruch in Chapter 3, of Cain in Chapter 4, and of Hilton and Lumsdaine in Chapter 5. The second issue

35

is addressed, directly or indirectly, in Chapters 2, 5, and 6, and particularly in Katz's discussion (Chapter 7) concerning organizational feedback and decision making. The third question, parts of which are also addressed by Katz, is the central concern of Edwards and Guttentag in Chapter 6.

If there is one issue on which we especially wish more could be said here, it is the fourth one, involving as it does fundamental questions of understanding versus decision, science versus application or technology, and shorter-term versus longer-term perspectives and payoffs. This issue, though at least touched on either explicitly or implicitly by several of the book's contributors, remains high on our agenda as a critical issue for future consideration. We return to it briefly in Chapter 8, where we try to suggest some of the facets of this complex question that call for further close attention.

REFERENCES

Astin, A. W., & Panos, R. S. The evaluation of educational
programs. In R. L. Thorndike (Ed.), Educational Measurement. Washington, D.C.: American Council on Education,
1971.

Campbell, D. T. Methods for the experimenting society.
Invited address presented at the annual meeting of the
American Psychological Association, Washington, D. C.
September 1971. In press.

Caro, F. Evaluation research: An overview. In F. Caro
(Ed.), Readings in evaluation research. New York:
Russell Sage Foundation, 1971.

Hayes, F. O'R. The process of policy formulation and
resource management. Session on Managing urban resources: A report on the mayor's seminar on policy formulation and resource management. Washington, D. C.:
Government of the District of Columbia, 1972.

Kimball, A. W. Errors of the third kind in statistical consulting. Journal of the American Statistical Association, 1957, 52, 133.

Light, R. J., Mosteller, F., & Winokur, H. S., Jr. Using
controlled field studies to improve public policy. In
President's report on federal statistics (Vol. 2). Washington, D.C.: U. S. Government Printing Office, 1971.

Rivlin, A. Systematic thinking for social action. Washington, D.C.: Brookings Institution, 1971.

Scriven, M. The methodology of evaluation. In R. W. Tyler,
R. M. Gagne, & M. Scriven (Eds.), Perspectives of curric-
ulum evaluation. AERA Monograph Series on Curriculum
Evaluation, No. 1. Chicago: Rand McNally & Co., 1967.

Scriven, M. Maximizing the power of causal investigations:
The modus operandi method. In W. James Popham (Ed.),
Evaluation in education: Current applications. Berke-
ley: McCutcheon, 1975.

Stufflebaum, D. L., et al. Educational evaluation and decision making. Itasca, Ill.: F. E. Peacock Publishers,
Inc., 1971.

Weiss, C. H. Between the cup and the lip. Evaluation,
1973, 1(2), 49-55.

Wold, H. A. D. Causal inference from observational data: A review of ends and means. _Journal of the Royal Statistical Society_, Series A, 1956, _119_, Part I, 28-61.

2

Assessing Social Innovations:
An Empirical Base for Policy

JOHN P. GILBERT, RICHARD J. LIGHT, and
FREDERICK MOSTELLER

I. THE GENERAL IDEA

How effective are modern large-scale social action
programs? To see how well such programs accomplish their
primary mission, we have reviewed the performance of a large
number. At the same time, we have also examined methods of
evaluation and their possible contribution toward social
improvements. We particularly focus on evaluations that
identify causal effects because they provide the most direct
means for learning how to increase program effectiveness.

Reviewing these programs and their evaluations nas led
us to some fresh insights. We invite the reader to join us
in looking at the data and considering some of their implications for choosing methods of evaluation. Our examples
are drawn from public and private social action programs,
from applied social research, and from studies in medicine
and mental illness. Thus, though our writing is oriented
especially to policy-makers in government, the findings
should also be informative to investigators in the fields of
applied social research and to those who fund them.

In our collection of well-evaluated innovations, we
find few with marked positive effects. Even innovations
that turned out to be especially valuable often had relatively small positive effects--gains of a few percent, for

example, or larger gains for a small subgroup of the population treated. Because even small gains accumulated over time can sum to a considerable total, they may have valuable consequences for society. In addition, understanding the causes of even small specific gains may form a basis for evolutionary improvements in the programs. The empirical findings for the programs described here emphasize the frequent importance of detecting small effects and, since these are difficult to measure, the need for well-designed and well-executed evaluations. Many would agree that, where practical and feasible, randomized field trials are currently the technique of choice for evaluating the results of complex social innovations. Our data suggest that such careful evaluations may be needed much more often in the future if society is to reap the full benefits of its expenditures for new programs.

While realizing the theoretical effectiveness of randomized trials, investigators often use nonrandomized trials for a variety of practical reasons, including apparently lower costs and easier execution. When we examine the findings of well-executed nonrandomized studies, we often find conflicting interpretations even after a large, expensive, time-consuming evaluation. Frequently the question is, "Were the differences found the result of how the samples were chosen or were they due to program effects?" In several large sets of parallel studies, the results of nonrandomized and randomized evaluations of the same programs conflict. These difficulties with nonrandomized trials lead us to re-examine some of the common objections to randomized trials.

Although we consider the force of these objections in some detail, we are not striving for completeness. The length of this paper arises from the discussions of numerous programs—almost two score—and their evaluations, rather than from an attempt to provide a manual to aid in carrying out field trials or from a systematic treatment of political and organizational programs. We understand only too well that such problems exist. Insofar as we do discuss them, our stimulus comes primarily from the empirical studies presented here, and secondarily from occasional considerations of constraints on evaluations where more freedom of action may be available than is often supposed. What we offer are data suggesting that a decision maker has more reason for carrying out a randomized field trial than he may suspect.

Despite the difficulties of organizing and implementing randomized field trials, our examples show that such trials have been done successfully in education, welfare, criminal justice, medical care, manpower training, surgery, and preventive medicine. The fact that these randomized trials were actually carried out and that valuable social and medical findings emerged, documents the importance and feasibility of randomized trials even in sensitive areas. Beyond this, we re-examine such issues as costs, timeliness, and flexibility, and suggest some steps that could improve the availability and effectiveness of the randomized controlled field trial as a method of evaluation.

II. INTRODUCTION

A. *THE PLAN OF THE PAPER*

Section I gives the general ideas of this paper, and Section II briefly describes methods of gathering information about social programs with emphasis on randomized controlled field trials and their merits. To give the reader a flavor of the innovations to be discussed and to exemplify randomized and nonrandomized field trials, in Section III we describe three instructive studies which are prototypes of material treated in Sections IV and V. Section IV explains the idea of ratings for innovations and why we want to make them. Our main empirical study of 29 innovations in Section IV reviews the frequency with which innovations offer clearly beneficial effects as evaluated by randomized controlled field trials, the innovations being drawn from social, socio-medical, and medical areas. Having looked at how often innovations turn out well, we provide case studies in Section V of what happens when innovations are evaluated by nonrandomized field trials, including comments on such issues as costs, timeliness, reliability, and validity of findings. Section VI deals at more length with special topics related to randomization, and with developmental needs. Three short sections deal with feasibility of making evaluations (Section VII), costs and timeliness (Section VIII), and the implementations of innovations (Section IX). Section X sums up our findings and recommendations.

In the course of describing various studies in Sections III, IV, and V, we occasionally sneak in a few methodological comments and prepare the way for our later treatment of special topics in evaluation. That later treatment is more systematic than the remarks sprinkled among the descriptions of evaluations, although we are not trying to provide a comprehensive statement on the design and execution of field trials. Instead, we try to offer an overview of some important matters related to evaluations.

For the reader who wishes a highly streamlined look at the main findings of this paper, we suggest the following path:

- Section III to get an idea of the studies being rated in Sections IV and V.

- Sections IV-A, B, C, and one or two further innovations, especially one that received a low rating; for example, Section IV-D-3 (Delinquent Girls), or IV-F-4 (Probation for Drunk Arrests), or IV-H-8 (Large Bowel Surgery). The reader will already have seen innovations with high ratings in Section III.

- Section IV-J, the summary of the ratings for the randomized studies.

- Section V-A-3 to get a feeling for nonrandomized studies, and Section V-C, the summary of Section V.

- Sections VIII-A and VIII-E to tune in on some facts about dollar costs and time in evaluations.

- Section X, the grand summary and recommendations.

B. *EVALUATING SOCIAL PROGRAMS*

Extensive public spending on many innovative social programs makes it essential to document their benefits and evaluate their impact. We trace here the results of a number of social, medical, and socio-medical programs, and present an empirical view of their effectiveness.

The review of these studies leads us to the conclusion that randomization, together with careful control and implementation, gives an evaluation a strength and persuasiveness that cannot ordinarily be obtained by other means. We are particularly struck by the troublesome record that our examples of nonrandomized studies piled up. Although some nonrandomized studies gave suggestive information that seems reliable, we find it hard to tell which were likely to be the misleading ones, even with the power of hindsight to guide us.

It is also true that not all randomized trials are successful in their quest for an accurate appraisal, and one of our chief concerns is that enough of these randomized studies be done so that both decision makers and the public may learn their strengths and weaknesses, just as they have learned to appreciate the strengths and weaknesses of sample surveys. In the course of such a development we would hope to see the emergence of the organizational and technical skills necessary for applying randomization effectively in field studies of program effectiveness, just as we have seen the development of both practical and theoretical aspects of sample surveys over the past few decades and their effect on decision making.

We recognize that the word "evaluation" has for some years had different meanings for different people. One form of evaluation involves examining managerial records, such as when one wants to find out who received what treatment. A second form focuses upon measuring inputs to a program, such as how much money per pupil is being spent in different school districts. We concentrate throughout this paper on a third type of policy-oriented evaluation. Such investigations usually ask the question, "What are the effects of a program on its intended beneficiaries?" Thus, our focus is upon the output, or result of the program, and the evaluative question generally before us is how to improve the program so that it may better serve its clients.

We are aware that the effectiveness of any program must be related to its costs by policy makers; nevertheless, we largely confine our discussion to the prior problem of rating program effects. If an effect is a slam-bang success and does not cost much, then it is almost certainly cost effective. If it is a slight success, its costs may put it near the borderline. For innovations that have no effect or even a harmful effect, obviously the net value is negative, and many of the innovations examined have these properties. Beyond this simple-minded thinking about cost effectiveness, we also discuss some aspects of the costs and cost effectiveness of different methods of conducting program evaluations in Section VIII.

C. *INITIAL IGNORANCE*

A knifelike truth that the policy maker, the economist, the social scientist, the journalist, and the layman--

indeed, all of us--need to learn to handle is that we often do not know which is the best of several possible policies and, worse yet, that we may not know if any of them betters what we are now doing. Economic reasoning, sophisticated analysis, sample surveys, and observational studies will give us some good ideas, suggestions--let's be plain, guesses--but we still will not know how things will work in practice until we try them in practice. This is a hard lesson and often an unwelcome one. We want medical and social helpers to know for sure what ails us and how to cure us. If there is some sort of dilemma, we want to know the comparative chances of success under each available regimen. Ironically, neither request can be answered unless the regimens have been studied in a controlled way, a way we call the randomized controlled field trial--a practical tryout under field conditions.

The theme of the policy man must always be that evaluative studies should provide information required for policy decisions and not necessarily that required, let us say, for progress in science. This position helps avoid policies that are obviously expensive and have but little yield, and often helps to choose a good way for carrying out a program. But the key question in many programs comes when we ask how much benefit will be derived from the program--How many points will IQ be raised? How many accidents prevented? How many fish will be saved? How many additional happy, disease-free days will be provided? How much will the air be cleansed? We can think and dream and compute and theorize and observe and temporize, but the answers to such questions, even approximate and uncertain answers, must finally be found in the field. We all know this; even our language knows it: "The proof of the pudding is in the eating." George Box (1966) put it well in addressing statisticians and the social science community in general when he said, "To find out what happens to a system when you interfere with it you have to interfere with it (not just passively observe it)" (p. 629). The social policy maker will find this advice particularly valuable when the system being investigated is complicated, and when there is no large body of experience available to predict reliably what happens when the system is actually changed. In contrast to more predictable effects in simpler laboratory investigations in the physical sciences, where considerable experience and proven theory offer guides, we focus here primarily on social and medical settings that are much more unpredictable. For example, it is difficult to foresee how effective a job training program will be before instituting it and systematically investigating its effects on trainees.

D. *METHODS OF INVESTIGATION*

Let us review the main ways of gathering information to assist us in policy decisions and in other forms of evaluation.

1. Introspection, theory, analysis, and simulation today form an important group of parallel methods for finding out how a policy might work. Although these methods can all have substantial inputs from empirical information, we put them first to emphasize that they often do not have a strong empirical base; indeed, sometimes they have none, except for casual observation and analogy.

2. Anecdotes, casual observation, and case studies are very commonly used in medicine, anthropology, law, sociology, business, and education. Like the first set of methods, they are likely to suggest theories and discover difficulties that we might not otherwise detect. They provide a firm record of a special event. They are especially weak, however, in giving us a bridge from the case at hand to the wider realm of situations that we wish to influence in the future. The inference from a case study to the more general practical policy may be a very long step.

3. Quantitative observational studies, including sample surveys and censuses, are very widely used now. They are especially good at telling us the current state of the world. Our own Section IV is an observational study to indicate how often innovations give clear benefits. This kind of study is ordinarily not designed to include the administration of new treatments. Usually sample surveys involve a stage of random sampling, but this randomness is designed to reduce certain kinds of bias in collecting information; it is not ordinarily connected with the administration of treatments, but rather is used for deciding which items should be observed. We may, for example, observe how people with various characteristics respond to different treatments. But in sample surveys we ordinarily do not initiate the treatments. The response observed in the survey may well not be to the treatment that we have in mind as the potential causal agent.

Censuses are a form of observational study. Again, they are ordinarily designed to aid our appreciation of matters as they stand, rather than to administer treatments and see what their effect might be.

Among quantitative observational studies we include searches of records and studies to see how various people fare under various treatments that have been imposed through the natural processes of society, without the investigator's interfering with those processes. From the evaluation point of view, the general feature of an observational study is that some individuals, groups, or institutions have in the course of events experienced one regimen, and others have experienced other regimens, and these regimens have led to outcomes on variables of interest. We hope to find out from a thoughtful examination of the outcomes following each regimen what the approximate effect of the regimen was. This hope has often been frustrated by a variety of difficulties.

Innovations and experiments. When we have an innovation in society, such as the establishment of social security, the adoption of Prohibition, a new child assistance program, or an employment training program, some people call such innovations "experiments." The word "experiment" is then being used in the sense of a new and sometimes tentative treatment. It is not being used in the sense of a scientific investigation. We try the innovation, and then if we don't care for it, we may change matters again. Since the word "experiment" is commonly used in this way, we need an expression for the social equivalent of the controlled scientific investigation. We shall call such investigations controlled field trials, and when they employ randomization, we shall prefix the word "randomized." The expression "field trial" is intended to emphasize the possibly substantial variation of effects from one place, person, or institution to another.

4. In <u>nonrandomized field trials</u>, the investigator initiates new treatments but without the use of randomization. For example, the investigator gives some people and not others treatment 1 and then compares the performance of those who got treatment 1 with that of others who got treatment 2. This nonrandomized method is a step forward from the observational study because the investigator rather than the social process chose the treatment, and so we can relate treatment and outcome. The difficulties of this procedure have to do with a variety of matters, but the key problem is that the effect of the treatment is not distinctive in all cases, so that the treatment cannot be proved to have caused the effect of interest. Selection effects and variability of previous experience have often led to biases and misinterpretations. In the famous Lanarkshire milk experiment ("Student," 1931), a controlled but nonrandomized study, the teachers tended to give the less robust children the milk, and so the value of the milk treatment was left uncertain. Biases arising from selection have on several occasions led to adopting therapies that seemed to have great prospects in the light of the nonrandomized study, but that have not proved out under randomized clinical trials. We document this point in Section V-B.

5. <u>Randomized controlled field trials</u> are currently our best device for appraising new programs. The word "trial" suggests the direct comparison of the effects of treatments. We shall also speak of these trials as "studies" because the investigators usually go beyond just the initial comparison of treatments. In these studies, the experimental units--individuals, families, school districts, whatever the unit--are randomly assigned to treatments or

regimens and carefully followed to find out what the effect
of the regimen might be. The randomization helps in several
ways. First, it avoids the dangers of self-selection or of
biased selection that we have mentioned earlier. It
provides objectivity to outsiders. If we hand select the
cases ourselves, then no matter how fair we may try to be,
we may tend to choose on some basis that will confuse the
effects of the variable of primary interest. If we use a
random method, we assure the reader or consumer, as well as
ourselves, that we have constructively protected against
selectivity. (We still may want to examine the outcome for
balance and perhaps adjust if nature has given us a bad
break.) Second, it helps us control for variables we may
not otherwise be able to control. We explain this further
in Section VI.

Since "randomized controlled field trials" is rather a
mouthful, let us spell out its parts. The expression "field
trial" implies that the treatment or treatments are being
studied in the field rather than in the laboratory, and that
they are being tried out in practice rather than through
simulation or theory. A field trial might consist of one
treatment only, but it could refer to several. For
instance, a field trial of a new medication might be for the
purpose of discovering side effects. "Controlled" refers to
two matters: 1) that the choice of treatment for a site or
an individual is primarily that of the investigator rather
than the individual (once he agrees to participate) or the
natural or market processes; 2) that at least two treatments
are being compared. "Randomized" refers to the use of
chance at some stage to choose which units get which
treatments.

The purpose of randomized controlled field trials, like that of the other kinds of evaluative investigations we discuss, is marshalling information to aid decisions (Thompson, 1973). People tend to think of this device as especially important for the scientist rather than for the policy maker. This leaves us with the idea that a scientist needs a very fine tool to get information about a process, but the policy maker should be content with uncertain information. Although sometimes this may be true, one could argue that exactly the reverse holds: the policy maker needs not only fine tools, but also good efforts to develop better tools. This seems especially true in policy problems where large numbers of individuals are involved and large amounts of money are at stake or when lives and careers are being substantially affected.

E. *LARGE AND SMALL EFFECTS*

When is it that weaker tools are adequate? We usually think that in the presence of "slam-bang" effects, weaker methods work. For example, if there is a well-established disease which once had a 100% chance of leading to death in a short time, and if someone begins to keep 30% of the patients alive and well for more than two years, we would say that a slam-bang effect was at work and that it looked as if the new treatment caused the cures.

This sort of dreamy situation is one that we tend to think of when we install new social programs. We will raise IQ by 20 or 30 points, advance education by four additional months per year of training, cut the death rate on the highways by 50%, and so on. These optimistic forecasts often play a crucial role in the political process that leads to a program being tried. These dreams lead people to suggest that if one has a first-class social program it will speak for itself. Statistics will not be needed. One cannot argue with this position, given its assumptions; such programs will indeed be beacons in the night. In the cold light of day, however, such slam-bang effects are few, as Section IV documents. For this reason we suggest that evaluations of these new social programs should be designed to document even modest effects, if they occur, so that new programs may be built upon these gains.

III. THREE INSTRUCTIVE EXAMPLES

For concreteness, we next give examples of three evaluations of medical and social innovations. These real-life cases give an opportunity to illustrate distinctions between randomized and nonrandomized controlled field trials, and also to focus on difficulties that arise in such evaluations.

A. *THE SALK VACCINE TRIALS* (Francis et al., 1955; Meier, 1972; Brownlee, 1955)

The 1954 trial to test a new preventive medication for paralytic polio, the Salk vaccine, is most instructive. First, it exposed children to a new vaccine, and thereby showed that we as a nation have been willing to experiment on people, even our dearest ones, our children. Secondly, the preliminary arguments over the plan instructed us, as did the way it was actually carried out--in two parallel studies.

In the initial design--the observed control method-- the plan was to give the vaccine to those second graders whose parents volunteered them for the study, to give nothing to the first and third graders, and then to compare the average result for the untreated first and third grade with the treated group in the second grade.

There are troubles here. In the more sanitary neighborhoods, polio occurs more frequently than in unsanitary neighborhoods, and the more sanitary regions are associated with higher income and better education. It is also a social fact that better educated people tend to volunteer more than less well educated ones. Consequently we could expect that the volunteers in the second grade would be more prone to have the disease in the first place than the average second grader, and than the average of the first and third graders. The comparison might well not be valid because of this bias. In addition, if only second graders got the vaccine, more of them might be suspected by physicians of having caught the disease because of possible exposure through the vaccine itself, and so there might well be differential frequencies of diagnoses in the volunteer and nonvolunteer groups. Another difficulty is that if an epidemic happened to confine itself largely to one of these school grade groups, this large-scale investigation might wind up an uninterpretable fiasco.

Some state public health officials noticed these difficulties and recommended instead a second design, the placebo control method, which randomizes the vaccine among volunteers from all grade groups; that is, these officials recommended a randomized controlled field trial. Half the volunteers got the vaccine and half a salt water injection (placebo), so that the "blindness" of the diagnoses could be protected. Thus the physician could be protected from his expectations for the outcome in making a diagnosis. This meant that the self-selection effects and their associated bias would be balanced between the vaccinated and unvaccinated groups of volunteers, and that the hazards to validity from an epidemic in a grade would be insured against.

In actuality, both methods were used: one in some states and the other in others. The result has been carefully analyzed, and the randomized trial (placebo control) shows conclusively a reduction in paralytic polio rate from about 57 per hundred thousand among the controls to about 16 per hundred thousand in the vaccinated group. (See Table 1.)

In the states where only the second-grade volunteers were vaccinated, the vaccinated volunteers had about the same rate (17 per hundred thousand) as those vaccinated (16 per hundred thousand) in the placebo control areas. The expected bias of an increased rate for volunteers as compared to nonvolunteers appeared among the whole group. Among the placebo controls, the volunteers who were not vaccinated had the highest rate (57 per hundred thousand) and those who declined to volunteer had 35 or 36 per hundred thousand. In the states using the observed control method, the first and third graders, who were not asked to volunteer and were not vaccinated, had a rate between the two extremes, 46 per hundred thousand.

Table 1. Summary of Study Cases by Vaccination Status for Salk Vaccine Experiment.

Study group	Study population (thousands)	Paralytic poliomyelitis cases: rate per hundred thousand
Placebo control areas: Total	749	36
Vaccinated	201	16
Placebo	201	57
Not inoculated*	339	36
Incomplete vaccinations	8	12
Observed control areas: Total	1,081	38
Vaccinated	222	17
Controls**	725	46
Grade 2 not inoculated	124	35
Incomplete vaccinations	10	40

*Includes 8,577 children who received one or two injections of placebo.

**First- and third-grade total population.

Source: Paul Meier, 1972; from Table 1, p. 11.

Brownlee (1955), referring to the observed control study as 59% of the total investigation, says, "59% of the trial was worthless because of the lack of adequate controls" (p. 1013). This illustrates how one informed skeptic views the observed control study. Thus for him, the biases and lack of reliability destroyed this part of the study. Others might not be so harsh. Uncontrolled biases can make interpretation difficult because it becomes necessary for the interpreter to guess the size of the bias, and when its size may be comparable to that of the treatment effect, the interpreter is guessing the final result. In the Salk vaccine study we happened to have two investigations in parallel and they support each other. But this does not help us in the situation where the observed control study is performed alone.

These results then instruct us that the size of a study is not enough. We need randomization and controls. And we have to worry not only about biases, but about the possibility that uncertainty in the answers may make the results not very useful even when they happen to come out in the right direction and in approximately the right size, for we will not be confident that these events occurred. From the policy maker's point of view, he is less sure of the direction and size of the effect and so is less sure to make appropriate decisions.

B. *THE GAMMA GLOBULIN STUDY* (U.S. Public Health Service, 1954)

The general success of the Salk vaccine randomized study can be contrasted with the results of a corresponding earlier study of gamma globulin which was carried out in a nonrandomized trial. In 1953, during the summer, 235,000 children were inoculated in the hope of preventing or modifying the severity of poliomyelitis. "The committee recognized that it would be very difficult to conduct rigidly controlled studies in the United States during 1953" (p. 3). They hoped to use mass inoculation in various places and compare differential attack rates at different sites, as well as to analyze other epidemiological data. In the end this approach turned out to be inconclusive, and the authors of that study describe the need for a more carefully controlled experiment. The general belief of Dr. Hammon, in commenting on the study, was that the gamma globulin was given too late, but that it seems to have an extremely limited application in the field of preventive medicine. If Hammon is right, the intended treatment may not have been given. This is a concern often raised about controlled social trials, as well.

What we have to recognize here is that whether or not gamma globulin was good for the purpose, the lack of randomization undermined the expert investigators' ability to draw firm conclusions, in spite of the large size of the study. The children were put at risk. Although it must be acknowledged that conducting randomized studies would have been difficult in 1953, those who argue today that randomized trials have ethical problems may wish to think about the problems of studies that put the same or greater numbers of people at risk without being able to generate data that can answer the questions being asked.

C. *EMERGENCY SCHOOL ASSISTANCE PROGRAM* (National Opinion Research Center [NORC], 1973)

The Emergency School Assistance Program (ESAP) was a federally funded program to assist desegregating schools to improve the quality of the education they offered. It was succeeded by the Emergency School Aid Act (ESAA), which has similar purposes. Both programs are intended, among other things, to improve academic performance. During 1971–72, a randomized controlled field study was performed under ESAP to see what benefits certain parts of the program had conferred.

This evaluation illustrates the possibility of a controlled field study being superimposed upon an ongoing large-scale program. In all, ESAP was distributing about $64,000,000. The funds going to the schools in the field trial amount to approximately $1,000,000 or less, perhaps about 1% of the total funds. The total funds available in ESAP were far from enough to distribute to all the schools and school districts that asked for aid (ESAP supported many kinds of programs, of which one kind was tested), and so it was not hard to justify a randomized controlled field study in which some schools did not get the funds and others did. Usually we prefer to compare two or more treatments, all of which are hoped to be beneficial, but here the comparison was between giving the funds and not giving the funds. The funds were used for two different purposes. First, all schools receiving funds (both elementary schools and high schools) used the money for teacher's aides, counseling, in-service education for teachers, and remedial programs. Second, in addition to these uses, the high schools also used some of the funds on programs intended to change the way the schools handled problems in race relations. Thus one difference between the elementary and the high school treatment was the program in race relations in the high school.

The designers of the field trial set up a rather straightforward plan whereby in the South 50 pairs of high schools and 100 pairs of grade schools were candidates for ESAP grants. In each pair, one school was randomly chosen to get the funds and the other was not. The objections to participation in the controlled field study were reported to have been few. (There can be problems; for example, it may be hard for a school superintendent to convice his constituency that it is reasonable for one school to get and another not to get what looks like a valuable contribution. Developing an understanding that such a move can be not only fair but wise may be important for our society.)

The academic performance of the children in the schools receiving the funds was compared with that of those not receiving funds. Several groups were studied: males versus females, blacks versus whites, elementary schools versus high schools. The major positive finding was that black males in funded high schools improved by half a grade level compared to those in high schools without the funds. Other groups were not detected as improving. The researchers suppose, but not with as strong convictions as they have for the existence of the improvement itself, that the race relations programs may have influenced attitudes for the male blacks, leading to improved school performance.

Without going into the details of the other findings, we would like to emphasize that this is one of the very rare large-scale randomized controlled field studies in education that have been done so far. It was installed without much difficulty in the midst of an ongoing program, and we have some evidence about an improvement. The funds necessary for this investigation were largely those of a program that was already being administered; extra funding was not required. Even though billions have been spent in other educational programs, and tens of millions in evaluations, this is the only one where a substantial randomized controlled field trial has been carried out, and it gives us a definite notion of which groups improved their school achievement. One policy recommendation flowing from this study is the desirability of trying out programs in race relations in the elementary schools as well as in the high schools, because the presence of this element in the high school program was the main difference in treatment between the elementary school program and the high school program, and was the source of the positive effect in the latter.

In commenting upon this evaluation, the National Opinion Research Center experimenters say, "It is difficult to overstate the importance of the experimental design. Had there not been an experiment, we would have had to compare schools that were deemed worthy of ESAP funds to those that were not; no matter what statistical tricks we attempted to make the two groups comparable, the question of whether or not the differences we believed to be the result of ESAP were due to some other differences between the two schools would have always remained open" (Vol. I, p. ii). This uncertainty haunts nearly every attempt to reach firm conclusions from observational studies and nonrandomized field trials about the effects of social or medical programs, no matter how clever the analysts.

In addition to the positive finding, a number of findings indicated small or no effects, and so we know in what areas of schooling we need new thoughts if money is to benefit others in addition to black male high school students. An extra half a grade improvement is a large increment in performance for one year. An extra half a grade for students who have traditionally done poorly is more than a 50% improvement, perhaps as much as 70% over the expected gains in the same time period. And so we are discussing a very valuable effect.

Because such positive findings about school performance of black males came from a randomized study, there should be relatively few disagreements about the results themselves. Thus the value of randomization in this ESAP study was great, for it gave us firm inferences about a program that was adopted on a wide scale and worked.

How should we regard the rest of the money spent that does not seem to improve achievement? First, the funds went into the school system, and so they represented a redistribution of finances. Second, the findings tell us where we did not get substantial gains, as well as where we did.

Finally, this program is one of very few in education that provide firm evidence of a substantial effect. The study went forward without excessive difficulty and was imbedded as an integral part of the main program. Perhaps a little less effort debating the merits of randomized controlled field studies and a lot more spent on actually doing them might benefit society a great deal.

D. *AFTERWORD*

The preceding three examples illustrate a variety of issues, at some length. In the next section we describe many studies, but usually much more briefly than those just given. Naturally, all such studies have complications and details that will be largely omitted in this short presentation.

After some of these studies, we remark on additional methodological points, but that is not the prime purpose of the section. Our primary purpose is to find out how often innovations are successful in carrying out their stated mission.

IV. RATINGS OF INNOVATIONS

In this section, we rate a substantial number of innovations. Our primary purpose is to find out something about how often innovations succeed and fail these days.

We include an innovation only if its evaluation seems well done and well documented. Each one involved a randomized controlled field trial. Furthermore, each trial is of sufficient size to reach some conclusion about the innovation it evaluates. For some studies the conclusion about the innovation has to be confined to the region, circumstances, or site where the trial was done. In others the study has been done in a broad enough way that its inferences may be more generalizable.

If all innovations worked well, the need for evaluations would be less pressing. If we forecast so nearly perfectly, the suggestion might even be made that we were not trying enough new things. Our findings in this section show that this happy state of affairs does not hold; they show, rather, that only a modest fraction of innovations work well. This finding makes clear that innovations need to have their performance assessed.

A. *SOURCES OF THE STUDIES AND THEIR BIASES*

We present the innovations in three groups. The first group is a collection of nine social innovations, the second is a collection of eight socio-medical innovations, and the third is a collection of twelve primarily medical studies. If we set aside for a moment two of these medical studies (Salk Vaccine and Gastric Freezing), the remaining ten come from a systematic MEDLARS search through the medical literature for a certain period (as described in more detail in the introduction to Section IV-H).

Our collection of randomized field trials has come from four main sources. First, Jack Elinson and Cyrille Gell prepared in 1967 for the Ross Conference on Pediatric Research abstracts of ten social action programs in the areas of health and welfare. These ten innovations were carried out in the 1950's and 1960's, and what they had in common was their use of field trials to test innovations. These abstracts not only aided us a good deal in and of themselves, but also their existence encouraged us to begin our study in the first place. From these studies we have chosen the seven with randomized field trials that seemed large enough to give us a reliable conclusion.

Second, we have been aided considerably by the work of Robert Boruch (Boruch, 1972; Boruch & Davis, in press), who has also been collecting results of field trials, both on his own initiative and in support of the Social Science Research Council's Committee on Experimentation as a Method for Planning and Evaluating Social Intervention. Boruch compiled a large list of field studies, including many that were not randomized field trials. At an early stage, we reviewed his list and selected for this section only the strong randomized field trials.

Third, in the social and socio-medical area we have been collecting information about randomized controlled field trials ourselves and making a collection. Because we have been corresponding with Boruch, it would be hard now to recollect which ones we have supplied ourselves, for Boruch's lists have grown and at last look contain nearly all we know about and much more. We also included a large medical investigation we thought appropriate: the Salk Vaccine trial.

Fourth, Bucknam McPeek, M.D., has helped us develop a list of ten surgical studies that used randomization. These studies arose from a systematic computer search (MEDLARS) through the medical literature for prospective studies in surgery. From the whole set we selected the first ten strong randomized studies picked out by the system. These ten studies might be regarded as coming from a more objectively defined population than do the social or socio-medical studies. Some readers may feel that in the case of the MEDLARS search we are examining a whole population, but this is not the interpretation we find useful. We think of the production of research papers as a process that goes on more or less continuously, and we are taking a sample in time, hoping the results for the period we study give a fair inference for other periods in the near future.

Some additional studies from the first three sources are discussed under nonrandomized trials in Section V.

The reader should also know that we had available a substantial number of studies of family planning through the good offices of Arthur Lumsdaine and Elizabeth J. Hilton.

After reviewing and discussing them, we decided not to include them because, although some were randomized, most did not have measures on the basic payoff variable: the number of births. (These studies are described, though not given ratings, in Chapter 5.)

All these collections have their biases. For example, we have only used published studies. The surgical studies are the ones chosen by the MEDLARS search and are subject to the limitations of the instructions and the MEDLARS flexibility. The social and socio-medical studies are the ones drawn to our attention from our own knowledge and from lists we have been able to gather. Both kinds probably have an upward bias in the quality of the study described, compared to the average study in its field. Holding constant the quality of the study, there is likely a further upward bias in the performance of the innovation compared to all the studies done of that quality because of selective publication. Some may feel that social innovators would be more willing to publish the failures of reforms than physicians to advertise disasters to their patients, but we have no evidence for this. And so we have no reliable evidence about the comparative biases of the several groups of investigations.

Our interest in the problem continues, and we will be grateful to readers who call our attention to further randomized field trials in the social and socio-medical areas. We have not yet made a large-scale effort in the medical and surgical areas.

The Databank of Program Evaluations (DOPE) described in Wilner et al. (1973) should make it easier to do studies like the one reported here, and, along with parallel efforts in other fields, should give a better basis for describing some populations of innovations.

B. *MEDICAL AND SOCIAL INNOVATIONS*

The idea that the exact techniques that have worked so well in agriculture or physics can be directly applied to the evaluation of social programs is naive. Medicine is, however, a field that suffers many of the same difficulties that beset the evaluation of social programs. Physicians, in general, and surgeons, in particular, have been diligent in their attempts to evaluate the effects of their therapies on their patients. Many of the currently used techniques for implementing and analyzing randomized controlled field trials have been developed in this context. Medical programs have problems that parallel those often faced by social programs; for example:

- There are multiple and variable outcomes and often negative side effects.

- The diagnosis of whether the patient has the condition the treatment is designed to cure is sometimes in doubt.

- In multi-institutional trials the treatments may differ from place to place.

- Patients often differ in their general condition, in the state of their disease, and in their response to treatment.

- Ethical tensions may exist between the study protocol and the perceived best interests of the patients.

- Patients may adapt their lives so as to minimize their symptoms and thus prevent their disease from being diagnosed.

- Patients may receive additional treatments, unprescribed and uncontrolled, that are unknown to the physician.

Beyond these areas of similarity, it is often true that the problems under investigation are urgent and that the costs of investigating them are high. It is largely because so much good work has been done in medical evaluation, despite these problems, that we have chosen to present a number of medical trials as part of this study. We feel that the social evaluator will find a closer parallel to his own work in medical and health investigations than in those of the laboratory scientist.

C. OUR RATINGS OF SOCIAL INNOVATIONS

We rate the innovations according to a five-point scale, from double plus (++), meaning a very successful innovation--it does well some of the major things it was supposed to do; to double minus (--), meaning a definitely harmful innovation. A single minus (-) indicates a slightly harmful or negative innovation. A zero (0) means that the innovation does not seem to have much if any effect in either the positive or negative direction. It could mean also that the innovation has both small positive and small negative effects, neither overwhelming the other. A plus (+) means that the innovation seems to have a somewhat positive effect, but that one would have to weigh particularly carefully whether it was worth its price. We have not carried out detailed cost- benefit analyses here.

Several caveats are in order. The reader might disagree with our ratings, but this worry is not as substantial as one might at first suppose. We shall try to give enough detail as we go along so that the reader can get a feel for the studies. We doubt if any zeros would move up to double pluses, and we would be surprised if many single pluses moved up to double pluses. Similarly, we doubt if many double pluses would be reduced to single pluses. The double pluses are probably the items to watch especially. In a few studies we shall explain some special difficulties in making the ratings.

The surgical innovations are probably less subject to unreliability of ratings than the two other groups. The reason is twofold: first, the translation from the summaries of the original investigators' findings to the pluses or minuses is almost automatic; secondly, we have had expert surgical advice.

We wish to stress again that we are not rating the methodology of the field trial. All of the field trials we discuss were in our judgment of sufficient size and quality to give strong evidence of the efficacy of the innovation. Thus the rating applies to the <u>innovation</u> as measured by the field trial.

We are also not rating the study for its help in establishing a base line for future research, or for its dismissal of the innovation, or for some new approach discovered during the research. We merely rate as best we can whether the innovation itself, if cost-free, looks like a substantial success. When the innovation has multiple goals, we rate its success in achieving the primary goal. We regard all the studies as successes, even when the innovations they evaluate are not.

All told, we have in this section an observational study of randomized trials. Innovations that reach the stage of having a randomized trial have already gone through preliminary theoretical, intellectual, and pilot work. In general the trials we review were intended to be the final clinching documentation of the ability of the innovation to do its job. Every item in the list, therefore, was originally expected to be an absolute winner. Insofar as observational studies, pilot work, clinical practice, and theory can help, they already have made their contribution. The randomized field trial is the final hurdle. This is most important to bear in mind while reviewing these studies. We shall return to this point after discussing the studies themselves.

If two treatments perform equally well and one is much cheaper, then the latter would be preferred, especially if both treatments are helping society. We happen not to have examples of an innovation that did as well as the standard treatment but was cheaper. On the other hand, we have several where the innovation was more expensive and did no better than the standard treatment, which was sometimes "no treatment."

Similarly it is possible for two treatments to be equally beneficial, but for a certain innovation to be much preferred because the quality of life was substantially improved. For example, if a very limited operation helped patients with breast cancer as much as a radical operation, then the limited operation would be preferred. This particular issue (not among our lists of studies) is still under investigation, and we do not have any innovation in our group that falls into this category. The reader will readily appreciate that the decision as to what is especially beneficial in an innovation or a standard treatment is somewhat case-specific.

D. *SOCIAL INNOVATIONS*

We turn now to our collection of evaluations of social innovations. The ESAP study given in Section III should be considered a member.

In giving descriptions of studies, we inevitably idealize and oversimplify. Some of these investigations have had whole books to describe them. Infelicities trouble every substantial investigation. It is our hope that the reader will be provided with a much more extensive statement about each of these studies when Robert Boruch publishes his summaries of randomized field trials.

The reader who does not wish to read descriptions of the randomized trials and wants to move directly to summaries will find them in Section E for the social innovations, Section G for the socio-medical innovations, and Section I for medical innovations, while Section J provides a grand summary for our complete set of randomized controlled field studies.

1. The New Jersey Graduated Work Incentive (Negative Income Tax) Experiment (Department of Health, Education and Welfare [HEW], 1973)

The purpose of the negative income tax experiment was to see what the labor response of the working poor might be to a system of support that added directly to their income. The idea was to give a guaranteed minimum income to such a working family, but the more the family earned, the less would be the contribution of the government. The family was allowed to keep part of what it earned itself according to a "tax" scale.

The experiment was carried out in New Jersey, using three levels of "taxation," 30, 50 and 70%, and several different sizes of guarantee. In the original year the poverty line was about $3300 for a family of four. The sizes of guarantees expressed in fractions of the poverty line were 1/2, 3/4, 1, and 1 1/4. Not all taxation levels were used with all guarantee levels—some pairs were omitted because the effect was believed to be too small for useful measurement. In addition to the several treatment groups involving originally 1,216 families with 141 added later, there was also a control group of 491 families that received no benefits, except that they were paid modest sums for filling out questionnaires from time to time.

Economic theory strongly suggested that the result of such a negative income tax would be a reduction in the number of working hours a family contributed, but the theory did not have much to say about the amount of that reduction. That was an important reason for doing the experiment. Some people argued that if the working poor had a guaranteed minimum income, they would stop working altogether. The experiment was completed in 1973, and the results are largely in.

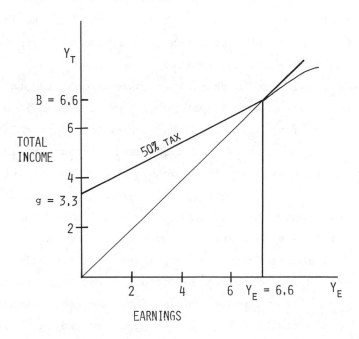

Fig. 1. *Relation between family earnings* Y_E, *for a family of four, and the total income* Y_T, *when g (the guarantee) is $3300 (that is, g = 3.3) and the tax rate is 50%. When the family earns* Y_E *= $6600, it receives no money from the program and its total income is B = $6600. The 45° line shows what the earnings would be if there were no negative income tax; it curves a bit to the right of $6600 because of ordinary income taxes.*

73

The most striking finding is that the reduction in hours worked is small--less than 10% for most groups. The work of the wives did decrease, in some cases a substantial percentage of their own total work, but since wives were not contributing a great deal in working hours outside the home (to qualify, all families had at least one able-bodied male worker), their contribution to this reduction was small in total effect. Even with the overall reduction in hours, the earnings remained about the same.

Thus the evidence is that a negative income tax to the working poor does not create a large reduction in work effort. Since many had feared that it would create a large reduction, the proposed innovation can be regarded as a considerable success; that is, a double plus. Again, let us emphasize that what is being rated here is the innovation, not the experiment, and the comparison is the observed small loss in work effort against the feared large losses.

We might mention that the assignment of the families to the various taxation-guarantee groups was designed to maximize the information received from the investigation (Conlisk and Watts, 1969); this was a very sophisticated randomized assignment. Inevitably and realistically, economists express concern that full-scale implementation of such a program may lead to consequences different from those of the trial.

RATING: ++

2. Social Workers for Multi-problem Families (Wallace, 1965)

Because of concern that a small group of families seems to receive an excessively large proportion of overall welfare expenditures, an investigation was undertaken to study the effects of intensive professional casework with multi-problem families. The treatment involved assigning these families experienced social workers with limited caseloads and extra cooperation from the Welfare Department.

From the population of multi-problem families 50 treatment families and 50 control families were randomly selected. In addition, a third group of 50 control families was selected, known only to research staff. The average participation time per family in this study was just under two years. Data were collected from the first group (treatment) and second group (control) at the beginning and end of the study, but from the third group ("hidden" control group) only at the end.

Outcome variables included family relationships, care and training of children, social activities, household practices, health conditions, and use of community resources. There were no statistically significant differences found between the two control groups and the treatment group at the conclusion of the investigation, although there was the interesting finding that the variance of outcomes increased for the treatment group relative to that for the control groups. That is, the level of family functioning for the treatment group had more extremes at the conclusion of the study.

RATING: 0

3. <u>Delinquent Girls</u> (Meyer, Borgatta, & Jones, 1965)

The investigators tried to reduce juvenile delinquency among teen-age girls in two ways: first, by predicting which girls were likely to become delinquent; and secondly, by applying a combination of individual and group treatment to girls who exhibited potential problem behaviors. The population was four cohorts of girls entering a vocational high school; of these, approximately one quarter were screened into this study as indicating potential problems. These girls were randomly assigned to a treatment group which was given treatment at Youth Consultation Service (YCS), a social agency; and to a nontreatment group given no special services. The assignments were 189 to YCS, 192 to the nontreatment group.

The result was that in spite of the group and the individual counseling, delinquency was not reduced. The investigators were successful in identifying girls who were likely to become delinquent, but that was not the primary purpose of the study. They report that, "on all the measures ... grouped together as school-related behavior ... none of them supplies conclusive evidence of an effect by the therapeutic program" (p. 176). Similar findings were reported for out-of-school behavior.

We view this innovation as rating a zero, though the detection ability might be of value on another occasion.

RATING: 0

4. Cottage Life Intervention Program (Federal Bureau of
   Prisons, 1964)

The Bureau of Prisons undertook a randomized field study of a Cottage Life Intervention Program. Boys convicted of interstate crimes and of robberies and burglary in the District of Columbia were randomly allocated either to the regular training school for convicted boys where there was no special treatment or to a substantial counseling, recreation, and incentive program in hopes of improving their in-house behavior and also of reducing their recidivism rate. The experiment had 75 to 80 boys in the experimental group and 300 to 500 (depending on release) in the controls.

Over a period of two years, the boys' in-house behavior was found to improve. Further, while the recidivism rate did not decrease, the time for staying out of trouble was longer for the experimental group than for the controls.

We view this as a slightly positive result, and give the innovation a plus, though this may be generous.

RATING: +

5. Manhattan Bail Project (Botein, 1964-65)

The purpose of the Manhattan Bail Project experiment was to see whether arrested persons who have close ties to the community will return for trial even if they are not required to put up bail. Based upon interviews with the defendants prior to arraignment, staff of the Vera Foundation chose on the basis of a scoring system some thousands of defendants they thought were suitable to be recommended for release. (Persons arrested for very severe crimes were not eligible for Vera consideration.) Then they randomly split defendants deemed suitable for release into two groups, half (the recommended group) that they recommended to the court for release without bail, and half (the control group) for which no recommendation was made. The court followed 50% of the recommendations for release without bail in the recommended group, and in the control group it released 16%. Of all those released in this way, 15--that is, about 7/10 of 1%--failed to show up in court. We see here an example of a "slam-bang" effect. The result is so overwhelming that, as Botein says (p. 331), "One need not struggle with recondite statistics to gauge such results."

RATING: ++

The idea of the bail bond innovation has been taken up all across the country. Vera has gradually increased from 28% to 65% its recommendation for release. The judges have increased to 70% their acceptance of the Vera recommenda- tions, and the District Attorney's office increased its agreement from about 50% to 80%, all in a period of about four years (1961-64). It would be helpful if someone could gather the results of the many applications of the bail bond idea and give a continuing evaluation under the various and changing uses.

With such large effects one might argue that a field trial was scarcely needed. But additional valuable infor- mation would probably not have been firmly gathered without the field trial. It turns out that in the recommended group

60% of recommended parolees were acquitted or had their cases dismissed, as opposed to 23% in the control group. Of those 40% of the parolees found guilty in the experimental group, about 16% were sentenced to prison, while 96% of those convicted in the control group were sentenced to prison. All told, then, we learned not only about the reliability of the word of those released, but also rather unexpectedly about the huge differential consequences of the treatments on the ultimate outcome of the case for the experimental and control groups.

The whole enterprise has been a most notable success, starting with an observational study on the lack on the part of the accused of available funds for bail, followed by the field trial just described, and then followed by further developmental exploration intended to improve the process of justice further. (See discussion of Dunn and George that follows.)

Although this pathbreaking work is most impressive in its own right, it is even more important as an illustration in one field of what can be done, and of the need to develop an investigational process. Botein (p. 320) quotes Abraham S. Goldstein of Yale: "Increasingly, law is seen as a decisional process in which men use institutions to shape norms, to interpret them and to enforce them. Inevitably, such an approach brings with it an effort to appraise legal institutions in terms of the functions they are called to play. And this can be done only if more information is fed into the process ..." (emphasis ours). He goes on to point out that this drive has led us to "frame issues in ways which make empirical research essential if a meaningful body of scholarship is to grow" (p. 320). And Botein says that law students need to be trained to work with others who are better equipped to carry out field research. In commenting on these remarks, Botein emphasizes that a major impact of the Manhattan Bail Project has been generally overlooked; that is, "the spur and stimulus it has given to empirical experimentation and study in criminal law throughout the country" (p. 320).

We would emphasize more generally that these experiments are part of the current development of gathering data carefully and cumulatively for social problems.

A study of the applicability of pretrial release in Des Moines, Iowa used the questionnaire and the point system of the Manhattan Bail Project (Dunn & George, 1964). The investigators proposed to the judges the pretrial release without bond of 740 out of 940 prisoners. Of these 740, the judges released 716 with the following results: 98% appeared in court when they were supposed to; 10 people never showed up; and 6 people came to court several days late. Of the 10 who did not show up, 7 were charged with traffic violations, 2 with forgery, and 1 with breaking and entering. This is an example of a one-treatment observational study. For another site, it supports the idea that community-based arrestees will almost always return to court even without the requirement of bail.

6. Los Angeles Sheriff's Academy (Earle, 1973)

The Los Angeles County Sheriff's Academy has created an innovative training program that reduces the militaristic and authoritarian aspects of the regular police training program and makes the training much more like that in a college. The Assistant Sheriff, with the cooperation of the Sheriff's Office, ran a randomized experiment to study the new training program. Half of the officers were trained the standard way, and half were trained using the innovative program. In the first year there were 74 officers; that is, 37 matched pairs with one from each pair randomly assigned to the special training group. The experiment was repeated in the succeeding year with a new class involving 100 officers in 50 matched pairs.

Performance in the field for the two kinds of officers, as measured by complaints, commendations, and supervisors' reports, showed that officers trained in the innovative program had higher job proficiency, higher levels of job satisfaction, and better overall work quality.

How do we judge this innovation? It deserves at least a plus from the point of view of the Los Angeles Police Department. Because Los Angeles is a large city, many people are favorably affected by this innovation. Also, since Los Angeles is large, the results are suggestive for trials in other large cities.

Viewing this study from a national perspective, however, we must be cautious. This is not because we don't believe it will work, but rather because the success of a program can sometimes depend upon a special charisma of the innovators or some special features of the site. (See also Section IV-A.) We thus assign no rating to this innovation on a national scale, but we note the importance with an innovation such as this one of trying a treatment in more than one site. Many writers discuss this topic under the heading "external validity." If this innovation were tried using randomized field trials in several cities, and the results were reasonably consistent over the cities, there would be a major national success as well as a Los Angeles success.

RATING (for Los Angeles only): + or ++

7. The Pretrial Conference (Rosenberg, 1964)

The pretrial conference is a meeting of the concerned parties and their lawyers with the judge before the formal trial. The purpose of the conference is to clarify which issues are in contention. By 1959 pretrial conferences were mandatory in at least 36 states, and they were thought by their proponents to make trials not only shorter but fairer. A body of critics claimed that their effects were just the opposite--that they made the legal process longer and that the procedure resulted in a less fair trial. The Project for Effective Justice at Columbia University carried out a randomized trial to evaluate the effectiveness of the pre-trial conference in the New Jersey civil courts during 1960-63.

The experiment involved three groups: Group A was the mandatory pretrial conference group; Group B was invited to forgo the conference but chose to have it; and Group C was invited to forgo the conference and did forgo it. Three groups were needed because it was felt that none could be denied the right to such a conference. Group A had over 1500 cases, and groups B and C combined also had over 1500 cases. Group B contained 48% of all the cases in Groups B and C. The principal comparison in the study and the randomization was between Group A and the other two combined.

Thus the treatment was the choice of forgoing the conference, not whether they did in fact forgo it. The study findings were that the mandatory pretrial conference did improve the quality of the trial; however, it did use more of the judge's time and increased the time required to obtain recovery for damages. Since the conference was shown to have some modest good and some modest bad features and we are not in a position to weigh their relative merits, we have given this treatment a zero. Others might differ a bit.

This was a test of an ongoing program, and it was therefore rather creative to think of a way of evaluating this program without violating the requirements of the law. This is a frequent problem, and when everyone in a program has received a perceived desirable good, it takes a creative investigator to think of an ethical way to test the innovation. We note that the experiment does seem to have pointed out the strengths and weaknesses of the pretrial conference in a way that almost unlimited opportunity for observation had not.

RATING: 0

8. Emergency School Assistance Program (NORC, 1973)

This study has already been described in Section III-C.

RATING (for high schools only): ++

9. Harvard Project Physics (Welch, Walberg, & Ahlgren,
   1969; Welch & Walberg, 1972)

Project Physics was an effort to construct a new high
school physics curriculum that would be both more interesting and more effective than traditional instruction. A
national experiment in curriculum evaluation for Project
Physics was carried out during academic year 1967-68. From
among the 16,911 physics teachers listed by the National
Science Teachers Association, a random sample of 136 teachers was drawn using random numbers, 124 being actually
reached by registered mail. They were asked to participate
and told that to participate they would have to be able to
agree in advance to teach the experimental or control
course, whichever they were chosen for. The experimental
teachers further had to attend a 6-week course, the control
teachers a two-day session. (This difference in amount of
time devoted to training and attending to the teachers is
one source of possible criticism of the investigation. This
is not so much because of the actual physics training, since
these teachers were continuing with their own course, but
because of the additional enthusiasm and freshness of
treatment and of examples that such a long session can
produce. However, the two-day session seems much better
than none.) Of the 124 teachers responding, 52 declined for
various reasons (previous commitment, change in situation,
lack of interest, and so on) and 72 accepted. Of the 72, 46
were randomly assigned to the experimental, 26 to the
control group. Transfers, illness, and other events brought
the final experimental group to 34 teachers and the control
group to 19 teachers.

Welch and Walberg (1972) report that cognitive performance of students in the two groups was much the same, and so Project Physics seemed not to reach one of its goals; namely, increased science-process understanding as compared with the standard physics course. We rate the gain in cognitive performance a zero. Project Physics students scored higher on a measure of course satisfaction, and thought the historical approach interesting, their text enjoyable to read, and physics understandable without an extensive mathematics background. Students in control courses more often found physics to be one of the most difficult courses and concluded that physics has to be difficult. We rate the gain in enthusiasm and palatability a double plus. We have therefore a program with multiple goals, the ratings for their achievement being very different. This shows the importance and feasibility of doing studies that evaluate programs with multiple goals.

In all the other investigations rated in Section IV, we were able to identify a single primary goal for the purpose of our ratings, but here we could not, and so this study does not fit smoothly into the summary we give below in Table 4.

The authors report that the added cost of this national randomized controlled field study, over and above the costs for a regional nonrandomized investigation, was less than $10,000 all told. They highly recommend (Welch & Walberg, 1972) such national studies, especially considering the millions often spent in the development phase of such curriculum work. So far such studies are rare in education itself, let alone in curriculum work.

RATING: 0 (cognitive performance)

++ (enthusiasm, palatability)

E.   *SUMMARY FOR SOCIAL INNOVATIONS*

Of the eight innovations rated for single goals in this section, we gave three double pluses--that is, three innovations were recorded as definitely successful. These were the Emergency School Assistance Program, the Manhattan Bail Project, and the Negative Income Tax--one program from education, one from the legal area, and one from welfare. Of the other five, three received zeros and two a plus. Thus none of the social innovations seemed definitely harmful. We did not assess the costs of the innovations, and so for the zeros the total impact on society might be somewhat negative if a program receiving a zero is continued. Since our rating scale is so simple, it is reassuring to find only two where a simple summary is inadequate. The pretrial conference seemed to have pluses and minuses in sufficiently complicated and hard- to-evaluate directions that probably the rating must be tempered by further examination. Harvard Project Physics required two ratings: zero for cognitive gain; double plus for palatability. In a different direction, the Cottage Life program had such slight advantages that the reader may prefer to give it a zero rather than a plus, while the Los Angeles police training program may deserve a double rather than a single plus.

In the Negative Income Tax investigation we gave the double plus primarily because the beneficiaries continued to work nearly at the previous rate of hours, and because they earned as much as they did before. It had been feared that they would drastically reduce their working hours. The reader might wish to argue that we should evaluate the whole package on a cost benefit basis, but that is beyond our goals in this paper.

Since our rated innovations all come from published sources, there is probably an upward bias in successful outcomes compared to the population of innovations evaluated by randomized controlled field studies. That is, an evaluation of a clearly unsuccessful innovation may be less likely to be published than an evaluation that found a success. In laboratory experiments we observe a much higher failure rate than we observe here, and so even if the population rate of highly successful social innovations were only half of what was observed in this set, we could afford to be pleased.

F. *EVALUATIONS OF SOCIO-MEDICAL INNOVATIONS*

The next series of evaluations deals with innovations that have strong components of both social and medical treatment. Although the reader might prefer to recategorize a few of our studies, these categories are more for convenience in exposition than for making inferences to types of innovations. The third category--medical--does represent an exception to this remark because it has a more objective basis for selection.

1. Outpatient Treatment (Hill & Veney, 1970; Gorham
   Report, 1967; Alpert et al., 1968)

The Gorham Report pointed out that the general medical insurance practice of paying only for procedures done in the hospital was encouraging doctors to send their patients to the hospital when they did not require full hospitalization. To investigate the possibility of savings by paying for outpatient treatment, Blue Cross-Blue Shield set up a large field trial in Kansas to see what would happen by giving people, in addition to their usual policy, coverage that would pay for certain procedures done outside the hospital (Hill & Veney, 1970). An experimental group of 5,000 people was given the new coverage at no extra cost, and a control group of 10,000 had the regular coverage only.

After a year the amounts of hospitalization for the two groups were compared, and it was found that, contrary to expectation, the group with the new extended coverage had 16% more days in the hospital than they had had the year before, while the controls, without the new coverage, had increased only 3%. Thus the new program did not have the hoped-for overall effect. More was learned from the field trial, though. The extended coverage group did indeed have 15% fewer short-stay admissions (supporting the idea in the Gorham Report), but this decrease was more than offset by additional long stays. The extra cost for the outpatient coverage was found to be about $40 per patient.

RATING: −

We rate this innovation minus since it did not have the savings in cost that were forecast. Indeed, it cost more, not less. It is interesting to note that the effect suggested by the Gorham Report did exist, so that if it had not been for the unforeseen effects on the longer stays, this change in coverage would have been a beneficial policy change. This illustrates the value to the decision makers of controlled field trials: the ideas in the Gorham Report warrant serious consideration, but instituting the new policy on a wide scale with the expectation of reduced costs would have been a serious fiscal mistake. Whether a sustained program of this kind would find that the long stays were reduced in later years would require a further evaluation, because part of the problem here may be due to the treatment of accumulated illnesses, as the following reference suggests.

In a related study, Alpert et al. (1968) reported pediatric experience comparing a comprehensive medical care service with regular medical service. This comparison was based on a randomized controlled field trial. They found that in the first six months, the hospitalization rate per hundred children was over twice as high in the comprehensive care group as in the regular medical group, but that in each of the next four six-month periods the rates were lower. The average rates for the 30 months, per six-month period, were for the comprehensive care children 2.8 and for the regular medical care 3.3. These data offer some support for the position that the costs associated with initial examination and treatment may be larger because of accumulated ills.

2. Operations and Education (Skipper & Leonard, 1968)

A field study was done at Yale New Haven Community Hospital to reduce the stress that a young child experiences when having a tonsillectomy. The theory underlying the trials was that if mothers knew in more detail, step by step, what their child would be undergoing both in the hospital and during the week following the hospital stay, they would provide emotional support and information to the child that would reduce his or her postoperative stress. Notice that the treatment here did not involve a direct intervention on the part of the investigators with the children who had operations. The hope was to improve the children's postoperative reactions by using the mothers to "carry" the treatment.

Eighty patients were in the study. They were randomly assigned to treatment and nontreatment groups, 40 per group. The patients were all children between three and nine years old. Upon entry to the hospital all 80 mothers were asked whether they were willing to fill out a questionnaire that would be administered one week after surgery, giving information about their child's and their own level of stress and information before, during, and after the surgery. All consented.

The outcome measures were children's stress, as indicated by temperature, systolic blood pressure, and pulse rate. These were recorded at admission, preoperatively, postoperatively, and at discharge. The data were collected by nurses who did not know which children were in which group.

The 40 mothers in the "treatment" group were randomly subdivided into 24 who met with a special nurse several times during the hospital stay, and 16 who received extra information only during the admission process. None of the 40 controls received any special nurse's briefing.

The results were positive in the hoped-for direction. Children in both treatment subgroups had temperatures, blood pressures, and pulse rates upon admission similar to those of the children in the nontreatment group. Yet differences showed up between the treatment and nontreatment groups at the preoperative stage, and continued through the postoperative and discharge stages. This was true for both treatment groups. In addition, the treatment-group children had less postoperative vomiting, voided earlier, and drank more fluids than control-group children, all good signs. Finally, the mail-back questionnaire filled out by the mothers gave information one week after surgery; differences between the groups were again substantial. More control-group children ran fevers their first week at home, and only half as many treatment-group mothers as controls indicated they were worried enough about their child's condition to call a physician. Most striking was that 39 out of the 40 treatment group children were reported by their mothers to have recovered from the operation one week after discharge, while this was true for less than half of the control-group children. (As far as the questionnaire results go, it is possible that the treatment group mothers have essentially been told what their response should be, and they are more or less seeing and reporting what they have been told by authority to expect.)

RATING: ++

3. Teaching Comprehensive Medical Care (Hammond & Kern, 1959)

Hammond and Kern wanted to improve the understanding and ability of medical students to give comprehensive medical care. In particular, the goals were:

- To teach maximum responsibility for the "whole" patient.

- To give more contact with the patient.

- To explain family relations and their importance to medicine.

- To teach the relation between social and psychological problems in proper medical care.

The investigators began by stratifying the 80 students in the fourth-year medical class at the University of Colorado into approximate thirds by class standing. They then randomly divided each third into a control group and an experimental group. The experimental group got the innovative education, while the control group got the usual clinical clerkship. The experiment lasted for three years, thus encompassing three senior classes.

The outcome was that the innovative teaching program did not improve students' attitudes in any of the directions hoped for. It left the experimental group about where they were to begin with, while the controls became a little more negative toward both comprehensive care and the social and psychological side of medical care. We rate the innovation (not the investigation) zero.

Before leaving this field trial, let us notice that a pure comparison between treatment and control groups may be difficult because the students in the two groups could have talked to one another across groups. This social interaction may have led to a partial blurring of the distinction between treatment and controls.

Such a partial blurring is common in many social investigations, whether they are randomized experiments or nonrandomized studies. For example, this blurring was found in a recent investigation of the innovative preschool program for children, Head Start. In many schools some children were enrolled in Head Start classes, while other children were in non-Head Start comparison groups in classrooms next door. These children played together, and their parents met outside school. A recent nonrandomized evaluation of Head Start effects on children, which found few differences between experimental and control children, noted that this contamination of pure treatment-versus- control comparison may have lessened the differences that were ultimately measured (Smith, 1973).

These difficulties suggest that when it is possible and realistic to use isolated groups for treatments, differences in treatments may be more readily detected.

RATING: 0

4. <u>Probation for Drunk Arrests</u> (Ditman et al., 1967)

Encouraged by preliminary work on the use of probation with suspended sentence as a way of getting chronic drunk offenders into treatment, Ditman et al. developed with the cooperation of the San Diego Municipal Court a randomized controlled field study. Offenders who had had either two drunk arrests in the previous three months or three in the previous year were fined $25, given a 30-day suspended sentence, and then assigned by judges to one of three groups: 1) no treatment, 2) alcoholic clinic, and 3) Alcoholics Anonymous. The primary payoff variables were number of rearrests and time before first rearrest. The total study included 301 individuals, divided randomly into the three groups. The results, based on the 80% of the subjects for whom good records are available, were that the "no treatment" group did as well as or better than the other two groups, which performed practically identically. Tables 2 and 3 show the detailed results. Ditman et al. conclude that the study gives no support to a general policy of forced short term referrals, on the basis of the suggestive evidence contained in the paper.

Table 2 shows that 44% of the "no treatment" group had no rearrests (in the first year) as opposed to about 32% in the other two groups. Table 3 shows that all three treatment groups had about the same percentage of rearrests, 21 or 22%, within the first month of treatment. Although the missing 20% of the data might change this picture somewhat, the overall result is compelling. (The missing data arise because of difficulty in getting complete data from two distinct sources of records.) Since the difference, though favoring the control, is well within the range of chance effects, we rate this zero rather than minus.

RATING: 0

Table 2. Number of Drunk Rearrests Among 241 Offenders in Three Treatment Groups.

	Rearrests			
Treatment Group	None	One	Two or More	Total
No treatment	32 (44%)	14 (19%)	27 (37%)	73
Alcoholism clinic	26 (32%)	23 (28%)	33 (40%)	82
Alcoholics Anonymous	27 (31%)	19 (22%)	40 (47%)	86
Total	85	56	100	241

Source: Ditman et al., American Journal of Psychiatry, 1967, 124, 160-63. Copyright © the American Psychiatric Association.

Table 3. Time Before Drunk Rearrest in Three Treatment
          Groups.

Treatment Group	No Rearrests	After Month of Treatment	Within First Month of Treatment	Total
No treatment	32 (44%)	25 (34%)	16 (22%)	73
Alcoholism clinic	26 (32%)	39 (47%)	17 (21%)	82
Alcoholics Anonymous	27 (31%)	40 (47%)	19 (22%)	86
Total	85	104	52	241

Source: Ditman et al., <u>American Journal of Psychiatry</u>,
         1967, <u>124</u>, 160-63. Copyright © the American
         Psychiatric Association.

5. Psychiatric After-Care (Sheldon, 1964)

Mental hospitals in England had high readmission rates,
so a field study was undertaken to see if "after-care" of
discharged patients could reduce readmission significantly.
Women between the ages of 20 and 59 were randomly assigned
to psychiatric after-care treatment or to their general
practitioner, the latter being viewed as the standard
treatment. The after-care involved 45 women; the standard
involved 44. The psychiatric after-care group was further
divided into a day center nurse treatment mode and an
outpatient clinic with a doctor; this assignment was also
random.

After six months, the general practitioners returned their patients to the hospital in about 47% of the cases, while the nurse and the MD (the psychiatric team) sent back about 18% of theirs. The psychiatric team kept their group under care for a longer period than the general practitioners, but had less rehospitalization. The investigation found that the better the attendance, the less the readmission in all three groups. But the psychiatric team was more frequently associated with good attendance by the patient than was the general practitioner.

We rate this innovation plus. The lower return-to-hospital data make it seem like a double plus, but since the innovators may be biased in keeping the patients out, we think caution is in order. Were the decision for rehospitalization being made by a separate decision group, the research would be tighter.

RATING: +

6. <u>Rehabilitation of Mentally Ill</u> (Fairweather, 1964)

The purpose of this investigation was to help chronic mental patients move into the outside world more effectively. As a treatment the investigators formed small, autonomous, problem-solving groups to provide mutual support and prepare patients for the outside world.

Patients from the neuro-psychiatric section of a V.A. Hospital were randomly assigned between two treatment programs. One was the small-group innovation with 111 patients; the other was a standard "traditional" program with 84 patients. The treatment lasted for six months within the hospital, and the follow-up outside the hospital took another six months.

Outcome measures included both in-hospital data and community behavior after release on variables such as employment, friendships, communication, residence, and physical and social activity indices.

The findings were that the innovation succeeded modestly in most of its goals. The small group patients had a greater degree of social participation, had more cohesiveness, and had better employment and active community involvement. The small group program had no effect, however, on general attitudes toward mental illness.

RATING: +

7. <u>Rehabilitation of Nursing Home Patients</u> (Kelman, 1962)

Could patients in nursing homes be given training in self-care that would improve their abilities to function in ways such as locomotion, transfer (changing positions), feeding, dressing, washing, and handling toilet problems? The hope was to help patients without extreme physical impairments to care for themselves.

The investigators assigned 200 patients randomly to two treatment groups and assigned 100 patients to a nontreatment group; 11 nursing homes were involved. In addition 100 more nontreatment patients were selected from an additional four nursing homes. The testing team collected the data blindly; they did not know the subject's group.

The conclusion after one year was that rehabilitation treatment did not substantially alter functional status. The quality of self-care was unimproved, and the rehabilitation programs also did not reduce hospitalizations and mortality.

RATING: 0

8. Family Medical Care (Silver, 1963)

This study examined the effectiveness of "team practice" using teams of an internist, social worker, and public health nurse in combining prevention and treatment of both physical and emotional disorders. For a family to be eligible for the study, it had to have both parents alive, father not more than 45, and at least one child. The specific treatment included family guidance and emotional support from the health team, as well as literature, meetings, films, and conferences.

Families were randomly assigned to treatment or nontreatment groups. The experimental group had 124 families (150 were invited, but 124 accepted), and the nontreatment group had 150 families. Outcome variables included physical condition, nutrition, educational achievement of children, recreational adjustment, and various intrafamily relationships. Data were collected from the treatment group both at the beginning and end of the study, but only at the end from the nontreatment group.

The results indicated that treatment families in general did not outperform the nontreatment families on most outcome variables. The two groups were similar in physical health and children's educational achievement. Controls actually did better in 9 out of 12 evaluation areas.

RATING: 0

G. *SUMMARY FOR SOCIO-MEDICAL INNOVATIONS*

Of the eight innovations rated here, one on tonsillectomy was rated double plus. The two innovations treated here on psychiatric care were rated plus. The zeros included a training program for medical students in comprehensive medical care, an attempt at treatment of persons arrested for drunkenness through legal assignment to therapy, a physical training program for the elderly in caring for themselves, and a team approach to family medical care. The one innovation scoring a negative was the outpatient payments for people with medical insurance. These subscribers had more hospital days than those with the ordinary policies. It is possible that the long-run effect of such a program would be more positive, as we have noted in the text.

H. *EVALUATIONS OF MEDICAL, MAINLY SURGICAL, INNOVATIONS*

Ten of the twelve studies presented in this section were found through a systematic MEDLARS search of the surgical literature (see close of this introduction). Our surgical advisers, who checked the ratings, were somewhat uneasy about associating 0's with some of these evaluations even though they agreed in these instances that the innovation itself was no improvement. They asked us to be sure to emphasize that some of these investigations are milestones in surgery--landmark studies--and that current surgical research and practice are building on these important studies. Their point is, of course, quite general.

First, when one has a solid finding, one can reason from it for some distance with assurance. Second, the value of an evaluation comes not only from the appraisal of the innovation or program it reviews, but also from the related findings which can be used in later work. Elsewhere, we emphasize the value that a substantial body of information has for long-run policy. Third, when an innovation widely expected to be successful does not perform as anticipated, either as therapy or according to theory, such firm knowledge points researchers in new directions.

To these three ideas, we would add a fourth. On first realizing that our systematic method of collecting had produced several milestone studies in surgery, we felt quite lucky. But on second thought, perhaps randomized clinical trials described in medical journals are just where one finds landmark studies. Maybe well-done randomized clinical trials create landmark studies.

When discussing these evaluations with others, we were asked by many to describe the illnesses and the operations in everyday terms. We authors could not do this, and we are grateful to Bucknam McPeek, M.D. for providing these descriptions. His initials follow his descriptive paragraphs. He also provided the following description of the MEDLARS search:

> For the past ten years, computer-produced bibliographies on biomedical subjects have been provided through the National Library of Medicine's Medical Literature Analysis and Retrieval

System (MEDLARS). At present, about 2,300 separate journals are indexed into the system. Most
journals are indexed cover to cover. However,
general scientific journals, such as Science and
Nature, are indexed for their biomedical coverage
only. At present, the MEDLARS data base comprises
well over one million citations, beginning January
1964. This data base is now growing at the rate
of 200,000 citations annually. Approximately 50
percent of the articles cited are written in
English.

The indexing process involves the careful
analysis of articles, and description of their
contents by the use of specific subject headings
selected from a list of 8,000 subject headings.
Articles are indexed with as many subject headings
as are needed to fully describe the subject matter
discussed.

A MEDLARS search request asks for a retrospective search through the indexed citations in
the data base to retrieve those that deal with a
particular subject matter. A search analyst goes
through a two-stage process: first, he must
decide what articles are wanted; and second, he
must translate his interpretation of the request
into a search statement in MEDLARS subject heading
terms that can be processed by computer against
the citation file. In practice, this is a system
of asking for articles which are indexed under one
or more terms. In the development of the MEDLARS
search used in this paper, we requested articles
dealing with prospective studies in surgery,
written in the English language, and available
from medical libraries in the Greater Boston area.
From this MEDLARS search, we selected the first
ten randomized clinical trials encountered.

1. A Prospective Evaluation of Vagotomy-Pyloroplasty and

    Vagotomy-Antrectomy for Treatment of Duodenal Ulcer

    (Jordan & Condon, 1970)

We do not have an exact understanding of the causes of
duodenal ulcers, but most standard treatments for ulcers are

aimed toward decreasing the production of stomach acid. A very common surgical treatment for serious ulcer disease involves cutting the vagus nerves in an effort to decrease acid production. This procedure, vagotomy, is almost always performed either in association with an operation to enlarge the exit through which food leaves the stomach, or as a part of an operation to remove the lower portion of the stomach where the bulk of acid production is located. These two operations are called vagotomy-drainage for the former or vagotomy-resection for the latter. This study attempted to compare these two forms of surgical treatment. (B. McP.)

Patients were assigned to one of two groups using a "randomized series held in the custody of the study secretary" (p. 547). The two groups were 108 patients who had vagotomy-drainage (V-D) and 92 patients who had vagotomy-resection (V-R). There were two operative deaths in the V-D group, whose causes were believed not relevant to the treatment. "It is concluded ... that vagotomy and antrectomy (V-R) is superior to vagotomy and drainage (V-D) ... in the majority of patients because of its lower recurrence rate without the association of increased morbidity or mortality" (p. 560). Eight patients were reoperated on for recurrence, all in the V-D group, and two of the three patients suspected of having recurrences were also in the V-D group.

RATING: ++

2. Comparison of Symptoms after Vagotomy with Gastrojejunostomy and Partial Gastrectomy (Cox, 1968)

Like the preceding study, this paper compares two surgical treatments for serious ulcer disease. Studied were a
vagotomy-drainage operation (vagotomy with gastrojejunostomy), and a resection-only operation; i.e., removal of the
lower portion of the stomach without cutting the vagus nerve
(partial gastrectomy). (B. McP.)

"The choice of operation was determined by random
selection after exploration of the abdomen had confirmed the
diagnosis and shown that either operation could be performed
with safety" (p. 288). Fifty-five patients had partial
gastrectomy. Fifty-one patients had vagotomy with
gastrojejunostomy.

The study showed that the difference, if any, was small
and seemed to favor the vagotomy group so far as symptoms
are concerned; however, other factors (recurrent ulceration
and survival) showed a slight advantage for the gastrectomy
group.

RATING: 0

3. Selective or Truncal Vagotomy? A Double-Blind Randomized Controlled Trial (Kennedy & Connell, 1969)

There are two ways by which the vagus nerve may be cut
to perform a vagotomy for the surgical treatment of ulcer
disease. In a truncal vagotomy, the vagus nerve is cut as
it approaches the stomach. In a selective vagotomy, only
those nerve fibers which appear to be supplying the acid-
forming portions of the stomach are cut. A selective

104

vagotomy is technically more difficult and more time consuming. If it could be shown that there are no advantages in selective vagotomy, surgeons would prefer to do the quicker, more easily performed truncal vagotomy. (B. McP.)

"The early results of a double-blind, randomised controlled trial of selective and truncal vagotomy, each combined with pyloroplasty, in the treatment of 100 patients with duodenal ulcer are described" (p. 899). After one year, "No patient had died, and there was no difference in clinical grading between the two groups" (p. 899). There were 50 patients in each group. Further follow-up is planned.

RATING: 0

4. Five-Year Follow-up of the Medical Research Council Comparative Trial of Surgery and Radiotherapy for the Primary Treatment of Small-Celled or Oat-Celled Carcinoma of the Bronchus (Miller, Fox, & Tall, 1969)

Cancer of the lung is a dread disease. The outlook for most patients is bleak regardless of the treatment used. Cancer kills not only by direct growth of the original tumor, interfering with a vital structure, but also because of the tendency of the cancer to metastasize and spread at a distance by seeding itself in other tissues of the body. Two common treatments are to remove the portion of the lung containing the affected bronchus and cancer (surgery), or to attempt to destroy the cancer cells with powerful radiation. The surgical treatment involves a major operation with all its attendant hospitalization, pain, and risk. Radiation therapy is lengthy and has its own risks. Patients frequently become ill from side effects of the treatment. (B. McP.)

There were 71 patients allocated at random to surgery and 73 to radical radiation therapy. "The mean survival for the surgery series was 199 days and for the radical-radiotherapy series 284 days, a statistically significant difference (P=0.05). It is concluded that in this trial radical radio-therapy has given, in terms of survival, a somewhat better result than surgery ..." (p. 501).

We found this innovation hard to rate. On the one hand, the percentage increase in life expectation is large; on the other, it is not absolutely large. Further, there are questions about the relative quality of life under the two treatments.

RATING: + or ++

5. Factors Influencing Survival after Resection in Cancer of the Colon and Rectum (Dwight, Higgins, & Keehn, 1969)

The standard treatment for cancer of the colon and rectum is to remove the affected area surgically. The surgeon is ordinarily able to remove all of the primary tumor, but he usually cannot tell whether or not it may have already spread or metastasized to other areas. In an effort to kill microscopic seedings of tumor cells which may have been left behind, surgeons have considered treatment of their patients with anti-cancer drugs such as TSPA, in addition to operation. (B. McP.)

This study is a trial of triethylenethiophosphoramide (TSPA) as an adjuvant (a help) to surgery in cancer of the colon and rectum. Patients were assigned to this additional treatment or to a control group at random. There were 469 in the treatment group and 595 in the control group. This difference in size arises because the treatment was suspected of causing increased post-operative mortality and was discontinued for six months. It was then decided that the suspicion was not correct and the treatment was reinstated, although at a lower dosage schedule. The study concluded that this additional treatment produced no improvement in five-year survival. (The discussion suggests that not even the surgery is very effective for this type of cancer.)

RATING: 0

6. Conclusions from a Controlled Trial of the Prophylactic Portacaval Shunt (Callow et al., 1970)

A number of liver diseases (chronic alcoholism, hepatitis, etc.) have, as a final stage, scarring or cirrhosis of the liver. Among other effects, cirrhosis of the liver causes an obstruction to venous blood flow from the intestinal tract. This venous obstruction leads to the development of varicose veins in the esophagus (esophageal varices) which are prone to rupture and produce massive (frequently fatal) bleeding. Treatment of advanced cirrhosis of the liver and esophageal varices is very unsatisfactory. One of the methods is to attempt to bypass the scarred liver, shunting the blood around the block through an artificial pathway between the portal vein and the vena cava. This is a long, difficult and hazardous operation. (B. McP.)

The patients all had moderate-to-advanced cirrhosis of the liver and had had esophageal varices (lumps and irregularities on veins) demonstrated by barium swallow. Of these, 48 were randomized to surgery and 45 to medical treatment. The main conclusion was that "In this type of patient from the lower socioeconomic group with poor nutritional habits, prophylactic portacaval shunt does not exert a beneficial effect upon survival ... Although surgical therapy greatly reduced the incidence of esophageal bleeding ... it failed to improve longevity" (p. 103).

This study is related to the clinical trials discussed in Section V-B. Our surgical advisers note that this study is very important for society because it showed that an expensive, high-risk procedure was not an effective treatment for this class of patients. That remark emphasizes again that the value of the innovation can be small or negative, as here, but the value of the field trial very high.

RATING: 0

7. Topical Ampicillin and Wound Infection in Colon Surgery
   (Nash & Hugh, 1967)

Operations on the colon inevitably involve the risk of spreading small amounts of fecal material from within the colon to contaminate the surgical wound. With the development of antibiotics over the last generation, surgeons have considered the prophylactic use of antibiotics as a means of reducing wound infections. (B. McP.)

"Seventy patients undergoing operations on the large bowel were divided by random selection into two groups. In one group the use of topical powdered ampicillin in the main abdominal wound was associated with a significant reduction in wound sepsis. No side-effects were noted" (p. 472).

This study was not done blind, although a placebo powder could perhaps have been used.

RATING: +

8. A Controlled Trial of Inverting Versus Everting Intestinal Suture in Clinical Large-Bowel Surgery (Goligher et al., 1970)

The standard method of joining two segments of bowel together is to suture the bowel together in such a fashion that the outside layer of both segments are approximated. Technically this is called inverting, as the cut edges are turned toward the center of the bowel. Recently some have advocated the reverse; i.e., joining the bowel in such a fashion that the inner layers are approximated with the cut edges being everted or directed toward the outer surface. This new method also uses a different style of suturing. (B. McP.)

This trial was done to compare the new method, everting, to the old method of suturing the bowel, inverting. Thirty-five patients were assigned to each treatment at random, and the numbers of patients who developed wound infections, peritonitis, or overt fecal fistulation were observed. The conclusion was that "These experiences are considered to provide a clear condemnation of the use of an everting technique of suture in the large intestine in clinical practice" (p. 817). Thus the new technique was judged to be definitely poorer than the older one.

RATING: --

9. The Use of Chlorhexidine Antisepsis in Contaminated Surgical Wounds (Crosfill, Hall, & London, 1969)

This study is similar to surgical study No. 7 in that an antibacterial agent (in this case chlorhexidine) is used to wash the surgical wound in an effort to prevent post-operative infection. In one group of randomly chosen patients the wound was washed with a solution that was saline and in another randomly chosen group the washing solution contained the drug. The surgeon did not know which solution was which. Every third patient got neither treatment. There were in total 97 patients treated with a saline solution, 99 drug-treated patients, and 92 additional patients with no treatment. All groups were virtually identical, both with respect to wound sepsis and to hospital stay.

RATING: 0

10. Early Pituitary Implantation with Yttrium-90 for Advanced Breast Cancer (Stewart et al., 1969)

The pituitary is the source of some hormones which may affect the growth of breast cancer. Yttrium-90 is a radioactive isotope which, if implanted in the pituitary gland, will destroy pituitary cells and decrease hormonal production. (B. McP.)

"A controlled randomised trial was carried out in 119 patients with advanced cancer of the breast, to establish whether yttrium-90 implantation of the pituitary, performed early in the course of metastatic disease, results in longer survival than the initial use of other methods of palliation. The results indicate that, in general, there is no advantage and that in some instances early suppression of pituitary function may actually do harm" (p. 816).

RATING: —

11. Gastric Freezing (Wangensteen et al., 1962; Ruffin et al., 1969)

Gastric 'freezing' was introduced as a treatment of ulcers by Dr. Wangensteen on the basis of extensive work with animals as well as clinical observations on his own patients. It was suggested that the production of acid in the stomach could be permanently decreased by freezing the interior wall of the stomach. The treatment consisted of placing a balloon in the patient's stomach which was then irrigated with a coolant at -10° C for about an hour. The treatment was thought to offer a safer, simpler alternative to patients who would otherwise have gone to surgery. Although the procedure was widely used, there were reports of complications and some reservations about its acceptance by many physicians. After many small studies with conflicting results had been published (see Section V-B), a cooperative randomized trial involving several different institutions was performed (Ruffin et al., 1969). This trial failed to document any significant benefit to the patient from this treatment as compared to a sham treatment in which the patient's stomach was not cooled.

RATING: 0

12. Salk Vaccine (Francis et al., 1955; Meier, 1972; Brownlee, 1955)

This study was described in Section III.

RATING: ++

I. *SUMMARY OF MEDICAL RATINGS*

The 10 randomized trials found through the MEDLARS search gave one double plus for a vagotomy operation, and two pluses, one for ampicillin and the other for radiation treatment of cancer of the bronchus. There were five zeros and two negatives, one being a double negative. Thus great successes were hard to find. To the ten trials found through the MEDLARS search we have added Gastric Freezing, a zero; and Salk Vaccine, a double plus. By excluding these two, we have a rather objectively drawn sample.

J. *SUMMARY OF RATINGS*

Table 4 summarizes the ratings of the 28 single-goal studies we have now described. We should make clear that some of these studies may have had more goals, but we chose to rate only the one that we regarded as central. Since the gamma globulin study and the Des Moines Bail Study were not randomized trials, we do not include them in the ratings. Harvard Project Physics also is not included in the table of ratings, because it required the rating of two goals.

Overall, six innovations, or about 21% of the total, were scored double plus. The rate of double pluses does not differ sharply among the three groups. The pile-up at zero, 13 out of 28, or 46%, suggests that we have a rather broad interval for zeros.

We warn again that there may be some upward bias owing to selective reporting and selective finding by our searches. Even so, when we consider the high rate of failure of laboratory innovations, we can take pleasure in a success rate as high as the one seen here.

Except for the surgical innovations where we have a rather solid description of our population, the skeptical reader may feel we have no grounds for discussing rates of successful innovations in the absence of a population and in the presence of several possible selection effects. The difficulty is not unique--if one wants to know the percentage of new products that succeed or the percentage of new businesses that succeed, the same problems of definition of population and success arise.

Table 4. Summary of Ratings.

Rating	--	-	0	+	++
Social Innovations (Total 8)	0	0	3 D2. Welfare Workers D3. Girls at Voc. High D7. Pretrial Conf.	2 D4. Cottage Life D6. L.A. Police (or ++)	3 D1. Neg. Income Tax D5. Manhattan Bail D8. ESAP
Socio-medical Innovations (Total 8)	0	1 F1. Kansas Blue-Cross	4 F3. Comp. Med. Care F4. Drunk Probation F7. Nursing Home F8. Family Medical Care	2 F5. Psychiatric After-care F6. Mental Illness	1 F2. Tonsillectomy
Medical Innovations (Total 12)	1 H8. Everting	1 H10. Yttrium-90	6 H2. Vagotomy (Cox) H3. Vagotomy (Kennedy) H5. Cancer H6. Portacaval Shunt H9. Chlorhexidine H11. *Gastric Freezing	2 H4. Bronchus (possibly ++) H7. Ampicillin	2 H1. Vagotomy (Johnson) H12. *Salk Vaccine
Grand Total	1	2	13	6	6

*These two studies did not emerge from the MEDLARS search. All the other medical innovations did.

114

To repeat briefly our remarks in Section IV-A, we guess that a higher proportion of better studied programs with published reports are likely to be successful than those less well studied. Further, more successful programs are more likely to have come to our attention. Consequently, we believe that the estimate of about 21% successful innovations is high compared to what a census would yield.

Beyond the question of the adequacy of our sample, the programs in our series that have had little or no success are in themselves an important source for concern, since they each represent a serious but unsuccessful attempt to solve a problem.

We have pointed out how even successful innovations often lead to small gains, how important such gains are for building on in the future, and the value of a randomized controlled field trial for detecting these gains. It is worth noting further that small gains can come about in more than one way. For example, nearly everyone in a program may gain a little bit, leading to a modest but widespread overall average gain. Or, some fraction or subgroup of people in a program may gain substantially, while other subgroups and perhaps most participants show no gains. The ESAP investigation, where black males in high school were found to benefit substantially while other groups did not show improvement, illustrates this latter possibility. Society may find such information useful when deciding what programs to implement.

To sum up, the major findings of this section are that 1) among societal innovations studied here, about one in five succeeded; and 2) among those that succeeded, the gain was often small in size, though not in importance.

Both findings have important consequences for the policy maker considering methods of evaluation and for the attitudes toward programs that society needs to develop. We should treasure and try to strengthen programs that have even small gains. After we gather further information in later sections, the implications are taken up in Section X.

V. FINDINGS FROM NONRANDOMIZED STUDIES

A. *NONRANDOMIZED STUDIES*

Section IV treated ratings of innovations, ratings obtained from randomized controlled field trials. Next we explore the results of investigations that for the most part did not use randomization. We will see the consequences of this approach for both weakness of the findings and the ultimate time taken to gather firm information.

1. The Baltimore Housing Study (Wilner et al., 1962)

D. M. Wilner et al. (1962) undertook a study to see what the effects of improved housing were on physical, mental, and social health of low-income families. These effects were regarded as additional possible benefits over and above the improved shelter, cooking, and toilet facilities. This was a landmark study involving a large number of investigators from different fields, the development of new instruments for measuring outcomes, and improved methods of data collection, as well as careful analysis of the results. The treatment group of 300 families was given public housing with improved room, heat, toilet, refrigeration, and garbage disposal facilities. The control group consisted of 300 families matched with treatment families on social and demographic background characteristics. This study was not a randomized trial. Housing was assigned by the Baltimore Housing Authority and the matched control group was picked from the waiting list. Over a three-year period the two groups were compared on housing quality, physical morbidity, social-psychological adjustment, and children's performance in school.

The results showed that on several outcome variables the group that received the better housing had improved life circumstances. Mortality was substantially lower in the housing group, and morbidity (illness) in the housing group was lower for persons under 35, although not for older people. Accidents in the housing group were reduced by one third. While the children in the housing group did not improve on standardized tests, they were more likely to be promoted on schedule and had better school attendance.

Overall the results of the housing can be described as a success, and if the evaluation of this innovation had been based upon a randomized controlled field trial, we would have included it in the examples given in the preceding section. The crux of our problem is that we do not know the effect of the criteria used by the housing authority to choose those most deserving of housing from their large field of applicants. If, for example, the perceived potential of the applicant to develop in other ways if relieved of the disadvantages of poor housing were a conscious or unconscious factor in choosing the families to get the new housing, the study would in large part be verifying this assessment rather than the effect of the housing. If, on the other hand, the assignment was to give the new housing to the applicants most in need, the effectiveness of housing on the social outcomes measured might be seriously understated by the data. And, of course, the reverse could occur using other criteria, such as first come, first served.

If selection procedures positively biased the Wilner study, society could be badly disappointed with the results of a social program based on its findings. Let us notice that by not having done the randomization to begin with, the study has made it more difficult for someone later to try to find out, because the original finding is so agreeable to our prejudices.

2. Nutrition Delivery in the Philippines (Salcedo, 1954)

A study was done in the Philippines to see if the death rate from the disease beriberi could be reduced by substituting fortified rice for white rice. Here is a case where it was extremely difficult to carry off a genuine randomized experiment. If neighbors received different "treatments" as part of the experiment (that is, if one person received white rice and his neighbor received fortified rice), how could one be sure that the neighbors would not share their different rices? Or, how could one be sure that neighbors would not trade their rices, or even perhaps sell them to other people?

To overcome these problems, the Bataan Peninsula was divided into two parts, control and experimental; 29,000 people got regular white rice, while 63,000 got enriched rice. The results were that after one year the beriberi death rate decreased by 56% in the experimental zone and increased 10% in the control zone. The incidence of beriberi in the experimental area dropped from 14.3% to 1.5%, while in the control area it rose from 6.7% to 8.7%.

It is instructive to examine some of the issues illustrated by this study. First, although the fortified rice was not randomly distributed over the entire Bataan Peninsula, and therefore did not constitute a true randomized field study, we view the results as positively convincing. We are willing to assume that people on one side of the Bataan Peninsula were not different in important ways from those on the other. We also assume that some other innovation did not come in to confuse the findings--this is always a possibility to consider. The study was large and based upon nearly the whole Bataan population. The medical situation was such that there was solid reason for believing that the fortified rice would reduce the death rate from the disease. While it is possible that people might not have been eating the new rice, the reduction in beriberi deaths encourages us to suppose that they were. The result would have been important even if it worked in only the half that actually got the fortified rice.

Second, a major concern of this innovation was whether the new rice would be accepted in the regular rice trade. The study answered this. The new rice was accepted.

3. Head Start Planned Variation: A Nonrandomized Experiment

In the field of preschool education, one of the most widely known innovations is the compensatory program called "Head Start." Its purposes as outlined in the enabling legislation are several, but a clearly important component is the development of academic skills, the better to prepare children from relatively poorer families for school.

Head Start worked in a very decentralized manner. From the beginning, local groups applied for funding, and as long as certain minimum legal requirements were met, they received funding to develop centers and enroll children. Thus, by 1968, there were hundreds of centers scattered throughout the country, with essentially no centralized coordination for learning about program effectiveness.

Because of this general lack of information about the program's effectiveness, and the fact that it was costing several hundreds of millions of dollars per year, the Office of Economic Opportunity commissioned in 1968 an evaluation of Head Start. This report was issued in 1969 by Westinghouse Learning Corporation and Ohio University (Cicirelli et al., 1969). It examined summer-program effects and full-year program effects. Its basic conclusion in the area of cognitive development was that in the aggregate, Head Start children had insignificantly better performance than comparable children not in the program.

Because Head Start was and still remains a politically popular program, the Westinghouse Report had major repercussions in the educational research community. In particular, a number of critics (e.g., Smith & Bissell, 1970) pointed out two major flaws of the study: first, it was entirely retrospective; and second, it lumped together dozens of different kinds of Head Start programs under the single rubric "Head Start" and then compared these aggregated children with another group of aggregated nonrandom "control" children. The critics argued that Head Start programs could not be thrown together helter skelter, and that a more organized study of the program's effectiveness was needed. The Westinghouse evaluators had anticipated some of these criticisms themselves, noting especially the retrospective nature of the study and their inability to perform a randomized field trial under the existing conditions.

This led in 1969 to Head Start Planned Variation (HSPV). HSPV was a large national investigation, and was actually a downward extension of a study developed for a follow-up program to Head Start for older children, called Follow Through. We discuss the HSPV evaluation here at some length because it provides a valuable illustration of what we can and cannot learn from a nonrandomized field study. HSPV was a three-year study designed to compare the different kinds of effects that different kinds of Head Start centers were having on children. It was built upon the assumption that by selecting "sponsors" for different types of programs, and by systematically varying the kinds of programs offered to children, much could be learned about which kinds of programs most benefited which kinds of children. Thus the words "planned variation"; the sponsors were selected to participate in this investigation precisely because they were able to specify their goals and their curriculum structure, and the sponsors who were selected had a substantial amount of variation in their goals and teaching strategies. In addition, each sponsor had developed a laboratory model of its curriculum, and wanted to try it out in the field.

The concept behind HSPV was excellent: to vary Head Start curricula and then study the effects of the different kinds of curricula. The full benefit of this idea in the field was never achieved. In particular, there was no randomization anywhere in the assignment process--no randomization of sponsors to sites, no randomization of children to sponsors.

To illustrate what happened in this investigation, we focus on the data from the 1971-72 academic year. This was the last of the three years of the HSVP study. During this academic year, 11 sponsors were distributed over a total of 28 sites. In addition, for comparison purposes, 11 of the 28 sites also had "nonsponsored" Head Start classrooms. Finally, three sites had "control group" children not enrolled in any preschool program. According to Herbert Weisberg (1973), "these children were contacted by direct recruitment or from Head Start waiting lists."

The evaluators of HSPV, Smith (1973) and Weisberg (1973), tried to disentangle the various confounded effects that made inferences difficult because of lack of randomization. But their studies illustrate how crucial randomization is for facilitating inferences.

Overall, each sponsor had somewhere between two and four sites, except for one sponsor who had only one site. Within each site, there were a variable number of classrooms that were "operated" by the appropriate sponsor. At some sites there were both sponsored classrooms and nonsponsored, regular Head Start classrooms, while at other sites there were only sponsored classrooms. Several important variables were unequally distributed across the sponsors. In particular, such variables included (according to Weisberg) race, age of children, prior preschool experience, and socio-economic status. To choose one extreme example, one sponsor had almost no black children at his sites, while another sponsor had almost no white children.

What policy conclusions were drawn from the HSPV study? First, Weisberg found that, overall, both the sponsors' programs and the regular Head Start programs seemed to accelerate certain kinds of specific academic performance, such as letter and number recognition. Second, pooling together the 11 sponsored sets of centers and comparing them to the regular, nonsponsored Head Start centers revealed no large differences. Third, when the 11 sponsored centers were compared among themselves, some differences between sponsors emerged on performance on the several cognitive tests. That is, certain types of curricula seemed to enhance different kinds of cognitive development.

Despite the lack of randomization in HSPV, many valuable lessons were learned. In particular, viewing HSPV as a pilot study gives us important information about the difficulties and the time required to install a complex curriculum in the field, even after it has been developed in the laboratory. Let us note, though, that these sorts of findings are not the ones we were scoring in Section IV.

We view HSPV not as a randomized experiment, but rather as a sort of pilot study of implementing new curricula. Let us see what the very existence of HSPV tells us about the willingness of federal agencies to experiment to learn more about the effectiveness of their programs. HSPV involved a few dozen sites for three years. It was initially conceived as a three-year project, which indicates that program developers were willing and able to organize more than a "one-shot" study. According to Wilson (1974), the entire investigation cost $50.4 million and involved a total of 39,900 students. (Note that since much of it was the cost of the substitute program and its management, the marginal cost of the field trial was vastly less.) Thus we see that a federal agency was willing to spend a substantial amount of time, planning, and resources, and involve a large number of children in an effort to learn something about the effectiveness of Head Start and about how to improve it. Further, the argument that "the big program should be held up until we spend several years with an experiment" was not applied. HSPV illustrates, then, that a small study, involving several dozen sites and costing a modest fraction of the overall program budget, can be mounted in the field to provide information as to how the program is working and how it might be improved. Let us draw this further positive message from HSPV. But, again, recall that our information about the success of the innovation is weak, and since it was not a randomized study, we do not score it.

4. Performance Contracting (Gramlich & Koshel, 1973)

The idea of accountability for instruction in education led to the concept of performance contracting. This means essentially that those doing the teaching get paid in accordance with the amount the pupil learns. This idea is rather old and was used in England in the eighteen hundreds.

Recently some companies felt that they could teach children better than the public schools, at least in some subjects, and they were willing to contract to do so, being paid according to performance. The Office of Economic Opportunity found a number of school districts that were willing to participate in a field trial using such contractors. The contractors apparently believed that they could improve performance substantially--perhaps by gains of one or two hundred percent.

The Office of Economic Opportunity (OEO) did not do a randomized trial, but rather assigned schools to the contractors. (OEO might have randomized the schools as in our ESAP description, but probably could not randomize pupils directly.) Each contractor taught about 100 pupils. It turned out that the students assigned to the performance contractors were not initially achieving as well as those in the control groups because the experimental schools had lower averages. That is, the performance contractors were initially at a disadvantage. Thus the companies doing the performance contracting probably had more trouble teaching their children than the regular school groups did theirs. In addition, there was an even deeper problem. The OEO had decided to run the experiment for only one year. The companies had to begin teaching four months after they bid on the contract and two months after being informed that they had won. This is in very marked contrast to the two- or three-year period used in installing the programs in the Planned Variation studies of Head Start and Follow Through. One might have expected that the performance contracting idea would have been developed and implemented more gradually. In the end, as near as one can tell, the contractors did, after adjustment for initial inequality, a little better, perhaps 9%, than the control groups. Recall that the control groups were not rushed for installation, as they were already installed in existing schools. We do not feel strongly about the value of performance contracting, but we do think it unwise to start and stop experiments so rapidly. For instance, contractors had no time to adjust to the new set of financial incentives.

There were, of course, political problems with performance contracting. Most teachers' unions didn't like the idea. The companies had signed contracts that let them in for potentially large financial losses, and the possibility of only modest gains. (It is not clear why.) The rush to installation might have been caused by a now-or-never atmosphere in Washington (Gramlich & Koshel, 1973).

It is difficult to say with a high degree of confidence how well the contractors did. The analysis necessarily depends very heavily on adjustment methods because of the initial lack of randomization. Thus we see a study that inflicted all the pains of innovation and gathered little of the fruits of knowledge.

It could be argued, of course, that this is just an example where the political problems took precedence over careful development of findings. Whether they did or not, society missed out as far as firm findings were concerned. Furthermore, once people learn that a procedure is effective, the political system has a way of adapting so as to use the new procedure. For example, it appears that some of the school systems involved in the performance contracting study have now adapted some of the contractors' materials into their ongoing programs.

5. Manpower Training

We shall not treat here the Department of Labor's manpower training programs, except to say that they offer another setting where many evaluative studies have been done but have led to little information about either the effectiveness of the training or how to improve the programs. In Section VIII-A we treat this program in some detail.

6. Rehabilitating Schizophrenics (Meyer & Borgatta, 1959)

Generally we have not explained the sorts of troubles that can arise with randomized controlled field trials. Lest the reader suppose that we do not recognize real difficulties that occur, we describe an investigation carried out by outstanding investigators on a disease of considerable importance.

Schizophrenic hospital patients between 20 and 40 years old were randomly assigned into a treatment group of 41 people who were to receive post-hospitalization psychiatric care and jobs in a sheltered workshop, and a control group of 40 people who received no such care and no workshop. The treatment group did not all get the treatment: one third had no contact with the workshop, one third had limited contact, and one third entered the workshop.

The outcome measure was avoidance of recommitment. In the treatment group 76% had not been rehospitalized at follow-up, compared with 62% of the control subjects. Within the treatment group, 83% of the group participating in the workshop were not recommitted, compared with 72% from the other two thirds combined. Thus, although the treatment looks promising, the numbers actually taking the treatment are so small that we cannot be very confident about the size of the effect. Meyer and Borgatta write, "The strongest conclusion that can be stated on the basis of these data about the effectiveness of Altro [the treatment] ... is that actual participation in the program seems slightly advantageous" (p. 97).

We decided not to rate this innovation, even though a randomized study had been attempted, on the ground that it had failed in execution because the treatment group did not accept the treatment.

B. *NONRANDOMIZED STUDIES IN MEDICINE*

We have mentioned earlier the value for social investigators of learning from the medical experience. What we have been observing recently in medicine are systematic attempts to appreciate the interpretative difficulties in ordinary nonrandomized investigations as compared with randomized controlled clinical trials. Much experience is building up, and we can profit from a short review of very extensive work in a few medical areas.

About 1945 an operation called portacaval shunt was introduced to treat bleeding in the esophagus for certain patients, and this operation has been extended for other purposes. After 20 years of experience with this operation and 154 papers on the subject, it still was not clear (Grace, Muench, & Chalmers, 1966) what advice a physician should give to a patient with esophageal varices. In Section IV-H-6, we have already described this operation and an associated randomized controlled trial. That trial was performed several years after Grace, Muench, and Chalmers reviewed the literature to see whether they could resolve such questions as whether the operation would prevent further hemorrhage, what disabling side effects there might be, or what expectation of life went with the operation as compared with not having it.

They rated the investigations on two variables: degree of control in the investigation and degree of enthusiasm for the operation as expressed in the article reporting the trial. The degrees of enthusiasm after the study are: marked, moderate (with some reservations), and no conclusion or enthusiasm. The degrees of control are: 1) well-controlled--random assignment to treatment groups; 2) poorly controlled--selection of patients for treatment (compared with an unselected group or some other experience); and 3) uncontrolled--no comparison with another group of untreated patients.

For the physician, the details of the relationship for three types of shunt operations (emergency, therapeutic, and prophylactic) would have high interest, but for our purpose, it is enough to look at their grand total table, our Table 5, for studies with 10 or more patients.

Table 5 shows clearly that following their uncontrolled studies, investigators almost invariably express some enthusiasm for the shunt, and more than two thirds of the time express marked enthusiasm. Poorly controlled investigations have much the same outcome. On the other hand, in the six instances where the study was well-controlled, three investigators expressed moderate enthusiasm; the rest none. We assume that the investigators using the well-controlled field trials had better grounds for their degree of enthusiasm than did those with no controls or poor controls. (See footnote to Table 5 for more detail on the operations.)

Table 5. Degree of Control Versus Degree of Investigator Enthusiasm for Shunt Operation in 53 Studies Having at Least 10 Patients in the Series.

	Degree of enthusiasm			
Degree of control	Marked	Moderate	None	Totals
Well-controlled	0	3*	3*	6
Poorly controlled	10	3	2	15
Uncontrolled	24	7	1	32
Totals	34	13	6	53

Source: Revised from Grace, Muench, & Chalmers (1966), Table 2, p. 685. Copyright © 1966 The Williams and Wilkins Co., Baltimore.

*In the original source, the cell "well-controlled - moderate enthusiasm" had one entry, but Dr. Chalmers informed us by personal communication that two studies can now be added to that cell. Furthermore, he told us that the "well-controlled - moderate enthusiasm" group is associated with therapeutic shunts, and the "well-controlled - none" with prophylactic shunts.

Some other findings in the Grace, Muench, and Chalmers review of portacaval shunts were that after four years, the survival rates of patients undergoing elective therapeutic shunts were much the same as those who did not get them (the initial operative mortality was about 15%, based on 1244 patients). Although bleeding was reduced in the pro- phylactic group of operations, survival was not improved (the initial operative mortality was over 4%, based on 137 patients). We shall not go into the side effects problem here.

This investigation is informative because we can put the results of uncontrolled, poorly controlled, and well- controlled studies side by side. In all, the results of the investigation show that uncontrolled and poorly controlled studies led to greater enthusiasm than was warranted on the basis of the well-controlled studies. If the poorly controlled studies had suggested conclusions similar to those of the well-controlled trials, we, the surgeons, and policy makers, could be more comfortable with the results of related studies in similar contexts. But we see instead that the results are far from the same. By performing many poorly controlled trials we waste time and human experience and mislead ourselves as well. The argument that we do not have time to wait for well-controlled trials does not seem to have been applicable here.

Chalmers, Block, and Lee (1972) carried out a similar investigation in connection with estrogen therapy for car- cinoma of the prostate. This investigation had only two levels of enthusiasms (enthusiastic or negative) and two degrees of control (well-controlled or uncontrolled). The data of Table 6 show again the considerably higher rate of enthasiasm from investigators who have uncontrolled trials. They also show how few controlled trials there are compared to uncontrolled.

Table 6. Clinical Trials of Estrogen Therapy of Carcinoma
of the Prostate.

| | Conclusions of authors | | |
Degree of control	Enthusiastic	Negative	Totals
Well-controlled	1	1	2
Uncontrolled	16	1	17
Totals	17	2	19

Source: Chalmers, Block, & Lee (1972), Table 3, p. 76.
Reprinted by permission from the New England
Journal of Medicine (Vol. 287, p. 75-78, 1972).

Chalmers, Block, and Lee point out that in spite of 57
papers in five years on the cancer chemotherapeutic agent
L-asparaginase, no one knows how it compares with other
possible therapies. They note that in 1972 the number of
clinical studies of this agent was decreasing. They take
this to mean that the drug may be considered more toxic than
beneficial. They point out that many more patients have
been used in these uncontrolled trials, from which no firm
evidence has been forthcoming, than would have been
necessary to conduct a modest randomized clinical trial. Of
the five controlled human trials of this agent, none deal
with comparisons with other treatments.

In 1972 at the annual meeting of the American Heart
Association, cardiologists and cardiovascular surgeons
expressed the need for caution in connection with operative
therapy for coronary artery disease, and urged controlled

clinical trials, according to Chalmers (1972). He points out that in 152 trials reported in the literature up to that time, only two were controlled, and that both of these found internal mammary artery ligation of no value. He goes on to explain the problem of making comparisons between medical treatment and surgical treatment, including especially the selective reporting of outcomes and the special selectivity of the patients in the uncontrolled series.

Lillian Miao (1974) has reviewed the literature on gastric freezing as a treatment for duodenal ulcer. This technique was proposed by Dr. Owen Wangensteen and his colleagues in 1962. Miao reports the results of 16 studies of this problem published in the following seven years. Nine were uncontrolled observational studies and involved a total of over 700 patients. The results varied from over 70% of patients with complete relief to less than 20%. Of the five reported controlled studies that were both randomized and double blind, two favored gastric freezing and three found no difference. All five randomized studies were small, the largest having 30 patients in each group, experimental and control. White, Hightower & Adalid (1964) estimated that at the time 1,000 freezing units were being used on 10,000 patients. Gastric freezing was finally abandoned after the publication of the negative results of the large, multi-institution, double-blind, randomized field trial by Ruffin et al. (1969), described in Section IV-H-11. It thus took a large randomized trial carried out at several institutions to convince the medical community of the value (or lack of it) of gastric freezing as a medical innovation.

C. *SUMMARY FOR SECTION V*

Now that we have reviewed a number of nonrandomized studies, what overall conclusions emerge? One characteristic of nonrandomized studies that shows up in context after context is that even after repeated studies had consistently gotten the same result, there was always room to doubt the validity of the finding. Indeed, in several medical areas--portacaval shunt, estrogen therapy, and gastric freezing--the findings were not backed up with the same degree of investigator enthusiasm when put to the test of a carefully controlled randomized trial. This weakness of uncontrolled trials poses a particularly difficult problem for the policy maker faced with what appears to be more and more evidence in favor of a particular course of action, when he knows that he may just be seeing the same biases again and again.

Nonrandomized trials may not only generate conclusions with doubtful validity--they may actually delay the implementation of better evaluations. If a series of nonrandomized studies indicates that a certain treatment is highly effective, some investigators will point out the ethical difficulties of withholding this apparently valuable treatment from some persons in a randomized trial. Yet the evidence in this section suggests that nonrandomized studies may often artificially inflate our estimate of a treatment's value. Whenever this happens, and a randomized trial is postponed as a consequence, an ineffective treatment or program may be administered for years. The opportunity cost of such a mistake can be high.

VI. ISSUES RELATED TO RANDOMIZATION

This section deals with topics in controlled field studies that are closely related to the matter of randomization.

A. *THE IDEA OF A SAMPLE AS A MICROCOSM*

In discussing both sample surveys and controlled trials, people often suggest that we not take random samples but that we build a small replica of the population, one that will behave like it and thus represent it. Then, to assess the effect of a treatment, the investigator would simply treat one small replica and not treat another, thereby getting a perfect measure of the treatment effect. This is such an attractive idea that we need to explain why it is not done more often, and to mention circumstances when it nearly can be done. We confine ourselves to discussing the construction of one small replica or microcosm because if we can make one we usually can make two.

When we sample from a population, we would like ideally a sample that is a microcosm or replica or mirror of the target population--the population we want to represent. For example, for a study of types of families, we might note that there are adults who are single, married, widowed, and divorced. We want to stratify our population to take proper account of these four groups and include members from each in the sample. Otherwise, perhaps by chance we would get none or too few in a particular group--such as divorced--to make a reliable analysis. This device of stratifying is widely used to strengthen the sample and bar chance from playing unfortunate tricks.

Let us push this example a bit further. Do we want also to take sex of individuals into account? Perhaps, and so perhaps we should also stratify on sex. How about size of immediate family (number of children: zero, one, two, three, ...)--should we not have each family size represented in the study? And region of the country, and size and type of city, and occupation of head of household, and education, and income, and .... The number of these important variables is rising very rapidly, and worse yet, the number of categories rises even faster. Let us count them. We have four marital statuses, two sexes, say five categories for size of immediate family (by pooling four or over), say four regions of the country, and six sizes and types of city, say five occupation groups, four levels of education, and three levels of income. This gives us in all 4x2x5x4x6x5x4x3 = 57,600 different possible types, if we are to mirror the population or have a small microcosm; and one observation per cell may be far from adequate. We thus may need hundreds of thousands of cases! Clearly this approach is getting too fine for most purposes, and such an investigation will not be carried out except when enormous resources are available. We cannot have a microcosm in most problems. What we can do instead is pick a few of the most important and controllable variables, stratify on these few, and then randomly select from within each of the groups or cells thus formed. The randomization is intended to control (make other things equal on the average) for other variables on which we have not been able to stratify. It prevents bias that would arise if, for example, a treatment group and control group, or several treatment groups, were quite different with respect to an important background variable, such as age of participants. This feature of making other things equal on the average applies as well to variables we have not thought of as to those we have. Randomization thus makes possible certain mathematical tests that might not otherwise be readily justified.

Why isn't the microcosm idea used all the time? The reason is not that stratification doesn't work. Rather it is because we do not have generally a closed system with a few variables (known to affect the responses) having a few levels each, with every individual in a cell being identical. To illustrate, in a grocery store we can think of size versus contents, where size is 1 pound or 5 pounds and contents are a brand of salt or a brand of sugar. Then in a given store we would expect four kinds of packages, and the variation of the packages within a cell might be negligible compared to the differences in size or contents between cells. But in social programs there are always many more variables and so there is not a fixed small number of cells. The microcosm idea will rarely work in a complicated social problem because we always have additional variables that may have important consequences for the outcome.

One can readily think of some circumstances when randomization might not be needed. In a chemical investigation, if we want to treat several samples of the same liquid, all of whose components are miscible, there seems to be little need to pick and choose among several aliquots as to which gets which treatment. The homogeneity of the liquid equates the basic material.

In a metallurgical study, the investigator may cut a piece of metal into chunks and treat them. Although these chunks may not be quite as homogeneous as the liquid in the chemical example, still they may be so much alike compared with the effect of the treatment we are about to administer that there is little reason to worry about randomization.

As a general rule, randomization has less value when the effect of the treatment is large enough to dominate both the biases in selection and the natural variability from one group or cell to another. When dealing with social problems, we must usually cope with variability among regions, families, schools, hospitals, and neighborhoods, often from several sources simultaneously. Consequently, the randomization matters a great deal, as does getting enough replications so that averages are sufficiently stable to give us a good estimate of the effects of treatments.

In discussing random sampling we do not limit our consideration to the simplest case of drawing two samples (one called the treatment group and the other called the control group) randomly from the population. Many variants of this idea can strengthen inferences. For example, in the ESAP study described in Section III, schools were paired, and then one of each pair was randomly assigned the treatment. Such a step improves the reliability of inference because the treatment-no treatment comparison is made over many pairs. Other procedures that can strengthen inference include stratification of the sort mentioned earlier, and sequential treatments where the choice of treatment that the next person or site receives depends upon all the information received up to the present time. Although we do not go into all the details of such procedures here, we expect that they will be increasingly used in the future. It is adequate for our purposes to recognize that these methods are waiting in the wings, and are sometimes used now. For example, as mentioned earlier, the New Jersey Work Incentive Program allocated its families to treatment in a special way which, while randomized, was designed to maximize the information developed by the investigation.

B. SEARCHING FOR SMALL PROGRAM EFFECTS

Sometimes it helps to distinguish between sampling errors and nonsampling errors in investigations. Sampling errors are the ones which would disappear if somehow we were able to take the entire population into the sample. Nonsampling errors arise from the various sorts of biases that occur from a variety of measurement and selectivity problems. For example, selectivity could bias the fractions of various kinds of individuals entering different treatment groups. Measurement error may produce biases because of poor recall, recording mistakes, nonresponse, and so on. In assessing small differences, as the sample grows, the biases from the nonsampling errors become more important, and then the big problems with assessment and evaluation have to do with these nonsampling errors.

This point is well illustrated by the Salk Vaccine trials described in Section III, where in the placebo control method the study was able to document selection effects by comparing the disease rate for non-vaccinated volunteers with that of those who declined to volunteer (57 versus 36 per hundred thousand). The bias amounts to about half the effect (57 versus 17 per hundred thousand) for volunteers. Increasing the size of the study would not have changed this effect substantially, if at all. It was only by comparing the two randomized groups that one obtained a good assessment of the treatment effect. As we search for smaller and smaller effects, it becomes more and more difficult to know whether these are due to the treatment or rather to some artifact or disturbance. Thus, a crucial property of randomization is the protection it offers from many sources of bias, some not even suspected of being important. Randomization greatly increases the confidence one can have in the results of a large trial, especially when treatment effects are small.

Let us now consider two circumstances when an investigation will require substantial numbers of participants. One is the case just discussed, where the occurrence of an event, such as poliomyelitis, is quite rare. Here, a large sample is needed simply to turn up a reasonable number of occurrences in either the treatment or nontreatment groups. The second case is when program effects are small. Here, whether or not an event is rare, small samples even in a randomized study may not have much chance of detecting small program effects.

What attitude might an investigator take when such small effects are found? We have noted earlier that when a social program is mounted, there is often great expectation for spectacular effects: gains of the order of a 50% improvement in performance, or a doubling in the rate of reading, or a drop of 50% in automobile fatalities. Our empirical study found, however, that for an innovation to achieve gains of such magnitude is an uncommon event. Let us think about this question of small gains a bit further.

To take an example from education, suppose that students exposed to an innovation were in general the poorer students in their school system, and that in the past their average gain score per academic year was in the neighborhood of 0.7 of a grade-equivalent unit. This is a realistic value. What kind of improvement for such students would we consider a "success"? Obviously, bringing about an enormous change, such as a doubling of the rate of gain, would be a wonderful achievement. Yet, in view of our empirical study of innovations, would not changing the gain rate incrementally, say by an additional 0.2 of a grade-equivalent unit, represent a valuable achievement? It is true that these students, who would now be gaining an average of 0.9 of a grade-equivalent unit per year, would on the average still be below the national norms. But their rate of gain, using the numbers just suggested, would have increased by 2/7, or better than 28%. Is a 28% annual increase in achievement educationally negligible? The authors believe not. This view would especially hold if the gain was achieved by students having the most trouble in school, and further served as a basis for additional future improvement. In the end, costs and alternative values decide whether society will pay a fair amount for this kind of progress, especially when there is a paucity of alternative treatments available, expensive or inexpensive, known to assure such gains. And, once again, the sensitivity offered by a randomized field trial is necessary to get good estimates of such modest yet important gains.

C. STUDYING THE INTERACTION EFFECTS IN SOCIAL PROGRAMS

Program evaluators frequently address the question, "How on the average does one treatment group compare with another?" In addition to this question about main effects, evaluators also need to consider questions about interaction effects. Two such questions are, "Does a treatment work well at some sites and poorly at others?" and "Does a program work better for some types of people than for others?" For example, although natural variation in effectiveness will account for some differences, features of the sites or the assignment of people to treatments at each site may cause the program to be more effective at some sites than at others. We may need a specially designed study to help us understand these different features and to adjust for their influences.

An example from the field of preschool education illuminates these issues. In the late 1960's, several studies examined the comparative effectiveness of three different kinds of preschool curricula. They involved three-year-old children of both sexes, who came from a broad cross section of socio-economic backgrounds and ethnic groups. The three different kinds of curricula were characterized as 1) highly structured academic; 2) traditional development curricula, relatively lacking in teacher-structured activities; and 3) Piagetian, with emphasis on student initiative.

Joan Bissell (1971) gathered raw data from three major studies, each evaluating these three types of curricula. One was conducted in New York, sponsored by the State Department of Education. The second was conducted in

Urbana, Illinois, sponsored by the U.S. Office of Education. The third was conducted in Ypsilanti, Michigan, also sponsored by the U.S. Office of Education.

The results from each of the three sites suggest that the highly structured academic program was the most successful in promoting cognitive growth. Yet as Bissell points out, since children were not randomly assigned to treatments at any of the three sites (through randomization of schools or individuals), the validity of this finding is open to doubt. An alternative interpretation says that these results are largely an artifact of self-selection. Perhaps parents who "drill" their children at home and work with them in other ways tend also to send them to programs with highly structured curricula. These children may differ on the average from children enrolled in the other two curriculum groups in the level of overall academic "load" they have received. If this possible selection effect were similar across all three sites, it would explain the seemingly consistent result (see further related remarks in Section VI-F). Randomization would have eliminated this self selection possibility. Because of replication, the evidence appears quite strong at first glance that the highly structured curriculum is most effective. Yet because of the lack of randomization we do not have great confidence in this result.

Let us turn to person-treatment interaction, whose presence could mean that a treatment best for one child need not be best for all. We want to know what treatments are best for which children. If we knew, then the policy implication would be to match treatments with children to get optimum payoff. (Although this idea is a perennial favorite in educational discussions, its application has been slight, except at the level, say, of choosing electives or long-run educational plans.)

Bissell (1973) extended her analysis of the preschool curricula to search for such interactions. She found that at all three sites, children from higher socio-economic backgrounds gained more in the "traditional preschool" with less structure, while children from lower socio-economic backgrounds did better in the highly structured academic program. Thus, she found a similar person-treatment inter-action at all three sites. The finding implies a substan-tial and consistent interaction. But as Bissell points out, the lack of randomization in the initial assignment of children among treatments severely threatens the validity of the interaction inference.

D. *UNMEASURABLE EFFECTS*

Some suggest that the results of effects of particular social action programs are unmeasurable. Clearly any such program will be difficult to evaluate by objective criteria. Administrators of such programs are going to have a difficult time with any but the most sympathetic of funding agencies. How can unmeasurable effects arise? Several possibilities come to mind:

- The effect may be too subtle to measure easily or inexpensively. Thus although in principle the effect could be measured, the decision may be made to avoid spending the large amount of money and effort required. It is worth noting that such an effect need not defy definition in terms of an operational test, but it may defy a cost-benefit analysis for evaluation.

- A long time interval lapses between the application of the treatment and the period when the effect is evident: for example, changing the diet of pregnant women to improve the academic performance of their children. Such a long period makes it hard to follow participants and the intervening events weaken the inferences.

- The measurement process may cause damage or actually destroy the treatment effect. Very special circumstances would be required, for example, for an investigator to be willing to test directly whether a particular treatment had increased a child's resistance to psychic trauma.

We conclude that occasional situations exist where we cannot or should not measure the result of a treatment. These cases are, by and large, exceptional, and we should be careful that these few exceptions do not encourage a generalized resistance to evaluation. It is important not to underestimate the ingenuity of a determined investigator, or the efficiency that is possible with a good design, and thus deprive a program's administrator of the evaluative data he so badly needs.

E. *VALIDITY OF INFERENCE FROM ONE-SITE STUDIES*

We have studied some multi-site investigations. Examples include the preschool curriculum investigation by Bissell (1971) that examined curricula in three different preschool centers, the Work Incentive Program which was applied in several cities, and the portacaval shunt trial which was a cooperative study in several institutions. Other investigations focused on a single site. For example, the Los Angeles Sheriff's Academy training program took place entirely within a single county, and we had to be extremely cautious about extending our inferences from Los Angeles to other cities. The value of the multi-site investigation, when it is feasible, is that it gives us a much stronger basis for making inferences to broader populations. If randomized trials of a new program tried in five cities show the program outperforming a comparison group in all five, then we gain confidence that if the program were adopted in similar cities, it would probably be successful in many of them as well. Thus an investigator must keep in mind the population to which he wishes to generalize. Studies done at a single site, even if well designed and executed, must necessarily have inferences restricted to sites like it, "like" being more narrowly defined than when the effect has already been verified at a variety of sites.

F. *DOES RANDOMIZATION IMPLY COERCION?*

Let us suppose that in a social innovation three treatments are to be compared: A, B, and C. We have argued extensively that a randomized controlled field study is necessary to get sensitive results. This implies the need to assign treatments randomly among many sites. Does this also imply coercion? Must some sites (cities, for example) be forced against their will to participate in the field study for randomization to do its good work?

The answer is NO; there is no need for any city, or school, or group, to accept a treatment that it does not find acceptable. Suppose, for example, that out of hundreds of cities contending for money to engage in the social program, a subset of 50 are willing to accept either treatment A or treatment B, but are absolutely opposed to C. In this event, a randomized comparison between the two treatments A and B is still possible.

Two points we have touched upon earlier tie in to this discussion. First, if only a total of two cities are willing to accept either A or B, then even random assignment of the two treatments between the two cities will not yield a comparison in which we have confidence. This is simply because of the tiny sample of cities involved. As more cities are willing to accept one of a subset of treatments, better estimates of the differential treatment effects can be developed. In addition, with more cities it becomes possible to estimate the city-to-city variation in outcome within any one treatment.

A second matter concerns the generalizability of treatment comparisons when some cities are willing to accept only a subset of treatments. Caution is required in generalizing results from a field study in a few cities to a larger population of cities. We are not in a good position to judge how a program would have fared in a school system that would not accept it as a possibility. Yet until they change their position, this is not as important as learning reliably how the program performs in systems that will accept it. These caveats notwithstanding, the major point

147

here is that randomization can be used in field studies without any treatment recipient feeling he has been "coerced" into participating, provided some are willing to accept either of a pair of treatments. It is an attractive feature of controlled field studies, not just randomized ones, that they offer the opportunity of achieving a flexible mix between centralized control of an investigation and local site options as to what treatments are acceptable.

G. *THE ETHICS OF CONTROLLED FIELD STUDIES*

Although many social investigators are aware of the advantages of randomization for evaluating programs, a common reason offered for doing so few randomized studies focuses on the ethics of conducting such investigations. Some people think that using randomized trials implies that people will be abused or mistreated. They say, "You can't experiment with people!" Let us examine this position a little more carefully.

We change our social system—for example, our educational system—frequently and rather arbitrarily; that is, in ways ordinarily intended to be beneficial, but with little or no evidence that the innovation will work. These changes are routinely made in such an unsystematic way that no one can assess the consequences of these haphazard adjustments. By using this casual approach, we are frittering away the valuable experiences, good and bad, of the participants. This action devalues both their pleasure and suffering, to say nothing of their achievements and failures, by not learning from them for society's benefit;

indeed, for the benefit of the participants themselves, their families, and their children.

This is not to say that all ethical and technical problems can be overcome. Far from it; there are important questions that for ethical reasons should not be investigated by controlled trials, randomized or not, on children or on adults. We stress, however, that for the same ethical reasons these same questions should not be investigated by haphazardly trying an innovation on a number of likely subjects to see how it works out.

Most people are willing to accept randomization when resources are limited. For example, if only 100 pills are available and 200 people volunteer for the treatment, a randomized assignment is relatively uncontroversial. However, even when a program has enough funds to benefit all, there is still plenty of room for the sort of study we are discussing because there may be many alternatives for program delivery. If one has a food distribution program, is it better to give out stamps, deliver the food to the poor, give people the money for food, or what? It would be good to know also whether under various circumstances people ate it themselves, sold it, fed it to cattle, or threw it away.

When we object to controlled field trials with people, we need to consider the alternatives--what society actually does. Instead of field trials, programs currently are instituted that vary substantially from one place to another, often for no very good reason. We do one thing here, another there in an unplanned way. The result is that we spend our money, often put people at risk, and learn little. This haphazard approach is not "experimenting" with people; instead, it is <u>fooling around with people</u>. It is most important that we appreciate the difference between these two ideas. We need to decide whether fooling around with people's lives in a catch-as-catch-can way that helps society little is a good way to treat our citizens, and we need to understand that in current practice this is the principal alternative to randomized controlled field trials.

H. *NEED TO DEVELOP METHODOLOGY*

In looking forward to the contribution that randomized controlled field trials have to make to the administration and evaluation of social programs, we are hampered because there have been so few. Consequently we are still developing the necessary skills, techniques, and theory to facilitate and strengthen such field trials. Evaluators of social programs will have to devise their own special methods of applying randomization in the context of ongoing and often shifting programs, just as agriculture, experimental laboratories, quality control departments, and opinion polls have each had to produce their own variations on the theme of randomization.

We cannot map from an easy chair just how such developments would go, since in large part this will depend upon the experience gained as more randomized trials are integrated with social programs. Thus we will be learning not only more about the effectiveness of programs but also how to integrate field trials smoothly into social programs with fewer problems and possibly at lower cost.

Shifts in the goals of a program, for whatever reason, will pose difficult problems for any evaluative process.

Most of these problems are not specific to randomized trials. Their occurrence is a warning that the background and base-line data collected at the start of a project should be as broad as possible since this increases the chance that they will retain their relevance even after some changes in program goals.

I. *NEED FOR AN ONGOING CAPABILITY FOR DOING RANDOMIZED CONTROLLED FIELD STUDIES*

What should society think of carefully evaluated innovations that work well? First, it should be pleased to find a fair proportion of them working. Second, it needs a mature attitude toward both reforms and evaluations. It needs to accept, though not without grumbling, the variety of performances that new ideas provide, from very poor to very good. It needs to learn to tolerate this groping for solutions and the mistakes in the attempts. It is astounding how mature America has become about accepting mistakes in forecasts and estimates. For example, we continue to take a tolerant and constructive attitude toward polls in spite of the Literary Digest failure, the Truman-Dewey election, and the two Heath-Wilson "failures" in England (we use quotes because neither was very far off). Society understands that these measuring devices are fallible, just like weather forecasts, but that they nevertheless have their practical uses and their successes as well as failures.

The nation accepts the idea that a good deal of data about a problem can be routinely gathered through the sample survey approach. This positive attitude goes along with the existence of a substantial number of survey organizations which are able on very short notice to field an investigation for a client, helping him design and carry it out from start to finish. We are less used to the idea of the randomized controlled field study, and have less experience in carrying it out. Once people come to understand it and its role better, we can expect more appreciation for its utility.

This suggests that policy makers should push for the development of an ongoing capability to mount well-designed randomized field studies. This capability will be developed gradually over time, as several organizations gain experience in the conduct of such field studies. It may then become part of the normal course of events for policy makers to call on such organizations to provide information about program effectiveness and program improvement.

VII. ISSUES OF FEASIBILITY IN INSTALLING PROGRAM EVALUA-
TIONS

In this section we take up a variety of feasibility matters where the randomization issue is not always central. Later sections deal with costs and timeliness (Section VIII), and with the implementation of programs (Section IX).

A. *SPECIFYING THE TREATMENT*

The notion of doing a controlled field study implies that whoever is doing the study can specify approximately what treatment, or set of treatments, is being investigated. Sometimes this is relatively easy. For example, in the series of Graduated Work Incentive experiments (Negative Income Tax experiments) done in New Jersey, Seattle, and Gary, each treatment consisted of a specific monetary payment to a family together with a certain marginal tax rate. Having such well-defined treatments simplifies any examination of their comparative effects.

In contrast, developing a Follow Through center to serve several hundred preschool children is quite different. One of Follow Through's educational programs was called Bank Street. A Bank Street program in New York may not be the same as a Bank Street program in Detroit or Fort Worth. It is not uncommon for treatments to differ among several sites (as was found in an evaluation done by Weisberg [1973]). Such flexibility makes it valuable to have ways of measuring the properties of the programs actually installed. At a Brookings Institution conference on Follow Through, program leaders frequently mentioned that creating better measures of the properties of the programs as they were actually installed would help researchers. The sponsors had trouble in knowing and documenting the extent of installation of their models for teaching. Had they exported their program? Or how nearly had they implemented it? A system for monitoring the field installation of programs should be part of most field trials.

What lessons can we draw from this example? Perhaps there are two. First, treatments in innovative programs require careful specification. This requirement especially applies to relatively more complex treatments, such as those in educational programs. Local program managers may "declare" that they are running a Bank Street model of the Follow Through program, when they are actually running a set of very different programs. The second point is that both the program developer and evaluator need to be able to tell what the installed program is.

One complication that can arise in any controlled study is that a treatment found to have an effect in a carefully monitored and supervised setting may fail in widespread implementation. This may happen for a number of reasons. Perhaps people will not take a pill voluntarily, perhaps parents will not send their children to schools using a new program, or perhaps a treatment is only effective in the dedicated atmosphere of the experimental situation and not in the everyday classroom. This problem is not unique to randomized studies but rather is one of when and how to investigate what treatments.

One of the advantages of evaluations using field trials embedded in larger programs is that they are not so susceptible to the "being in an experiment" effect since they tend to be run more nearly under actual field conditions.

Another example of implementation is given by the Kansas Blue Cross-Blue Shield outpatient investigation described above (Section IV-F-1). In this study the treatment may not always have operated consistently. Lewis and Keairnes (1970) reported that 41% of the experimental group knew about their change in coverage and 23% of the control group thought they were covered for outpatient visits. Although different ways of measuring what the participants "knew" or "thought" might give different results, the data just given do warn us that when an important part of the treatment depends on communicating information, we may often fail to supply a specified treatment. How much this matters will depend on the circumstances. It may not matter, for example, that some members of the experimental group did not know they were covered if their physician knew.

The need for constant monitoring out in the field as part of the evaluation process has been discussed extensively in the educational research literature. For example, Michael Scriven (1969) has described "process evaluation," or "formative evaluation," as opposed to "summative evaluation." When a "summative evaluation" of a program is done, external measures of a program's performance are examined primarily. For example, pretest and posttest scores may be studied in a preschool setting. In contrast, "formative evaluation" requires the careful analysis of how a program is actually progressing in the field, together with feedback to the program managers about how well their theoretical curriculum design, or treatment, is in fact being implemented. Formative evaluation can thus achieve two purposes. It informs program managers about the extent to which their original conception of a program actually exists in a field setting. Also, it provides data about implementation so that policy makers can assess the relative effectiveness of different versions of a program. Both the external evaluation and the "formative evaluation" provide important information to policy makers.

B. *INCENTIVES FOR PARTICIPATION*

How can we encourage people to participate in randomized studies? Since a controlled field trial requires random assignment of treatments to sites or of people to treatments, how do we get sites and people to go along with the experimental design?

An ideal solution, and one that is occasionally possible, is to guarantee that all who participate in the field study will (either with certainty or with very high probability) end up at least as well off as they would have been had they not participated. With every person in the study guaranteed zero or minimal loss and some reasonable chance of a gain, most potential participants in a study may be willing to accept the randomization process.

An example of the carefully planned use of incentives in a controlled field study is offered by the Health Insurance study being done by Joseph P. Newhouse (1972) and Charles Phelps and colleagues at the RAND Corporation. The RAND group is assessing how the demand for medical services might change under different insurance schemes. They have developed a 16-cell study design, combining different minimum deductible amounts, maximum payout amounts, and different proportions of total expenses to be paid by the medical service user.

As they planned to select the sample, they realized that some people in the target population might already have insurance coverage that would exceed the coverage offered to them by the RAND investigators. This would be especially likely for people who happened to fall into certain cells. Either such a subset of people would refuse to participate in the controlled field study, or if they participated and kept their old insurance, the inferences from the study might be meaningless.

The RAND group solved this problem by developing a procedure that requires people to give up their old insurance, and instead subsidizes in advance payments for medical care. The type of subsidy depends upon what cell of the design a family is in. To compensate for the risk of participating in this investigation, each family is given a lump sum of cash at the outset. This money is given whether or not medical expenses are actually incurred. The basic idea is that families are given an incentive to participate in the investigation by being compensated independently of how they use this extra money. This requires, as Newhouse and Phelps point out, assuming that families will treat the cash received for participating in this study as just another bit of general income, rather than income to be spent only on medical care.

C. *A MULTIPLICITY OF PROGRAM GOALS*

What about social programs such as Head Start or Model Cities that have, in their enabling legislation, a variety of goals? Are controlled field studies still appropriate for such programs?

We believe the answer is yes. There need not be just one set of goals for a program. A field trial can measure, count, or otherwise assess variables that concern different audiences, and the enlightened decision maker will realize the need for evaluating multiple outcomes. When several kinds of performance are reported, a more informed trade-off can be made between the various possible achievements that a program can offer. For example, suppose that one system of education produces higher scores on academic achievement tests and another program produces higher scores on satisfaction of those enrolled in the program, neither system being disastrous on either variable. Then, until someone invents a new system that combines these two virtues, society has to make hard choices. But knowing that these options are available would itself be of considerable value.

It may be desirable when programs have multiple goals to use more than one outcome measure. While in social programs the arithmetic mean is the most common outcome measure, others can be profitably used. For example, possibly a new educational curriculum will show no improvement in students' mean performance, yet have important effects as measured by changes in the variance of students' scores. This has been found in several studies of ability grouping for low achieving students; ability grouping in schools leaves mean performance unchanged but reduces the variance of these students' test scores. Still a different outcome variable would be the proportion of people falling above a minimum cutoff point in performance. This is the sort of variable used by the U.S. military services in their evaluation of the physical health of volunteers.

Goals in many programs can be divided into primary and secondary. By primary we mean the overall stated purpose of the program. We believe firmly in the idea of multiple goals, but we must assess progress toward a few of the major goals. For example, many social programs (such as manpower training) have as an important part of their task the redistribution of society's funds. One can accept this position and still feel that the program should be examined. Let us accept that such redistribution may be a major goal of a legislative body in passing the program. But society uses a variety of ways to redistribute funds, so we may well ask which ways will be especially good at accomplishing the secondary goals of the society, such as improved education, health, or job training.

VIII. COSTS, TIMELINESS, AND RANDOMIZED FIELD STUDIES

The policy maker, when considering whether to evaluate a program with a randomized controlled field trial, will weigh a number of matters. Thoughtful views of costs and timeliness associated with randomized studies differ with the occasion, and we bring out in this section some implications for short-run policy implied by long-term needs.

A. *COSTS AND BENEFITS OF DOING RANDOMIZED CONTROLLED FIELD STUDIES*

A number of people have called for more controlled field trials, and it is instructive to ask why more such trials have not been done in recent social and medical work (Campbell [1969]; Cochrane [1972]; Gilbert & Mosteller [1972]; Lasagna [1969]; Light, Mosteller, & Winokur [1971]; Orcutt [1970]; Rivlin [1970, 1971, 1973]; Rutstein [1969]). Despite the advantages of randomly controlled trials, three objections often emerge: 1) randomly assigning treatments to sites or to people raises political problems (see Sections V-B and VII-C for discussion); 2) randomly controlled trials take too long; and 3) they are too expensive to conduct. Let us examine the question of cost.

How much should society be prepared to pay for an evaluation of a program that leads to firm and reliable inferences about how well the program is working? The answer to this difficult question depends upon many features of the program: its size, its importance to society, and the alternatives. The answer to a related question is clearer. How much should society be willing to pay for an evaluation that does <u>not</u> lead to firm inferences about how well a program is working? Not much. Yet for years we have been paying enormous amounts for evaluations of this second kind. Had we earmarked a small portion of the budget expended on these efforts for a few randomized field studies, we might have realized three benefits: first, we might have learned with greater reliability how well or how poorly a particular program was working; second, we might have spent less on overall evaluation expenses; and third, we might have been able to use the results of the field trials to improve the operation of the program, so that it could better serve its intended beneficiaries.

These three possible benefits are mentioned in a somewhat abstract context because they apply to many programs in both the social and medical fields. Let us focus on a particular set of social programs that illustrate these three points—<u>manpower training programs</u>. These have been developed in the past decade to train people to get and hold jobs. The bulk of such federal spending between 1963 and 1973 was distributed among four particular program groups: the Manpower Development and Training Act (MDTA), the Neighborhood Youth Corps (NYC), Job Opportunities in the Business Sector (JOBS), and the Work Incentive Program (WIN).

Between 1963 and 1971 the Federal Government spent 6.8 billion dollars for training 6.1 million people. By any yardstick, this is a huge expenditure on an important social enterprise. The average taxpayer might feel safe in concluding that these programs had obvious benefits for the trainees because so much money was spent over such a long period of time.

What are the findings of the evaluations of manpower training programs? A report of the National Academy of Sciences (1974) says that although a total of 180 million dollars has been spent on evaluating these programs, we still know little about the effect of the programs on the trainees' job seeking and job holding behavior. In the words of the report, "Manpower training programs have been in existence a little over a decade, yet, with the possible exception of the Manpower Development and Training programs, little is known about the educational or economic effects of manpower training programs. This is troublesome, especially in light of the fact that about $180 million have been spent over the past ten years in an attempt to evaluate these programs. There are several reasons for lack of clarity ..." (p. 1). The report goes on to document the methodological inadequacies of the evaluations, primarily case studies, involving nonrandom samples with data collected retrospectively. It concludes that, "In short, while reliable evaluation is badly needed, it does not exist even after ten years of study and the application of large amounts of public resources" (p. 2).

In a staff study prepared for the Subcommittee on Fiscal Policy of the Joint Economic Committee, United States Congress, Jon H. Goldstein (1972) reaches a similar conclusion: "Despite substantial expenditure of public funds for research and evaluation, there is only limited reliable information about the impact of training. Some of the largest and most important programs have been subjected only to crude, preliminary investigations" (p. 14).

These two carefully developed reports show that the average taxpayer would have been disappointed in his expectations. Apparently little is known about the effectiveness of these programs. Although the many manpower- training studies that have been carried out in the past ten years tend to suffer from the difficulties mentioned earlier, they seem to show that most of the time, most programs had essentially no or little positive effect upon the trainees.

Sifting through this literature leads us to a single randomized controlled field study conducted in the Cincinnati Neighborhood Youth Corps program (Robin, 1969). There were far more volunteers for the program than there were places. The evaluators randomly assigned the volunteers, female teenagers, between a treatment and a control group. The treatment consisted of monetary payments and work training for part-time work while the teenagers were still finishing high school. The outcome measure was how much these extra payments reduced the dropout rate of these girls from high school. After a year, the evaluators found that indeed a statistically significant difference had developed: the treatment girls were more likely to drop out of school than the controls.

There are some hints from just a few reported studies that selected manpower training programs may be highly effective in achieving their goals. But these can be viewed only as promising rather than convincing, because randomization of trainees between treatment and control groups was not employed. For example, Brazziel (1966) reports on a training program that offered general education

162

and technical education, and compared the effects of these programs with two control groups. The general education training seemed highly effective, both during the training and after a one-year follow-up. The difficulty we have in generalizing such findings comes from the lack of any reported randomization of trainees among the several groups.

The accumulated evidence on manpower training programs told us little about their effectiveness, with the one exception of a small controlled field study that showed us an outcome in the opposite direction to that intended.

Manpower training programs thus exemplify an area where thoughtful public policy has broken down. The goal of these programs is laudable: to find a job for a person who doesn't have one and wants one. Society has found that it is not easy to train a person to get and keep a job; and therefore we need to learn more effective ways of delivering training services. Randomized controlled field studies might enable us to learn which, if any, versions of programs are succeeding in their mission, and might indicate good pairings between programs and kinds of trainees.

In the future, as a result of revenue sharing, new manpower training programs may be instituted by the states. They will want to consider what sorts of field trials they need to improve their own programs. Most states are now less well prepared for carrying out randomized controlled field trials than the federal government, and so the availability of organizations competent to carry out such trials would be crucial if evolutionary work is to succeed.

When thinking about the cost of a field trial embedded in an active program, we must realize that the entire cost of the field trial is not an extra expenditure. The people

in the trial are part of the program. We need only think of
the added cost associated with designing and monitoring the
investigation, and analyzing its results--the marginal cost
of the investigation.

Are randomized controlled field studies too expensive
to embed in such large ongoing programs? No. The manpower
training experience suggests that just the reverse is true:
it is too expensive to pour large sums of money into programs, year after year, with no reliable indication of their
value and no firm data on how to improve them.

B. *VALUE OF A FIELD TRIAL*

How can we measure the value of a field trial, or to be
more precise, the value of the information it generates? If
the alternative treatments have equivalent net payoffs, it
makes little or no difference to the policy maker which he
picks, and increasing one's knowledge has no direct payoff.
Knowing of the equality may have indirect value because each
alternative treatment can, and often does, have strong
proponents.

When alternative treatments differ in performance and
costs, then the value of the information depends both upon
the importance of this difference, and upon how much the
information increases the probability that the better decision will be made. Evidence pointing to the right decision
increases in value as it becomes more convincing. Recalling
how important it is to detect small differences in social
programs reminds us that randomized field trials may
generate information with a very high value. The increased

reliability gained from a randomized trial may improve the world for many people.

C. THE QUESTION OF "GRADUALISM"

One strategy we advocate, the idea of embedding within an innovation a carefully planned randomized field study, assumes the value of gradualism in social change. Gradual improvement is often valuable, important, and not so easy to achieve. Further, small changes continued through time often result in large changes. Consider the analogy to interest rates: a sum of money left on deposit at a modest interest rate grows surprisingly rapidly because of the effects of compounding.

As an example of the impressive improvements possible with gradualism, consider the changes in the effectiveness of the treatment of various forms of childhood leukemia. In reports from about 1937 to 1953, the median time of survival following diagnosis was about 3 months. From 1955 to about 1964, the reported median was about 13 months. In reports from 1964 to 1966, survival was about 30 months (Henderson, 1969).

A recent article (Pinkel et al., 1972) concludes that "One cannot be certain that the long-term leukemia-free survivors will not eventually develop recurrence or relapse. However the high frequency of long-term complete remission achieved with total therapy indicates that at this point in time ALL (acute lymphocytic leukemia) in children cannot be considered an incurable disease. Palliation is not an acceptable approach to its initial treatment. Every child with ALL deserves an opportunity for prolonged leukemia-free survival and possible cure." A long but steady series of small improvements in the treatment of leukemia is producing a revolution.

As another illustration, Sherwin & Isenson (1967) report that in Project Hindsight, a study to find out what innovations (called "Events" in this study) had been needed to improve weapons systems, several teams of researchers independently discovered the following truth. To make a big improvement requires not one big breakthrough, but many innovations. Some may be big and some small, but the collection of them rather than any one separately produces the improvement. "In the larger systems, 50 to 100 Events were common. Even for small pieces of equipment, a number of Events--18 in the case of the night-vision device, for example--were readily identified" (p. 1574).

D. *"STALLING" AND EVALUATING INNOVATIONS*

Should a social innovation be delayed for some years while we first mount a controlled field study and then await the results? We think not. The possibility seems politically unrealistic. We are not advocating that an entire social program be designed as a randomized controlled field study, but rather that a portion of the overall budget be set aside and devoted to such studies. The ESAP experience discussed in Section III shows that it is possible to allocate a small percentage of an education program's overall resources to a field study. Society learned a great deal about overall program effectiveness, and nearly all the funds for the field study went to finance participation in the program.

Often a good evaluation cannot be finished just when everyone wants it. Many studies are initiated under some important whip such as "The state government is going to spend $100 million on this area, and so we have to give them the answer right away." Well, of course, someone has to give them the best suggestions possible based upon what we know about the subject matter, but rarely can we give sudden, definitive answers. In the meantime anyone committed to spend $100 million will likely go ahead anyway. What we can do is build into the effort an opportunity to study the progress of the program in a controlled way so that we can effectively build upon its demonstrated strengths and correct its weaknesses.

E. *TIME AND DOING FIELD STUDIES*

Not all randomized studies take especially long periods of time. For example, in the field of family planning, many randomized studies of short duration have been carried out. The basic question about time required for a well-designed study is a comparative one. To design, organize, implement, and analyze the results of a randomized field trial may take a long time; some will think too long for the results to do any good. Let us ask, too long relative to what? Although a randomized field trial takes time, alternative evaluation procedures rarely provide the needed information about the program. In practice, the randomized field study may provide information about program effectiveness more quickly than alternative procedures, since they may never provide solid information. We have seen that the manpower and compensatory education programs continued for a decade without providing documentation of their effectiveness.

Doing poor evaluations has not helped us much, and urgency seldom leads to good evaluations, though it has been an excuse for doing weak ones. If we do too many poor evaluations, they reduce the probability of getting good ones done. Consequently, doing stronger evaluations earlier may end up with our saving both time and money.

IX. ISSUES THAT ARISE IN IMPLEMENTING INNOVATIONS

In addition to questions of feasibility and cost, evaluators and program developers alike face a series of questions that arise when field studies are implemented. We now turn to some of these.

A. *EVOLUTIONARY DEVELOPMENT OF PROGRAMS*

When an evaluation shows that a social program has small but nevertheless measurably positive effects, we should examine the results of the field trials to discover the program features associated with the more successful outcomes. Programs in new sites should incorporate features that the controlled field studies have found to be promising. By refining the "settings" of program features gradually, toward levels which lead the overall program to function more effectively, a social or medical reform can be improved incrementally. This approach has been described in the chemical engineering and statistical literature extensively by George Box (see, for example, Box & Draper,

1969) and is called "evolutionary operation." As we mention (Section VII-A), the educational literature speaks of formative evaluation in the same sense.

For evolutionary operation to be successful, three preconditions are necessary. First, decision makers must be willing to give up a "go, no-go" approach to judging a program that shows modest success. Successes in social reforms are so infrequent that managers should adopt the attitude that an initial modest success in the "first iteration" of the evolutionary operation promises greater success in the future if the program is gradually improved.

Second, some degree of centralized control over the field trial is necessary. If a program is assigned over several sites, and if, as information comes in, new versions are developed, with program features changed in ways that look promising, some agency must process the incoming information and develop the new versions. This approach to program improvement is incompatible with total local control of social programs, where local control means independence of local site managers from the agency accumulating data on program performance.

The third precondition for a successful evolutionary approach is somewhat more philosophical than statistical. The root problems of society that most social reforms hope to ameliorate--problems such as inadequate housing, school performance, job training, nutrition, and others--have been with us for a very long time. Few of them have just emerged as major social problems, although many have received extensive publicity in recent years. It is important, then, to remember that these problems are unlikely to be solved, especially in a massively successful way, in a short period of time. If these problems were so easy to solve, they would not be as persistent and plaguing as they are. This realization, if accepted by society, should lead to general acceptance of the principle that difficult and long-standing social problems will be at best slowly responsive to social programs. Once this principle is accepted, the idea of actually achieving slow but steady improvement in a program's effectiveness begins to sound much more attractive. Since slow and steady improvement requires time, society must learn not to be disappointed when a program is only a small success at first.

Here is where Congress, or state legislatures, could make a major contribution. By mandating in a program's enabling legislation the spirit of evolutionary program improvement, they could turn managers toward developing systematic ways of both generating information and then using it. Many large federal programs have in the past required, in rather vague terms, some sort of evaluation. Writing a requirement that information should be collected to form a basis for future program modification would be a helpful legislative action. While such bodies cannot set out in detail a step-by-step blueprint for a technical evaluation, they can and should encourage the implementation of evolutionary program development.

B. *FIELD TRIALS AND POLICY INACTION*

Some evaluators become discouraged when information retrieved from field trials is not instantly acted upon by administrators or decision makers. We find this view politically naive. First, nothing happens in a moment. One good study may not be enough to satisfy the people in charge. There may be commitments in certain programs that preclude immediate changes of the sort that have been found to be especially beneficial. Evaluators have to understand that they are involved in a political process, and that the success and palatability of the total political process is a part of the evaluation system to which the evaluator of a particular program may not be tuned.

On the other hand, we find little reason to be discouraged. For one thing, so few strong evaluations exist that one can scarcely plead that the results are not being considered. To quote Donald Campbell (Salasin, 1973), "I don't see the store of red hot findings that are being neglected ... [and] at the moment I'm not panicked by the failure to utilize them." It is true that the overall political situation does much to determine the next step in any program. But we have no reason to suppose that when a systematic body of knowledge has been acquired, the political system will ignore it. Inaction does not necessarily mean lack of consideration. There may, of course, be ways to help the political system appreciate new results, but the more urgent problem is to get them.

There is plenty of room for educating decision makers and policy workers by people who do studies--that is, room for helping to get the message of the results over to legislatures and agency heads. But when one has so few studies that are strongly based, it is hard to argue that decision makers are neglecting them. Legislators should be asking, "Where are they?" Not so much because any one study is invaluable to instant legislative decision, but because the overall process of gathering this information is what we need. We need to quit thinking in terms of the single evaluation of the single program and regard randomized studies as a way of life. Collecting such sets of good studies leads to accumulating patterns of information that are much more important and interpretable than the results of single investigations. With a collection of weak investigations it becomes hard to interpret any picture that emerges, particularly since few studies give adequate notice of their weaknesses.

A related point is a common criticism leveled against the very idea of evaluating social programs: that evaluations sometimes provide a political excuse for ending a program. How does this criticism tie in to the consequences of doing evaluations via randomized controlled field studies? We believe that if the stopping of a social program is due to political considerations, and independent of real program results, then no methodology will save this program. That is, if a program will be stopped independent of what an evaluation shows, then randomization will not lead to an evaluation's being an input into the policy process. Thus, there is no good argument that calling for randomized studies is a proxy for wanting to discontinue a program.

C. POLITICAL OBSTACLES

Social innovations and hence their evaluations often have complicated political and legal implications. We recognize that sometimes political reasons exist for not having good evaluations. A detailed discussion of such political reasons falls outside the scope of this paper. Here we view the goal of evaluation as providing data for the political decision process, not as deciding the value of an innovation for society.

We have reviewed a variety of objections to good evaluations, randomized or nonrandomized, where complaints such as "the information won't be quite good enough," "it will take too long," "it costs too much," "the program is too complex," or "it won't be generalizable" are given for not carrying out a trial. A more fundamental reason that often underlies such objections is much more direct: a program manager simply may not wish to have his program evaluated. He may prefer poor information to good information, or no information at all to a modest amount. If a program manager has a career trajectory that depends more upon the size of the programs he controls than the effectiveness of those programs, his first interest may be in expanding a program, rather than considering its effectiveness for its clients.

D. T. Campbell (1969) has made the suggestion that to combat this difficulty, program managers should be rewarded less for the size or actual effectiveness of their program, and more on the quality of the procedures they employ for evaluation. This would encourage more widespread adoption of randomized trials, since generating good information would become a primary objective of the manager.

The history of program evaluations suggests that adopting Campbell's idea might change sharply the attitudes of program managers and their sponsoring agencies. Political expediency has in the past led to suppression of information about programs, and in some extreme cases even lying about what the effects were. An even more common occurrence, illustrated in the recent history of manpower training program evaluations and the early history of Head Start, involves program managers' commissioning evaluations that because of their retrospective nature are bound from their moment of inception to yield findings that are ambiguous. This will not surprise the politically sophisticated observer. To the extent that managers correctly perceive they will be rewarded only if their programs demonstrate a double plus rating, they are acting quite rationally in their self interest to either develop an evaluation that artificially inflates their program's success, or to commission an evaluation with a design that will not allow even the most competent investigator to pin down program effects with any reasonable degree of reliability. Until we find ways to reward them for good evaluations, only program managers who are totally confident that well-designed randomized field trials will show their programs to be big successes will find it in their self interest to commission such desirable evaluations.

We hope that these attitudes will change, and we see some evidence that they are beginning to change already. The public is demanding greater accountability for its tax monies, and large-scale programs being developed by government agencies are slowly but steadily beginning to build in the idea of embedding controlled field studies as integral parts of the program.

X. FINDINGS AND RECOMMENDATIONS

A. *THE RESULTS OF INNOVATIONS*

To see how effectively new ideas for helping people worked out in practice, we have collected a series of innovations from social programs and medicine that have been well evaluated (Section IV-D, E, H). The overall findings are that 1) about a fifth of these programs were clear and substantial successes; 2) a similar number had some small to moderate positive effects; and 3) most of the remaining programs either had no discernible effects or were mixed in their effects, while a few were even found to be harmful rather than beneficial. These proportions do not differ sharply among the social, medical, and socio-medical studies (Section IV-J and Table 4).

How should we interpret these findings? If most innovations had worked, one might well feel that we were not being expansive or broad enough in our attempts to ameliorate social problems. If hardly any had worked, one might conclude that not enough thought and planning were being put into these programs and that they were wasting society's resources. Although our results fall between these two extremes, we would have liked to see a higher proportion of successful innovations, particularly since we feel that the selection biases of our observational study are probably causing the data to overestimate the proportion of successful innovations rather than underestimate them. Thus it seems to us that the more successful innovations would be both more likely to have been well evaluated and more likely to have come to our attention (Section IV-A). If it is true

175

that we are less apt to evaluate programs that are feared to have little effect, society should be concerned that so many very large programs have only been evaluated with nonrandomized studies if at all.

B. FINDINGS FOR NONRANDOMIZED TRIALS

Although we are often pushed to do them for reasons of expediency, uncontrolled trials and observational studies have frequently been misleading in their results. Such misdirection leads to the evaluations' being ineffective and occasionally even harmful in their role as tools for decision makers. This was well illustrated in the medical studies described in Section V-B, and we are concerned because similar troublesome features are present in many evaluations of social programs. Nonrandomized studies may or may not lead to a correct inference, but without other data the suspicion will persist that their results reflect selection effects, as we discussed in Wilner's study of housing (Section V-A-1). This suspicion leads to two difficulties for the decision maker. First, his confidence in the evaluation is limited, and even when he does believe in the result, he may be reluctant or unable to act because others are not convinced by the data. Second, because of this lingering suspicion, observational studies are rarely successful in resolving a controversy about causality (Section V-C). Though controversy about policy implications may of course persist, few controversies about the effects of new programs survive a series of carefully designed randomized controlled trials.

C. *BENEFICIAL SMALL EFFECTS*

The observation that many programs do not have slam-bang effects stresses the importance of measuring small effects reliably (Sections II-B, VI-B). Once small effects are found and documented, it may be possible to build improvements upon them. The banking and insurance businesses have built their fortunes on small effects--effects the size of interest rates. Ten percent per year doubles the principal in a little over seven years. Similarly, a small effect that can be cumulated over several periods--for example, the school life of a student--has the potential of mounting up into a large gain. Naturally, small effects require stronger methods for their accurate detection than do large ones. One must be sure that the observed effects are not due to initial differences between groups, or to other spurious causes. Randomized controlled field trials are virtually essential for controlling these sources of bias, and so are necessary for the accurate measurement of small effects. The examples of randomized controlled field trials given in Section IV show that in practice when such trials have been carried out, they have been helpful for understanding the process, for bringing out the issues, and for suggesting policy implications.

D. *COSTS AND TIME*

Although it contradicts our intuition, the cost of randomized controlled field trials may well be less than the cost of nonrandomized methods or observational studies

(Section VIII-A). Although the cost of a particular randomized trial may exceed that of an observational study, even repeated observational studies often yield unreliable results (Section V-B). In some situations it may take a few years to design, implement, and analyze a randomized study. But this is an extremely short time compared to the generations that problems such as poverty, unemployment, hunger, and poor education have been with us. We should also note that often randomized studies take no longer than nonrandomized studies. The cost of not doing randomized studies can be extremely high--we may never find out the effectiveness of our programs (Section VIII-E).

One must sympathize with the decision maker who suggests that information that will be available in a few years is not of much value for his immediate decisions. But looking a step ahead, we see that information that is not available in a few years will not be available for decisions even then, let alone now. As we have stressed, the problems these innovations are treating are the more permanent ones of society, and a few years from now matters could be even more urgent than they are now. This suggests that the discount rate for information may not reduce the value of future information, but rather increase it, and so we should be more willing to invest in such long-term studies.

E. *FEASIBILITY OF RANDOMIZED TRIALS*

We find that randomized controlled field trials can be and have been carried out in situations that were made complicated and difficult by both ethical and technical problems. The Salk Vaccine field trial shows that society is willing to apply randomization to its children when the issues at stake are well known (Section III-A). Naturally, we recognize the constraint that some field trials would be impractical or unethical (Section VI-D) and should not be set up, and fortunately we have regulations to protect the public. These will continue to be developed. Inevitably, political problems can also arise that make evaluations hard or even impossible to carry out (Section IX-C). We have suggested the use of appropriate incentives as one way to encourage participation (Section VII-B), but we do not treat political problems in detail in this paper. We have outlined some of the flexibility that is available when participating individuals, groups, or institutions are willing to accept either one of a pair of treatments (Section VI-F). Further, we believe that the dichotomy of centralized control versus local options is a complication that can often be solved by special study designs and careful planning. A randomized field trial can frequently be conducted in a manner consistent with local units' (such as cities or schools) having a complete veto on treatments they consider undesirable (Section VI-F).

By carrying out the trials in the field we often discover additional facts of considerable value. An example is the finding of the Manhattan Bail Project that there were very different legal outcomes for those released than for those jailed among comparable groups of arrestees (Section IV-D-5).

F. *EVOLUTIONARY EVALUATIONS*

We do not advocate holding back large-scale programs until randomized trials can be held. Our reasoning is that political pressures often make this position unrealistic. Instead, we encourage embedding the trials in the program (Section VIII-D). Programs often continue for quite a long time. This presents the opportunity for evolutionary improvement when good evaluations are done within the program itself (Section IX-A). The crucial point here is that such evaluations should be directed toward improvement rather than being restricted to "go, no-go" decisions. It is more realistic to measure progress in an ongoing program than in a pilot study, because larger-scale studies can detect small but valuable effects at a low marginal cost. Of course, when advance studies can be made, as in the New Jersey Work Incentive Program, we naturally regard the special opportunity as beneficial. And we do encourage the use of pilot studies, whenever possible.

In many programs Congress makes available money through "set-asides" for mandatory evaluations. More of these funds should be used for randomized controlled field trials designed to indicate how to improve the programs. Sometimes components of a program can be studied and improved without involving the whole effort. Boruch has suggested to us that such component investigations may reduce the threat to the program administrator and leave him more comfortable with the evaluators than he would be with total program evaluations (Section IX-A).

G. LONG-RUN DEVELOPMENT

We need to develop a capability for doing randomized controlled field trials that will enable us to mount such trials as a natural part of new program development (Section VI-I). This facility exists today for carrying out excellent sample surveys, and we see no reason that similar capabilities could not be developed in the coming years to carry out randomized field trials. The existence of such institutions will not only enable us to set up field trials when appropriate, but in addition we will begin to accumulate substantial amounts of reliable data about social programs. As such experience and capability develop, the time required for doing randomized controlled studies may well be reduced. As part of this process, we must work on developing better incentives for participating in controlled trials, better methods of installing and assessing the installation of complex programs, and strategies for handling the problems associated with multiple goals. Over the past twenty years various organizations specializing in carrying out sample surveys have steadily improved their capability to conduct such surveys rapidly and accurately. They have accumulated experience and learned from mistakes that may have been made from time to time. As all policy makers know, survey organizations are now accepted as an important component of the information-gathering process in America. It is time to develop a similar place for groups carrying out controlled field trials (Section VI-H).

H. *CONTROLLED TRIALS VS. FOOLING AROUND*

Ethical problems have often been cited as reasons for not carrying out well-controlled studies. As we have discussed (Section VI-G), this is frequently a false issue. The basic question involves comparing the ethics of gathering information systematically about our large scale programs with the ethics of haphazardly implementing and changing treatments as so routinely happens in education, welfare, and other areas. Since the latter approach generates little reliable information, it is unlikely to provide lasting benefits. Although they must be closely monitored, like all investigations involving human subjects, we believe randomized controlled field trials can give society valuable information about how to improve its programs. Conducting such investigations is far preferable to the current practice of "fooling around with people," without their informed consent.

ACKNOWLEDGMENTS

We have benefited from a variety of resources which we gratefully acknowledge.

We have explained in the text our great debt to Jack Elinson and Cyrille Gell and also to Robert Boruch.

Bucknam McPeek, M.D. has helped us develop our list of randomized surgical studies as well as provided descriptions of surgical operations for our lay audience. And we appreciate the generosity of the surgeons John Lamberti, M.D., and Gary Fitzpatrick, M.D., for their review of ratings of the surgical innovations and their advice about the surgical studies themselves. Thomas C. Chalmers, M.D., has kindly given us substantial materials. Lillian Miao kindly gave us prepublication copies of her manuscript (1974) as did Edward Gramlich and Patricia Koschel (1973). D. G. Horovitz directed us to the Kansas Blue Cross-Blue Shield investigation. Harold Watts gave us helpful information about the New Jersey Negative Income Tax experiment.

Many individuals have given us the benefit of more comments than we could use: Robert F. Boruch; Michael L. Brown; John P. Bunker, M.D.; William B. Fairley; Edward M. Gramlich; David C. Hoaglin; Nan Hughes; Joel C. Kleinman; William H. Kruskal; Arthur A. Lumsdaine; Bucknam McPeek, M.D.; Julia A. Norton; Alice M. Rivlin; Marvin A. Schneiderman; John D. Steinbruner; Wayne W. Welch; and Richard J. Zeckhauser. Their suggestions have added about 50% to the length of the paper, against our active resistance.

Several of our advisers have encouraged us to write about good ways to do observational studies and nonrandomized controlled field trials. Although a systematic treatment of methods was not part of our plan, this request would be difficult for anyone to meet in 1974. What we now have are lists of techniques that advise us how to carry out such studies better, and lists of hazards that may be encountered, but little in the way of firm grounds for inference, either theoretical or empirical. We are well aware of the tremendous interest in these approaches, but the desired discussion must be put off to a later day.

We have benefited from relations with the Brookings' Panel on Social Experimentation of the Brookings Institution, Washington, D.C., and participation in the Faculty Seminar on Human Experimentation in Health and Medicine (facilitated by a grant from the Edna McConnell Clark Foundation) at Harvard University, and from our participation in the Conference on Evaluation at the Battelle Memorial Institute, Seattle, Washington. We have had critical discussions following talks on this subject with audiences at the University of Iowa in association with the Allen T. Craig Lectures; at Princeton University in connection with the Samuel S. Wilks Memorial Lecture Series; at Harvard University's South House Statistics Table, organized by Karen Rackley Credeur; at a lecture sponsored by the Department of Statistics at the University of Chicago; at the Graduate School of Education of Michigan State University; at the Washington Statistical Society; and at the joint Berkeley-Stanford Statistics Seminar.

We would like to thank Elizabeth J. Hilton for her help.

Majorie Olson and Cleo Youtz assisted in every stage of the preparation of this paper.

We gratefully acknowledge the permission of the following to reproduce table material: Thomas Chalmers, M.D.; Keith Ditman, M.D.; Paul Meier; American Psychiatric Association; Gastroenterology, Holden-Day, Inc., and the New England Journal of Medicine.

The preparation of this paper has been facilitated by United States Public Health Service Grant GM 15904 to the Harvard Anesthesia Center and by National Science Foundation Grant GS 32327X1 to Harvard University.

REFERENCES

At the end of each reference are the numbers of the section(s) and subsection(s) where that reference is treated. For example, the Alpert reference is treated in subsection F-1 of section IV.

Alpert, J. J., Heagarty, M. C., Robertson, L., Kosa, J., & Haggarty, R. J. Effective use of comprehensive pediatric care. American Journal of Diseases of Children, 1968, 116, 529-533. (IV-F-1)

Bissell, J. S. Implementation of planned variation in Head Start: Review and summary of first year report. Washington, D. C.: U.S. Department of Health, Education, and Welfare, Office of Child Development, 1971. (VI-C, VI-E)

Bissell, J. S. Planned variation in Head Start and Follow Through. In J. C. Stanley (Ed.), Preschool programs for the disadvantaged (Vol. 2). Baltimore: Johns Hopkins University Press, 1973. (VI-C)

Boruch, R. F. Abstracts of randomized experiments for planning and evaluating social programs. Compiled for the Social Science Research Council's Committee on Experimentation for Planning and Evaluating Social Programs and for the Project on Measurement and Experimentation in Social Settings at Northwestern University. Revised, Fall 1972. (Unpublished) (IV-A)

Boruch, R. F., & Davis, S. Appendix: Abstracts of controlled experiments for planning and evaluating social programs. In H. W. Riecken, et al., Social experimentation as a method for planning and evaluating social interventions. In press. (IV-A)

Botein, B. The Manhattan Bail Project: Its impact on criminology and the criminal law processes. Texas Law Review, 1964-65, 43, 319-331. (IV-D-5, X-5)

Box, G. E. P. Use and abuse of regression. Technometrics, 1966, 8, 625-629. (II-C)

Box, G. E. P., & Draper, N. R. Evolutionary operation. A statistical method for process improvement. New York: John Wiley & Sons, 1969. (IX-A)

Brazziel, W. F. Effects of general education in manpower programs. Journal of Human Resources, Summer 1966, 1, 39-44. (VIII-A)

Brownlee, K. A. Statistics of the 1954 Polio Vaccine Trials. Journal of the American Statistical Association, 1955, 50, 1005-1013. (III-A)

Callow, A. D., Resnick, R. H., Chalmers, T. C., Ishihara, A. M., Garceau, A. J., & O'Hara, E. T. Conclusions from a controlled trial of the prophylactic portacaval shunt. Surgery, 1970, 67, 97-103. (IV-H-6)

Campbell, D. T. Reforms as experiments. American Psychologist, 1969, 24, 409-429. (VIII-A, IX-C)

Chalmers, T. C. Randomization and coronary artery surgery. Annals of Thoracic Surgery, 1972, 14, 323-327. (V-B)

Chalmers, T. C., Block, J. B., & Lee, S. Controlled studies in clinical cancer research. New England Journal of Medicine, 1972, 287, 75-78. (V-B)

Cicirelli, V. G., et al. The impact of Head Start: An evaluation of the effects of Head Start on children's cognitive and affective development (Vol. 1). Westinghouse Learning Corporation and Ohio University (contractors). U. S. Department of Commerce/National Bureau of Standards/Institute for Applied Technology. Distributed by Clearinghouse, Springfield, Va., PB 184 328, 12 June 1969. (V-A-3)

Cochrane, A. L. Effectiveness and efficiency: Random reflections on health services. London: The Nuffield Provincial Hospitals Trust, 1972. (VIII-A)

Conlisk, J., & Watts, H. A model for optimizing experimental designs for estimating response surfaces. In American Statistical Association Proceedings of the Social Statistics Section, 1969. Washington, D. C.: American Statistical Association. (IV-D-1)

Cox, A. G. Comparison of symptoms after vagotomy with gastrojejunostomy and partial gastrectomy. British Medical Journal, 1968, 1, 288-290. (IV-H-2)

Crosfill, M., Hall, R, & London, D. The use of chlorhexidine antisepsis in contaminated surgical wounds. British Journal of Surgery, 1969, 56, 906-908. (IV-H-9)

Ditman, K. S., Crawford, G. G., Forgy, E. W., Moskowitz, H., & MacAndrew, C. A controlled experiment on the use of court probation for drunk arrests. American Journal of Psychiatry, August 1967, 124, 160-63. (IV-F-4)

Dunn, M. R., & George, T. W. Des Moines pre-trial release project 1964-1965. Drake Law Review, 1964, 14, 98-100. (IV-D-5)

Dwight, R. W., Higgins, G. A., & Keehn, R. J. Factors influencing survival after resection in cancer of the colon and rectum. American Journal of Surgery, 1969, 117, 512-522. (IV-H-5)

Earle, H. H. Police recruit-training: Stress vs. non-stress. Springfield, Ill.: Charles C. Thomas, 1973. (IV-D-6, VI-E)

Elinson, J., with abstracts prepared by C. Gell, School of Public Health, Columbia University. The effectiveness of social action programs in health and welfare. Working paper. Ross Conference on pediatric research: "Problems of assessing the effectiveness of child health services," March 15-17, 1967. (IV-A)

Fairweather, G. W. (Ed.) Social psychology in treating mental illness: An experimental approach. New York: John Wiley & Sons, 1964. (IV-F-6)

Federal Bureau of Prisons. Rational innovation: An account of changes in the program of the National Training School for boys from 1961 to 1964. Washington, D. C.: Federal Bureau of Prisons, 1964. (IV-D-4)

Francis, T., Jr., Korns, R. F., Voight, R. B., Boisen, M., Hemphill, F. M., Napier, J. A., & Tolchinsky, E. An evaluation of the 1954 poliomyelitis vaccine trials. Summary Report. American Journal of Public Health and The Nation's Health, 1955, 45, xii, 1-63. (III-A, VI-B, X-5)

Gamma globulin in the prophylaxis of poliomyelitis: An evaluation of the efficacy of gamma globulin in the prophylaxis of paralytic poliomyelitis as used in the United States in 1953. (Public Health Monograph No. 20, U. S. Public Health Service publication No. 358.) Washington, D. C.: U. S. Government Printing Office, 1954. (III-B)

Gilbert, J. P., & Mosteller, F. The urgent need for experimentation. In Mosteller, F., & Moynihan, D. P. (Eds.), On equality of educational opportunity. New York: Random House, 1972. (VIII-A)

Goldstein, J. H. The effectiveness of manpower programs. A review of research on the impact on the poor. In Studies in public welfare. Subcommittee on Fiscal Policy, Joint Economic Committee, Congress of the United States. Washington, D. C.: U. S. Government Printing Office, 1972. (VIII-A)

Goligher, J. C., Morris, C., McAdam, W. A. F., De Dombal, F. T., & Johnston, D. A controlled trial of inverting versus everting intestinal suture in clinical large-bowel surgery. British Journal of Surgery, 1970, 57, 817-824. (IV-H-8)

[Gorham Report] A report to the President on medical care price. U. S. Department of Health, Education, and Welfare. Washington, D. C.: U. S. Government Printing Office, 1967. (IV-F-1)

Grace, N. D., Muench, H., & Chalmers, T. C. The present status of shunts for portal hypertension in cirrhosis. Gastroenterology, 1966, 50, 684-691. (V-B)

Gramlich, E., & Koshel, P. Social experiments in education: The case of performance contracting. Washington, D. C.: Brookings Institution, December 1973. (V-A-4)

Hammond, K. R., & F. Kern. Teaching comprehensive medical care. Cambridge, Mass.: Harvard University Press, 1959. (IV-F-3)

Henderson, E. S. Treatment of acute leukemia. Seminars in Hematology, 1969, 6, 271-319. (VIII-C)

Hill, D. B., & Veney, J. E. Kansas Blue Cross/Blue Shield Outpatient Benefits Experiment. Medical Care, 1970, 8, 143-158. (IV-F-1)

Jordan, P. H., Jr., & Condon, R. E. A prospective evaluation of vagotomy-pyloroplasty and vagotomy-antrectomy for treatment of duodenal ulcer. Annals of Surgery, 1970, 172, 547-560. (IV-H-1)

Kelman, H. R. An experiment in the rehabilitation of nursing home patients. Public Health Reports, 1962, 77, 356-366. (IV-F-7)

Kennedy, T., & Connell, A. M. Selective or truncal vagotomy? A double-blind randomized controlled trial. The Lancet, May 3, 1969, 899-901. (IV-H-3)

Lasagna, L. Special subjects in human experimentation. Daedalus, Spring, 1969, 449-462. (VIII-A)

Lewis, C. E., & Keairnes, H. W. Controlling costs of medical care by expanding insurance coverage. Study of a paradox. New England Journal of Medicine, 1970, 282, 1405-1412. (VII-A)

Light, R. J., Mosteller, F., & Winokur, H. S., Jr. Using controlled field studies to improve public policy. In Federal Statistics: Report of the President's Commission (Vol. 2). Washington, D. C.: U. S. Government Printing Office, 1971. (VIII-A)

Meier, P. The biggest public health experiment ever: The 1954 field trial of the Salk poliomyelitis vaccine. In J. M. Tanur et al. (Eds.) Statistics: A guide to the unknown. San Francisco: Holden-Day, 1972. (III-A)

Meyer, H. J., & Borgatta, E. F. An experiment in mental patient rehabilitation: Evaluating a social agency program. New York: Russell Sage Foundation, 1959. (V-A-6)

Meyer, H. J., Borgatta, E. F., & Jones, W. C. Girls at vocational high: An experiment in social work intervention. New York: Russell Sage Foundation, 1965. (IV-D-3)

Miao, L. Gastric freezing: An example of the development of a procedure monitored by the results of randomized clinical trials. Memorandum NS-256, Department of Statistics, Harvard University, February 23, 1974. (V-B)

Miller, A. B., Fox, W., & Tall, R. Five-year follow-up of the Medical Research Council comparative trial of surgery and radiotherapy for the primary treatment of small-celled or oat-celled carcinoma of the bronchus. The Lancet, September 6, 1969, 501-505. (IV-H-4)

Nash, A. G., & Hugh, T. B. Topical ampicillin and wound infection in colon surgery. British Medical Journal, 1967, 1, 471-472. (IV-H-7)

National Academy of Sciences. Final report of the Panel on Manpower Training Evaluation. The use of Social Security earnings data for assessing the impact of manpower training programs. Washington, D. C.: National Academy of Sciences, January, 1974. (VIII-A)

National Opinion Research Center [NORC]. Southern schools. An evaluation of the effects of the Emergency School Assistance Program and of school desegregation (Vol. 1). Prepared for the Office of Planning, Budgeting and Evaluation, U. S. Office of Education of the Department of Health, Education and Welfare. (NORC Report No. 124A.) Chicago: University of Chicago, National Opinion Research Center, October 1973. (III-C, IV-D-8, IV-J, VI-A, VIII-D)

Newhouse, J. P. A design for health insurance experiment. Santa Monica: RAND, November 1972. (VII-B)

Orcutt, G. H. Data research and government. American Economic Review, May, 1970, 60(2), 132-137. (VIII-A)

Pinkel, D., Simone, J., Hustu, H. O., & Aur, R. J. A. Nine years' experience with "total therapy" of childhood acute lymphocytic leukemia. Pediatrics, 1972, 50, 246-251. (VIII-C)

Rivlin, A. M. Systematic thinking and social action. Berkeley, California: H. Polan Gaither Lectures, January, 1970. (VIII-A)

Rivlin, A. M. Systematic thinking for social action. Washington, D. C.: Brookings Institution, 1971. (VIII-A)

Rivlin, A. M. How can experiments be more useful? American Economic Review, Papers and Proceedings, May 1974. (VIII-A)

Robin, G. D. An assessment of the in-public school Neighborhood Youth Corps Projects in Cincinnati and Detroit, with special reference to summer-only and year-round enrollees: Final Report. Philadelphia: National Analysts, Inc., February, 1969. (VIII-A)

Rosenberg, M. The pretrial conference and effective justice. A controlled test in personal injury litigation. New York: Columbia University Press, 1964. (IV-D-7)

Ruffin, J. M., Grizzle, J. E., Hightower, N. C., McHardy, G., Shull, H., & Kirsner, J. B. A co-operative double-blind evaluation of gastric "freezing" in the treatment of duodenal ulcer. New England Journal of Medicine, 1969, 281, 16-19. (IV-H-11, V-B)

Rutstein, D. D. The ethical design of human experiments. Daedalus, Spring, 1969, 523-541. (VIII-A)

Salasin, S. Experimentation revisited: A conversation with Donald T. Campbell. Evaluation, 1973, 1 (3), 9-10. (IX-B)

Salcedo, J., Jr. Views and comments on the Report on Rice Enrichment in the Philippines. In Food and Agriculture Organization of the United Nations (Report No. 12). Rome, Italy: March 1954. (V-A-2)

Scriven, M. Evaluating educational programs. The Urban Review, February 1969, 3(4), 20-22. (VII-A)

Sheldon, A. An evaluation of psychiatric after-care. British Journal of Psychiatry, 1964, 110, 662-667. (IV-F-5)

Sherwin, C. W., & Isenson, R. S. Project Hindsight: A Defense Department study of the utility of research. Science, June 1967, 156, 1571- 1577. (VIII-C)

Silver, G. A. Family medical care. A report on the family health maintenance demonstration. Cambridge, Mass.: Harvard University Press, 1963. (IV-F-8)

Skipper, J. S., Jr., & Leonard, R. C. Children, stress and hospitalization: A field experiment. Journal of Health and Social Behavior, 1968, 9, 275-287. (IV-F-2)

Smith, M. S. Some short term effects of Project Head Start. A preliminary report on the second year of planned variation--1970-1971. Cambridge, Mass.: Huron Institute, 1973. (IV-F-3, V-A-3)

Smith, M. S., & Bissell, J. S. Report analysis: The impact of Head Start. Harvard Educational Review, 1970, 40, 51-104. (V-A-3)

Stewart, H. J., Forrest, A. P. M., Roberts, M. M., Chinnock-Jones, R. E. A., Jones, V., & Campbell, H. Early pituitary implantation with Yttrium-90 for advanced breast cancer. The Lancet. October 18, 1969, 816-820. (IV-H-10)

"Student." The Lanarkshire milk experiment. Biometrika, 1931, 23, 398-406. (II-D-4)

Thompson, M. S. Evaluation for decision in social programs. Unpublished doctoral dissertation, Harvard University, 1973. (II-D-5)

U. S. Department of Health, Education, and Welfare [HEW]. Summary report. New Jersey graduated work incentive experiment: A social experiment in negative taxation sponsored by the Office of Economic Opportunity, U. S. Department of Health, Education, and Welfare. Mimeographed, December 1973. (IV-D-1, VI-A, VI-E, X-6)

Wallace, D. The Chemung County research demonstration with dependent multi-problem families. New York: State Charities Aid Association, 1965. (IV-D-2)

Wangensteen, O. H., Peter, E. T., Nicoloff, D. M., Walder, A. I., Sosin, H., & Bernstein, E. F. Achieving "physiological gastrectomy" by gastric freezing. A preliminary report of an experimental and clinical study. Journal of the American Medical Association, 1962, 180, 439-444. (IV-H-11)

Weisberg, H. I. Short term cognitive effects of Head Start programs: A report on the third year of planned variation—1971-1972. Cambridge, Mass.: Huron Institute, September 1973. (V-A-3, VII-A)

Welch, W. W., & Walberg, H. J. A natural experiment in curriculum innovation. American Educational Research Journal, Summer 1972, 9(3), 373-383. (IV-D-9)

Welch, W. W., Walberg, H. J., & Ahlgren, A. The selection of a national random sample of teachers for experimental curriculum evaluation. School Science and Mathematics, March 1969, 210-216. (IV-D-9)

White, R. R., Hightower, N. C., Jr., & Adalid, R. Problems and complications of gastric freezing. Annals of Surgery, 1964, 159, 765-768. (V-B)

Wilner, D. M., Hetherington, R. W., Gold, E. B., Ershoff, D. H., & Garagliano, C. F. Databank of program evaluations. Evaluation, 1973, 1(3), 3-6. (IV-A)

Wilner, D. M., Walkley, R. P., Pinkerton, T. C., Tayback, M., with the assistance of Glasser, M. N., Schram, J. M., Hopkins, C. E., Curtis, C. C., Meyer, A. S., & Dallas, J. R. The housing environment and family life. Baltimore: The Johns Hopkins Press, 1962. (V-A-1, X-2)

Wilson, J. O. Social experimentation and public policy analysis. Public Policy, Winter 1974, 22, 15-38. (V-A-3)

3

Making the Case for Randomized Assignment to Treatments by Considering the Alternatives: Six Ways in Which Quasi-Experimental Evaluations In Compensatory Education Tend to Underestimate Effects

DONALD P. CAMPBELL and ROBERT F. BORUCH

I. INTRODUCTION

This chapter constitutes an indirect advocacy of randomized experiments.[1] Its illustrative focus is on compensatory education, an area in which randomized experiments are
particularly feasible. Our mode of approach is to go over a
variety of sources of ambiguity and bias in quasi-experimental evaluations, all of which would be eliminated or
greatly reduced by randomized experiments.

It is tempting, but probably misleading, to dramatize
this volume and the conference on which it was based by
seeing in them a controversy over the role of randomized
experiments in program evaluation and in science. Our paper
certainly joins with Chapter 2 (this volume) by Gilbert,
Light, and Mosteller (and the orthodoxy of statistical

[1] The preparation of this paper has been supported in part by
National Science Foundation Grant SOC-7103704-03 and by
National Institute of Education Contract NIE-C-74-0115.

experimental methodology) in support of random assignment. In view of the widespread tendency of Bayesian statisticians to disparage randomization[1] one might be tempted to classify Chapter 6 by Edwards and Guttentag in the opposition. This would technically be an error. What they provide is a mechanism by which decision-making groups can transform a wide variety of considerations, including evidence on the effectiveness of programs if they have such, into administrative decisions. They do feel that randomized experiments are oversold, that evidence on program effectiveness is usually

---

[1] This rejection of randomization is hard to document in writing but seems an important part of an oral tradition. Note this brief report, with demurrer, by one of the founding fathers: "The theory of personal probability must be explored with circumspection and imagination. For example, applying the theory naively one quickly comes to the conclusion that randomization is without value for statistics. This conclusion does not sound right, and it is not right. Closer examination of the road to this untenable conclusion does lead to new insights into the role and limitations of randomization but does by no means deprive randomization of its important function in statistics." (Savage, 1961, p. 585). In a letter of November 14, 1974, which he has kindly permitted us to quote, Ward Edwards amplifies this point: "I have always been puzzled about this topic. Heuristic justifications for randomization are easy; formal justifications for it seem impossible to me. Yet formally optimal procedures for choosing a pure strategy, instead of randomizing, seem not to be available. So I have always carefully

of minor influence in policy decisions, and that decision makers who seek out help in program evaluation usually need help with value clarification and rational value pooling for decision making more than they need precise evidence on program effectiveness. While Cain's comment in Chapter 4 is basically in agreement as to the theoretical superiority of randomization, he doubts that the validity difference between randomized and nonrandomized comparisons is as great as the present paper and its predecessors try to make it appear.

The other conference speaker whom one might, for the sake of drama, cast as an opponent of randomized experiments is Scriven (1975). This, too, is probably a miscasting. What he advocates is an alternate approach to knowledge of program effects, one based upon tracing the histories of particular persons or sub-classes of persons, and one much closer to ordinary, prescientific modes of knowing. This could better be seen as an advocacy of a precursor or supplement to formal experimental procedures rather than a substitute.

———————

avoided saying anything very explicit in print on this point. (I perhaps should mention that, as a general rule, I try to handle sequence effects in experimental designs by picking some appropriate sequence and putting all Ss through it, rather than by randomizing over possible sequences. This perhaps reflects a Bayesian bias--or perhaps simply reflects the uselessness of proving yet again that sequence effects exist.) Savage was equally baffled by this topic; he and I discussed it several times, always in a spirit of frustration."

II. COMMON SENSE AND SCIENTIFIC KNOWING

We are in essential agreement with Scriven that common-sense knowing and scientific knowing share the same epistemological setting. One doesn't know anything for certain, but one knows remarkably well; the procedure is that of guess and check (Campbell, 1974a). Moreover, scientific knowing builds upon common-sense knowing. Scientific knowing trusts common sense and uses it to assemble the evidence for doubting common sense in any specific instance. Scientific knowing goes beyond common-sense knowing, not by replacing it but by depending upon it and building upon it. If one were to look at the evidence whereby Eddington or others might become convinced that an apparently solid table is a loose lattice and that for many purposes its solidity is illusory, one would find that in the process of thus doubting ordinary perception, one was in fact trusting the same kind of common-sense perception of objects, instruments, locations, etc. This is analogous to the process by which a person convinces himself that the Müller-Lyer illusion is actually illusory. According to anthropological evidence (Segall et al., 1966), if the reader is a typical member of Western society, the horizontal line on the right looks longer than the horizontal line on the left. If he is

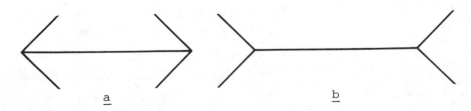

a   b

Fig. 1. A version of the Müller-Lyer illusion.

198

allowed to measure, or to exclude the diagonal lines from view, he will eventually convince himself that his eyes have been fooling him and that the left horizontal line is actually longer. In the process of discounting one product of perceptual evidence, it became necessary to trust a great number of other equally simple perceptual evidences. It was also necessary to make a lot of unverified assumptions: e.g., that the paper is not flexing in a synchronized pattern so that, as one brings up the ruler, the lines expand or shrink; assumptions of solidity and permanence; etc.

The implications of this orientation for evaluation research are manifold (Campbell, 1974b). The qualitative project history becomes absolutely essential to proper interpretation of the research results. The common-sense knowing involved at each stage of converting human experience and action into numbers (e.g., the transactions in the public opinion interview and coding room) becomes focal. The subjective impressions of the many participants and observers of the social experiment acquire a relevance equal to that of the computer output. If, as in the case of Head Start (Campbell & Erlebacher, 1970) or Job Corps (Director, 1974), the qualitative impressions are markedly at variance with the computer output, the validity of the latter should be suspected fully as much as the validity of the former; in particular, an attempt should be made to understand the source of the discrepancy. Thus, we join Scriven in the heretical belief that there are other ways of knowing than through experiment. We, more than he, would emphasize the equivocality of all ways of knowing--including experiments. In many areas, experimental data are much less equivocal than common-sense knowing or passive observational statistics, but his illustrations of inference through autopsy are convincing. We have used similar arguments:

> Yet we make assured causal inferences in many settings not involving randomization: The earthquake caused the brick building to crumble; the car's crashing into it caused the telephone pole to break; the language patterns of the older models and mentors caused this child to speak English instead of Kwakiutl. These are all potentially erroneous inferences, unproven, unsupported by deductive certainty. They are of the same type as experimental inferences, in that we are confident that were we to intrude experimentally, we could confirm the causal laws involved. Yet they are inferences available to the unintrusive observer. Cannot the social scientist as observer make some inferences as to sources of change on comparable grounds? The program of attempting quasi-experimental interpretation of observational sequences addresses itself to this problem.
>
> Some slogans: Experiments probe theory, but do not prove theory. Any data that probe theory are worth looking at. The only uncontrolled variables that invalidate an experiment are those to which we are willing to attribute the status of empirical laws comparable in standing to the law under investigation. When we have an evidence of change and wish to interpret it causally, the only relevant threats to that interpretation are other plausible, probable, causal explanations.
>
> Consider the inference as to crashing car and telephone pole. Our assurance of inference is due to the total absence of other possible causes. Combinations of termites and wind we have ruled out because the other data implications of these theories (e.g., termite tunnels and debris in the wood and wind records in nearby weather stations) do not occur. Spontaneous splintering of poles by happenstance coincident with the auto's onset does not impress us as a rival, nor would it explain the damage to the car. Analogously, in the quasi-experimental program, field observations will be given causal interpretation where (a) the interpretation in question squares with the data, and

(b) other plausible rival hypotheses have been ruled out.

Does this let down the bars and give approval to the descriptive journalism which so often passes for science in our fields? I think not, if we vigorously attend to the specific plausible rival hypotheses appropriate to each situation. In particular, I find the plausible rival hypothesis of regression (Thorndike, 1942; Campbell & Clayton, 1964) so compelling as to rule out totally these well-established customs in the reported observations of natural change: Chapin's (1955) "ex-post facto experiments" in all forms; matching as a substitute for randomization in providing pretreatment equivalence of groups; sociology's "qualifier," "elaboration," "turnover table," and other complex cross-classifications with percentages for comparison computed to part-sample bases; partial or multiple correlation when used to reject the hypothesis of cosymptom in favor of the hypothesis of distinctive determinant; and the division of pretest scores into extreme subgroups for the assessment of differential rates of change as a function of initial level. (Campbell, 1963, pp. 213-214)

As to our strategy of practical knowing, we agree with Scriven that practical proof (which is never logical proof) depends upon eliminating alternative hypotheses. This is in fact the key to our orientation toward quasi-experimental design. Any quasi-experimental design, or set of data assembled to argue for a causal hypothesis, is to be treated as valid unless there are plausible alternative explanations for the results. In Campbell and Stanley (1966) there are listed some common classes of uncontrolled variables, or threats to validity, that are characteristic of various quasi-experimental designs. By and large there are more of those threats for quasi-experiments than there are for randomized assignment to treatment, and there are many more for some quasi-experiments than for others, but our emphasis is that in many specific settings these threats may not be plausible. For some particular sets of pretest and posttest data, for example, it is incredible that the gain could be due to what people had read in the daily papers. Another example is provided by B. J. Underwood, who, in measuring memory for nonsense syllables, finds no need to control for what Campbell and Stanley call "history." There are so few opportunities of learning these particular nonsense sylla- bles that there is no need for control groups or lead- insulated rooms in which to retain subjects between pretest and posttest. Quasi-experimental designs are only weak insofar as there are plausible alternative explanations. This is essentially in the spirit of Scriven's emphasis, although when it comes to drawing practical conclusions, we may be a lot more cautious than he.

It may be that Campbell and Stanley (1966) should feel guilty for having contributed to giving quasi-experimental designs a good name. There are program evaluations in which the authors say proudly, "We used a quasi-experimental design." If responsible, Campbell and Stanley should do penance, because in most social settings there are many equally or more plausible rival hypotheses than the hypoth- esis that the puny treatment indeed produced an effect. In fact, however, their presentation of quasi-experimental designs could as well be read as laborious arguments in favor of doing randomized assignment to treatment whenever possible. Admittedly, there are also encouragements to do the second best if the second best is all that the situation allows. The arguments presented in this chapter continue the stragey of justifying randomized experiments by making explicit the costs in equivocality and the burdens of making additional estimations of parameters that result from a failure to randomize. We agree with those who say "Randomized experiments are expensive and difficult. Don't use them unless you really need to." Our only disagreement may be over when it is that randomized experiments are actually needed.

There is, in particular, one plausible rival hypothesis that invalidates most social experiments of a quasi-experimental design nature: that is, there is a profound underlying confounding of selection and treatment. If a quasi-experimental study shows that people who have had psychotherapy have a higher suicide rate than matched cases who have not had psychotherapy, one is correctly reluctant to conclude that psychotherapy causes suicide. It is clear that no amount of matching can completely correct for the fact that those seeking psychotherapy are more suicide prone. As another example, consider an experiment done with failing students, some of whom are randomly assigned to a group that receives twenty hours of high-quality tutoring. The results would show that this tutored group does better than those randomly assigned to the control group. However, if a correlation study were performed, it would show that the students who had more hours of tutoring got poorer grades on the subsequent final examination. This is because of the strong tendency for those students who do poorly to seek out the most tutoring. While this tutoring no doubt helps, it is not sufficient to correct the selection bias. Although the study needs to be done, we doubt if any amount of matching, covariance or regression adjustment on previous grades and other covariates would change the negative correlation into the correct positive one.

In these two examples, common-sense background knowledge would prevent the conclusion that psychotherapy and tutoring were harmful. But in many other settings, evaluation researchers are packaging similar under-adjusted selection differences as though they were treatment differences (Campbell & Erlebacher, 1970; Director, 1974). In aggregated economic data, where raw correlations are on the order of .99, this may not be a problem; in the area of education, where test-retest correlations in compensatory programs run as low as .30, this systematic underadjustment characteristic of present statistical procedures becomes a serious matter.

Settings no doubt occur in which there is no confounding of selection and treatment. One also can conceive of modes of analysis that would avoid the biases that are present in the commonly used methods of adjusting away the confounding, and thus make quasi-experiments less biased and more useful. As a matter of fact, the present authors' own research programs are addressed to the task of developing such modes of analysis. Even when developed, however, these "unbiased" adjustment procedures will require problematic assumptions and estimations that would be obviated by random assignment.

III. EXPERIMENTATION IN EDUCATION

In the particular area that we want to discuss--education--one has a setting in which randomized experiments are generally feasible because of features which make schools a natural laboratory. Pupils are arbitrarily fed doses of education. They assemble regularly for this process. What is being taught them is arbitrarily varied all the time. There is therefore a laboratory in which the treatment can be arbitrarily changed without difficulty. There are enough units to randomize: individual students, or, better yet, classrooms. It is even possible to randomly assign schools or school districts to treatments, since, even in the case of massive national programs such as Follow Through or Head Start, there is never enough of the treatment to go around. Nor is there usually enough certainty about the benefits of the treatment to create an ethical problem by withholding it. And even if deprivation of treatment were a problem, one could arrange the use of evaluation budgets to create true experiments in a way that expands rather than decreases the number of people having access to the program:

> The funds set aside for evaluation are funds taken away from treatment. This cost-benefit trade-off decision has already been made when quasi-experimental evaluation has been budgeted, or when funds are committed to any form of budgeting and accounting. Taking these evaluational funds, one could use nine-tenths of them for providing experimental expansions of compensatory instruction, one-tenth for measurement of effects on the small experimental and control samples thus created. Here the ethical focus could be on the lucky boon given to the experimentals. Since evaluation money would be used to expand treatment, the controls would not be deprived. In retrospect, we are sure that data from 400 children in such an experiment would be far more informative than 4,000 tested by the best of

quasi-experiments, to say nothing of an ex post facto study. (Campbell & Erlebacher, 1970, p. 207)

That randomized experiments in education are often feasible is clear. As further evidence for our contention, a bibliography on such efforts is included in the appendix to this chapter. These studies describe randomized experiments employed to evaluate an impressive range of programs, including teacher training programs; curriculum components, encompassing alternative media (T.V., radio) and support systems (CAI, typewriters); compensatory education programs; vocational training programs; specialized industrial, commercial, and public service training programs; and other educational efforts. These experiments also vary considerably along other dimensions. The unit of randomization, for example, varies from schools, through classrooms and teachers, to households, family units, and children. Though most such experiments have been performed within the formal school setting, many have taken place in new schools, industrial environments, hospitals, homes, and other field conditions. Most constitute a small part of a larger, integrated series of investigations. And indeed, some manage nicely to combine randomized experimental tests, quasi-experimental assessments, and completely qualitative evaluations in a single research effort (see, for example, the work by Goodwin and Sanders, 1972). Needless to say, in some experiments randomization was not complete or was corrupted. Most of the experiments listed in the appendix, however, were implemented well. It is encouraging to note that in most cases, the experiments provided good evidence for the superiority of at least one of the educational variations being tried.

Practical feasibility--the mere availability of a convenient laboratory for randomized experiments--does not cover all of the relevant feasibility issues. There are, of course, many other obstacles to doing randomized experiments. Boruch (1975) and others have surveyed anticipatory objections to such experiments. Some of these objections seem specious, some valid. They include the alleged Procrustean nature of quantitative experimental evaluation, the adverse impact of doing the experiments themselves, their disproportionate expense when evaluated against their survival utility, the real or perceived unfair deprivation of the control groups, and so on. Conner (1974), in a survey of the problems of implementing 12 randomized experiments, finds some of these anticipated fears unwarranted. But even the specious objections may reflect a valid underlying reality. Experiments are feared because in most settings they evaluate not only the program alternative, but also the administrators, teachers, or students involved. For soft-money programs they directly jeopardize budget renewal; the alternative is not bureaucratically present to support the same staff in attempting another program designed to alleviate the same problem. Program personnel intuitively know that their program is too weak and the problem too intractible for any complete cure or even substantial progress to result (Rossi, 1969). In the course of getting the program implemented, too much has been promised for the program (Campbell, 1969). All these factors really do justify a fear of hard-headed program evaluation, a fear which expresses itself through every available argument and rationalization. Solving this recurrent trap is not the purpose here. Until organizations have solved it, evaluation methodologists should often advise against program evaluation, and should certainly not force it on unwilling institutions. Since true experiments are less equivocal than quasi-experiments, and since they permit fewer excuses for unwanted results, this legitimate fear of evaluation may often lead true experiments to be more opposed than quasi-experiments. Probably the correct stance will often be to recommend no evaluation at all, particularly when the quasi-experimental alternative has biases such as are described below, which mistakenly tend to make a program appear not only more ineffective than it is, but also actively harmful.

If an experiment is not randomized, assumptions must be made that are often untenable and are even more frequently unverifiable. In addition, a mélange of parameters must be identified and estimated based on insufficient theory and data. These two problems in themselves are sufficiently formidable (and at times untractable) to justify eliminating them at the outset, by assuring through randomization that groups are identical to one another with respect to unknown parameters. The problems of making inferences based on nonrandomized data are not new, of course, nor are they confined to the evaluation of social programs. Their formal origins are evident in Galton's attempt to identify the size and stability of the effects of various plant fertilization methods based on some of Charles Darwin's observational data. Galton overestimated the conclusiveness of his own results, in part because he assumed that clever statistical manipulation would make possible essentially the same inferences one might obtain on the basis of randomized data

(Fisher, 1935). Essentially the same message has been delivered by H. Fairfield Smith (1957) and, in a more elegant way, by Herman Wold (1956). Their specific warnings to the biological and agricultural communities are nearly identical to those we try to make here. Simple applications of multiple regression, covariance analysis, and matching will usually be inappropriate vehicles for estimating effects. That these same problems occur chronically in naive applications of these techniques is evident in the engineering sciences (Box, 1966), the administrative sciences and operations research (Hilton, 1972), and the medical sciences (Chalmers, Block, & Lee, 1972), as well as in the social sciences and education, as we will detail below.

IV. SIX SOURCES OF UNDERADJUSTMENT BIAS

In what follows, we will sample six problems from this morass of assumptions and adjustments which quasi-experimental evaluation necessitates. Through the perversity of fate, it turns out that in all six problems the probable direction of bias is toward making compensatory education programs look harmful at worst, or ineffective at best, since usually the compensatory treatment is applied to the less able of the comparison groups.

A. *SYSTEMATIC UNDERADJUSTMENT OF PREEXISTING DIFFERENCES*

1. Matching and Regression Artifacts

In a paper by Campbell and Erlebacher (1970) on how regression artifacts in quasi-experimental designs can mistakenly make compensatory education look harmful, there was assembled a literature which has been persistent but never dominant in the psychology and education tests-and-measurement tradition (e.g., McNemar, 1940; Thorndike, 1942; Lord, 1960a). This literature points out how, when the experimental group and the comparison group come from different populations, efforts to correct for pretreatment differences lead to regression artifacts. The problem is so recurrent and so little understood that it seems worth an elementary pedagogical review here.

First, let us consider the simplest case of "regression to the mean" in a single group measured twice, as discussed in the classic paper by McNemar (1940). If we concentrate on extreme samples selected on the basis of the pretest, then, as shown in Figure 2, we will find that the subgroups which were so extreme and compact on the pretest will have spread out on the posttest, and that each subgroup mean will have regressed toward the total group mean. Presented as in Figure 2 this may seem like a rather mysterious process. The same facts presented in Figure 3 as a scatter diagram of the pretest-posttest relationship make it more understandable. The apparent regression is nothing more than a byproduct of a biased form of entry into a symmetrically imperfect relationship. The bias comes from constructing groups on the basis of extreme test scores on only one of the variables. Inevitably, if the correlation between the two tests is less than perfect, the extremes on the pretest will be less well defined on the posttest. If in Figure 3 the extreme groups had been defined by horizontal slices (e.g., all those with scores of 20 and above on the posttest as one extreme, all those with scores of 8 and below as the other extreme), these groups would have been better defined and more extreme on the posttest than on the pretest. There would then have been "regression toward the mean" working

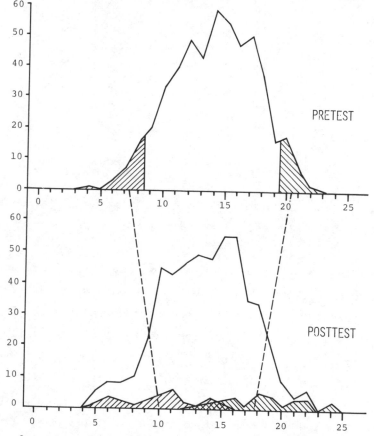

Fig. 2. Regression of pretest extremes toward mean on post-test (correlation = .55).

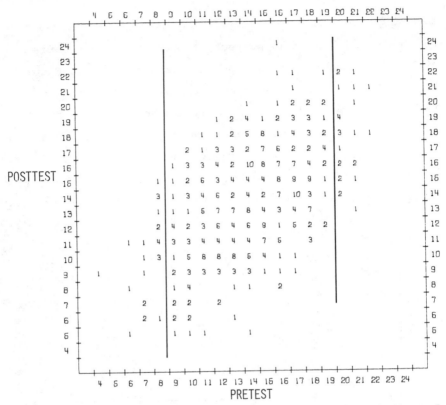

Fig. 3. Scatter diagram with pretest extremes indicated. Same data as in Figure 2 (r = .55).

backward in time. "Regression to the mean" is thus not a true process working in time, but a methodological artifact, a tautological restatement of imperfect correlation. To use McNemar's (1940) example, suppose the IQ of all the children in an orphanage is measured on two occasions, one year apart. If one looks at the children with initially high scores, they will have regressed down toward the mean on a second test, and will appear to have gotten worse. Those initially lowest will have improved. One may mistakenly conclude that the orphanage is homogenizing the population, reducing the intelligence of the brightest, increasing the intelligence of the less bright. However, if one were to look at the extremes on the posttest and trace them back to the pretest, one would find that they had been nearer the mean on the pretest, thus implying the opposite conclusion. If the whole group mean and standard deviation have been the same on both testings (as in Figures 2 and 3), these dramatic findings truly imply only that the test retest correlation is less than perfect.

The amount of "regression to the mean" is a direct function of the correlation coefficient. Indeed, Galton called it r for "regression" or "reversion," (Galton 1879; 1886). (Because of a generation gap between the present coauthors, the following will be stated here in the correlational algebra of the 1930's. The algebra in later sections will be more up-to-date.) If scores are expressed in standard score form (as deviations from the mean divided by their standard deviation), and if x is a pretest and y a posttest score, r the correlation coefficient, and the "hat," ^, indicates a predicted score, then $\hat{y} = rx$; but note also that: $\hat{x} = ry$. The regression artifact comes from failing to note that $\hat{y} \neq y$ and $\hat{x} \neq x$. $\hat{y}$ and y are different measures, with widely different variabilities, for one thing. If one solves $\hat{y} = rx$ for x, one gets $x = \hat{y}/r$, dramatically different from $\hat{x} = ry$.

Now let's shift to the more complicated two-group regression artifact case, such as that produced by matching. Figure 4 sets up a hypothetical case of two elementary schools with student populations that differ in ability, where the treatment is being given to the less able student

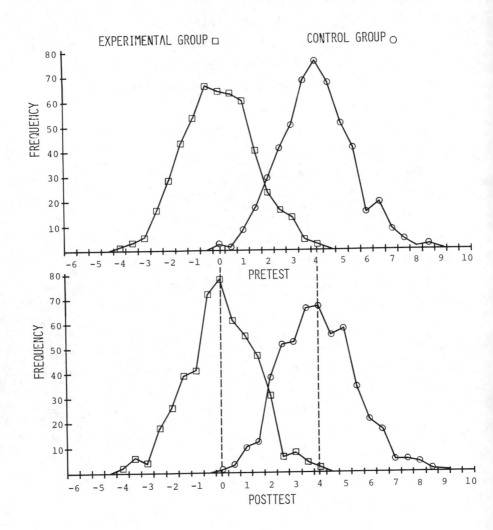

Fig. 4 (See legend on next page.)

Fig. 4. Simulated data for a nonequivalent group comparison with no true treatment effect, and in which the means and standard deviations are the same on both pretest and post-test except for independent sampling of error on the two testings. The two dashed lines connecting pretest and post-test means are seen to be essentially parallel. The data have been generated using normal random numbers for both true score and error. For the experimental group, the formula was: Pretest = True + Pretest Error; Posttest = True + Posttest Error. For the advantaged control group, a constant of 4 has been added to the random true score. 500 cases have been generated for each group. For these data, the pretest means come out to be .045 and 3.986, the post-test means .011 and 3.924, where the universe values are 0 and 4. The four standard deviations are 1.436, 1.424, 1.411, and 1.469 for the data grouped as shown, where the universe value is 1.414. The pretest-posttest correlations are .535 for the experimental group and .485 for the control, where the universe value is .500.

population, and the other group is being used as the control. As shown in Figure 4, the mean difference between the two groups and the variance within each group remain essentially the same on the pretest as on the posttest. Given only this evidence, the obvious conclusion would be that the hypothetical treatment given to the experimental group between the pretest and posttest had had no effect whatsoever. The status of the two groups, relative and absolute, is the same on posttest and pretest. While this conclusion involves some assumptions that we will lay out in more detail later, it is the correct conclusion, in that it was built into our simulation.

In contrast to this conclusion, several seemingly more sophisticated approaches, such as matching and covariance, produce "significant effects"--actually pseudo effects. We will attempt to illustrate this in intuitive detail in the case of matching.

Suppose one were bothered by the conspicuous pretest dissimilarity of our experimental and control groups, and felt that this dissimilarity made them essentially uncomparable. It might be noted that in spite of this overall noncomparability, the two groups did overlap, and must therefore contain comparable cases. This would suggest basing the quasi-experimental comparison not on the whole group data, but only on subsets of cases matched on the pretest. Figure 5 shows what happens in this case. Each of the two purified, compact, matched subgroups on the pretest spreads out widely on the posttest, although each remains within the boundaries of its whole group distribution. Since the subgroups on the posttest are no longer as pure, extreme, and compact as they were on the pretest, their means have been distorted toward the mean of their respective whole group distributions. The result is a separation in posttest means for the matched groups which has often been mistaken for a treatment effect. It is instead, once again, a product of a biased mode of entry into an imperfect relationship. The intuition to look for comparable subsets is not necessarily wrong, but the employment of the fallible pretest scores to define comparable subsets is fundamentally

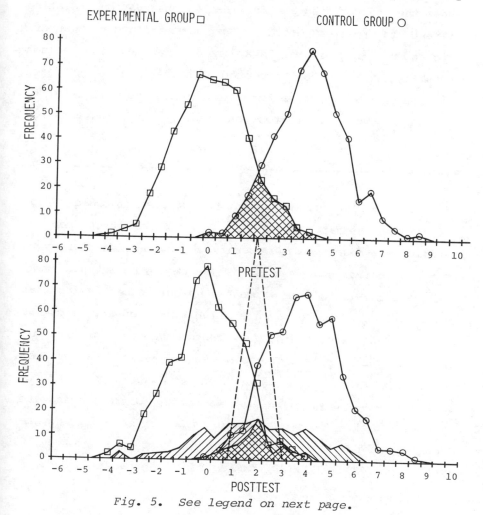

Fig. 5. See legend on next page.

217

misleading. Were one to have matched scores on the post-test, tracing these back to the pretest would have produced a pretest separation. One would be unlikely to do this, however, because the temporal order of the testing tends to be associated with the temporal order of the hypothesized causal sequence.

Once again, approaching the problem through scatter diagrams may make the effect more comprehensible. Figure 6 shows the scatter diagram for the 500 observations relating pretest to posttest for the experimental group. Super-imposed on this diagram is a line connecting the column means, i.e., the mean expected posttest value for each specific pretest value. (For convenience we will refer to this as the "unfitted regression line." The least squares

---

Fig. 5. The posttest distribution of cases matched on the pretest for the data of Figure 4. To illustrate how the matching was done, consider score 0.0, for which there were only two control group cases. These two were matched with the two first-listed experimental group cases having that score, out of the 64 such available. Since all cases had been generated from independent random numbers, no bias was produced by this selection rule. There resulted a total of 86 matched pairs. For each of the two subgroups, the pre-test mean was 2.104. The two subgroup posttest means are .878 and 3.145. The two subgroup pretest standard devia-tions are .805. The two subgroup posttest standard devia-tions are 1.331 and 1.323, reflecting the greater spread.

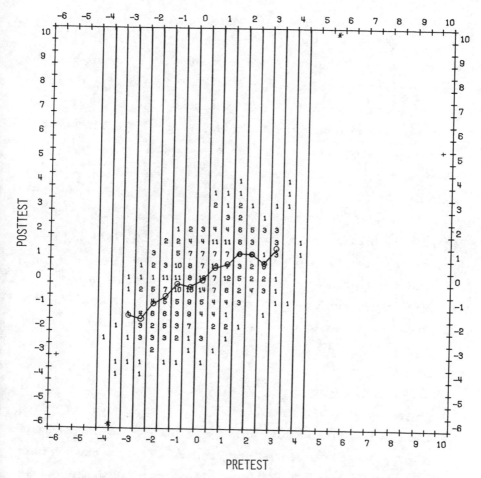

Fig. 6. Scatter diagram for the pretest-posttest correlation for the experimental group of Figure 4. The correlation coefficient is .535. Also indicated is an "unfitted regression line" connecting the mean posttest value corresponding to each of the various pretest values, except for those columns with fewer than five observations. The corresponding <u>linear</u> regression line can be drawn in by connecting the two +'s. Connecting the two *'s provides the reverse regression line, predicting pretest values from posttest scores.

straight line fitting these data can be drawn in by connecting the two + points.) Note that this is only one of two such lines. The other would connect the row means--the mean _pretest_ score corresponding to each specific posttest value. (The linear fit to this second regression line can be drawn by connecting the two *'s.) Whereas the illustrated regression line has a slope of about $28°$, the other regression line would have a slope of about $62°$. Had the correlation been 1.00--that is, perfect, without scatter-- both regression lines would have been the same, and at a $45°$ angle in this case. Figure 7 shows the pretest-posttest scatter for the control group, and the regression line predicting posttest scores from specific pretest values. In Figure 8 these two scatters are superimposed. While we have not found it convenient to tag the specific matched cases in this graph, the vertical distance between the two regression lines makes the point clearly. For example, for pretest scores of 2.0, right in the middle of the matching area, the 23 experimental cases have a mean posttest score of only .98, while the 29 control group cases have a mean posttest score of 3.02--two whole points higher. The expected values in the absence of any treatment effect thus show the inadequacies of matching on a fallible pretest. Note that as the correlation between pretest and posttest becomes higher, the underadjustment of the preexisting differences resulting from matching (or covariance adjustment) becomes less. Before matching, the experimental and control groups differed by four points. After matching (or covariance adjustment) on the pretest, and when the within-group pretest-posttest correlations are .50, the group difference becomes two points. Had the pretest-posttest correlations been .75, only a one-point difference would remain; had they been 1.00, the matching would have completely adjusted away the initial group difference. Referring back to Figure 8, note that as the correlation gets higher, the linear slope of the regression line gets closer to 45°. Were the correlations to reach 1.00, the two regression lines would connect, the expected posttest values for any given pretest

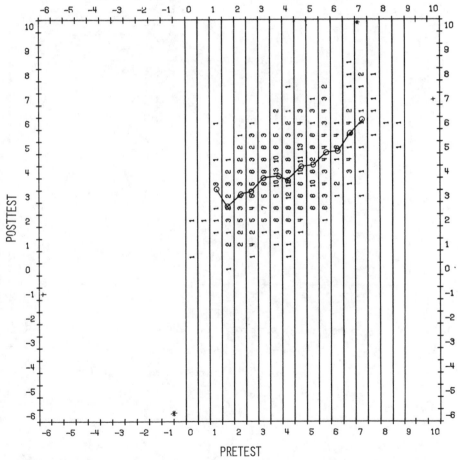

Fig. 7. Scatter diagram, etc., for the pretest-posttest correlation for the control group of Figure 4. The correlation coefficient is .485.

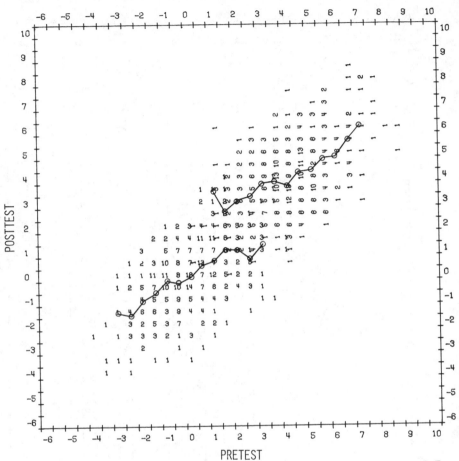

Fig. 8. Superimposed scatter diagrams from Figures 6 and 7, showing both experimental group and control group. The ver- tical differences between the regression lines indicate the magnitude of the "regression artifact" produced by matching on pretest scores.

value would be the same for both experimental and control groups, and matching would achieve its intended aim.

2. Covariance Adjustment

What we have described is the regression artifact produced by matching (Thorndike, 1942). As Lord (1960a), Cochran (1968), Porter (1967) and others have made clear, ordinary covariance adjustment results in analogous biases in the same direction. The "adjustment" in covariance is usually made by subtracting from the raw dependent measures a function of measures of a covariate; i.e., an analysis is made of

$$Y_i - \beta_T (T_i - \bar{T})$$

instead of Y_i, where

Y_i = posttest score of the ith person,

T_i = pretest true score of the ith person, and

β_T = the regression of Y on T from the covariance analysis.

With no errors of measurement of T_i, the adjusted mean differences between two groups may be represented as

$$\Delta \bar{Y} - \beta_T \Delta \bar{T},$$

where $\Delta \bar{Y}$ represents the mean difference on Y between treatment and control group members, and $\Delta \bar{T}$ represents the mean group difference on the covariate. When errors of measurement (ξ) are present, we may represent the fallible observations coarsely by the model

223

$$X_i = T_i + \xi_i$$

where

$$T_i \sim I(0, \sigma^2), \quad \xi_i \sim I(0, \sigma_\xi^2),$$

$$Cov(T_i \xi_i) = 0.$$

Then the observed regression of Y_i on X_i, β_X, will differ from the true regression, β_T. Specifically,

$$\beta_X = \beta_T \, \sigma^2/(\sigma^2 + \sigma_\xi^2).$$

Consequently, the adjusted means will be biased, since

$$\Delta\bar{Y} - \beta_X \, \Delta\bar{X} = \Delta\bar{Y} - \beta_T \, \Delta\bar{T} \, \sigma^2/(\sigma^2 + \sigma_\xi^2),$$

and

$$\Delta\bar{X} = \Delta\bar{T} \neq 0,$$

so that

$$\Delta\bar{Y} - \beta_X \Delta\bar{X} > \Delta\bar{Y} - \beta_T \, \Delta\bar{T},$$

if β_T and $\Delta\bar{T}$ have the same sign.

One class of approaches to unbiased adjustment is reliability-corrected covariance analysis. In most cases, the situation considered is identical to that described above: constant differences between treatment and control group, complete predictability of those differences from perfectly measured covariates (i.e., complete specification) except for sampling error, and the usual assumptions about homogeneity of variance and regression, and independence of error.

Lord (1960a) derived a test statistic based on repeated measures of a fallible covariate and proved that in large samples, the statistic is distributed as z and can be used to make unbiased tests of the hypothesis that the mean difference between groups, adjusted for the covariate and error in the covariate, is zero. Porter's (1967) approach, like Lord's, assumes that the simple mental test model holds for observations ($X = T + \xi$), but Porter's approach accommodates two or more treatment groups when an estimate of the reliability of the covariate is available. He prefers first to estimate true scores on the covariate, and then to conduct conventional F tests in covariance analysis. The estimated true scores ($\hat{T}_i$) for each member (i) of the sample are computed from

$$\hat{T}_i = \bar{X} + rel\ (X_i - \bar{X}),$$

where X_i represents the fallible observation on the covariate, rel represents the reliability of the observations on the covariate, and $\bar{X}$ is the sample mean.

This formula begins to point up some of the difficulties implicit in various approaches that are being developed to accommodate the errors-in-variables problem. There is an unpublished dialogue between Porter and Campbell concerning the choice of reliability to use in Porter's formula. Porter (e.g., Porter & Chibucos, 1974) has observed that a parallel forms reliability or a short time lapse test-retest coefficient might be used under certain conditions. Campbell argues that this procedure usually undercorrects, in that as the time lapse between pretest (X_i) and posttest (Y_i) increases, the correlation between these variables decreases; consequently, the degree of undercorrection can increase. More specifically, a correction of the sort under discussion amounts to computing a corrected regression coefficient for the covariate of the form

$$\beta_T = \beta_X / \text{rel} .$$

Suppose that an internal consistency reliability of the form

$$\text{rel(IC)} = \sigma_T^{\,2} / (\sigma_T^{\,2} + \sigma_\xi^{\,2})$$

is used, when in fact a correction which recognizes temporal errors (η) in temporal consistency (TC), as well as internal errors (ξ), should be used; e.g.,

$$\text{rel(TC,IC)} = \sigma_T^{\,2} / (\sigma_T^{\,2} + \sigma_\xi^{\,2} + \sigma_\eta^{\,2}) .$$

Then the estimate of β_T will be biased by an amount

$$- \beta_T \sigma_\eta^{\,2} / (\sigma_T^{\,2} + \sigma_\xi^{\,2} + \sigma_\eta^{\,2})$$

and, in the absence of any treatment effect, the adjusted mean difference between groups will differ from its true value of zero; i.e.,

$$\Delta \bar{Y} - \beta_X / \text{rel(IC)} \cdot \Delta \bar{X} \neq 0 .$$

Where $\Delta\bar{Y}$, $\Delta\bar{X}$, β_X are greater than zero, the adjustment will be imperfect and can lead to a conclusion that the treatment is not as effective as it in fact is; or even that the treatment is harmful. Campbell has suggested that in the simplest case, the simple correlation between pretest and posttest might be used as the "reliability" in Porter's formula (assuming that X and Y have the same internal consistency reliability).

We suggest that the disagreement can be resolved if it is reinterpreted as a disagreement about background assumptions regarding the nature of the group differences in the world of application. To do this, in what follows we first expand on the observation that the longer the time lapse involved, the lower the test-retest correlations tend to be. We subsequently consider several alternate assumptions about the history over time of the selection bias for which a correction is being attempted.

Table 1 presents an idealized version of the pattern of correlations that might be found among repeated achievement tests given in grades one through six. The "temporal erosion" of relationships that is almost universally found is strikingly illustrated in this table. One-year lapses produce a .78 correlation at all age levels, two-year lapses a .68 correlation, and so on to a five-year lapse correlation of .47. This pattern of correlations is now most commonly identified as a Guttman simplex, or as an autoregressive process. We will model it in terms of an underlying first order Markov process upon which is superimposed measurement error.

Before proceeding to the model, however, let us consider what the fact of such test-retest correlation matrices

Table 1. Hypothetical correlations among repeated testings and selection; treatment having no effect given in the first grade.

Grades	1 X₁	2 Y₂	3 Y₃	4 Y₄	5 Y₅	6 Y₆	Alt. A	Alt. B	Alt. C
Pretest X₁	(.92)						.50	.50	.50
Posttest Y₂	.78	(.92)					.50	.43	.55
" Y₃	.68	.78	(.92)				.50	.37	.59
" Y₄	.59	.68	.78	(.92)			.50	.32	.63
" Y₅	.52	.59	.68	.78	(.92)		.50	.29	.66
" Y₆	.47	.52	.59	.68	.78	(.92)	.50	.26	.69

Bias in selection to treatment administered between X and Y, expressed as a correlation coefficient.

228

imply for our psychological concepts of ability. Such matrices are found for intelligence as well as for achievement (Humphreys, 1960). They force us to abandon the concept of a fixed true score for each person, which is imperfectly measured on various occasions. Instead, that true score is itself changing in some autoregressive or moving average manner. The stochastic input of learning opportunities--the slings and arrows of outrageous fortune--make this a plausible model for learned abilities. A genetic model is also possible; we assume that several thousand genes affect test scores, and of these genes, different subsets are operative at different ages, with adjacent ages having the more overlapping sets.

The pattern of relationships underlying Table 1 assumes that within both the experimental group and the control group, the underlying process conforms to a first order autoregressive (Markov) scheme:

$$Y_t = \rho^\delta Y_{t-\delta} + \eta_t$$

where

$$\delta < t = 1, 2 \ldots k, \quad \eta_t \sim I(0, \sigma_\eta^2),$$
$$Cov(Y_{t-\delta}, \eta_t) = 0.$$

Any perfect observation at time t, (Y_t), is a function of the regression parameter (ρ); a perfectly observed score $(Y_{t-\delta})$ at time $t-\delta$; the time between test and retest (δ); and a random independent component (η_t) with mean 0 and variance σ_η^2, introduced by nature at time t, that becomes part of the "true score" at subsequent times. Under this model, longer lapses show lower correlations; one-year intervals show the same correlation early and late in the series. In generating Table 1, ρ has been set at .8 within groups. In conformity with our preferred interpretation of the persisting selection bias, this autoregressive process within groups has been combined with a sustained group difference, producing a constant correlational component when groups are taken together. This component is such that if the temporal erosion within groups were to proceed to the point where test-retest correlations within groups were essentially zero, the test-retest correlation for the pooled experimental and control groups would asymptote at .27. This figure corresponds to a selection bias expressed as a correlation coefficient of .50.

The tabulated correlations also reflect <u>not only</u> temporally linked random perturbations, but also some additional error attributable to internal inconsistencies. That is, we have assumed, as is usually the case, that any observation Y'_t is a function of the combination of the true Y_t and a random independent error of measurement ξ_t:

$$Y'_t = Y_t + \xi_t,$$

where

$$\xi_t \sim I(0, \sigma_\xi^2).$$

Hence, the internal consistency of the observations is

$$rel(IC) = \frac{\sigma_y^2}{\sigma_y^2 + \sigma_\xi^2} \, .$$

In the development of Table 2, this reliability has been set at .92 for each measurement occasion, corresponding to a reliability within groups of .90.

We are now ready to consider models of what happens to the selection bias over time, in the absence of a treatment effect. Our examples of the bias due to matching, in Figures 4 through 7, assumed that the selection bias remained the same on both pretest and posttest in the absence of any treatment effect; i.e., the relative separation of experimental and control groups remains constant. In the discussion to follow, we are going to express this selection bias as a point-biserial correlation coefficient, in which assignment to treatment is used as a "dummy variable," with the superior control group being assigned a value of 1 and the experimental group 0. (In Figure 4, the corresponding computed values are .809 for the pretest and .805 for the posttest. In a randomized experiment these values would, of course, be zero, except for sampling errors.)

The three right-hand columns of Table 1 illustrate three alternative assumptions as to the course of the selection bias over time. The Alternative A column illustrates the constant bias assumption. In recommending the use of the test-retest correlation as the proper coefficient in Porter's true score covariance adjustment, Campbell is assuming Alternative A. In the Alternative B column, the selection bias itself erodes with time, just as do the test-retest correlations. If this were the real-world state of affairs regarding selection bias, then Porter's recommendation of the use of the pretest internal consistency reliability would be appropriate. For completeness, Alternative C illustrates a steadily increasing selection bias, such as would occur if the control school not only had superior pupils but also had superior instruction, or if pupils in both schools learned vocabulary from each other. We will come back to this very plausible alternative as the sixth of our list of biases. At present, we will concentrate on Alternatives A and B.

Table 2 exemplifies the statements of the preceding paragraph by using partial correlations in a way analogous to covariance. The first row repeats the data from the Alternative A and Alternative B columns of Table 1. The second row attempts to adjust for selection bias by means of partialing out the pretest. Since a null case is being simulated, the values in this row would all be zero if this were an adequate correction. It is not, however, and the values of the partial correlation coefficient which remain correspond to the regression artifacts due to matching and the underadjustment produced by ordinary covariance. The third row corresponds to Porter's reliability-corrected covariance, using the .92 internal consistency value as the pretest reliability. These values were obtained by correcting the two correlation coefficients involving the pretest for attenuation due to unreliability of the pretest only (i.e., by dividing by $\sqrt{.92}$), and then computing the partial correlation coefficient between posttest and assignment to treatment, holding the pretest constant). This correction,

Table 2. Three Modes of "Adjusting Away" the Selection Bias of Table 1.

| | Alt. A | | | | | | Alt. B | | | | | |
| | Pretest | Posttest | | | | | Pretest | Posttest | | | | |
Grade	1	2	3	4	5	6	1	2	3	4	5	6
Raw selection bias	.50	.50	.50	.50	.50	.50	.50	.43	.37	.32	.29	.26
Residual bias after partialing out pretest,		.20	.25	.29	.32	.35		.07	.05	.04	.03	.03
Partial corrected for internal consistency unreliability in pretest (rel = .92)		.15	.22	.27	.30	.33		.00	.00	.00	.00	.00
Partial corrected for unreliability in pretest using pretest-posttest correlation for that reliability		.00	.00	.00	.00	.00		-.19	-.29	-.37	-.43	-.49

too, fails to adjust the values to zero under Alternative A, and the underadjustment or residual bias gets larger as the time between pretest and posttest increases, going from .15 in the second grade to .33 in the 6th. However, for the Alternative B selection bias, this adjustment removes the bias in each posttest year. The fourth row provides values of another corrected partial correlation coefficient, using the test-retest correlation as the pretest reliability. This procedure corrects Alternative A adequately at all delay levels, a different "reliability" being used for each delay; however, it overcorrects for Alternative B. Thus, the choice of reliabilities cannot be made on algebraic grounds alone, but must involve assumptions about the nature of the real world, assumptions which hopefully can be evaluated by further data collection.

In a previous paper (Campbell, 1971) a case was presented for an Alternative B type eroding selection bias. This is the case in which exposure to the treatment is in itself a symptom of the momentary state of the student. In this respect, the treatment would be like a test score, and would be expected to become less similar to other momentary states the more it was removed in time. For a hypothetically pure case, let us imagine that the choice of a course in Latin was freely made by a pupil at the beginning of the seventh grade. A pretest on English vocabulary was administered to the pupil at the same time, but independently of his selection of the Latin class. The pupil's choice of the Latin class was a symptom of momentary ability, momentary scholarly commitment, motivation, etc. This choice will correlate substantially with English vocabulary scores taken at the same time. It will probably correlate to decreasing degrees with vocabulary tests taken one, two, three, or four years earlier. Were it not for the impact of the course itself on English vocabulary, the choice of Latin would probably correlate in decreasing degrees with vocabulary tests administered one, two, three, or four years later, just as the seventh grade vocabulary test would.

In arguing, as we do, that Alternative A is the more appropriate model, we are assuming that factors such as social class, racial segregation, parental education, neighborhood, and school characteristics, which determine a child's presence in a compensatory program, have trivial degrees of temporal erosion, being symptoms of enduring states rather than dated, time-specific attributes. There are numerous school records relevant to this problem. We probably can be sure that with respect to intelligence or achievement tests, performance differences resulting from social class and neighborhood characteristics are sustained rather than diminished when presented in this relativistic correlation form. Furthermore, they increase when expressed in age or grade equivalents, as is discussed in the next section. Race differences found in the Coleman report are remarkably constant across ages when expressed in these terms. For school achievement tests in Milwaukee, when results are expressed in correlational form and are corrected for reliability differences, the inner-city suburb difference remains essentially constant between the fourth and sixth grades (Kenny, 1975; Crano, Kenny, & Campbell, 1972).

To combine sustained group differences with our autoregressive true score model requires that the group differences be continually renewed. To refer back to the formula

$$Y_t = \rho^\delta Y_{t-\delta} + \eta_t,$$

groups must differ on the mean value of η_t, the new random component entered at each time period, and this difference must remain constant relative to the within-group variances. While Alternative A is no doubt the more plausible, and while we are convinced that in some general way environmental differences sustain and renew the group differences, it is still unlikely that these group differences would be sustained to exactly the same degree at all ages and grades. While Alternative A is a better assumption in compensatory education experiments than Alternative B, it is unlikely to be exactly so. Clearly, it would be much better to randomize, thereby avoiding the necessity of having to make such assumptions.

The selection bias could also be considered in terms of a hereditarian model for the autoregressive pattern of correlations among repeated tests, assuming social class differences on all of the thousands of genes involved. While a different subset of genes would be active at each age level, each subset would show the same social class bias. But again, why would the social class bias be exactly the same at each age level? Would we not on the contrary expect it to be largest for that subset operative at the ages in which ability differences were most determinative of social mobility?

Even where the delay between pretest and posttest is short (one week, one month, etc.), the pretest-posttest coefficient is likely to be more appropriate than is the internal consistency reliability of the pretest. The internal consistency reliability is probably too high, due to correlated errors that increase the correlation among all item-sets administered at the same time. Stanley (1967), Cronbach and Furby (1970), and others have pointed out that the correlation between Y and X measured under identical conditions and the correlation between Y and X measured under independent conditions will ordinarily differ, and that difference must be recognized to obtain unbiased estimates of true change. The linked case and independent case are recognized explicitly by a measurement error element that is correlated if observations are linked and uncorrelated if observations are made independently. The relevant algebra leads to an analogous point made with regard to temporal erosion: the specific character of the measurement must be recognized if reliability-adjusted methods of estimating true program effects are to be useful.

Porter's reliability-corrected covariance formula is

$$SS'_{t_y} = SS_{t_y} - \frac{(\text{rel } SS_{w_{xy}} + SS_{b_{xy}})^2}{\text{rel}^2 SS_{w_x} + SS_{b_x}},$$

where

SS_{t_y} is the total sum of squares for the dependent variable,

$SS_{w_{xy}}$ is the within-groups sum of products,

$SS_{b_{xy}}$ is the between-groups sum of products,

SS_{w_x} is the within-groups sum of squares for the covariate,

SS_{b_x} is the between-groups sum of squares for the covariate, and

rel is a reliability coefficient.[1]

However, before we can employ the pretest-posttest correlation in this formula, we must consider several additional complexities that will emerge in an actual situation. First, our recommendation was based on the assumption that pretest and posttest had the same internal consistency reliability. Each of these reliabilities should be computed. If they are not the same, it will be necessary to solve for the value that would have been obtained had the posttest had the same internal consistency reliability as the pretest-- another limited correction for attenuation:

$$\text{Corrected } \rho_{\text{Pre-Post}} = \rho_{\text{Pre-Post}} \left(\frac{\sqrt{\text{rel}_{\text{Pre}}}}{\sqrt{\text{rel}_{\text{Post}}}} \right).$$

Second, if there has been a real treatment effect, this will modify the posttest variance for the pooled experimental and

---

[1] It should be noted that if rel = 1.00 in both numerator and denominator, we would have the usual $SS'_b = SS'_t - SS'_w$, where SS'_w is the usual adjusted within-groups sum of squares.

control group, and this modification will in turn affect the pretest-posttest correlation for the pooled population. To avoid this complication, the process just discussed should be done separately for experimental and control groups. It should then be expanded into an inferred pooled pretest-posttest correlation, such as would be obtained if the overlap between the experimental and control groups—i.e., the selection bias correlation—had been the same on the posttest as it was on the pretest. Even here, there are at least three ways to do this, and our projected computer program will generate computations using all three. One method is to obtain a weighted average of the pretest-posttest coefficients for experimental and control groups, assuming that these coefficients are independent estimates of the same value, and that the experimental treatment has not affected the coefficient for the experimental group. The second method is to use only the control group coefficient, assuming 1) that the experimental coefficient would have been the same had it not been for the effect of the treatment on it, and 2) that there is an experimental effect, and therefore excluding use of the experimental group data in estimating the reliability. The third method is to assume that the experimental and control groups had basically different pretest-posttest coefficients (as will be argued in Section IV-E, below), but that the experimental treatment did not disturb the coefficient. If this latter model is preferred, it might be easiest, both conceptually and practically, to use covariance on regressed pretest scores, as Director (1974) has done so effectively. In this case, the coefficient should be adjusted for pretest-posttest internal consistency reliability differences where this information is available.

Another major assumption is that pretest and posttest have a similar factorial composition. This is certainly a more plausible assumption for pretests than for other covariates, although Cronbach (1970) warns against it for children's tests, especially for individual tests in the preschool years and for group tests in the early grades when reading is just being mastered. There is substantial empirical support for the contention that the factorial composition of achievement tests, IQ tests, and the like vary with age of the respondent. Research on the Stanford-Binet, the Wechsler Scales, the California tests of Mental Maturity, and others suggest that with age, patterns of factor loadings change, factors become more distinct, and the number of factors increases. Osborne's (1966) work on the WISC, for example, shows an increase in number of factors from preschool to one year after entry to school. Similar changes occur for samples of adolescents and adult populations (Cohen, 1957; Berger et al., 1964; Owens, 1966; and others). For adult populations, these changes are less marked, except for the very aged and for long intertest intervals.

We believe that making the assumptions and the adjustments reviewed here would provide substantial gains over current practice in quasi-experimental analysis, perhaps removing the systematic biases now present. But we are appalled at the number of assumptions and estimates required. Again, randomization can avoid this.

Though the methods of Lord (1960a) and Porter (1967) have been most thoroughly investigated in simulation studies, other methods of covariance correction are being developed and tested. The most recent techniques try to accommodate a notable shortcoming of earlier work: restriction to a single covariate. The estimated true score approach, for example, has <u>not</u> yielded satisfactory results in simulation studies conducted by Pravalpruk and Porter (1974). Wayne Fuller (Warren, White, & Fuller, 1974), on the other hand, has derived method-of-moments estimators for regression coefficients which are unbiased to $O(N^{-1/2})$ and have finite variance; these estimators can be used in formal, unbiased tests of hypotheses about the nature of adjusted mean differences between groups when estimates of reliability are available. Stroud (1974) makes the less likely assumption that population measurement error variances are available and derives large sample maximum likelihood tests for the hypotheses about equal regressions and conditional variances within each regression. The relations among these and other complex tests are not well documented, and their relative benefits and limits are unclear. Further, most of these tests assume that the simple true score model holds (with errors and true scores distributed independently and normally) without additional specification; consequently, most are likely to be susceptible to the difficulty previously discussed regarding the choice of reliability coefficient.

3. Regression Adjustments Based on Multiple Covariates

The commonest approach to "correcting" for biased assignment to treatments, in both education and economics, is some kind of regression adjustment. Such a method, for example, has been used as though adequate in all three analyses and reanalyses of the Westinghouse-Ohio University data on Head Start (Cicourelli et al., 1969; Smith & Bissell, 1970; and Barnow, 1973--Barnow's being done as a Ph.D. dissertation in Economics). While explanation of the problem involved should by now be redundant, we would like to make clear that these procedures, too, lead to systematic underadjustment, and in practice are packaging underadjusted selection differences as though they were treatment effects.

Table 3 presents a set of simulated correlations based upon a simple, single-factored model in a setting where regression adjustments are commonly applied. In this hypothetical study, children are given achievement tests prior to and subsequent to a Head Start program. Both pretest (Pr) and posttest (Po) have 80% of their variance determined by a common "social advantage" factor. The assignment to

Table 3. Hypothetical correlations among variables for regression adjustment demonstration, where T = Treatment variable (1 or 0), Pr = Pretest score, Po = Posttest score, and C_1, C_2, C_3 = covariates 1, 2, and 3.

	T	Pr	Po	C_1	C_2
Pr	.505				
Po	.505	.800			
C_1	.399	.632	.632		
C_2	.399	.632	.632	.500	
C_3	.399	.632	.632	.500	.500

Head Start and control conditions is biased, and 50% of its variance comes from the social advantage factor. (Since this factor is a dichotomous variable, the correlations are lower than if it were a continuous variable.) The covariates might be father's income (C_1), mother's educational level (C_2), and socioeconomic level of residence (C_3). Each of these hypothetical covariates derives 50% of its variance from the social advantage factor and 50% from unique determinants, including error. This is a simulation of a null case, in that the correlation of treatment with posttest, like that of treatment with pretest, reflects the social advantage factor but no true treatment effect. Thus $r_{PrT} = r_{PoT} = .505$. Rather than adjusted means, let us use partial correlation coefficients, which will be zero when the difference between adjusted means is zero. Our focus is on r_{TPo}; that is, on the correlation between the treatment and the posttest.

First, let us consider an ex post facto analysis where good covariates are available but a pretest is not. r_{TPo} starts out at .505 before adjustment. Using one covariate, the partial

$$r_{TPo \cdot C_1} = .355,$$

somewhat smaller but still far from the zero that it should be if one covariate were providing adequate adjustment for pretreatment differences or for the biased assignment to treatment. Using two and three covariates makes the partial smaller yet:

$$r_{TPo \cdot C_1 C_2} = .277;$$

$$r_{TPo \cdot C_1 C_2 C_3} = .229.$$

However, these partial correlations are still of a magnitude that would be mistakenly reported as impressive treatment results. Even if we had ten such marvelously good covariates and a large number of cases, the difference between adjusted means would remain impressive:

$$r_{TPo \cdot C_1 C_2 C_3 C_4 C_5 C_6 C_7 C_8 C_9 C_{10}} = .104.$$

In a situation such as Table 3 simulates, the only way in which a finite number of such covariates could provide adequate adjustment would be for one or more of them to be a perfect measure of the common factor, without irrelevant variance or error. Such covariates simply do not exist. In an ordinary situation, few, if any, of the covariates are as good as the ones in Table 3.

Suppose, however, that we do have a pretest and adjust on it. Then

$$r_{TPo \cdot Pr} = .195.$$

What if we use both pretest and covariates? Then,

$$r_{TPo \cdot PrC_1 C_2 C_3} = .136.$$

These are still of a magnitude frequently packaged as treatment effects in the form of adjusted mean differences. Other likely models produce similar biases. For example, a common view of regression adjustment is that each covariate picks up a different aspect of the variance shared by assignment to treatment and a pretest. Idealized, this concept would produce a matrix like Table 3, except that all of the intercorrelations between covariates would be zero. Here, too, significant underadjusted residuals remain. Other likely patterns all produce underadjustments if the covariates contain any irrelevant variance or error. The kinds of covariates that economists working in education are using as "errorless" (race, sex, father's occupation, income, and years of schooling) are dominated by irrelevant variance when used for the purpose of estimating a child's achievement, and lead to profound underadjustments.

We are working on a double corrected regression adjustment, analogous to the Lord and Porter reliability corrected covariances. The practical insight involved is the recognition that for the covariate set to be adequate for adjusting the selection bias, the multiple correlation within the control group of the covariates with the dependent variable (Posttest) should be 1.00 except for unreliability in the posttest. Knowing the posttest internal consistency reliability, we can solve the old correction-for-attenuation formula

$$1.00 = \frac{R_{Po \cdot C_1 C_2 C_3}}{\sqrt{rel_{Po}} \; \sqrt{rel_{C_1 C_2 C_3}}}$$

and generate a coefficient $rel_{C_1 C_2 C_3}$ appropriate to the covariate set, which we call its coefficient of "relevance" rather than "reliability," to stress the fact that in addition to measurement error, all types of independent variance are involved. Practical problems emerge in estimating what the pooled experimental plus control group posttest variance would be in the absence of a treatment effect, as well as in applying the shrinkage formula. Nevertheless, we believe these to be soluble on the basis of a number of strong but plausible assumptions. Also needed are strong assumptions about the factor pattern among covariates, selection bias, and posttest, and the assumption that the treatment has not disturbed the correlation between covariates and posttest within the experimental group. While our double adjusted regression adjustment will be much less biased and more useful than the present practice, it is still undesirable to have to make all of the assumptions involved. The need for such assumptions can be avoided by randomized experiments.

The bias of underadjustment can fallaciously make programs look good or look bad depending upon the direction of the preadjustment differences. The general pattern in quasi-experimentation is to select the treatment group first and then to search around among the untreated residual population for a control. When applied to the class of treatment that goes to those who need it least, such as college education, advanced training, etc., this pattern usually results in an experimental group that is superior prior to treatment and statistical adjustment. Therefore, the underadjustment masquerades as a desirable treatment effect.

In the case of compensatory education, the experimental group is inferior to the remainder of the population; it is also, as a rule (but not always), inferior to the specific comparison group chosen as a control. In this setting, the underadjustment makes the compensatory treatment look harmful, when in fact it may be only worthless. This setting clearly was the case in the Westinghouse-Ohio Head Start evaluation (Cicirelli et al., 1969) and is certainly the most plausible explanation of the fact that the short summer programs showed up as significantly harmful (Porter, 1969). It was also the preponderant bias in the Performance Contracting experiment and in Follow Through. It is clearly present in the Hardin and Borus (1971) study of Job Corps training, in which the surprisingly confident conclusion was reached that such training had been harmful; it is also prevalent in other manpower training program evaluations (Director, 1974). It is not present in the case of Sesame Street; this program, like college education, is given most to those who need it least and is probably increasing rather than decreasing the social-class gap in reading readiness for children entering the first grade (Cook et al., 1975).

In other compensatory education studies, it must sometimes happen that it is the superior group which receives treatment and the control group is selected from the remainder. Imagine, for example, a Head Start study design using pupils with 100% attendance as the experimental group and pupils with attendance of 20% or less as the control group. As a result, in terms of family support, interest in achievement, or whatever, the experimental group would start out superior to the control group, and underadjustment of these differences would work to exaggerate program effectiveness. It is our opinion, however, that in the main, underadjustment for selection bias has served to stack the deck against compensatory education programs. Even though a hard look at most of these programs shows them to be weak and half-hearted efforts, we are nonetheless convinced that methodological biases are making them appear worse than they are. Thus, this chapter has a second theme that is perhaps more political than methodological. Compensatory education programs have been good enough, have avoided "creaming" (Miller et al., 1970) well enough, so that in most studies those receiving treatment have been to some degree inferior to the pool from which the control group had to be selected. As a result, the evaluations have had an inadvertent, systematic political bias in the direction of discouraging compensatory education and accepting racist interpretations of the test scores accompanying poverty.

For Head Start, Follow Through, and Performance Contracting, randomized assignment to treatment (by schools, residential blocks, classrooms, or pupils) would have been possible, had there been an awareness of the problems of inference that would result from nonrandom assignment. It would be more difficult to provide randomization for Sesame Street (although Educational Testing Service did local randomized experiments with home visitor encouragement and Cable TV). Job Corps, too, might be a more difficult setting for randomized experiments. This program is, however, an appropriate setting for the regression-discontinuity design (Campbell, 1969; Riecken et al., 1974). Randomized tests of special vocational education and of manpower training programs have been achieved, among them Robin's (1969) evaluation of summer Neighborhood Youth Corps projects in Detroit; Brazziels' (1966) assessment of manpower programs in Virginia; and Earle's (1973) experimental tests of police training strategies.

B. *DIFFERENTIAL GROWTH RATES*

The second frequent source of bias in nonrandomized evaluations of compensatory education programs stems from differential growth rates of program recipients and non-recipients. For a wide variety of measures used in such evaluations--raw achievement test scores, mental age scores, age or grade equivalents, estimate of vocabulary size, and so forth--it is reasonable to assume that groups higher on a pretest are higher because of a more rapid growth rate in previous years, and that the more rapid rate will continue at least for a time. Figure 9 illustrates one plausible form of differential growth rate for two groups, one of which (the lower scorers) receives a compensatory program.

Figure 9 also illustrates how the use of grade equivalent scores (or mental age, achievement age, etc.) limited to one pretest and one posttest, with the results expressed either graphically or as a comparison of gains scores, will make a treatment given to the less able of the two groups seem harmful when it is in fact only ineffective. Covariance analysis, too, will be misleading, even when corrected for measurement and temporal errors in the covariate, if the differential growth goes unrecognized. The analysis will be biased because the relation between the dependent variable and the covariates differs between groups, while covariance analysis assumes that the relation is the same across groups. The heterogeneity of within-group variance that goes along with differential growth rates would, if unrecognized, lead to significance tests which are not commensurate with size and power advertised for conventional F tests.

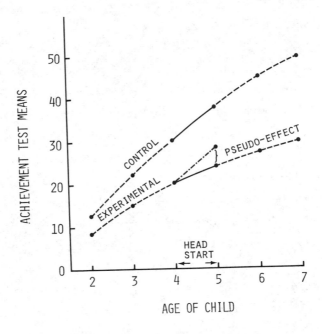

Fig. 9. Pseudo effect generated by assuming the growth rate in the experimental group to be the same as that found in a superior control group. (After Campbell & Erlebacher, 1970). Solid lines represent data observed by the experimenters. Dashed lines represent the unobserved real situation. The dot-dash line represents the wrongly assumed null condition employed when comparing gain scores, which generates the apparently harmful pseudo effect under truly no-effect conditions.

To clarify problems like these, we need to have a better understanding of the methods used to analyze such data and their shortcomings when differential growth rates prevail. We also need to investigate more thoroughly the empirical character of the growth rates. With a greater understanding of factors such as these, we will be in a better position to offer suggestions that avoid the biases implicit in conventional analyses, as well as to specify conditions under which randomized experiments are essential.

Consider the age equivalent scores, for example. These are manufactured by administering tests to representative children at various ages, then computing averages within each age range. The mean points are plotted and smoothed, and the smoothed plot is used as a basis for identifying the age equivalent of a child who achieves a certain test score. Typically, test publishers and school districts maintain completely aggregated data: the scales do not recognize explicitly how various subgroups within the sample differ in level or rate of growth. Such curves imply that all students follow the same growth curve, when in fact their development may depend heavily on subgroup membership, as indicated in Figure 9. Often the samples on which published scales are based are irrelevant to the samples of control and experimental students at hand, and they usually fail to recognize explicitly either individual or group differences among students. Even locally derived scales are difficult to interpret to the extent that they depend heavily on curriculum and promotion schemes within schools (age and grade level becoming uncoupled), in which case the general shape of the curve may vary notably from school to school. Under such conditions, comparisons between schools will be difficult if not impossible. Angoff's (1971) paper contains a fine review of these and other problems that, if ignored, can lead to biased inferences about the program effects that are purportedly reflected in such scores. It is encouraging to note that in the American Psychological Association's revised standards for tests, age and grade equivalent scores have come in for specific disapproval.

If one abandons the equal growth rate assumption, the next simple model is the constant growth rate assumption. For example, one might assume that an undereducated group one year behind at grade 1, age 6, would be two years behind at grade 6, age 12, if education has been evenly distributed and no special treatment or school effects have been involved. This is a great improvement over the equal growth rate assumption, but neglects the fact that the growth rate for all groups will eventually tend to level off. The constant growth rate assumption was built into the traditional definition of IQ as mental age divided by chronological age (X100), a formula that becomes unworkable some place between ages 12 to 18. A superior approach, which achieves the same purposes while accommodating decreasing growth rates during adolescence and early maturity, is to base IQ's on the mean and standard deviation of the normal population of each age group. Applied to group differences in growth rates, this method involves the assumption that differential growth is taking place within groups to the same extent as between groups; that is, as the gap between groups increases, so does the variability within each group, and to a comparable extent. This has been called the "fan spread" assumption (by Campbell & Erlebacher, 1970, and no doubt others). The visual imagery appropriate to distinguishing this concept from the constant growth rate assumption would have been better, however, had they called it the "limp" or "droopy" fan spread hypothesis, thus indicating the change in growth rates toward an asymptote. If the fan spread assumption is correct, then standardizing scores (to mean zero and variance one) at each age level will produce a metric which eliminates the differential growth rate, insofar as a group mean of -1 in pretest standard score would be expected to be -1 in scores standardized on the posttest. This approach is better than any based on a constant growth rate assumption, in that the standardized scores will be interpretable whether the growth is constant or whether it is asymptotic, as in Figure 9. Such standardized scores have been assumed in Figures 2 through 8, so that the underadjustment problem due to error and unique variance in variables would be presented uncluttered by the differential growth problem.

Even though the fan spread assumption is more plausible than any of the others that we have examined, it is still a weak reed upon which to estimate the effects of a compensatory program. Note that it implies that the group-to-group gap will remain constant when expressed in units of within-group standard deviations, assuming no differential treatments or changes in differential opportunities. Translated into the dummy-variable selection bias correlations of Table 1, this assumption corresponds to the Alternative A column. Again, while this assumption is plausible as a general model, it is unreasonable to expect the selection bias or relative group difference to remain exactly constant, as one has to assume in making our recommended quasi-experimental adjustments.

There is some good evidence for the contention that cognitive test scores do follow fan spread patterns in a general way, although we may also be sure that when examined, the fit will not be exact, as indicated in the following examples:

1. Osborne's longitudinal studies (1966; Osborne & Suddick, 1972) involved samples of white and black students who completed the California Reading Achievement Test and the California Arithmetic Tests three times (6th, 8th, and 10th grades). White students began at higher levels and developed at a more rapid rate than blacks did; i.e., means conformed to the fan spread pattern. Cross-sectional studies by Baughman and Dahlstrom (1968) and others confirm early results in that mean differences among racial and sex subgroups increase over time for the Stanford Achievement tests administered to similar age groups.

2. Burket's (1974) analysis of children's achievement test scores is based on Carroll's (1973) highly articulated model for achievement as a function of time and of important stratification variables, such as aptitude. The data for grades 1-12 conform to a fan spread pattern, with increasing mean differences between groups which differ initially in achievement, and increasing variance within groups. The fit of Carroll's analytic models, which are based on educational/learning theory, is good.

3. Similarly, cross-sectional data on the Metropolitan Achievement tests for students in grades 1-6 were analyzed by Fennessy (1972) and show characteristic increases in variance and mean which conflict with the publisher's normative data for the same age range.

This is but a small sample of the available empirical evidence that can and should be collected to assure that the nature of the differential growth rate phenomenon is understood. If growth equations and curves can be developed on the bases of relevant samples, we will be in a much better position to understand growth of achievement and, in those cases where randomized experiments are impossible, we may be able to obtain less equivocal estimates of program impact than are usually available from nonrandomized evaluations. For most evaluation work, however, these curves will be of limited utility: they are growth indicators that are legitimate with respect to specific populations, in specific regions, and at a specific time. Test publishers are unlikely to be able to develop these curves for each and every target population of interest in evaluations of contemporary compensatory programs. Normative curves would have to be developed locally and, to be useful, would have to be based on empirical data collected over a wide range of students and over a considerable period of time. Without such longitudinal data, nonrandomized evaluation is hazardous at best; with the data, evaluation will in some cases be possible. Even then, considerable expenditure in time and energy will be required for collection of the data, and the evaluation may _still_ be equivocal relative to results based on randomized experimental tests. Again, we can avoid making unreasonable assumptions about differential growth rates and expending energy in developing empirical growth curves, which we then use to produce equivocal evaluations, _if_ we conduct randomized tests. So why not do so?

C. *INCREASES IN RELIABILITY WITH AGE*

There is increasing awareness that reliability differences between scales (e.g., Chapman & Chapman, 1973) and between subgroups (e.g., Gorsuch, Henighan, & Barnard, 1972) can create spurious mean differences, or differences in mean differences. In a conclusion directly relevant to the theme of this section, Chapman and Chapman state, "With two tests of differing reliability, the test with the higher reliability will yield greater performance deficit for the less able subjects" (p. 380). The combination of this fact with the general tendency for tests given to older children to have higher reliabilities generates the prediction that in the absence of any treatment effects, posttests will tend to show greater group differences than pretests. When the supposed treatment has been given to the less able of two comparison groups, the increased posttest reliability, unless corrected for, will tend to make the treatment look harmful by seeming to produce an increased group difference.

If we use the traditional simple "true score" model of test theory,

$$X_i = T_i + \xi_i$$

$$\xi_i \sim I(0, \sigma_\xi^2)$$

$$T_i \sim I(T, \sigma_T^2)$$

this conclusion holds only for the relativized, standardized group comparisons advocated in the previous section. It does not follow for raw scores, age or grade equivalents, total vocabulary estimates, or other "absolute" scores. For the above model, X is an unbiased estimate of T, since ξ has a mean of zero. Changes in reliability are changes in the variance of ξ. These changes do not affect the mean X, and hence do not change the difference in means between two groups. The variance of X is, however, changed, becoming larger as the variance of ξ grows larger (holding the variance of T constant). This changes the divisor when the mean difference is expressed as a standard score. Increased reliability implies smaller variance, which in turn implies a larger relative mean difference.

But both the Chapmans and Gorsuch et al. (1972), persuasively argue the presence of the effect for absolute scores like simple totals. It seems likely that the simple true score model is inappropriate for tests of ability. For most such tests, the assumption that errorful responding is just as likely to raise the observed score ($\underline{X}$) above the true score (T) as it is to lower it seems basically wrong. Errorful responding can obviously lower a true score substantially, but the amount it can raise a true score is limited to rare combinations of lucky flukes.

Suppose one translated the hypothetical true score for a test into a specification of the items a child would get correct if he and the test performed without error. One could envisage the items ordered by degree of difficulty for the child, so that all items below the child's ability threshhold would be answered correctly and above it incorrectly. Now, let us conceptually add error to this ideal test performance, in greater amounts for one test (pretest) than for the other (posttest). For the pretest, there might be 20% error, which we could simulate by randomly selecting 20% of the items for errorful responding (e.g., choosing a response alternative at random on a multiple-choice test, or wild and usually unsuccessful guessing on a free-response item). Where the true response had been a pass, this error substitution would usually turn it into a failure. Where the true response had been a fail, the error substitution would occasionally produce a pass, though almost never on a free-response item. For the posttest, let us consider the same true scores and the same test, but with errorful responses affecting only 10% of the items. In this case, two groups differing in mean true score will differ more on the posttest than on the pretest, in <u>raw</u> scores as well as in standard scores or other relative measures.

This can be illustrated by considering the score of the average child in each of two groups for which the mean true scores on a 100-item test are 60 and 40. For this illustration it will be assumed that each item has five alternatives that are equally popular under random response conditions, that the test is unspeeded, and that each child chooses one alternative on each item. Under the 20% error condition, the scores of the average child become:

$$
\begin{array}{cc}
\text{T} & \text{E}
\end{array}
$$

$$
\text{Advantaged Group:} \quad X_1 = .80(60) + .20(20) = 52
$$
$$
\text{Disadvantaged Group:} \quad X_2 = .80(40) + .20(20) = 36
$$

$$
\text{difference} = 16
$$

Under the 10% error, the scores become:

$$
\begin{array}{cc}
\text{T} & \text{E}
\end{array}
$$

$$
\text{Advantaged Group:} \quad X_1 = .90(60) + .10(20) = 56
$$
$$
\text{Disadvantaged Group:} \quad X_2 = .90(40) + .10(20) = 38
$$

$$
\text{difference} = 18
$$

Under this model, the apparent group differences become smaller the more errorful the testing, disappearing entirely under conditions of 100% error.

The model just examined can be expressed in more familiar terms. For example, let

$$X_i = pT_i + (1 - p)E_i,$$

where
$$T_i \sim I(T, \sigma_T^2), \quad E_i \sim I(E, \sigma_E^2).$$

This formula can be rearranged to obtain

$$X_i = p(T_i - E_i) + E_i.$$

We can then define

$$\tau_i = p(T_i - E_i)$$

where

$$\tau_i \sim I[p(T - E), p^2(\sigma_T^2 + \sigma_E^2)]$$

and

$$\xi_i = E_i$$

where

$$\xi_i \sim I(E, \sigma_E^2)$$

and substitute to obtain

$$X_i = \tau_i + \xi_i$$

where ξ_i is <u>not</u> independent of τ_i. In fact, the correlation between ξ_i's (the errors of measurement) and the τ_i's (the "true" scores which contain an element of error) is

$$\rho_{\tau\xi} = \frac{- \sigma_E^2}{\sqrt{(\sigma_T^2 + \sigma_E^2)\, \sigma_E^2}}.$$

The observed mean and variance under this model are biased indicators of the mean and variance of the true scores to the extent that $p \neq 0$, since

$$\bar{X} = pT + (1 - p)E \quad \text{and}$$

$$\sigma_X^2 = p^2(\sigma_T^2 + \sigma_E^2) + \sigma_E^2.$$

For this case, a test-retest correlation is not an especially informative index of conventionally defined reliability since it does not reflect the ratio of true score variance to observed variance. Specifically, the correlation between the test and retest is

$$r_{X_1, X_2} = \frac{p^2 \sigma_T^2}{p^2 \sigma_T^2 + (1 - p)^2 \sigma_E^2}.$$

In fact, ordinary test-retest reliabilities will be an inappropriate vehicle for correcting a regression coefficient for attenuation in either bivariate regression or simple covariance analysis. For in this case, if in nature

$$Y_i = \beta\tau_i + e_i, \quad e_i \sim I(0, \sigma_e^2),$$

but we use a fallible measure of τ_i, we will have

$$Y_i = \beta'X_i + e_i',$$

where

$$X_i = \tau_i + \xi_i,$$

and the observed coefficient will be a biased estimate of the parameter β:

$$\beta' = \frac{\beta p \sigma_T^2}{p^2 \sigma_T^2 + (1 - p)^2 \sigma_E^2} \ .$$

Dividing by a test-retest coefficient

$$rel = \frac{p^2 \sigma_T^2}{p^2 \sigma_T^2 + (1 - p)^2 \sigma_E^2}$$

yields a still biased parameter; i.e.,

$$\beta' (\text{"corrected"}) = \beta/p.$$

Note that E need not have a mean of zero. What is essential is that the mean E be constant across persons and subgroups, so that the heavier E's weight, the more similar all subgroup means are to E, and hence to each other. In the above illustration, a mean E of 20 was assumed. The same point could have been made using a mean of 0, which is more appropriate for free-response testing or with discouraged children who refuse to guess.

This model is still very primitive and oversimplified. But if the reader joins us in finding it more plausible than the simple model that we started with, then it follows that the higher posttest reliabilities generally found will produce increased mean differences in absolute or raw scores, as well as in the relativistic standard scores we started out with. Again, where the disadvantaged group is the experimental group and the more advantaged group is the control, reliability increases make programs look harmful.

This analysis suggests that we should estimate the reliabilities and guessing behavior and "correct" group means for both attenuation and guessing. No doubt reasonable assumptions and appropriate algebra could be found that would greatly reduce the systematic biases in present practice. The analysis also suggests that we seriously consider alternative models for test scoring, such as those suggested by Rasch (1960) or the more complex true score models offered by Lord and Novick (1968). (We need to archive item response data as well as total scores so that alternative models can be tested in reanalysis.) Where we must use quasi-experimental designs, these are important lines of improvement. But they all add their costs in unverifiable assumptions, each of which becomes an argument for random assignment to treatment.

That the reliability of many tests increases with the age of the child tested is much better documented in the psychometric literature than in the contemporary evaluation research literature (published and otherwise). In fact, the relevant statistics are infrequently computed in compensatory program evaluations. Reliability estimates need to be made available for each group on each testing. Nonetheless, we can rely on good work in the psychometric tradition to get some feel for the character of reliability changes as a function of age. If we consider reliability in test-retest terms, for example, we find from Osbourne and Suddick (1972) stability coefficients in the range .35-.66 for subtests of the WISC given to children in preschool and first grade, and stability coefficients in the range .56-.72 for the same children in the third and fifth grades. Replications are not hard to identify; e.g., Klonoff's (1972) results for the total WISC show correlations of .76 between test scores of five- and six-year-olds, and .92 between scores of 13- and 14-year-olds. Cronbach (1970) has reported similar results from studies of the Detroit tests and the Terman intelligence tests. The same phenomenon occurs for measures other than achievement and intelligence tests. For example, a similar pattern can emerge in high quality rating scales. Cronbach (1970) reports one-year interval stability coefficients of ratings on behavior of very young boys (obtained by Macfarlane) showing a steady increase of .38, .50, .56, .67, .73, .70, and .86 for scores obtained at ages 2-3, 3-4, 4-5, 6-7, 7-8, 9-10, and 11-12.

D. *LOWER RELIABILITY IN THE MORE DISADVANTAGED GROUP*

It is a common experience in research on compensatory education that the disadvantaged group (usually the experimental group) has lower reliabilities than the advantaged group on both pretest and posttest. Following the same logic used in Section IV-C, we can see that this tendency further biases the analysis in the direction of an increased gap. Let us expand our illustration to include a 10-point true score gain between pretest and posttest for both groups, keeping advantaged and disadvantaged reliabilities the same:

Pretest

Advantaged Group: .80(60) + .20(20) = 52

Disadvantaged Group: .80(40) + .20(20) = 36

difference = 16

Posttest

Advantaged Group: .90(70) + .10(20) = 65

Disadvantaged Group: .90(50) + .10(20) = 47

difference = 18

Now let us substitute lower reliability for the disadvantaged group:

Pretest

Advantaged Group: .80(60) + .20(20) = 52

Disadvantaged Group: .70(40) + .30(20) = 34

difference = 18

Posttest

Advantaged Group: .90(70) + .10(20) = 65

Disadvantaged Group: .80(50) + .20(20) = 44

difference = 21

Again, in a nonrandomized study, where the disadvantaged group receives the treatment, the lower reliability of the disadvantaged group has the effect of making the treatment look harmful. And again, algebraic invention and estimates of reliability are necessary to remove the bias.

The pattern of measurement error laid out here will not ordinarily give biased estimates of a program effect in a randomized experiment when the treatment is ineffective. Specifically, we may represent means for groups 1 and 2 as

$$\bar{X}_1 = p_1 T_1 + (1 - p_1)E_1$$

$$\bar{X}_2 = p_2 T_2 + (1 - p_2)E_2$$

and the mean difference as

$$\bar{X}_1 - \bar{X}_2 = p_1 T_1 - p_2 T_2 + (1 - p_1)E_1 - (1 - p_2)E_2$$

In an experiment, we would expect the equivalent groups to react similarly to testing, so that

$$p_1 = p_2 = p \quad \text{and} \quad E_1 = E_2 = E$$

and

$$\bar{X}_1 - \bar{X}_2 = p(T_1 - T_2).$$

If there is no treatment effect, then

$$T_1 = T_2 = T$$

and

$$\bar{x}_1 - \bar{x}_2 = 0;$$

that is, the observed difference between groups is an unbiased indicator of the true mean difference between groups under null conditions. However, if the treatment is effective in producing a true difference of $T_1 - T_2$, then the estimate based on observed X's will be biased downward. Since $p < 1.00$, the observed mean difference will always be lower in absolute magnitude than the true mean difference between groups. The program effect will be underestimated to the degree that p is less than 1.00, but unlike the non-randomized case discussed above, this underestimation will not make the program look harmful.

Empirical data on the relation between achievement test scores and level of social or economic advantage are often unavailable. Test publishers usually do not publish such data. Local evaluations of compensatory programs typically fail to compute measures of internal consistency, and are even less likely to go to the trouble of obtaining test-retest reliabilities separately for each group. In some of the better evaluations, however, the relevant statistics are computed. Small differences in socioeconomic level of Electric Company viewers were reflected in small differences in reliability of testing in the Ball and Bogatz (1973) evaluations of the TV program's impact. To the extent that the level of economic or social advantage correlates with true scores, one might expect true scores to be linked with error and to yield different intergroup reliabilities. Indeed, the linkage between true score and variance of the error has been established for some achievement tests. Lord's (1960b) use of cumulants to better understand skewness and nonindependence of measurement errors is a nice illustration of how one might go about characterizing the problem in other areas; see also Mollenkopf (1949).

Though the focus here has been on achievement tests, demographic and other variables used either as response variables or as covariates in evaluations can also be susceptible to the problem described here. The best documented cases are perhaps the economic indicators. Siegle and Hodge (1968), for example, show that because conventional reports of income and education level have lower variance than the more accurate (nearly true) reports taken during censuses, there must be some negative correlation between the true state and errors in measurement, and proceed to estimate the correlation. Ferber (1965) has done similar work with reports of savings. He, like others engaged in such research, has found a distinctive association between accuracy of reporting and size of error as a function of true financial condition.

It would be helpful to have a greater consolidation of information on the way in which reliability varies with the characteristics of groups similar to those typically used in evaluations. Still more important would be side-studies which yield this type of information in the context of field evaluations. Without such empirical estimates, it is difficult to design sensitive and efficient randomized experiments. These estimates are also essential in correcting for social class differences in reliability, age changes in reliability, or reliability-corrected covariance analyses.

E. *TEST FLOOR AND CEILING EFFECTS*

It has been a frequent error in compensatory education evaluations to underestimate the degree of disadvantage in selecting tests, and therefore to use tests which are too difficult. This produces a test floor effect, resulting in an underestimation of the deficit on the pretest, particularly for the more disadvantaged group. If the same children are tested on the same test a year later, the expected growth in abilities will have reduced the floor effect, making the difference between two comparison groups appear greater in magnitude on the second testing. If a compensatory education program has been given to the less advantaged of the two groups, this test floor effect will make that program look harmful in cases where in fact there has been no effect at all.

To illustrate this problem, suppose that a full range test would have shown the following pretest distribution of experimental and comparison group abilities:

	\-4	\-3	\-2	\-1	0	+1	+2	+3	+4	N	$\bar{X}$
					Ability Level						
Comparison	0	0	0	10	20	40	20	10	0	100	1.00
Experimental	0	10	20	40	20	10	0	0	0	100	−1.00
									difference = 2.00		

If the pretest used has restricted range, the following outcome might be found:

	Pretest Ability Level							
	-1	0	+1	+2	+3	+4	N	X̄
Comparison Group	10	20	40	20	10	0	100	1.00
Experimental Group	70	20	10	0	0	0	100	-.60

difference = 1.60

If the same test is used a year later, and if each group has gained one unit through normal growth, and if there has been in fact no treatment effect, then the posttest results could look like this:

	Posttest Ability Level							
	-1	0	+1	+2	+3	+4	N	X̄
Comparison Group	0	10	20	40	20	10	100	2.00
Experimental Group	30	40	20	10	0	0	100	.10

difference = 1.90

It is obvious from such examples that a bias in the same direction would occur even if the test floor effect curtailed the range of both groups to some extent. It is also obvious that test ceiling effects can influence the results in the opposite direction, making the less advantaged group seem to catch up on the posttest.

The general principle involved has been stated by Chapman and Chapman (1973) in terms of item statistics. Group differences will appear greatest in magnitude in the middle range of difficulty. Items that are too easy (ceiling effects) or too difficult (floor effects) will produce smaller estimates of group difference. Reductio ad absurdum, if the test is so difficult that no persons of either group pass any items, then group differences will disappear entirely; the same situation will occur if the test is so easy that all persons in both groups pass all items. Approximations to either extreme by either group produce reduced mean differences.

In the typical hurried-up study of compensatory education programs, with group testing being done by outside evaluators on two occasions a year or less apart, the floor effect bias is probably most common. On the other hand, in experiments which carry the child over many waves of testing and use individually-administered tests, ceiling effects may be more common. In cases where the treatment has been given to the less advantaged, an overoptimistic catch-up interpretation will result.

In randomized experiments, both test floor and test ceiling biases lead to underestimates of the magnitude of the effect if the program is in fact effective. This is true even with covariance and reliability-corrected covariance adjustments. But in randomized experiments, floor and ceiling effects produce no bias, no pseudo-effects, under null conditions.

Assuring that such biases will not occur is a matter of good research design as well as of measurement. Pilot studies using the achievement tests on representative samples of the target population prior to the evaluation are essential. And the results of those pilot tests ought to be made public just as the results of the main evaluation are; otherwise, we will be unable to learn how to better use such results to modify the main design so as to reduce biases.

Understanding and reducing the biases is also a fundamental measurement problem, one which demands that alternative models be postulated and alternative scoring schemes be developed. There are in fact some more realistic and well articulated alternatives to the conventional test score theory model, though the latter has probably been most thoroughly investigated. Lord's (Lord & Novick, 1968) work on binomial models, for example, greatly increases our understanding of how to better link observable properties of the test scores to the unobservable stochastic processes which generate them, how to identify the important characteristics of those processes, and how to develop more informative indicators of reliability. Similarly, the work of Noack and Wolins (Noack, 1973), and Wright's (Wright, 1968; Wright & Panchapakesan, 1969) work on the one-parameter logistic model developed by Rasch (1960) suggest strongly that for at least some ability measures the Rasch model and scoring scheme yield estimates of true ability, based on observed scores, which are robust with respect to item discriminating power and fairly invariant with respect to item difficulty; moreover, important parameters in the model are easy to estimate. Again, the importance of archiving item data for use in reanalysis becomes apparent.

The improvement which this work implies is essential, but also adds both physical and presumptive costs to evaluation. To obtain decent estimates of important parameters of some less conventional test models, higher moments must often be used. Since these higher moments are subject to large sampling variations, sample sizes must be quite large. Similarly, the additional assumptions required by some approaches may increase the costs of incorrect decisions. Again, these improvements are justified for randomized experiments to assure that measurement-generated biases in the estimates of effects are negligible. The improvements are justified for nonrandomized evaluation to assure that at least programs will not be made to look harmful. But again, the randomized tests are preferred, given the state of the art in measurement and the potential costs attached to using less conventional models.

More generally, we should go over all aspects of testing practice and scoring theory to assess their implications for the comparison of groups over conditions of growth. Group testing is certainly different from individual testing for these purposes. We should pay close attention to the frequent anecdotes of chaos in group testing sessions and of children's mass refusals to humiliate themselves by responding to the tests at all. The traditional distinction between speeded and unspeeded tests should be examined, with recognition that in compensatory education, all group tests become speeded in effect. Since time limits have a real effect upon performance, their accidental or deliberate misuse in test administration becomes a major source of group-to-group and year-to-year differences in performance. Overall, testing and test theory need to be thoroughly reviewed and revised for use in compensatory education evaluations.

F. *GROUPING FEEDBACK EFFECTS*

Consider a setting in which experimental and comparison groups come from different schools, with the mean differences favoring the comparison schools. We can then ask whether the grouping of children into schools in itself has an effect. The answer is that it almost certainly does. Consider vocabulary, which is a major component of intelligence and achievement tests. Some of it is certainly

272

learned from classmates, so that children whose classmates have a lower level of vocabulary would learn less. Lower student vocabulary also lowers the vocabulary used by the teacher in classroom interaction and reading assignments. Neighborhoods and play groups have a similar effect. Thus, the feedback effects from the fact of social aggregation and segregation are almost certainly in the direction of increasing real group differences, and tend to reduce group overlap, both in relativistic scoring systems and on raw or absolute scores. To express this possibility as dummy-variable correlations with the selection variable in Table 1, the Alternative C Treatment column is the most appropriate, even after correction for increasing relia- bility, discussed in Section IV-C.

Therefore, even if we could correct for all of the psychometric problems raised in Sections IV-A through IV-E, we would still be wrong in assuming that a superior group could be an appropriate comparison for an experimental treatment applied to an inferior group. Note in particular that with regard to the fan-spread assumption discussed in Section IV-B, grouping feedback effects render untenable the assumption that the processes (of growth, etc.) that produce increasing differences in group means would also be pro- ducing proportional increases in within-group variability. On the contrary, the feedback effect would tend to reduce within-group variance while increasing between-group vari- ance. Again, neglect of this effect tends to make a treat- ment given to the less able group look harmful when in fact it is ineffective, and will in general lead to the under- estimation of the true effect of the treatment.

What we have called feedback effects can be described analytically in any number of ways. In the simplest case, for example, the effect may exercise an influence on variances within a school but not on means between schools. This heterogeneity can be treated more readily than the more realistic presumption that both means and variances are affected. If means but not variances are influenced by feedback, but the influence goes unrecognized in nonrandomized evaluations, the problem can be boiled down to misspecification of the model, a problem discussed, for example, in Goldberger and Duncan (1973). The consequences of misspecification are, in principle, related to those of measurement error in conventional covariance analysis: the estimates of parameters, and consequently of adjusted mean differences between groups, will be biased.

What we do about such a problem depends in part on how well we can measure the level of feedback. In fact, we know very little about measuring feedback because measures of classroom environment and the like often do not recognize the interaction of students and teachers that produces the effect. There may be a "critical mass" phenomenon associated with feedback, in that the effect will be minimal as long as there are substantial subgroups at every ability level in each school. The opportunity to capitalize on process-oriented measures in this respect, and to combine this information with more quantitative data on program impact, ought not to be ignored. Such information will enable us to understand better what seems to occur under normal conditions, as well as what happens under the extraordinary conditions produced by a novel program.

In the absence of more reliable information about the grouping effect, randomization is a relevant vehicle for our ignorance. It is also a cure, insofar as it prevents our ignorance, or our inability to observe the effect reliably, from becoming damaging, as it does in nonrandomized evaluations based on misspecified models. Where randomization is not possible, we should, of course, seek quasi-experimental approaches which avoid or reduce the bias. Perhaps in a study such as Follow Through, where hundreds of schools are involved, one could use populations of school means as the raw material for analysis. Perhaps for such means, the grouping feedback effects would be homogeneous enough so that a fan-spread assumption for group means would be reasonable. That is, if the mean of the means of fifty experimental schools and that of fifty control schools moved farther apart on the later tests, one should expect a similar spreading within each of the sets. The feedback process from grouping on individual learning would not have a differential effect here. There is a great deal of relevant data in school system files, although its retrieval might be difficult. But until such data is analyzed and the parameters of the feedback process known in detail, randomization of treatments seems essential.

V. SUMMARY COMMENTS

This chapter has enumerated six common sources of bias in quasi-experimental designs for evaluating compensatory education programs. Of these six sources of bias, four (Sections IV-A, IV-C, IV-D, and IV-F) are in our judgment present in almost every major evaluation, and the other two are frequently present. Quasi-experimental methodology will not be adequate until it incorporates specific adjustments for these sources of bias, or means of excluding them. There is no such methodological package available at the present time. When such methods become available, they will involve numerous additional assumptions, plausible but often unverifiable.

Collectively, these biases, together with the inventions and assumptions required to correct them, cumulate as powerful arguments for randomized assignment to treatments—that is, for true experiments rather than quasi-experiments. In the field of classroom education, such experiments are much easier to achieve than in most social settings. Since there are never enough funds to make a new compensatory program universally available, randomized experiments are also highly defensible on moral grounds as an equalitarian mode of distributing a scarce resource.

Another theme, one which is more political, has also been presented. It happens that all of the biases discussed in this chapter have probably operated toward making our compensatory efforts look harmful or worthless, because the most common quasi-experimental setting has involved a superior comparison group. The cumulative effect of these biased analyses has undermined our political will to readjust educational inequalities and has reinforced hereditary interpretations of social class differences in test performance.

Randomized experiments would have avoided much of this bias. In compensatory education, the few existing randomized experiments have produced optimistic, encouraging, and informative results (see appendix). Had those same experiments not been randomized, in most cases they would have produced estimates of effect that were biased in a pessimistic direction. The existence and nature of those biases is clear from studies which, for example, compare an unbiased estimator based on randomized data to an estimator based on statistical manipulation of data from the same (randomized) experimental group, as well as from an allegedly equivalent, nonrandomized comparison group, also available in the original experiment (Boruch, 1975).

But even the common setting for randomized experiments in school systems produces biases leading to underestimation. Saretsky (1972) has pointed to the "John Henry effect," the tendency for a control school to be spurred to competitive striving, particularly when teachers are confronted with a threatening new technology. Fennessey (1972) has noted a similar phenomenon. Equally biasing is compensatory budgeting. To have an experimental school and a control school in the same district creates a perceived inequity when the means of treatment involves additional equipment, staff, and funds. Superintendents inevitably become more responsive to budgetary demands from control schools and less so to those from experimental schools. Whatever budgetary discretion exists is used to reduce the experimental-control contrast. It is rumored that in the big Follow Through experiment, many of the controls got equivalent programs through use of Title I funds. To get away from these two effects, experimental and control schools should be selected from different administrative units whenever possible. The two biases are a matter of mislabeling the treatment variable, a problem which afflicts nonrandomized evaluations as well as randomized ones.

To make any headway at all in reducing the potential bias in experiments, we must consider the notion of treatment as dichotomy to be an oversimplification, and we must set aside the notion that measurement is independent of design. There are good precedents for doing so (see Riecken et al., 1974, Chapter 5), and we now have sufficient statistical theory to begin to accommodate these problems, provided that we are willing to obtain the data necessary to do so.

The social-political process that produces compensatory educational efforts already has a bias toward underfinanced token efforts, designed as much to create the image of governmental action as to make real changes. It is indeed tragic if evaluation methodology inadvertantly adds to the resulting image of social impotence.

REFERENCES

Angoff, W. H. Scales, norms, and equivalent scores. In R. L. Thorndike (Ed.), Educational measurement. Washington, D. C.: American Council on Education, 1971.

Ball, S., & Bogatz, G. A. Reading with television: An evaluation of the "Electric Company" (Vol. 1 and 2). Princeton: Educational Testing Service, 1973.

Barnow, B. S. The effects of Head Start and socioeconomic status on cognitive development of disadvantaged children. Unpublished doctoral dissertation, University of Wisconsin, Department of Economics, 1973.

Baughman, E. E., & Dahlstrom, W. G. Negro and white children: A psychological study in the rural South. New York: Academic Press, 1968.

Berger, L., Berstein, A., Klein, E., Cohen, J., & Lucas, G. Effects of aging and pathology on the factorial structure of intelligence. Journal of Consulting Psychology, 1964, 28, 199-207.

Boruch, R. F. Bibliography: Illustrative randomized field experiments for program planning and evaluation. Evaluation, 1974, 2(1), 83-87.

Boruch, R. F. Contentions about randomized experiments for evaluating social programs. In H. W. Riecken & R. F. Boruch (Eds.), Proceedings of the 1974 SSRC Conference on Social Experiments. Washington, D. C.: Science Technology and Policy Office, National Science Foundation, 1975.

Box, G. E. P. Use and abuse of regression. Technometrics, 1966, 8, 625-629.

Brazziel, W. F. Effects of general education in manpower programs. Journal of Human Resources, Summer 1966, 1, 39-44.

Burket, G. R. Empirical criteria for distinguishing and validating aptitude and achievement measures. In D. Ross (Ed.), The aptitude-achievement distinction. New York: CTB/McGraw-Hill, 1974.

Campbell, D. T. From description to experimentation: Interpreting trends as quasi-experiments. In C. W. Harris (Ed.), Problems in measuring change. Madison: University of Wisconsin Press, 1963.

Campbell, D. T. Reforms as experiments. American Psychologist, April 1969, 24(4), 409-429.

Campbell, D. T. Temporal changes in treatment-effect correlations: A quasi-experimental model for institutional records and longitudinal studies. In G. V. Glass (Ed.), The promise and perils of educational information systems (Proceedings of the 1970 Invitational Conference on Testing Problems). Princeton: Educational Testing Service, 1971.

Campbell, D. T. Evolutionary epistemology. In P. A. Schilpp (Ed.), The philosophy of Karl Popper (Vol. 14, I & II, The library of living philosophers). La Salle, Ill.: Open Court Publishing, 1974. (a)

Campbell, D. T. Qualitative knowing in action research. Kurt Lewin Award Address, Society for the Psychological Study of Social Issues, Meeting with the American Psychological Association, New Orleans, September 1, 1974. (b) (To appear, after revision, in The Journal of Social Issues.)

Campbell, D. T., & Clayton, K. N. Avoiding regression effects in panel studies of communication impact. Studies in Public Communication, 1961, 3, 99-118. (Also, Indianapolis: Bobbs-Merrill, Reprint series in the social sciences, S-353, 1964.)

Campbell, D. T., & Erlebacher, A. E. How regression artifacts in quasi-experimental evaluations can mistakenly make compensatory education look harmful. In J. Hellmuth (Ed.), Compensatory education: A national debate (Vol. 3, Disadvantaged child). New York: Brunner/Mazel, 1970.

Campbell, D. T., & Stanley, J. C. Experimental and quasi-experimental designs for research on teaching. In N. L. Gage (Ed.), Handbook of research on teaching. Chicago: Rand McNally, 1963. (Also published as Experimental and quasi-experimental designs for research. Chicago: Rand McNally, 1966.)

Carroll, J. B. Fitting a model of school learning to aptitude and achievement data over grade levels (Research bulletin RB-73-51). Princeton: Educational Testing Service, August 1973.

Chalmers, T. C., Block, J. B., & Lee, S. Controlled studies in clinical cancer research. New England Journal of Medicine, 1972, 287, 75-78.

Chapin, F. S. Experimental designs in sociological research (Rev. ed.). New York: Harper, 1955.

Chapman, L. J., & Chapman, J. P. Problems in the measurement of cognitive deficit. Psychological Bulletin, 1973, 79(6), 380-385.

Cicirelli, V. G. et al. The impact of Head Start: An evaluation of the effects of Head Start on children's cognitive and effective development. (A report presented to the Office of Economic Opportunity.) Ohio University, Westinghouse Learning Corporation, June 1969. (Distributed by Clearinghouse for Federal Scientific and Technical Information, U. S. Department of Commerce, National Bureau of Standards, Institute for Applied Technology (PB 184 328).

Cochran, W. G. Errors of measurement in statistics. Technometrics, 1968, 11, 637-666.

Cohen, J. The factorial structure of the WAIS between early adulthood and old age. Journal of Consulting Psychology, 1957, 21, 283-290.

Conner, R. F. A methodological analysis of twelve true experimental program evaluations. Unpublished doctoral dissertation, Northwestern University, August 1974.

Cook, T. D., Appleton, H., Conner, R. Shaffer, A., Tamkin, G., & Weber, S. J. Sesame Street revisited: A case study in evaluation research. New York: Russell Sage Foundation, 1975.

Crano, D. C., Kenny, D. A., & Campbell, D. T. Does intelligence cause achievement?: A cross-lagged panel analysis. Journal of Educational Psychology, 1972, 63(3), 258-275.

Cronbach, L. J. Essentials of psychological testing. New York: Harper, 1970.

Cronbach, L. J., & Furby, L. How we should measure "change" -- or should we? Psychological Bulletin, 1970, 74, 68-80.

Director, S. M. Underadjustment bias in the quasi-experimental evaluation of manpower training. Doctoral dissertation, Northwestern University, Graduate School of Management, August 1974.

Earle, H. H. Police recruit-training: Stress vs. nonstress. Springfield: Charles C. Thomas, 1973.

Fennessey, J. Incentives in education project: Impact evaluation report (Final report to U. S. Office of Education, Department of Health, Education, and Welfare). Washington, D. C.: The Planar Corporation, 1972.

Ferber, R. The reliability of consumer surveys of financial holdings: Time deposits. Journal of the American Statistical Association, 1965, 60, 148-163.

Fisher, R. A. Design of experiments. London: Oliver and Boyd, 1935.

Galton, F. Typical laws of heredity. Proceedings of the Royal Institute of Great Britain (Proceedings of 1875-1878), 1879, pp. 282-301.

Galton, F. Regression toward mediocrity in hereditary stature. Journal of the Anthropological Institute of Great Britain and Ireland, 1886, 15, 246-263.

Goldberger, A. S., & Duncan, O. D. Structural equation models in the social sciences. New York: Seminar Press, 1973.

Goodwin, W. L., & Sanders, J. R. The use of experimental and quasi-experimental designs in educational evaluation (Research report). University of Colorado, Laboratory of Educational Research, 1972.

Gorsuch, R. L., Henighan, R. P., & Barnard, C. Locus of control: An example of dangers in using children's scales with children. Child Development, 1972, 43, 579-590.

Hardin, E., & Borus, M. E. Economic benefits and costs of retraining courses in Michigan. Lexington, Mass.: Heath Lexington, 1971.

Hilton, G. Causal inference analysis: A seductive process. Administrative Science Quarterly, March 1972, 44-54.

Humphreys, L. G. Investigations of the simplex. Psychometrika, 1960, 25(4), 313-323.

Kenny, D. A. A quasi-experimental approach to assessing treatment effects in the nonequivalent control groups design. Psychological Bulletin, 1975, 82, 345-362.

Klonoff, H. IQ constancy and age. Perceptual and Motor Skills, 1972, 35, 527-534.

Lord, F. M. Large-scale covariance analysis when the control variable is fallible. Journal of the American Statistical Association, 1960, 55, 307-321. (a)

Lord, F. M. An empirical study of the normality and independence of errors of measurement in test scores. Psychometrika, 1960, 25, 91-104. (b)

Lord, F. M., & Novick, M. R. Statistical theories of mental test scores. Reading, Mass.: Addison-Wesley, 1968.

McNemar, Q. A critical examination of the University of Iowa studies of environmental influences upon the I.Q. Psychological Bulletin, 1940, 37, 63-92.

Miller, S. M., Roby, P., & Steenwijk, A. A. V. Creaming the poor. Trans-action, June 1970, 7(8), 38-45.

Mollenkopf, W. G. Variation of the standard error of measurement. Psychometrika, 1949, 14(3), 189-229.

Noack, H. R. Application of latent trait models to the ACT mathematics usage test. Unpublished doctoral dissertation, Department of Psychology, Iowa State University, 1973.

Osborne, R. T. Stability of factor structure of the WISC for normal Negro children from preschool to first grade. Psychological Reports, 1966, 18, 655-664.

Osborne, R. T., & Suddick, D. E. A longitudinal investigation of the intellectual differentiation hypothesis. Journal of Genetic Psychology, 1972, 121, 83-89.

Owens, W. A. Age and mental abilities: A second adult follow-up. Journal of Educational Psychology, 1966, 57, 311-325.

Porter, A. C. The effects of using fallible variables in the analysis of covariance (Doctoral dissertation, University of Wisconsin, 1967). (University Microfilms, Ann Arbor, Michigan, 1968.)

Porter, A. C. Comments on some current strategies to evaluate the effectiveness of compensatory education programs; Comments on the Westinghouse-Ohio University study. Two memoranda prepared for R. D. Hess, Symposium on the Effectiveness of Contemporary Education Programs in the Early Years: Reports from Three National Evaluations and Longitudinal Studies. Meeting of the American Psychological Association, Washington, D. C., August 1969.

Pravalpruk, K., & Porter, A. C. The effect of multiple fallible covariables in analysis of covariance and two correction methods. Presented at the annual meeting of the American Educational Research Association, 1974.

Rasch, G. Probabilistic models for some intelligence and attainment tests. Copenhagen: Nielson and Lydiche (for Danmarks Paedogogiske Institut), 1960.

Riecken, H. W., Boruch, R. F., Campbell, D. T., Caplan, N., Glennan, T. K., Pratt, J., Rees, A., & Williams, W. Social experimentation: A method for planning and evaluating social intervention. New York: Academic Press (For the Social Science Research Council), 1974.

Robin, G. D. An assesment of the in-public school Neighborhood Youth Corps projects in Cincinnati and Detroit, with special reference to summer only and year round enrollment (Final report). Philadelphia: National Analysts, February 1969.

Rossi, P. H. Practice, method, and theory in evaluating social-action programs. In J. L. Sundquist (Ed.), On fighting poverty. New York: Basic Books, 1969.

Saretsky, G. The OEO P.C. experiment and the John Henry effect. Phi Delta Kappan, 1972, 53, 579-581.

Savage, L. J. The foundations of statistics reconsidered. In Proceedings of the fourth Berkeley symposium on mathematical statistics and probability. Berkeley: University of California Press, 1961.

Scriven, M. Maximizing the power of causal investigations: The modus operandi method. In W. James Popham (Ed.), Evaluation in education: Current applications. Berkeley: McCutcheon, 1975.

Segall, M. H., Campbell, D. T., & Herskovits, M. J. The influence of culture on visual perception. Indianapolis: Bobbs-Merrill, 1966.

Siegle, P. M., & Hodge, R. W. A causal approach to the study of measurement error. In H. M. Blalock (Ed.), Methodology in social research. New York: McGraw-Hill, 1968.

Smith, H. F. Interpretation of adjusted treatment means and regressions in analysis of covariance. Biometrics, 1957, 13, 282-307.

Smith, M. S., & Bissell, J. S. Report analysis: The impact of Head Start. Harvard Educational Review, 1970, 40, 51-104.

Stanley, J. (Ed.) Improving experimental design and statistical analysis. Sponsored by Phi Delta Kappa, University of Wisconsin, Madison. Chicago: Rand McNally & Co., 1967.

Stroud, T. W. F. Comparing regressions when measurement error variances are known. Psychometrika, 1974, 39(1), 53-67.

Thorndike, R. L. Regression fallacies in the matched groups experiment. Psychometrika, 1942, 7, 85-102.

Warren, R. D., White, J. K., & Fuller, W. A. An error in variables analysis of managerial role performance. Journal of the American Statistical Association, 1974, 69(348), 886-893.

Wold, H. Causal inference from observational data: A review of ends and means. Journal of the Royal Statistical Society, Series A, 1956, 119 (Part I), 28-49.

Wright, B. D. Sample-free test calibration and person measurement. Proceedings of the 1967 Invitational Conference on Testing Problems. Princeton: Educational Testing Service, 1968.

Wright, B. D., & Panchapakesan, N. A procedure for sample-free item analysis. Educational and Psychological Measurement, 1969, 29, 23-48.

APPENDIX

ILLUSTRATIVE BIBLIOGRAPHY: EXPERIMENTS FOR PLANNING
AND EVALUATING EDUCATIONAL PROGRAMS

This appendix lists some randomized field experiments which have been mounted to plan and evaluate educational programs. The list is illustrative and not necessarily representative, and covers teaching and teacher training; curriculum and communications; and special programs, such as counseling systems, developed in the context of educational institutions.

Most of the references listed here concern experiments which have been completed. Some concern field experiments which are under way at this writing. In all cases, the initial evaluation design included a _randomized_ design as the main architecture for the program evaluation, or as a vehicle for evaluating components of a larger program. Most but not all of the experiments achieved randomization.

Abstracts of some of these references are available in Riecken et al. (1974). A more complete listing of randomized field tests of social programs in general (socio-medical, economic, etc.) is given in Boruch (1974), from which this bibliography was abridged.

For convenience, the bibliography is organized under the following outline:

1. Teacher Impact, Teacher Training
2. Curriculum and Other Learning Conditions
3. Instructional Objectives

4. Electronic and Mechanical Assistance for Instruction
5. Compensatory Education: Preschool and Primary Grades
6. Special Training: Disadvantaged Groups (Including Manpower Training and Career Education)
7. Post-Secondary Training, Education, Communications
8. School-based Systems for Social and Psychological Adjustment
9. Systems for Improving Quality of Educational Measurement
10. Aptitude-Trait Interaction

1. *TEACHER IMPACT, TEACHER TRAINING*

Amidon, E. J., & Flanders, N. A. The effects and indirect teacher influence on dependence prone students learning geometry. Journal of Educational Psychology, 1961, 52, 286-291.

Bausell, R. B., Moody, W. B., & Walzel, F. N. A factorial study of tutoring versus classroom instruction. American Educational Research Journal, 1972, 9, 591-597.

Berliner, D. C. Microteachings and the technical skills approach to teacher training (Technical Report No. 8). Stanford, Calif.: Stanford University Center for Research and Development in Teaching, 1969.

Carroll, J. B. Research on teaching foreign languages. In N. L. Gage (Ed.), Handbook of research on teaching. Chicago: Rand-McNally, 1963.

Centra, J. A. Effectiveness of student feedback in modifying college instruction. Journal of Educational Psychology, 1973, 65, 395-401.

Ellson, D. G., Barber, L., Engle, T. L., & Kampwerth, L. Programmed tutoring: A teaching aid and a research tool. Reading Research Quarterly, 1965, 1, 77-127.

Filson, T. N. Factors influencing the level of dependence in the classroom. Unpublished doctoral dissertation, University of Minnesota, 1957.

Goodwin, D. Training teachers in reinforcement techniques to increase pupil task-oriented behavior: An experimental evaluation. Unpublished doctoral dissertation, Stanford University, 1966.

Hammond, K. R., & Kern, F. Teaching comprehensive medical care. Cambridge: Harvard University Press, 1959.

Harrison, G. V. The results of professional and nonprofessional trainers using prescribed training procedures on the performance of upper grade elementary school tutors. Unpublished doctoral dissertation, University of California at Los Angeles, 1969.

Watson, F. G. Research on teaching science. In N. L. Gage (Ed.), Handbook of research on teaching. Chicago: Rand-McNally, 1963.

Weikart, D. P. Relationship of curriculum, teaching and learning in preschool education. In J. C. Stanley (Ed.), Preschool programs for the disadvantaged. Baltimore: Johns Hopkins University, 1972.

2. CURRICULUM AND OTHER LEARNING CONDITIONS

Anderson, R. C. The comparative field experiment: An illustration from high school biology. Proceedings of the 1968 Invitational Conference on Testing Problems. Princeton: Educational Testing Service, 1969.

Berliner, D. C. The effects of test-like events and note taking on learning from lecture instruction. Unpublished doctoral dissertation, Stanford University, 1968.

Bryk, J. A. Learning performance in the Defensive Driving Course (DDC) and the DDC Self Instruction Program (Research Report). Chicago: National Safety Council, 1973.

Far West Laboratory for Educational Research and Development. Internal summative evaluation plan: FY 74. San Francisco: Far West Laboratory, 1973.

Goldberg, L. R. Student personality characteristics and optimal college learning conditions: An extensive search for trait-by-treatment interaction effects. Instructional Science, 1972, 153-210.

Hagens, R., et al. Prospectus: Employer based career education program development. Portland: Northwest Regional Educational Laboratory, 1972.

Schuman, S. H., McConochie, R., & Pelz, D. C. Reduction of young driver crashes in a controlled pilot study. Journal of the American Medical Association, 1971, 218, 233-237.

Walther, R. H. A study of the effectiveness of the Graham Associates demonstration project on NYC-2 education programming. Washington, D. C., George Washington University, Manpower Research Projects, 1974. (Abstract)

Welch, W. W., & Walberg, H. J. A national experiment in curriculum evaluation. American Educational Research Journal, 1972, 9, 373-384.

Zener, T. B., & Schnuelle, L. An evaluation of self-directed search: A guide to educational and vocational planning (Research Report No. 124). Baltimore: Johns Hopkins University, Center for the Social Organization of Schools, 1972.

3. INSTRUCTIONAL OBJECTIVES

Baker, E. L. Effects on student achievement of behavioral and nonbehavioral objectives. Journal of Experimental Education, 1969, 37, 5-8.

Dalis, G. T. Effect of precise objectives upon student achievement in health education. Journal of Experimental Education, 1970, 39, 20-23.

Huck, S. W., & Long, J. D. The effect of behavioral objectives on student achievement. Paper read at the annual convention of the American Educational Research Association, Chicago, 1972.

Jenkins, J. R., & Deno, S. L. Influence of knowledge and type of objectives on subject-matter learning. Journal of Educational Psychology, 1971, 62, 67-70.

McNeil, J. D. Concomitants of using behavioral objectives in the assessment of teacher effectiveness. In R. C. Anderson, G. W. Faust, M. C. Roderick, D. J. Cunningham, & T. Andre (Eds.), Current research on instruction. Englewood Cliffs, N. J.: Prentice-Hall, Inc., 1969.

Moffett, G. M. Use of instructional objectives in the supervision of student teachers. Unpublished doctoral dissertation, University of California at Los Angeles, 1966.

Morse, J. A., & Tillman, M. H. Effects on achievement of possession of behavioral objectives and training concerning their use. Paper read at the annual convention of the American Educational Research Association, Chicago, 1972.

Nwana, E. An investigation into an objective way of examining student teachers in practical teaching in West Cameroon teacher training institutions. Unpublished doctoral dissertation, University of California at Los Angeles, 1968.

4. ELECTRONIC AND MECHANICAL ASSISTANCE FOR INSTRUCTION

Ball, S., & Bogatz, G. A. Reading with television: An evaluation of the "Electric Company" (Vol. 1 and 2). Princeton: Educational Testing Service, 1971.

Bogatz, G. A., & Ball, S. The second year of Sesame Street: A continuing evaluation (Vol. 1 and 2). Princeton: Educational Testing Service, 1971.

Fletcher, J. D., & Atkinson, R. C. Evaluation of the Stanford CAI program in initial reading. Journal of Educational Psychology, 1972, 63, 597-602.

Fuhr, N. L. The typewriter and retarded readers. Journal of Remedial Reading, 1972, 16, 30-32.

Goodwin, W. L., & Sanders, J. R. The use of experimental and quasi experimental designs in educational evaluation (Research Report). Boulder, Colo.: University of Colorado, Laboratory of Educational Research, 1972.

Holtzman, W. H., & Diaz-Guerro, R. Learning by televised Plaza Sesamo in Mexico. Journal of Educational Psychology, 1974, 66, 632-643.

Hornik, R. C., Ingle, H. T., Mayo, J. K., McAnany, E. G., & Schramm, W. Television and educational reform in El Salvador (Research Report No. 14). Stanford, Calif.: Stanford University, Institute for Communications Research, August 1973.

Searle, B., Friend, J., Jamison, D., Suppes, P., Tilson, T., & Zonotti, M. Radio mathematics project: Research plan. Stanford, Calif.: Stanford University, Institute for Mathematical Studies in the Social Sciences, June 1974.

5. COMPENSATORY EDUCATION: PRESCHOOL AND PRIMARY GRADES

Crain, R. L., & York, R. L. Evaluation with an experimental design: The Emergency School Assistance Program. To be published in a book of readings on evaluation by James G. Albert, National Center for Resource Recovery.

DeLoria, D., Love, J. M., et al. The National Home Start Evaluation interim report IV: Summative evaluation results. Ypsilanti, Michigan: High/Scope Educational Research Foundation, June 1974.

Feshbach, S. et al. A training, demonstration, and research program for the remediation of learning disorders in culturally disadvantaged youth (Final Research Report). University of California at Los Angeles, Fernald School, (Psychology Department), 1970.

Goodwin, W. Evaluation in early childhood education. In Colvin, R., & Zaffino, E. (Eds.), Developing personnel for the education and care of young children. New York: Springer, in press.

Heber, R., & Garber, H. The Milwaukee Project: A study of the effect of early intervention to prevent mental retardation in high risk families. Presented at the American Statistical Association and Allied Social Sciences Meetings, New York, December 1973.

Hudson, W. W., & Daniel, D. L. Project Breakthrough: A responsive environment field experiment with preschool children from public assistance families. Chicago: Cook County Department of Public Aid, 1969.

Klaus, R. A., & Gray, S. W. The Early Training Project for Disadvantaged Children: A report after five years. Monographs of the Society for Research in Child Development, 33(4), 1968.

Kraft, I., Fuschillo, J., & Herzog, E. Prelude to school: An evaluation of an inner-city preschool program (Children's Bureau Research Report No. 3). Washington, D. C.: U.S. Department of Health, Education, and Welfare, 1968.

McDill, E. L., McDill, M. S., & Sprehe, J. T. Strategies for success in compensatory education. Baltimore: Johns Hopkins Press, 1969.

McKay, H., McKay, A., & Sinisterra, L. Stimulation of intellectual and social competence in Colombian preschool children affected by the multiple deprivations of depressed urban environments (Progress Report 2). Cali, Colombia: Universidad del Valle, University Center for Child Development, Human Ecology Research Station, September 1973.

Mervielde, I. Research project concerning the stimulation of development and learning abilities of socially deprived children (Unpublished Research Memo). Belgium (Blandijhbergz, 9000 Gent): University of Gent, 1973.

Palmer, F. H. Minimal intervention at age two and three, and subsequent intellective changes. In Parker, R. K. (Ed.), Preschool in action. Boston: Allyn and Bacon, 1972.

Risley, T. Spontaneous language and the preschool environment. In J. C. Stanley (Ed.), Preschool programs for the disadvantaged. Baltimore: Johns Hopkins University Press, 1972.

Sinisterra, L., McKay, H., & McKay, A. Stimulation of intellectual and social competence in Colombian preschool children affected by multiple deprivations of depressed urban environments (Progress Report). Cali, Colombia: Universidad del Valle, University Center for Child Development, Human Ecology Research Station, November 1971. (Mimeo)

Wargo, M. J., Campeau, P. L., & Tallmadge, G. K. Further examination of exemplary programs for educating disadvantaged children. P.S. 115, Alpha One Reading Program, New York City. Final Report. Palo Alto: American Institutes for Research, July 1971.

6. SPECIAL TRAINING: DISADVANTAGED GROUPS (INCLUDING MANPOWER TRAINING AND CAREER EDUCATION)

David, J. Report on the design of the Follow Through Summer Effects Study (Follow Through Program, Bureau of Elementary and Secondary Education, U.S. Office of Education). Cambridge, Mass.: Huron Institute, 1972.

Gonzales, J. P. Summer/in-school NYC vocational and exploration experiment. Stockton, Calif.: Stockton Unified School District, 1974. (Abstract)

Jolly, E. et al. Urban Career Education Center's Career Intern Program (Research Prospectus). Philadelphia: UCEC Program, 1973.

Mountain-Plains Education and Economic Development Program, Inc. Research Design: Career Education Model IV. Glasgow, Mont.: Mountain-Plains Educational and Economic Development Program, 1973.

Robin, G. D. An assessment of the in-public school Neighborhood Youth Corps Projects in Cincinnati and Detroit with special reference to summer only and year round enrollment (Final Report). Philadelphia: National Analysis, February 1969.

Yinger, J., Ikeda, K., & Laycock, F. Middle start: Supportive interventions for higher education among students of disadvantaged backgrounds (Final Report). Oberlin, Ohio: Oberlin College, Psychology Department, November 1970.

7. POST-SECONDARY TRAINING, EDUCATION, COMMUNICATIONS

Centra, J. A. Effectiveness of student feedback in modifying college instruction. Journal of Educational Psychology, 1973, 65, 395-401.

Earle, H. H. Police recruit-training: Stress vs. non-stress. Springfield: Charles C. Thomas, 1973.

Fiedler, F. E. Predicting the effects of leadership training and experience from the contingency model. Journal of Applied Psychology, 1972, 56, 114-119.

Hand, H. H., & Slocum, J. W., Jr. A longitudinal study of the effects of a human relations training program on managerial effectiveness. Journal of Applied Psychology, 1972, 56, 412-417.

Hill, R., Stycos, J. M., & Back, K. W. The family and population control. Chapel Hill: University of North Carolina, 1959.

Holding, D. H. (Ed.). Experimental psychology in industry. Baltimore: Penguin, 1969.

Kupst, M. J. Experiments in communication of medical information (Research Report). Chicago: Children's Memorial Hospital, 1973. (Mimeo)

Rosen, H., & Turner, J. Effectiveness of two orientation approaches in hardcore unemployed turnover and absenteeism. Journal of Applied Psychology, 1971, 55, 296-301.

8. *SCHOOL-BASED SYSTEMS FOR SOCIAL AND PSYCHOLOGICAL ADJUSTMENT*

Hill, R. An experimental study of social adjustment. American Sociological Review, 1944, 9, 481-494.

Meyer, H. J., Borgatta, E. F., & Jones, W. C. Girls at vocational high. New York: Russell Sage, 1965.

Myers, J. R. A classroom preventive mental health program: Preliminary progress report. Chicago: Children's Memorial Hospital, September 1974.

Schulman, J. School-based Program for Primary Prevention of Mental Disorders (Introduction to prevention project). Chicago: Children's Memorial Hospital. (Mimeo)

Schulman, J., Ford, R. C., & Busk, P. A classroom program to improve self-concept. Psychology in the Schools, 1973, 10(4), 481-487.

9. *SYSTEMS FOR IMPROVING QUALITY OF EDUCATIONAL MEASURE-MENT*

Astin, A. W., & Panos, R. J. An analysis of the effectiveness of different (mailed questionnaire) followup techniques (Appendix D). In Astin & Panos, Vocational and educational development of college students. Washington, D. C.: American Council on Education, 1969.

Cronbach, L. J., Gleser, G. C., Nanda, N., & Rajaratnam, N. The dependability of behavioral measurements: Theory of generalizability for scores and profiles. New York: Wiley, 1972.

Education Research Centre Staff. The consequences of introducing educational testing: A societal experiment. Education Research Centre, St. Patrick's College and Boston College, Center for Field Research and School Services, 1972.

Medley, D. M., & Mitzel, H. E. Measuring classroom behavior by systematic observation. In N. L. Gage (Ed.), Handbook of research on teaching. Chicago: Rand-McNally, 1963.

Miltz, R. J. Development and evaluation of a manual for improving teacher's examinations. Unpublished doctoral dissertation, Stanford University, 1971.

Pike, L. W. and Evans, F. R. The effect of special instruction for three kinds of mathematics aptitude items (College Entrance and Examination Board Research Bulletin RB-72-19). Princeton: Educational Testing Service, 1972.

Schantz, B. M. B. An experimental study comparing the effects of verbal recall by children in direct and indirect teaching methods as a tool of measurement. Unpublished doctoral dissertation, Pennsylvania State University, 1963.

Welch, W. W., & Walberg, H. J. Pretest effects in curriculum evaluation. American Educational Research Journal, 1970, 6, 605-614.

Yates, A. Symposium on the effects of coaching and practice in intelligence tests: I. An analysis of some recent investigations. British Journal of Educational Psychology, 1953, 23, 147-154.

10. APTITUDE-TRAIT INTERACTION

Atkinson, J. W. Motivational determinants of intellective performance and cumulative achievement. In J. W. Atkinson & J. O. Raynor (Eds.), Motivation and achievement. Washington: Winston, 1974.

Atkinson, R. C., & Paulson, J. A. An approach to the psychology of instruction. Psychological Bulletin, 1972, 78, 49-61.

Cronbach, L. J. Beyond the two disciplines of scientific psychology. American Psychologist, 1975, 30, 116-127.

Cronbach, L. J., & Snow, R. E. Aptitudes and instructional methods. New York: Irvington, in press.

Domino, G. Differential prediction of academic achievement in conforming and independent settings. Journal of Educational Psychology, 1968, 59, 256-260.

Domino, G. Interactive effects of achievement orientation and teaching style on academic achievement. Journal of Educational Psychology, 1971, 62, 427-431.

Dowaliby, F. J., & Schumer, H. Teacher-centered vs. student-centered mode of college classroom instruction as related to manifest anxiety. Journal of Educational Psychology, 1973, 64, 125-132.

Goldberg, L. R. Student personality characteristics and optimal college learning conditions: An extensive search for trait-by-treatment interaction effects. Instructional Science, 1972, 1, 153-210.

Majasan, J. K. College students' achievement as a function of the congruence between their beliefs and their instructor's beliefs. Unpublished doctoral dissertation, Stanford University, 1972.

McKeachie, W. J., Isaacson, R. L., & Milholland, J. E. Research on the characteristics of effective college teaching (ERIC Document ED 024347). Ann Arbor, Mich.: University of Michigan, 1964.

McKeachie, W. J., Milholland, J. E., Mann, R., & Isaacson, R. Research on the characteristics of effective teaching (ERIC Document ED 024347). Ann Arbor, Mich.: University of Michigan, 1968.

4

Regression and Selection Models to Improve Nonexperimental Comparisons
GLEN G. CAIN

I. INTRODUCTION

This chapter is organized around two points.[1] The first is a restatement of the main thesis of the preceding chapter by Campbell and Boruch in the framework of a regression model. The second concerns strategies for obtaining unbiased estimates of parameters of interest from nonexperimental data. Before developing these points, let me raise briefly a larger and perhaps philosophical issue of whether there are lessons offered by economic research for the problems with which we are dealing. At the conference on which this volume is based, I was struck by the emphasis on the necessity for "true" experiments as a way of getting unbiased measures of the effects of various programs or

---

[1] Roughly the first half of this chapter adheres fairly closely to my oral presentation at the 1973 Battelle conference. The last half attempts to summarize points which emerged during the discussion with the conference participants. One section, noted in the text, has been added to help clarify a point. I am grateful to my colleague, Arthur S. Goldberger, for a number of clarifying comments on a first draft.

program inputs. If this impression is correct, then I see an implicit but definite challenge to economic research, or at least to empirical economics.

In my view economics is an empirical science. There is very little predictive power that can be derived directly from economic theory--solely, that is, from axiomatic economic theory. Even the simple proposition that demand curves slope downward is an empirical proposition, not a theoretical one. The predictive power, therefore, depends on the measurement and estimation of relationships among variables. This essential task of measurement is all done with nonexperimental data. The negative income tax experiment, with which I have been associated, is quite exceptional.[1]

Like evaluation research, economic research seeks to measure the effects of policy variables--taxes, subsidies, training programs, etc.--which are part of programs of intervention in the social processes. If we conclude that controlled experimentation is the only trustworthy way to measure the effects of these social-action programs, a shadow of doubt is cast on empirical research in economics. On the other hand, we could reach a contrasting and optimistic conclusion if evaluation research were approached from the perspective of a "believing" economist. That is, if the

---

[1] A report of the negative income tax experiment, formally entitled "The Graduated Work Incentive Experiment," is provided in the Spring 1974 issue of The Journal of Human Resources. The issue includes six articles which describe the experiment and some of its principal research results.

research findings of economics are valid and reliable, then this may indicate that the necessity for experimentation is overdrawn. This is not an issue that can be resolved in this volume, but it may serve as an interesting and perhaps provocative perspective.

II. AN ALTERNATE APPROACH TO BIAS IN TREATMENT EFFECTS

I will now turn to the substance of the previous chapter. The main thesis may be summarized and, I think, clarified, in the framework of a regression model. We can look upon the outcome of a program as the dependent variable, y, and the program itself (or, perhaps, some specified set of program inputs) as the independent variable, T. Let us adopt the simplest specification of T: T = 1 if the person is in the treatment group, and T = 0 if the person is in the control group. There is, of course, an error term, e, which will include all the omitted variables, X_1, X_2, ... X_k, which affect y and "pure" measurement error in y. Thus:

$$y_i = f(T_i) + e_i$$

(i = 1,2 ... N subjects in the sample).

This function may be represented by a linear model, $y_i = a + bT_i + e_i$, without sacrificing the generality of the argument. If we randomly assign groups to treatment and control status, we are assured that the measured relationship, $\partial y / \partial T (=b)$, is an unbiased measure of the effect of T

on y.[1] Formally, we are assured of the unbiasedness of b
because randomization assures us that T is uncorrelated with
the error term in the sample, and, therefore, the estimated
b is what we can expect to observe if T were changed in
replications of the program. Changes in T correspond, of
course, to administering the program to previously untreated
members of the population.

Let me digress briefly to discuss the strategy of trying to include some of the omitted "X" variables as explicit
independent variables in models which assume random assignments. Clearly, we never design an experiment without any
theory; we have some a priori knowledge of variables
(besides the treatment) that affect the outcome. Generally,
there are compelling reasons for including some of these
other variables in a multiple regression model used to estimate the relationship.

First, including relevant X variables will reduce the
amount of error variance, and in so doing increase the precision of our estimates of the effect of T on y. Clearly,
we seek a significant reduction in error variance which

---

[1] I use "unbiasedness" to mean that the effect we measure is,
on the average, the same as the effect that would emerge
from an application or implementation of the program to the
relevant population. Some degree of ambiguity in the term
may arise when there is uncertainty about whether the estimated model accurately represents the process or experiment
about which we wish to make inferences. The issue will be
discussed further below. Hopefully, the term will be sufficiently clear in context.

reduces the standard error of estimate and thus makes up for the loss in degrees of freedom when using more independent variables.

Second, there are often scientific or policy reasons for measuring the effects of the X's upon y for their own sake. The X's may be variables measuring father's education, mother's education, family income, the subject's health status, and so on. Some of these variables are amenable to policy manipulation. Others, like age, are not, but there may be some scientific interest in measuring their relationship. Moreover, in the light of our principal interest in the treatment (or program) effect, we might be interested in interaction effects between the treatment and some of these other independent variables; these interactions could be estimated explicitly in the multiple regression model.

Finally, by including the important X variables we afford ourselves some protection from misestimating the **treatment effect, in the event** a <u>sample</u> correlation exists between T and one or several of the X's. Given the high costs of controlled experiments, we can seldom rely on replications to "wash out" these sample correlations and the resulting biases in measured treatment effects.

Now let me turn to the main point of Campbell's and Boruch's argument, which concerns the biases in treatment effects that can result from statistical analysis of uncontrolled experiments. The general problem is precisely that the assumption of zero correlation between the error term, e, and the treatment variable, T, is incorrect; that the nonrandom assignment to treatment and control groups has resulted in some variable or set of variables (that affect

y) being correlated with T. If these go unmeasured or (if they are included in the model) are mismeasured, then we will in general get a biased estimate of the treatment effect. If the omitted variables are essentially unmeasurable, then the problem may be intractable.

The bias can be displayed with our linear, additive regression model. Let y measure educational achievement, and let "true ability," A, and the treatment (the program), T, be variables determining y, along with an error term which is assumed to be uncorrelated with A and T. In the regression equations written below, I will drop the subscript i and suppress all constant terms, which are irrelevant to the analysis. Thus,

$$y = a_1 T + a_2 A + e.$$

An unbiased measure of the effect of T on y would be obtainable from this model, if we could measure A. Without this measured variable, we have instead:

$$y = bT + e',$$

where $e' = a_2 A + e$ is correlated with T if A is correlated with T.

Now, there is a well-established relationship between the correct measure of treatment effect, a_1, and the observed measure, b; namely:

$$b = a_1 + ca_2,$$

where c denotes the regression coefficient in the auxiliary regression of ability on treatment:[1]

$$A = cT + u.$$

If we know the signs of these two parameters, c and a_2, then we know the direction of the bias in b. Clearly, the sign of a_2, the effect of true ability on achievement, is positive. The sign of c, the relation between treatment and true ability, can be plus, minus, or zero. It would be zero if treatments were assigned randomly with respect to true ability, and then there would be no bias. It would be minus in the case that Campbell and Boruch have discussed, where the most disadvantaged children (i.e., those with the lowest true ability) receive the treatment. Finally, the sign of c would be positive in the case of "creaming." There are many social programs for which we have reason to suspect such positive selectivity. Clearly, the magnitude of the bias in b will depend on the magnitude of a_2 (the size of the omitted variable's effect on y) and c (the size of the relation between A and T).

It will come as no surprise to note that the problem in avoiding the bias in the measure of T in the model with nonrandom assignments is that we are never able to measure the "true ability" variable, A. Note that A is merely a one-variable representation of all the unmeasured factors

---

[1] The auxiliary regression measures a sample relationship between A and T, but it does not purport to express "causality" as between the two variables.

that vary in the process described by the program and that systematically affect the outcome (y). So defined, A would generally represent test-taking ability in educational program evaluations, earning ability in manpower training evaluation, the "ability" to avoid some specific disease in a disease prevention program, and so on.

Now that I have presented the thesis of the preceding chapter using regression notation, let me summarize this thesis in words. Campbell and Boruch are certainly correct to claim that: 1) if two populations differ in mean true ability; 2) if one is the source of a treatment group and the other of a control group; and 3) if we do not control for this difference in ability when measuring the treatment effect, <u>then</u> the treatment-control difference will be confounded with the ability differences. Phrased in this terse way, the point will probably strike many readers as quite obvious. Furthermore, it is also intuitively clear that 4) if partially controlling variables are used, the bias (in the measured treatment effect) will be small or large as the control variables do a good or a bad job in controlling for the ability difference.

We can distinguish two types of selection processes that are relevant to this question of a bias in the measured treatment effect; namely, those that are known and those that are unknown to the investigator. Indeed, the critical difference for avoiding bias is not whether the assignments are random or nonrandom, but whether the investigator has <u>knowledge of and can model</u> this selection process. Recall that the sufficient condition for achieving no bias is that T and e are uncorrelated. Random assignment is just one way of knowing the selection process and ensuring the zero correlation between T and e. There are other ways of selecting subjects for treatment and control groups, and these ways may be fully specified in a regression model, in which case we could again attain the desired goal of a zero correlation between T and e.[1]

I will discuss a polar case in which no random assignments are permitted. (Mixed models are mentioned below.) For example, let the selection procedure be one in which the order of application for admission is the sole basis for assignment to the treatment group. If the order--1st, 2nd, ... 100th, etc.--is available, then the first 50, say, could be assigned to the treatment group. Let us assume that the order of application is correlated with true ability, although we do not need to prejudge the sign of this correlation. If, for example, the most "able" parents were the early applicants, the correlation would be positive; if, say, mothers on welfare first heard about the program and applied earlier, then the correlation could be negative. In either case, the fact that only order of application determines the assignment permits an unbiased measure of the treatment in the model:

$$y = b_1 T + b_2 X + e,$$

where X is the order or position number in the queue.

---

[1] My understanding of the material in the following several paragraphs has been improved by references to two papers by Arthur S. Goldberger (1972 [a] and [b]).

For another example, assignment to the treatment group could be made strictly and solely on the basis of family income--only subjects in families with incomes below a certain level are treated. Family income could then be the X variable in the above model. It is only slightly more complicated in form, if not in substance, to think of a well-defined set of indicators which determine the subject's assignment and which could then be included in the model as a vector of control variables.

Finally, a convenient illustration of modeling the selection procedure is offered by using a pretest score as a basis for assignment to an education program. Suppose all children who score less than X_0 are assigned to the treatment group. Here, X will represent that part of ability which is related to the treatment. Note that there is an ability component, $v = X - A$ (where A, as before, is the "true-ability" score for an individual), but this component is unrelated to the treatment. If the linear and additive specification of X and treatment is reasonably correct, then the following model (Figure 1) will provide an unbiased measure of the effect of T:

$$y = c_1 T + c_2 X + e.$$

Figure 1 is obviously drawn on the basis of an optimistic assumption that the treatment has a positive effect on y. Also, the flatter-than-$45°$ slope of $\partial y / \partial X$ $(= c_2)$ is intended to capture the realistic assumption that the pretest score, X, is a fallible measure of (test-taking) "ability." In principle, the assumptions of additivity and nonlinearity are not crucial, although if an interactive,

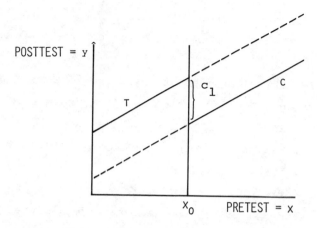

POSTTEST = y

T

c_1

C

x_0 PRETEST = x

Fig. 1. Nonrandom assignment to T and C groups, based on a pretest score, X. Dashed lines represent non-observed extrapolations of y, given X and the treatment/control status.

nonlinear model applies there may be practical difficulties in getting reliable estimates of the more complicated parameter, $\partial y/\partial T$.

One shortcoming with the model graphed in Figure 1 is that the precision of the estimate of $\partial y/\partial T$ is less than in the case of random assignments (in which T is independent of ability and, of course, independent of X). Also, if "true ability" were known and included in place of X, the precision of $\partial y/\partial T$ would be further increased.[1] But these shortcomings can be offset by larger sample sizes or by various

_____

[1] These statements are made without proof. See Goldberger (1972 [a] and [b]) for further discussion. Intuitively, uncorrelatedness between X and T provides for a larger

307

ways of reducing the error variance in the model, such as stratifying the sample or improving the accuracy of measures of y.

I should make clear a point which led to some misunderstanding during the discussion at the conference. The design shown in Figure 1 provides for a nonzero (indeed, negative) correlation between T and X, a correlation which is larger in absolute value than that between T and A. However, the correlation is not perfect: if one knows the value of T (either 1 or 0), one cannot perfectly predict the pretest value (X). If, on the other hand, the selection variable was also dichotomous--i.e., boys or girls, black or white, passed-the-pretest or failed-the-pretest--then our design would break down. A perfect correlation between T and X would exist, and we could not estimate $\partial y/\partial T$, given X, nor $\partial y/\partial X$, given T.

---

residual variance in T (i.e., the variance in T, holding X constant), and the larger residual variance in T produces a more reliable estimate of the regression coefficient of T. The claim that using A instead of X improves the reliability of the estimates of T is explained, again intuitively, as follows: Because A is a true measure of ability, using it would increase the R^2 more than would X (a fallible measure of ability). This higher R^2 means that the error variance in the model is less, and a significant reduction in error variance serves to increase the reliability of estimated regression coefficients.

At this point it is instructive to consider a mixed selection model, in which some randomization is combined with nonrandom selection. Let the probability, P, of selection depend on X, such that:

$$0 < P(X) < 1.$$

Note that the previous examples of nonrandom selection required that the probability of receiving the treatment was 1 if $X < X_0$, and 0 if $X \geq X_0$. In the mixed model the program administrators might select more disadvantaged children for the program, but not all such "low X" children would be placed in the treatment group and not all "high X" children would be placed in the control group. Given this stratification, however, some randomization would be necessary to determine which low-X (or high-X) children were assigned to the treatment and control groups. The selection process is fully represented by a random assignment that is conditional upon a known value of X. The previously defined regression model, with T and X as independent variables, allows as before an unbiased measure of the treatment effect, but with more precision than in the previous case of only an X-based assignment. The mixed model is very close to the "regression discontinuity" model Campbell has suggested as an acceptable quasi-experimental design (Campbell, 1969).

With a mixed model, even a dichotomous X variable and a dichotomous treatment/control status would not produce a perfect correlation between X and T, as discussed above. The polar case of a completely nonrandom selection process is nevertheless instructive, because we see explicitly the nonessentiality of randomization for the purpose of estimating an unbiased treatment effect.

Given the potential control that program directors have over the selection and allocation procedures, the model just described may have great practical significance under conditions when randomization is not feasible; again, see Campbell's discussion (1969). The model and example also serve to illustrate that a post hoc observed difference between treatment and control groups--i.e., they differ in population mean values of y--does not necessarily produce a situation in which the treatment effect is biased. The contrary impression is given by Campbell's articles on the problem. (This issue will be further discussed below.)

III. ESTIMATION OF MODELS UNDER CONDITIONS OF UNKNOWN BIAS

Now let us examine the second of the two fundamental situations in an evaluation design, wherein the selection process is not fully known. We cannot escape the requirement that the correlation between T and e must be zero (or, of course, small enough to be ignored) if we are to accept as unbiased the measured effect of T. Therefore, the burden falls on the theoretical specification to provide the relevant set of X variables. Generally, all those X's that are correlated with both y and T must be included, although special contrary cases, mentioned below, may arise which preserve a zero correlation between T and e. Whether this task of theoretical specification is feasible obviously depends on the given problem. Each program is intended to be operated in a certain way and in a specified environment.

Consequently, the task of the model builder is limited, at least, to a specification that applies only to these contexts.

There is no question but that the theory must convincingly "close" the system defined by the process and environment of the program.[1] In other words, the model must be "complete" in the following sense: variables correlated with y must be 1) included in the model as "control variables; or, if excluded, they must be 2) known to have a net or partial zero correlation with T; or 3) known to be unvarying in the given environment or process; or 4) known to be themselves completely determined by included variables (in which case we could say that the former have no "net" relation to y); or 5) known to be part of a set of omitted variables which tend to "offset" each other in their effects on y--i.e., where the expected value of y, given the omitted X's, is zero.

The informational requirements for such a complete model are formidable, of course. Incidentally, I would not object if someone claimed that the requirements amount to

---

[1] The term "closed system" was used by F. Mosteller, who raised the question at the conference and in subsequent correspondence of whether the theory provided a closed system (i.e., a complete model) for the purpose at hand. Mosteller quite properly remarked that the question of "bias" in the effect of a given variable, whether T or some other variable, has no meaning in the absence of such a complete model.

knowing the "selection" process in a more fundamental sense than that which is narrowly implied by the "direct selection" procedures which are determined by the administration of the program. If economists, for example, claim to estimate the net effect of labor unions on wages, we must have a model to "capture" (specify) the selection mechanism which distinguishes union member from nonunion member (or, perhaps, a worker covered by a union contract compared with one not covered). Here, the union status variable represents the T variable in our evaluation model, and all the caveats for estimating a union effect in a context of nonrandom assignments must apply. As I mentioned at the outset of this discussion, whether economics provides examples of credible empirical models--credible in the context in which they are intended to apply--is a large question.

Campbell's and Boruch's criticism of the estimated treatment effect in models where the selection process is not directly or explicitly specified is most effective when they are able to persuade their audience of a specific selection bias. Recall (from Figure 1) that an unconditional difference in population means is not sufficient to produce a bias; the difference in means must be one that is conditional upon the variables which appear in the theoretical model but are not included in the empirical model actually employed. There are undoubtedly many cases when there is sufficient knowledge about the selection procedures that the qualitative judgment about the difference in conditional means is warranted.

However, as I view the Campbell-Erlebacher criticism of the Head Start evaluation by the Westinghouse Learning Corporation (Campbell & Erlebacher, 1970), I find that their source of information about the selectivity bias is unclear. How do they know that the Head Start and control children, who came from the same neighborhood, differ in their conditional mean ability? A negative selectivity among children from the same neighborhoods for participation in compensatory education programs is not inevitable. We can visualize circumstances in which the Head Start administrators might "cream" or, what comes to the same situation, exclude "hopeless cases" or "disruptive" children.

If Campbell's and Erlebacher's "knowledge" comes solely from some observable characteristics (or set of characteristics) then we have a right to ask: If these are the characteristics that discriminate between the two groups, then why not use these variables in the model? If they "know" because there are nonmeasurable variables which are known to discriminate between the two groups--perhaps on the basis of some subjective or testimonial expressions of opinion--why don't they make clear that this is the source of their knowledge and permit the reader to assess this ad hoc judgment? Actually, I suspect that many observers would share Campbell's judgment that in the WLC Head Start study, differences in abilities between the Head Start and control groups remained even after the WLC control variables were used. That is, a net difference remains. But this conclusion is based on our subjective empirical impressions of the Head Start selection procedures. Such a conclusion should not be a product of an analysis of a hypothetical model in which the net difference is assumed at the outset, which it was in the simulation model used by Campbell and Erlebacher in their paper.

It may be helpful to consider adopting an explicit convention which, I believe, expresses the Campbell position

313

on the question of selectivity bias. The convention is that whenever the treatment and control groups differ in observed indicators of ability, in situations where the selection procedure is unknown, we should simply assume that this difference understates the "true" difference. Thus, the mean differences in preprogram test scores (if available) could be assumed to understate the true ability difference. If the treatment group's preprogram score were lower, we would assume that they are even worse off than indicated; if their preprogram test score were higher, they would be assumed to be "creamed" to a greater extent than was revealed by their test score advantage.

In the WLC Head Start study, there was no preprogram test score, but in a reanalysis of this data by Barnow, a measure of gross differences in ability was obtained as follows:[1] Using the <u>control</u> group, the postprogram test score, y_C, was regressed on a large number of ability indicators, such as child's age, parents' income, and parents' education, which we shall label X's. The regression equation measured the effect of these commonly used predictors of cognitive achievement on a test score that was, of course, unaffected by the Head Start program. Now, assuming the coefficients of these X's are the same for the treatment group, a predicted mean score, $\bar{\hat{y}}_T$, for the treatment group was calculated based on these coefficients and the treatment

---

[1]This procedure is specified in detail by B. S. Barnow (1973). The suggestion for this procedure came from my colleagues, Robert Avery and Harold Watts.

group's own X-values. A comparison of $\bar{y}_C (=\bar{\hat{y}}_C$, by construction) and $\bar{\hat{y}}_T$ reveals the extent to which the control and treatment groups differed in the set of ability indicators, where the ability indicators (the X's) are "weighted" by their effects (i.e., regression coefficients) on y_C. This method of comparing the abilities of the two groups seems to us to be far superior to any simple or multiple comparison of X values, per se, since we do not know whether a difference in a given X--say, "mother working,"--has a plus, minus, or zero effect on y. The regression-prediction equation not only combines the various X's but does so in a way that takes into account their effect on y.

Recall that controlling for the X's in the test of the Head Start program provokes Campbell to claim that the treatment group (whose $\hat{y}_T$ was less than $\hat{y}_C$) is still worse off. If this view is maintained consistently, it is equivalent to saying that any mean difference in indicators understates the true difference, when, to repeat, we have no relevant information about how the selection procedures "really" discriminated on ability. Perhaps we could adopt this convention as a "conservative" procedure in evaluation studies. I am not persuaded, however, that it is justified in general, although perhaps it was appropriate for the WLC study.

I would conclude by agreeing with Campbell and Boruch on the general desirability of random assignments. I would agree also to be suspicious of evaluations in which we know little about the selection methods, although I am more hesitant to assert a direction of bias in these circumstances. On the other hand, I am undoubtedly more sympathetic to the

315

use of theoretically justified models for analysis of non-experimental data. This sympathy is not totally owed to my membership in the economics profession. I am one of the few members who has hedged his bets with research in a controlled experiment.

REFERENCES

Barnow, B. S. The effects of Head Start and socioeconomic status on cognitive development of disadvantaged children. Unpublished doctoral dissertation, University of Wisconsin, Department of Economics, 1973.

Campbell, D. T. Reforms as experiments. American Psychologist, April 1969, 24(4), 409-429.

Campbell, D. T., & Erlebacher, A. How regression artifacts in quasi-experimental evaluations can mistakenly make compensatory education look harmful. In J. Hellmuth (Ed.), Compensatory education: A national debate (Vol. 3, Disadvantaged child). New York: Brunner/Mazel, 1970.

Goldberger, A. S. Selection bias in evaluating treatment effects: Some formal illustrations (Discussion paper 123-72). Madison: Institute for Research on Poverty, 1972. (a)

Goldberger, A. S. Selection bias in evaluating treatment effects: The case of interaction (Discussion paper 129-72). Madison: Institute for Research on Poverty, 1972. (b)

5

Field Trial Designs in Gauging the Impact of Fertility Planning Programs
ELIZABETH T. HILTON and ARTHUR A. LUMSDAINE

I. INTRODUCTION

A. *PURPOSE AND RATIONALE*

This chapter is based on a review of several dozen field studies conducted to determine the impact of various program innovations or alternative treatments on behavior relevant to the curbing of human fertility rates in countries concerned with excessive population growth.[1] Our main interest in this survey was with the use of behavioral data for assessing the accomplishments, and thereby improving the effectiveness, of both short-term and continuing population

---

[1] Most of the support for the survey of field studies of program impact on which this chapter is largely based was provided by the Battelle Population Study Center (BPSC), a component of the Battelle Human Affairs Research Centers. This paper, though not presented at the July 1973 Battelle conference, was drafted concurrently, and parts of it were discussed informally with some of the conference participants. The present chapter draws on portions of a working paper sponsored by UNESCO and reported by Lumsdaine at a

planning (fertility regulation) programs. Three purposes of the survey were: 1) to examine the kinds of program-oriented research and evaluation that have been conducted in family planning or other fertility regulation programs; 2) to clarify some concepts and pervasive problems of methodology in such evaluative research; and 3) to look for ways in which research and evaluation on population and other social programs can be improved in the future.

The term "fertility planning" is used herein in a comprehensive sense to include programs, program innovations or treatments utilizing any of a rather wide range of methods in order to increase the acceptance or continued use of fertility regulating practices, all for the end purpose of

———————

UNESCO conference in Davao City, Philippines, in April 1974. His work in revising the chapter for inclusion here was facilitated by a Russell Sage Foundation grant on social program evaluation reanalysis. The abstracting and analysis of field study reports and data, initiated at the East-West Center Communication Institute by Lumsdaine and D. Lawrence Kincaid in the winter of 1973, was done mainly at BPSC during 1973-74 by Hilton, to whom also belongs the primary credit for drafting the portions of the chapter that report specific studies of program innovations. A related UNESCO-sponsored report (Lumsdaine, Hilton, and Kincaid, 1975) describes some studies on process evaluation which are not included in the present chapter, and omits some of the details of impact-assessment studies reported here. (See also the footnote accompanying the recommendations presented at the end of this chapter.)

reducing population growth through the reduction of birth rates. These methods include instructive or educational communications--either interpersonal (as in family visits, individual counseling, or village meetings), or via mailings or mass media--as well as the provision of contraceptive or other fertility control devices or materials.

The studies we have examined display, within the purview of this one major social problem--control of population growth--an instructive variety of research design types. These span a substantial range in terms of the security of the basis they provide for valid attribution of outcomes to the impact of reasonably well defined program innovations.

The various research design types are exemplified in programs operated in a relatively homogeneous set of contexts. (In addition to having common basic objectives, all were conducted in developing nations of greater Asia and Latin America.) This general similarity of objectives and settings should facilitate comparison of relations between the design of the field researches and the conclusions they appear capable of supporting. The studies also suggest some of the socio-political factors that enter into the feasibility of carrying out studies which differ in the quality of evidence they afford for ascertaining program impacts.

B. *PERSPECTIVES*

Our present focus on the design of studies for assessing program impact should be viewed in the more general context of the various main classes of program evaluation, such as those suggested by Bennett and Lumsdaine (Chapter 1, this volume). Thus we may distinguish evaluation of <u>needs and</u>

goals for programs; evaluation of plans for progressing toward the goals sought; evaluation of ongoing program processes or operations, sometimes referred to as program monitoring or operational feedback; evaluation research to ascertain the impact(s) of the program on immediate or on later, more ultimate outcomes; and overall evaluation as a basis for decision, taking into account programs' goals, their demonstrated impacts, the alternatives available, and their costs and other constraints. Our focusing in this chapter on just the fourth of these classes (studies of measurable program impact) is in no way meant to deprecate the great practical importance of process evaluation in monitoring and improving the conduct of program operations, nor the basic importance of assessing program needs and goals as key inputs to program planning.

1. Goal Evaluation

The net merit of a program innovation in the end must obviously be judged both in terms of the desirability of the goals or outcomes sought and of the extent to which the goals are furthered by the demonstrable effects (impacts) of the particular innovation. Thus, our present concern with ways in which program impacts can be ascertained most efficaciously is clearly but one factor--though, obviously, a crucial one--in the determination of overall program merit on which major program decisions should be based.

One wants, obviously, programs that can be counted on to produce substantial impacts but also, of course, programs whose impacts are, on balance, socially desirable, considering both their planned and unplanned effects. Further, programs should be economically efficient in terms of the use of input resources. Program decisions thus must involve complex and difficult subjective judgments even after program impacts have been rather accurately identified and measured.

We largely bypass goal or output-value assessment in this chapter by simply accepting the desirability of fertility reduction per se as a given in the present context. This presumption emphatically does not deny that the final merit of a program or innovation also depends on numerous other factors as well (including side effects and cost of implementation). We recognize, also, that opinions may differ on the relative importance of empirical research to ascertain the impact of program innovations (on fertility-related outcomes, in this case) as compared with other phases of a total evaluation cycle. (See Edwards' and Guttentag's analogous calculus of impact probability and outcome desirability in Chapter 6, this volume.)

2. Process Evaluation

Likewise, we would strongly endorse the need for careful and thorough "process" evaluation, as a highly important factor in assuring that program impacts will not be compromised or attenuated because of failure to carry out a program's intended operations effectively. The survey from which this chapter derives included, in fact, the examination of a number of ways in which such process evaluation has been helpful in the conduct of population programs. The findings of this aspect of our survey are summarized elsewhere.[1]

The importance of adequate operational reports, showing the extent to which program functions are being carried out as planned, is quite apparent. In the present context such process evaluation includes, for example, information on dissemination of informational messages and materials, delivery of supplies, job performance of field personnel, and so forth. Included here also is the "pretesting" of informational program components (such as appeals, themes, slogans, messages, and instructions) to improve their clarity; and of training materials, operating procedures for field personnel, etc. to improve their effectiveness and efficiency in contributing to program output.

But despite the importance of such process-evaluation activities in monitoring the efficacy of day-to-day or month-to-month operations, they do not afford valid evidence of overall program impact. It is true that there are various recurrent features of program operations which experienced observers regard as generally important for programs to incorporate in order to operate effectively.[2]

---

[1] See Lumsdaine, Hilton, and Kincaid (1975); also, for a somewhat more detailed description, see UNESCO (1974), an earlier working document prepared by these authors.

[2] See, for example, the compendium by Lumsdaine and Hilton (1973) summarizing conference recommendations of a group of experts including, among others, Donald J. Bogue, H. C. Chen, L. P. Chow, Gordon W. Duncan, James Fawcett, Philip

However, such "process" criteria must be considered as only a basis for judging a program's <u>predicted</u> or potential impact. By contrast, our present concern focuses on <u>actual</u>, demonstrable program impacts, as assessed in terms of data on effects measured by adequately controlled field studies.

3. Program Outcomes

The underlying, accepted aim of the population programs that we consider here is, as noted above, to contribute to the ultimate goal of slowing down excessive fertility rates. However, more immediate or proximal outcomes of fertility regulation programs obviously are also of interest. These include program effects on persons' knowledge and attitudes concerning family size limitation, as well as on various forms of behavior that may lead directly or indirectly to changes in fertility. In a few of the studies surveyed here, the indices of impact reported are limited to measurement of program effects on knowledge or attitudes. However, the majority of studies used some measure (not always a clearly interpretable or valid one) of reported behavior indicating acceptance of contraceptive methods. In a number of instances, data were also given to indicate <u>continued use</u> of a method and/or of consequent birthrate decline, which we take to be the terminal or "payoff" impact criterion for the

---

Harvey, Peter S. King, John F. Marshall, K. J. Mette, J. Y. Peng, Gordon W. Perkin, D. Malcolm Potts, Denis J. Prager, Richard Reynolds, Everett M. Rogers, Thomas G. Sanders, Evan R. Spalt, and Nicholas Wright.

present purpose. In Section V we consider the use of various impact measures in somewhat more detail.

4. Specific Treatment Impact Versus Total-Attainment Outcome

On the input side, a distinction should be made between studies for ascertaining the impact of specific program innovations or treatments, considered herein, versus studies that seek to reveal the cumulative outcome of a totality of efforts, in national or regional programs, to attain such a social goal as reducing the rate of population growth. The latter, broader assessments normally do not attempt to isolate the contribution of specific program treatments, but nevertheless can, of course, be of great value in assessing the stage of progress that, due to whatever sources of influence, has been achieved over a period of time. They thus identify, as a basis for planning new program efforts, the magnitude of the future change that still is to be sought in order to attain desired goals.[1] For this broader purpose the stage of progress attained at a given date can usefully be gauged from data on changes in fertility and fertility-related behavior (contraception, abortion, etc.) over a period of years, even though the specific impacts of various contributing programmatic factors may be difficult or impossible to identify.

---

[1] See, for example, Rogers (1973), Lapham & Mauldin (1972), and Nortman (1972).

5. Methodology for Ascertaining the Impact of Specific
Program Innovations

As indicated above, the present review is concerned
primarily with features of field study design and procedure
that influence the validity and efficiency of data from
which the amount of program treatment impact can be ascertained. We take it as axiomatic that, other things equal,
the most secure basis for this determination derives from
controlled field studies in which comparisons among differently treated or nontreated population groups are such as to
eliminate bias in the assignment of treatment conditions to
the individuals or population units concerned, through
proper use of randomization and associated procedures.[1] The
result to be achieved by such procedures is that one can
identify clearly the changes that actually result from the
particular program innovations or treatments being studied,
so that these impacts are not confused with other changes
that would have occurred even if a given treatment had not
been introduced.

---

[1]Additional basis for this presumption is afforded both by
the empirical evidence supporting the argument presented by
Gilbert, Light, and Mosteller in Chapter 2, and by the
analysis given by Campbell and Boruch in Chapter 3.

II. FIELD STUDIES OF FERTILITY PROGRAM IMPACTS

A. *THE NATURE OF THIS SURVEY*

1. Scope and Purpose

For the present analysis, about 40 studies were selected, out of a larger group of reports initially identified, that seemed of particular interest in relation to attempts to gauge the outcomes of fertility planning program innovations in Asian and other developing countries. These studies are examined here primarily with respect to methodological aspects of their design and procedure. That is, our concern is primarily with how well the evidence obtained supports the causal attribution of measured outcomes to the impact of the treatment or innovation studied. For the present purpose, we are less concerned with evaluating whether the outcomes themselves were qualitatively or quantitatively satisfactory. This purpose of evaluating the quality of evidence thus contrasts with the further concern of Gilbert, Light, and Mosteller (Chapter 2, this volume) in also evaluating the success of the innovations.

2. Studies Reviewed

Table 1 lists the programs for which evaluation reports were reviewed in relation to the outcomes associated with the programs, indicates the source or sources of these reports, and identifies the broad category of research design employed.

The abbreviation "EXPT." in the right-hand column of Table 1 denotes what we have classed as true experiments, employing randomized or otherwise unbiased ("pararandom") assignment of treatments. The "quasi" designations include various forms of stronger ("QUASI") or weaker ("Quasi") quasi-experimental designs, involving nonequivalent control groups and/or supporting time series data. "Corr." means studies of essentially correlational design. These (regardless of whether relationships are presented in terms of correlation coefficients or by displaying concomitant variation in other ways) rely on comparison of groups identified as having different histories of treatments received, but where treatment differences were identified after the fact rather than being assigned for purposes of the study. The treatment differences thus are confounded, to varying and generally unknown degrees, with other causal factors. In some borderline cases, as will be seen, it is a toss-up whether to classify a study as correlational or quasi-experimental. "Post hoc" means case studies that present posttreatment data with no direct basis for comparison with pretreatment status or with nontreated groups.

The collection of reports reviewed is not an exhaustive one. The paper has the more limited purpose of reviewing a fairly broad selection of available studies which suffice to indicate the range of studies conducted and to illustrate important distinctions in the methodologies employed. We suspect, however, that the coverage is sufficiently comprehensive to give a rough indication of the prevalence of various kinds of impact studies that have been conducted in the population-program area. The studies reviewed are not all equally important, and information available on some of them was much more complete than on others.

Table 1. Studies Reviewed, with Reference Sources.

Locale and Nature of Program	Reports (see Bibliography)	Study Type*
1. Taiwan Studies		
T-1 Taichung Home Visits or Mail	Takeshita, 1969; Freedman & Takeshita, 1969	EXPT.
T-2 Free IUD Offer	Chen & Chow, 1973	EXPT.
T-3 Group Meetings	Lu, Chen, & Chow, 1967	EXPT.
T-4 Agent Incentives	Chang, Cernada, & Sun, 1972	EXPT.
T-5 Kaoshiung City Campaign	Cernada & Lu, 1972	Quasi.
T-6 IUD Demographic Impact	Chang, Liu, & Chow, 1970; Chow, Chang, & Liu, 1969	Corr.
T-7 Post-partum Mailing	Cernada, Chow, & Lee, 1970	Post hoc
T-8 Area Fertility Analysis	Hermalin, 1968	Corr.
T-9 Evaluation of Field-worker Types	Schultz, 1972	Corr.
2. Korea Studies		
K-1 Sung Dong Gu Mail-Meetings-Visits	Park, 1968; Lee & Kim, 1972; Takeshita, 1969; Kwon et al., 1970	QUASI.
K-2 Mothers' Clubs	Yang, 1972	EXPT.
K-3 Mothers' Clubs Intensity	Yang, 1972	EXPT.
K-4 IUD Check-ups	Bang, 1970b	EXPT.
K-5 Koyang Traditional Methods Education	Bang, 1966; Bang, 1970a	Quasi.
K-6 Koyang IUD Services	Bang, 1968	Quasi.
K-7 S/K Marketing Survey	S/K Marketing Research Co., 1972	Corr.
K-8 Korea Postcard Mailing	Finnigan & Koo, 1970	Post hoc
3. East Central or Southeast Asia Studies		
E-1 Chulalongkorn Diffusion Study (Thailand)	Fawcett, Somboonsuk, & Khaisang, 1967; Fawcett & Somboonsuk, 1969	Post hoc
E-2 Pho-tharam Family Planning Program	Peng, 1965	Quasi.
E-3 Thailand Auxiliary Midwife Experiment	Rosenfield, 1972; Rosenfield & Limcharoen, 1972	EXPT.
E-4 Singapore Family Planning Communication	Kanagaratnam, 1968	Post hoc
E-5 Malaysia Population Education Study	Khoon, 1972	**

Locale and Nature of Program	Reports (see Bibliography)	Study Type*
E-6 Indonesia Education Study	Kline, 1972	Quasi.
E-7 Hong Kong Field-worker Visit Types	Mitchell, 1968	EXPT.
E-8 Hong Kong Reassurance	Chan, 1971	EXPT.
4. South Asia Studies		
S-1 Singur Field Agent Contacts	Mathen, 1962; Population Council, 1963b	QUASI.
S-2 Meerut Communications	Raina, Blake, & Weiss, 1967; Raina et al., 1967a,b	Quasi.
S-3 Hooghly Publicity	Balakrishnan & Matthai, 1967	Quasi.
S-4 South Delhi Media/Visits	Indian Institute of Mass Communication, 1967	Post hoc
S-5 Dacca Spouse(s) Education	Green, Gustafson, Griffiths & Yaukey, 1972	QUASI.
S-6 Hyderabad (Pakistan) Radio	Karlin & Ali, 1968	Post hoc
S-7 Lahore (Pakistan) Family Planning	Fayyaz, 1971	Quasi.
S-8 Khanna Family Planning	Population Council, 1963a; Wyon & Gordon, 1971	QUASI.
S-9 Isfahan (Iran) Mass Media Campaign	Liberman, Gillespie, & Loghmani, 1973	QUASI.
5. Latin America Studies		
L-1 PATER Media Campaign	San Salvador Demographic Association, 1970	Corr.
L-2 El Salvador Family Planning	Londoño, 1973	QUASI.
L-3 Honduras Barrios Mass Media	Stycos & Marden, 1970; Stycos & Marden, 1973	QUASI.
L-4 Puerto Rico Message Content and Milieu	Hill, Stycos, & Back, 1959; Stycos, 1962	EXPT.
L-5 Dominican Radio	Marino, 1973	QUASI.
L-6 Bogotá Pilot Study (Mail/Visits)	Simmons, 1973	EXPT.
L-7 Colombia Radio	Simmons, 1973	QUASI.

*See text.

**This experimental study was not completed at the time of Khoon's report.

3. Locales

About two-fifths of the 40 studies were conducted in Taiwan and Korea. These are designated by codes T-1 through T-9, for Taiwan, and K-1, K-2, etc. for Korean studies. Another one-fifth, coded E-1, etc. in Table 1, were conducted in other East Asian or Southeast Asian countries, including Thailand, Malaysia, Singapore, Indonesia, and Hong Kong. Studies in South Asia (coded S-1, etc.) included studies done in India and Pakistan; these accounted for another one-fifth of the studies. Studies in Latin American countries (L-1, L-2, etc.) made up the remainder.

References to the published reports on the studies are listed by author or source in the references at the end of the chapter. For brevity, studies are generally referred to herein by the reference codes (T-1, T-2, K-1, etc.) used in Table 1, in lieu of citing the published reports by author and date.

4. Types of Programs and Media Used

About half of the studies were concerned with programs primarily dependent on some form of communication by mass media, interpersonal or other informal contact, or both.[1] In

---

[1] Five of the programs studied employed radio (and, in one case, television) as the primary means of communication (S-6, L-1, L-3, L-5, and L-7); two others relied primarily on mailing of printed matter as a vehicle of communication (T-7, K-8); and four employed combinations of media, such as

many of the programs, family planning services were involved, either as such or in combination with the communication efforts. The informational and other elements in the latter type of program were often confounded, so that only the joint effect of services and communication could be assessed, rather than isolating the individual contribution of the various components. However, at least four studies attempted to make a clear determination of relative effectiveness for different media or channels of communication, rather than only for a combination of channels (T-1, K-1, L-4, L-6).

B. *RANDOMIZATION IN SAMPLE SELECTION AND EXPERIMENTAL ASSIGNMENT*

As widely recognized in the field of sampling and experimental design, randomization in some form is clearly the method of choice for eliminating potential sources of bias, both in surveys and in experimental studies. (See discussion by Gilbert, Light, and Mosteller in Chapter 2, this volume.) Randomization can insure that each unit in the population has an equal chance of appearing in the sample (or of being assigned to one treatment or condition rather than to an alternative condition in an experiment). The units sampled or assigned may either be individuals, or may

_____

the combination of radio and pamphlets (T-5, S-2, S-3, S-9). About 20 programs used individual contact or group meetings as the major communication channel (e.g., T-3, T-4, K-2, S-1, S-5, E-2).

be larger population groups such as neighborhoods, towns, schools, classrooms, etc.

Two quite different functions of randomization in field experiments should be more clearly distinguished. The difference between these is often glossed over by lumping both functions under the term "random sampling," even though only one, or both, or neither actually may be employed in a given study. The first function is that of random selection (of individuals or units) for inclusion in the study. Its purpose is to provide samples that are representative of specified populations. This is particularly important in surveys, to provide a cross-section (or estimate based on a sample) that is representative of the total population.

The second function, particularly stressed by Gilbert, Light, and Mosteller in discussing controlled field trials, is that of random assignment of population units to treatments, such that the treatment groups are strictly comparable to each other--that is, equivalent except for chance fluctuations. It is this equivalence that is the distinguishing characteristic of "true" experiments, in insuring that posttreatment differences in the observed behavior of the population groups studied can be validly attributed to differences in treatment--rather than being confoundable with preexisting or other irrelevant differences in the population samples that were identified with the various treatments, as in quasi experiments or in correlational studies.

In surveys, where experimental treatment is not involved, the sample selection aspect is especially important to insure the "external validity" or generalizability of the

findings. In experiments, on the other hand, though representative sampling is likewise highly desirable, it is random assignment which is most crucial to satisfy the minimum
essential requirement of "internal" validity.[1] Such assignment to treatments is unique in its ruling out unidentified
as well as known sources of bias in experimental treatments.

In some of the field studies we examined, the groups
selected as a total sample for study were selected so as to
be fairly representative of the general population, but
assignment of the experimental treatments unfortunately was
not made on a randomized basis. Some examples are the
Kaoshiung campaign (T-5), the Sung Dong Gu study (K-1), the
Koyang traditional methods study (K-5), the Hooghly campaign
(S-3), the Lahore project (S-7), the Isfahan campaign (S-9),
the Colombia radio campaign (L-7), and the Honduras Barrios
campaign (L-3). In some other studies, the reverse was
true: groups from a limited geographic area were randomly
assigned to treatments, insuring an unbiased comparison
("internal validity"), but there was no formal basis for
assessing the generalizability of the demonstrated impacts
to other regions.

In the next section we first identify and illustrate
some salient features of the simpler experiments we reviewed
in the experimental category (labeled "EXPT." in Table 1)

---

[1]Cf. Campbell's and Stanley's (1966) widely cited discussion
of "internal" and "external" validity and of factors influencing these attributes in experiments and quasi-experimental studies.

and in the stronger quasi-experimental categories (labeled "QUASI" in Table 1). We also look at an example or two of each of these kinds of studies in slightly more detail, and then look more briefly at some of the weaker quasi-experimental, correlational, and one-shot post hoc studies that have been reported in relation to inquiry into program impacts.

III. IMPORTANT ASPECTS OF VARIOUS CLASSES OF STUDY DESIGN EXEMPLIFIED

A. *MAJOR TYPES OF DESIGN EMPLOYED*[1]

Twelve of the forty studies reviewed approximate the requirements of true field experiments, with treatments assigned randomly or by pararandom procedures that provide for unbiased comparisons between treatment groups. These are grouped by region as "Class I" designs in the top rows of Table 2. Though the precision and validity of some of these studies were flawed to varying degrees by faults of execution and analysis of data, the basic pattern in most cases is that which would provide a valid basis for ascertaining the effects of a particular program on various indices of outcome, or the comparative effectiveness of two or more alternative programs.

---

[1] We employ here a variant of the Campbell and Stanley (1966) classification.

Another nine of the studies (which comprise Classes II-A and II-B in Table 2) represent the somewhat stronger forms of quasi-experiments; three studies (Class III) are somewhat less satisfactory quasi-experimental types. The former use time series data (II-A) and/or fairly well-matched comparison groups (II-B) as evidence to support their conclusions about effects attributed to programs (as distinguished from other, nonprogram influences which could operate to change the observed behavior of recipients of the program); the latter (Class III) use only rather poorly matched comparison groups.

Yet another dozen or so of the studies employ designs which also generally yield the more ambiguous kind of results. About half of these studies (Class IV) employ a single group with before-and-after data, but with no control or comparison group to rule out or estimate the effect of concurrent nonprogram influences which could also be responsible for any changes detected. Others (Class V) are correlational studies which compare post hoc differences among groups that for various reasons had experienced differing amounts of program involvement. The remaining studies (Class VI) are post hoc surveys indicating the current status of desired outcomes with no explicit basis for differentiating specific program impacts from prior influences, because of the lack of preprogram measures.

Table 2. Kinds of Fertility Programs Studied, by Locale and Design Type.

				Locale and Nature of Program		
		Northeast Asia:				
Design Type	Taiwan (T)	Korea (K)	East Central or Southeast Asia (E)	South Asia: India-Pakistan-Iran (S)	Latin America (L)
I. TRUE EXPERIMENTS A. Employing random-ization of units or persons, etc.	T-1 Taichung: home visits or mail T-3 Group meetings T-4 Agent incentives	K-2 Mothers' clubs K-3 Mothers' clubs intensity K-4 IUD checkups	E-3 Thailand nurse-midwife E-7 Hong Kong visit types E-8 Hong Kong reassurance		L-4 Puerto Rico message content and milieu L-6 Bogotá mail or visits
B. Treatment rotation (plus time series)	T-2 Free IUD offer				
II. STRONGER QUASI-EXPERIMENTS A. With nonequivalent comparison groups but also with time-series data				S-9 Isfahan (Iran) mass media	L-2 El Salvador family planning services L-3 Honduras barrios mass media L-5 Dominican radio L-7 Columbian radio
B. Pre-post differ-ences with matched comparison groups		K-1 Sung Dong Gu con-tacts—by mail, meetings, visits		S-1 Singur field agent contacts S-5 Dacca spouse (hus-band and/or wife) education S-8 Khanna family planning	
III. OTHER QUASI-EXPERIMENTS (with poorly matched compari-son groups)	T-5 Kaoshiung City family planning services	K-5 Koyang tradi-tional methods education K-6 Koyang IUD services			

IV. SINGLE GROUP PRE-POST		E-2 Pho-tharam (Thai) family planning E-6 Indonesia education study	S-2 Meerut communications S-3 Hooghly publicity S-7 Lahore family planning (Pakistan)	
V. CORRELATIONAL ANALYSES	T-6 IUD demographic impact T-8 Area fertility analysis T-9 Evaluation of field worker types	K-7 S/K marketing survey		(L-2) See above (L-5) See above L-1 PATER media campaign
VI. POST HOC ONLY ("case studies")	T-7 Postpartum mailing	K-8 Postcard mailing	E-1 Chulalongkorn diffusion study (Thailand) E-4 Singapore family planning	S-4 S. Delhi media and visits S-6 Hyderabad (Pakistan) radio

B. *PATTERNS OF COMPARISON IN POPULATION PROGRAM IMPACT STUDIES*

Experiments (or quasi-experiments) generally permit three types of comparisons:

- Type CX: Single treatment, with nontreatment control group, thus showing the "absolute" effect of that one treatment.

- Type XY: Two or more treatments, no nontreatment control group; this shows the difference in effect between the two, but not the "absolute" effect of either.[1]

---

[1]It might be noted why experiments (or quasi-experiments) of the XY type, which compare two or more treatments (say, treatment X and treatment Y), but lack a nontreatment control group, have the shortcoming that we cannot ascertain the absolute effects of either treatment X or treatment Y, but only their comparative merits. If we determine that X is better than Y, we still do not know the absolute effects of either treatment. For example, it is possible that: 1) X had no effect and Y had a negative effect on behavior that perhaps was changing anyway; 2) Y had no effect and X had some positive effect, perhaps in addition to ongoing change; or 3) Y had some positive effect, but X had a greater positive effect. Program decisions to be made obviously may vary considerably, depending on which of the above situations is the actual case.

- Type <u>CXY</u>: Two or more treatments <u>with</u> a nontreatment control group. This can show the absolute effects of each treatment <u>and</u> the difference between their effects.

The three patterns of comparison distinguished above are of particular relevance in experimental comparisons where treatments are randomly assigned (either by individuals or by units), but may apply also in quasi-experimental comparisons that attempt to identify the impact of a given program or the comparative effects of alternative programs.

We will look first at the three examples of the simpler forms of true experiments which exemplify these three patterns.[1]

C. THREE ILLUSTRATIVE "TRUE EXPERIMENTS"

Only a rather small number of studies (about a dozen in all) making one of the three types of comparisons just distinguished, in gauging the effects of population programs, meet all the conditions of a true field experiment (including use of appropriate randomization and associated procedures). Certain characteristics of the 12 such experiments we have reviewed are further considered in Section IV. Three of the simpler studies will be described here to illustrate some of the basic features common to this class of

---

[1] Further consideration of these patterns, including their incorporation in somewhat more complex experimental designs, is given in Section IV.

studies. We have selected one experiment of each comparison type (CX, XY, and CXY) for this purpose. The first experiment, of type CXY, assigned individual women to one of the treatments or to control. The other two experiments (one of type CX and one of type XY) randomly assigned entire counties or townships to the experimental conditions (see further discussion of such assignment, and its implications for data analysis, in Section IV).

1. **Hong Kong Field Worker Visit Types** (Mitchell, 1968 [E-7])

For this type CXY comparison, a target population of about 1400 potential subjects was located by a preliminary census that identified married women under 50 years old, not pregnant, living with husbands, and not practicing family planning. The target population was then randomly divided into three groups: the first one was to be visited by the traditional field worker, the second to be visited by the new "comprehensive" case worker, and the third group to be a control. The first two groups were visited over a period of two months. To avoid potential biases, standard experimental procedures were used.

The study used a new clinic to test the effectiveness of the two field worker approaches and to outline the process women go through in deciding whether or not to visit a family planning clinic. Five new workers were each used to test the traditional approach, with a brief home visit to provide family planning information and to encourage visits to the clinic. This was compared to a new, comprehensive case worker approach, with a longer home visit in which family planning was discussed in the larger context of the family's socioeconomic situation.

Of the women visiting the clinics during the period of the study, 8.6% had been visited by the comprehensive case worker as compared to 3.8% visited by the traditional worker and 1% of the control. However, the comprehensive case worker approach required six hours of work to recruit a woman while the traditional worker took less than four hours.

Of the women in the treatment group who visited the clinic, about half indicated that the field worker caused them to decide to attend the clinic. Husbands were reported to have the greatest influence on the decision of 11% of the women to go to the clinic. Of those women rated most likely to go to the clinic by the field workers but who did not go, 40% said they had expected the field workers to come for a second visit.

2. <u>Taiwan Field Agent Incentives</u> (Chang, Cernada, & Sun, 1972 [T-4])

In this 1971 type CX study of the Taiwan Committee on Family Planning, treatments were assigned by counties to avoid undesirable interaction between treatment and control groups, rather than by individuals, as in the preceding example. Ten counties were randomly assigned to the treatment and ten to control. Assignment by township had been considered, but was rejected due to increased chance of field workers from nonexperimental townships finding out about the incentives; they might have become unhappy and produced a "negative" program instead of a true control (see further discussion of unit sampling in Section IV).

343

Family planning field agents were offered, in addition to base salary, $2.50 for each IUD loop acceptor and $0.50 for each acceptor of pills (three cycles) or condoms (one dozen). Outcome measures used were acceptance rates for loop, pills, and condoms. Results showed that acceptance rates for all methods combined were, in the incentive counties, approximately two times the rates in the nonincentive counties (20.7% of eligible women versus 10.7%). For the loop, the acceptance rates for incentive and nonincentive counties, respectively, were 9.0% versus 2.9%, and for the pill they were 6.5% versus 3.8%; the rates for the condom were about the same in the incentive and control groups.

Because of the county sampling plan used, the sample of women visited was reported to be representative of all of Taiwan. Thus, it was concluded that a change in the island-wide program to provide an immediate monetary incentive to a full-time family planning worker could produce demonstrably improved results.

3. Taiwan Group Meetings (Lu, Chen, & Chow, 1967 [T-3])

Assignment to treatments by population units (villages, in this case) was also employed in this 1964 study of type XY, conducted under the Taiwan Provincial Health Department and Population Studies Center. Thirty-seven villages in two townships in central Taiwan were randomly assigned to one of two treatments. There were no nontreatment control villages. One treatment employed small-group meetings which were conducted by public health nurses in every neighborhood in a random sample of one-half of the villages. In the other half of the villages, meetings were held in _every other_ neighborhood.

Before the meetings were held, a random sample of 794 married women was interviewed by trained public health nurses. (To avoid bias, interviewers were instructed not to teach people anything about family planning and to invite all questioners to the small-group meetings.) Meetings emphasized three main points: the general idea of family planning, specific contraceptive methods, and reproductive physiology. Altogether there were about 3000 attendees, at some 300 meetings. About six months after the meetings, a postmeeting interview survey was conducted with the originally interviewed sample. Of the original 794 women, 758 were interviewed in the postmeeting survey. Analysis was based on the women who completed both interviews.

Holding meetings in every neighborhood produced only 12% more acceptances than holding meetings in every other neighborhood. At the same time, holding meetings in every neighborhood increased costs by 70%.

D. _QUASI-EXPERIMENTS VARYING IN STRENGTH AS TO EVIDENCE OF IMPACT_

When true experiments (with random experimental assignment in order to provide an unbiased control on extraneous nonprogram effects) are deemed not feasible, attempts to ascertain program effects must rely on some combination of other attempted control measures.

There are two principal substitute techniques resorted to in the quasi-experiments that we have examined in connection with this chapter. These techniques, used either alone or in combination, are the use of nonequivalent, more or less matched comparison groups in lieu of an equivalent, randomly assigned control group (Class II-B in Table 2); and the use of time series data to provide control information as to trends that existed before the experimental program was undertaken (Class II-A in Table 2).

In Class II-B are four studies, which did not include time series data, and which appeared to have had relatively well-matched comparison groups (Dacca [S-5], Khanna [S-8], Singur [S-1]--see below, and Sung Dong Gu [K-1]).

1. Value of Time Series Data

In the absence of an equivalent control group, time series data are obviously of considerable importance in interpreting changes in criterion indices that take place after the initiation of the experimental program treatment. For example, if there is already a strong declining trend in fertility in the experimental group, further decline after the experimental treatment begins is to be anticipated, even if the experimental treatment is itself completely ineffective, due to the continued operation of whatever factors were causing the decline before the program began. If time series data are provided, inferences can be drawn about differential changes in data trends as opposed to differential end results. Data from the Singur study (S-1) seem to indicate a dramatic decline in fertility in the experimental area as compared to the control area, with the two areas having identical fertility rates at the beginning of the program. Although it is rather unlikely, it is possible that the experimental area had a much higher fertility rate than the control area several years prior to the beginning of the program; also, the experimental area may have been compensating in some way to produce a greater rate of decrease.

Among the studies considered, there are several examples in which the provision of time series data does strengthen the conclusions that might be drawn from a design even weaker than the Singur design. Studies which used "suspect" comparison groups and which are strengthened by the provision of time series data (Class II-A in Table 2) include the Isfahan project's (S-9) comparison of Isfahan Province and Mazanderan Province; the Honduras Barrios (L-3) comparison of San Felipe Hospital and Las Crucitas Health Center; and the Dominican Republic radio campaign's (L-5) comparison of San José de Ocoa and Montecristi. The Kaoshiung Campaign (T-5), the Koyang traditional methods study (K-5), and the Koyang IUD extension project (K-6), each of which also had inadequate comparison groups, did not have, but would have been considerably strengthened by, the analysis of time series data.

Time series data are also useful when an experimental group serves as its own "control"; i.e., in cases where a treatment is provided, then removed, and then possibly reinstated. The fluctuations in outcome which accompany these changes provide an indication of program impact. This is later illustrated (Section IV-B) in the carefully designed Taiwan free offer study (T-2) which, however, also had a set of counterbalancing control groups.

In a Seoul agent system (Kwon, 1971), a natural quasi-experiment of this type occurred when, in July 1967, the number of agents was reduced from 21 to 7 per district.

Because the agents had been so successful in the early months of the program, funds to pay their fees were running low. The total number of acceptors dropped sharply, from 1,838 in June to 715 in July, 829 in August, and 854 in September. The mean number of acceptors per agent was reduced from 17.0 to 15.9 to 13.0 to 12.4 over the same period. When the agents were rehired in September, the fee was reduced from 50 won to 30 won. Although this resulted in an increase in total acceptors, the mean number of acceptors per agent remained fairly stable.[1]

On a larger scale, monthly acceptor data from the Singapore family planning program (E-4) has been plotted for 1966 and 1967 in order to investigate what aspects of the family planning program system may actually be responsible for changes in program impact that have been detected. Based on the number of acceptors prior to 1966, the data indicate that the family planning program itself was related to a substantial increase in acceptors during the first

---

[1]In some Chicago fertility control studies (Bogue, 1966), the West Side Planned Parenthood Clinic showed a sudden dramatic increase in monthly new patients during the mailing campaign in that area (more than double any previous month, with 195 new patients in June); there was a sudden drop to previous levels thereafter. Most of the established drug stores in the West Side area reported an unexpected increase in contraceptive sales, with the number of prescriptions for oral contraceptives increasing by 50% to 100% in several stores within a period of three months.

three months of 1967. This trend was strikingly reversed in March, when side effects from the new IUD led to negative rumors in the community.

Using time order as a criterion, it is suggested that deemphasizing the IUD program in favor of pills in Singapore led to another dramatic increase, or at least to a return to the rate of increase that existed before the onset of rumors. Conversely, it appears as if the initiation of the educational campaign actually depressed this new trend. The author's graph (Kanagaratnam, 1968) may be misleading in this respect, however. Although the educational campaign appears to have occurred after the increase in September, it may have been initiated early in September and, therefore, during that September increase in acceptors. The same problem of interpretation occurs at the peak associated with the increase in midwife follow-up. More precise knowledge of the timing of events is required to assess the time order of these temporal relationships.

The even more detailed information that would be needed to establish the relative effects of various specific program activities is unavailable. This evaluation was conducted after the fact and no systematic preprogram plans were made to provide answers to this type of question. This report does show the value of keeping accurate records of program activities so as to have available time series data on changes in the target population.

Time series data can strengthen inferences drawn from even properly (randomly) assigned control and experimental groups. If the two groups prior to the initiation of the experiment show, as they should, closely parallel trend lines and then if there is a marked departure in the trend of the data starting with the beginning of--or shortly after--the implementation of the experimental treatment for the experimental group and not for the control group, the evidence on impact of the program is indeed strong.

The following example of a quasi-experiment further illustrates some of the points we have noted. Abstracts of other studies mentioned above are contained in Hilton's technical memorandum (1973).

2. Colombia Radio Campaign: An Informative Example (L-7)

The first mass campaign to bring new patients into the PROFAMILIA clinics began in February 1969 and continued through November 1969. At the peak of the campaign, 33 radio stations were broadcasting 20 half-minute announcements daily. Announcements were designed to appeal to women to plan their families, to think of and know how many children they could support, and to tell them that PROFAMILIA could help them to do this.

To analyze the influence of radio programming on clinic attendance it was felt necessary to use older, established clinics where a trend line for attendance had already been established. Centro Piloto and Hospital San José, two of the longest-established clinics in Bogotá, were used. Both clinics had reached their peak attendance several years ago and had had rather constant negative growth rates since. Centro Piloto was identified in the radio announcements while Hospital San José was not. During and after the campaign, San José continued its downward trend while Centro Piloto reversed its trend and the number of new patients rose through October. At its peak, the number of new patients was four times what it would have been according to the precampaign trend. The number of new patients declined a little at Centro Piloto in November and December but still remained above the level prior to the campaign.

Two clinics in Baranquilla followed the same procedure as those in Bogotá. Atlántico was announced over the radio while Bautista was not. Before the campaign, both clinics were showing positive growth trends. During the campaign, Atlántico's gain in new patients rose substantially (371 more than expected) while Bautista continued on its trend line. Even after the campaign, Atlántico's growth in new patients remained above the precampaign trend.

In the city of Medellín, there was only one clinic, but it also surpassed its expected performance by 1,276 patients, based on previously established trends. In the smaller cities with relatively new clinics, the campaign appears, at best, to have postponed the transition from positive to negative growth rates which otherwise might have been expected after an initial peak.

The trend lines for these clinics deserve some additional discussion. They were computed in order to rule out each of two alternative explanations for the rise in new acceptors soon after the campaign began and for the decline soon after it ended. It is possible that the rise and decline was due to 1) extraneous influences, such as shifts in public opinion unrelated to the campaign; and/or 2) seasonal variation. (The natural monthly trend of rise and decline corresponds closely to the onset and cessation of the campaign.)

The six-month data base was apparently selected to avoid including data from the earlier peak attendance period, occurring shortly after the opening of the clinics a few years prior to the campaign. The investigators note, however, that the trend lines for this six-month period are scarcely different from those of a period beginning a year or more prior to the campaign. Unfortunately, the reviewers have no way of ascertaining the statistical strength of the trend, since the actual month-by-month data are not presented. There is some corroboration for the smoothness of the trend if we consider quarterly data for Centro Piloto Hospital (see Figure 1). This is, however, another instance in which better reporting of detailed data would be desirable.

In spite of this point, the question, "What would have happened without the treatment?" appears to be fairly well answered indirectly through comparison--first, with previous time periods for the same clinic by use of its trend line, and second, with data from a similar clinic not specifically mentioned over the radio. Replicative evidence from more than one city increases our confidence that the radio campaign was reponsible for the observed outcome.

E. WEAKER QUASI-EXPERIMENTAL DESIGNS

One of the more frequently used quasi-experimental designs in the evaluation of family planning campaigns is the One-Group Pretest-Posttest design (Class IV in Table 2). Pretest observations are recorded on a single group of persons who later receive a treatment, after which posttest

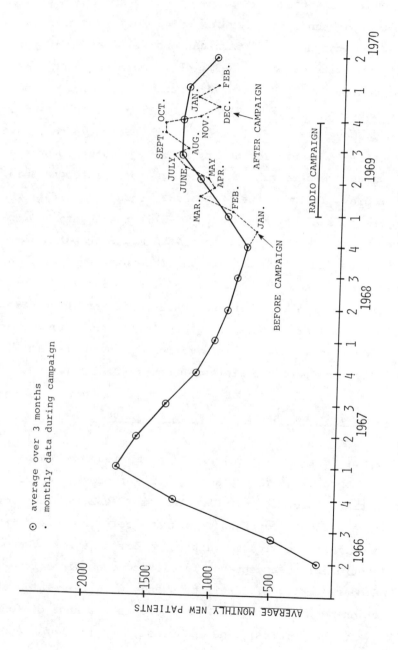

Fig. 1. *Colombia radio study time series data.*

observations are made. A weakness of this design is illustrated by considering examples of program evaluation in which it has been used. Studies which fall into this category include the Meerut Communications Program (S-2), the Hooghly Publicity Campaign (S-3), the Lahore Project (S-7), the Pho-tharam Family Planning Program (E-2), and the Indonesia education program (E-6). In addition, several studies mentioned above almost fall into this category; they have been considered previously due to special features or results which tend to make the findings more interpretable. These studies include the Kaoshiung campaign (T-5); the Koyang traditional methods study (K-5); the Koyang IUD extension project (K-6); the Isfahan mass media campaign (S-9) and its subsidiary, Functionary and Intensive Projects; the Honduras Barrios campaign (L-3); and the Dominican Republic radio campaign (L-5). In these cases, if one determines that the control or comparison group is so noncomparable as to provide little usable information, then the design is essentially the One-Group Pretest-Posttest design.

1. Fallacies to Which These Studies Are Liable

The typical case involves a communication campaign designed to promote family planning and/or provide specific contraceptive information, directed to a single group of people in a defined, contiguous geographical area, with the expectation that knowledge, attitudes or behavior of some sort (contraceptive acceptance rates, continuation rates, sales of contraceptives, fertility change, etc.) related to family planning will change. When there is a change of some sort between the pretest and posttest, researchers and, particularly, program personnel usually attribute responsibility for the change to the communication program.

However, other possible explanations cannot be refuted on the basis of this study design. For example, the change might alternatively be due to other events occurring between the pretest and the posttest that affected family planning knowledge, attitudes, or behavior. Some of these could have occurred within an overall family planning or fertility control program (e.g., additional clinics might have been opened; government policy on one or more contraceptive methods might have been changed; a shift of opinion might have occurred among religious leaders). Other events could have taken place outside a family planning program and also affected family planning behavior (e.g., changes in tax structures might have increased the saliency of family limitation; an unseasonably warm period might have encouraged more women to walk the necessary distance to the clinic; a new factory might have provided opportunities for housewives to be employed, thus increasing their desire to avoid bearing additional children). Any of these events, or others, could have affected fertility behavior, and it is incumbent upon the researcher to demonstrate that they did not operate or are not plausible. Otherwise, no confident conclusion can be drawn about cause.

2. Need for Caution in Interpreting "Findings"

Unfortunately, there are several instances in which there is a large disparity between the actual strength of the evidence and the conclusions drawn by the investigators from quasi-experimental studies such as these. For example, the Meerut investigators   (S-2) concluded that "a relatively modest   amount   spent for   publicity   purposes   can have   a sizable   effect   on   public knowledge about family   planning . . .   even   a   small, carefully planned programme will   pay enormous dividends   in increased public awareness" (emphasis added).

On inspection of the reported data,   we   find that this "sizable" effect consists of an increase from about   10%   to 20%   of   those who were "partially informed" and an increase from about   2%   to   7%   of those who were "poorly informed." (There was no increase   in   the percentage of those who were "highly informed.")   Many   would   disagree that the program effects are in fact "enormous."

F.   *CORRELATIONAL ANALYSIS OF IMPACT ON FERTILITY INDICES*

Most   studies using experimental and quasi-experimental designs tend   to   measure   program   impact in terms of rela- tively short-term indices, such as clinic attendance, condom purchases, IUD insertions, and in some cases, continued con- traceptive practice.   This situation results from the diffi- culty of   maintaining   control   over   the   experience of the various treatment and nontreatment   groups for a period suf- ficiently long to obtain useful measures of fertility.   Most of the research which has attempted to directly measure pro- gram effect   on fertility has therefore made use of correla- tional   designs (see Class V   in   Table 2).   In   these,   in essence,   post   hoc data from acceptors   or   high-acceptance groups   are   compared   with   those for nonacceptors or   low- acceptance groups. In interpreting   the   conclusions   that investigators have drawn from   such   studies,   it   should be borne in mind that their liability to being vitiated by selection biases is only partly offset by the analytic procedures that have been employed.

1. Matched-Area Comparison

The area analysis of fertility in Taiwan (T-8) used path analysis to determine the degree of influence of program variables on 1965 fertility when socioeconomic and demographic variables were "factored out." Data were collected from 78 urban areas and 204 rural areas on prior fertility of the area, IUD acceptance rates, numbers of health workers and doctors per capita, etc. The investigators concluded from the analysis that the early Taiwan program did have a negative effect on fertility even where socioeconomic factors were operating.

A second area-correlation analysis from Taiwan (T-9) compares the relative effect on fertility of varying allocations of two types of family planning field workers, holding environmental variables constant. Data were collected from 361 small administrative units of Taiwan on child mortality, schooling, agricultural composition of the male labor force, female educational attainment, the child death rate, and allocation of VHEN's (Village Health Education Nurses) and PPHW's (Prepregnancy Health Workers). The marginal effectiveness of each type of field worker is defined as the percentage reduction in age-specific birth rate associated with the employment of an additional (over the previous year) tenth of a person-month of field worker per thousand women of childbearing age. The results were interpreted to indicate that VHEN's are more effective in reducing the birth rate than are PPHW's.

A somewhat similar analysis is to be found in the 240-group matching system utilized in the Taiwan demographic study (T-6). This study appears to have provided a relatively good baseline of comparison in the absence of the program, and this is noteworthy in view of the difficulty of obtaining direct data on fertility in any other way.

The preceding three examples illustrate strong efforts to show program effect on fertility. However, it should be emphasized that the inferences made are not as strong as those which could be made from a well-controlled experimental design. For example, in the second study (T-9), it is not unlikely that a third factor, affecting fertility and allocation of health workers in a parallel manner, was indeed the cause of fertility decline. In general, of course, correlational studies can determine the degree of a relationship, but not necessarily its nature (i.e., that one event caused another).

2. Other Correlational Studies

Another interesting study of essentially correlational design is the El Salvador cost-analysis study (L-2). Although it was a post hoc comparison of users versus nonusers, this study employed carefully matched comparison groups and also made use of time series data. (The El Salvador study was also one of the relatively few in which explicit comparison was made in terms of cost in relation to program effectiveness.)

Among studies stressing informational impacts, the problems with drawing inferences from correlational data are also rather clearly illustrated by an example from the S/K marketing study (K-7) and the Honduras Barrios campaign (L-3). Both studies found that reported knowledge and practice of contraceptive methods was positively related to reported exposure to family planning mass communication.

Although it is possible to conclude that exposure to messages may have led to contraceptive use, the time-order could just as likely be reversed. Women already practicing family planning may be motivated to pay more attention to mass media messages about contraceptives, and they would probably remember them more easily. Other variables may also be responsible for the relationship observed. Better educated women are more likely to practice family planning, and they may be exposed to mass media more often and recall their content more readily. Statistical control of variables like education would be helpful with these data, but such analysis was not reported. Examples such as these should serve to point out the hazards of drawing causal conclusions from correlational data.

G. "PREEXPERIMENTAL" OR POST HOC STUDIES

One of the essentially uninterpretable research designs (at least with regard to assessment and attribution of effects) is the post hoc pseudoexperimental, or "preexperimental" (Campbell & Stanley, 1966) design, often called the "One-Group Posttest-Only Design." This design (Class VI in Table 2) is also sometimes called the "case study" (a term that has a rather confusing variety of meanings). Since observations are made only on the persons receiving the treatment with no measures on a control group of persons who did not receive the treatment, several potential threats to internal validity (ability to draw inferences) cannot be ruled out. Studies which fall into this category include the Taiwan postpartum mailing (T-7), the Korea postcard mailing (K-8), the South Delhi survey (S-4), the Hyderabad radio survey (S-6), the Chulalongkorn study (E-1), Singapore family planning (E-4), and the PATER campaign (L-1).

In most of these cases, the information collected is used, as it should be, only to suggest hypotheses to be subsequently tested by more rigorous methodology, or to collect process information (see Section I) relevant to future program planning (e.g., the number of people reached by certain radio stations, or the demographic characteristics of acceptors of the current programs). In some cases, however, overt or implied assessment of program effect is made. For example, the assumption that the program itself was responsible for subsequent acceptance is implicit in the cost-per-acceptor data for the Taiwan postpartum mailing (T-7). The Korean postcard mailing studies (K-8), on the other hand, were merely reported to indicate some difficulties with the process of mailing, making the recommendation that since the process could not be carried out, the program should be discontinued until such time as the mailing system could be improved. Had the process of mailing been carried out according to plan, however, the number of acceptors or some other measure would, because of the solely post hoc design, not necessarily indicate results attributable to such a program.

The Chulalongkorn Study (E-1) offers an interesting contrast, in that the pattern of word-of-mouth communication is described and, since no public information was given out about the service, it must be assumed that new acceptors (particularly those new patients living outside the immediate service area of Chulalongkorn Hospital) heard of the service by word-of-mouth (i.e., the effects can be rightly attributed to word-of-mouth communication). As a result of this information, a program was later carried out which attempted to stimulate and increase this word-of-mouth communication by giving each acceptor three "preferential treatment" cards for her friends or acquaintances (Fawcett & Somboonsuk, 1969).

It might be noted here that, in some rare cases, the changes from before the program to after the program are so dramatic or seem so unlikely a priori to have occurred in the absence of the program that one may be inclined to draw confident conclusions about causality even though the design is formally weak for this purpose. For example, in the Koyang traditional methods study (K-5), even if we do not consider the information from the comparison area of Kimpo, the results show that the percentages of women ever using contraceptives increased from 7.9% prior to the program to 49.6% after the program. It is very hard to believe that this dramatic increase of women who at least tried contraception was not due, at least in part, to program effect. In addition, it should be noted that in this case Kimpo, the comparison area, though not well matched with Koyang, does give us some valuable additional information to indicate the degree of program effect. Since in Kimpo the number of women who reported they ever used contraception increased from 11.7% to 28.5%, we would obviously not want to conclude that the total increase in the Koyang area was due to the program. (However, this is really a two-treatment, no-control comparison; Kimpo did have a "mild" national family-planning program.)

Some examples of situations in which, for reasons of logic, it is highly unlikely that a particular effect could have occurred without the program also occur with respect to knowledge of information presented in programs. For example, in the Honduras Barrios campaign (L-3), the percentage of women mentioning family planning as a service of Las Crucitas Health Center increased from 6% to 29%. Since this piece of information was a primary part of the campaign and since there were apparently no other efforts to bring this information to the attention of the people in the area, it seems quite likely that the knowledge gained resulted from the program.

To recapitulate by the main design types we have discussed, the reader may wish to review Table 2, which summarizes the studies falling in the main categories of design, ranging from randomized experiments to post hoc studies. In the following section, we examine more closely some special problems and features illustrated in the 12 "true" experimental studies.

IV. SPECIAL FEATURES OBSERVED IN FIELD EXPERIMENTS

A. MAIN FEATURES OF THE TWELVE "TRUE" EXPERIMENTS

As noted earlier, only a dozen of the impact studies reviewed met criteria which led us to claim them as true field experiments (including use of appropriate randomization and/or associated procedures). The 12 such experiments, including the three examples we have described in Section III-A, are listed in Table 3, along with brief notes on some of their primary characteristics.[1]

1. Patterns of Comparison

Two of the 11 controlled experiments on program effect listed in the table (T-3 and K-4) are examples of the XY type of comparison. The Taiwan group meeting experiment (T-3)—already described in Section III-A—compared the effects of having group meetings in <u>every</u> neighborhood with the effects of having group meetings in <u>every other</u> neighborhood in a given village. The Korea IUD check-up study (K-4) compared the effectiveness of asking acceptors to return in one week, two weeks, or one month, but did not compare these treatments to a treatment which did not ask the acceptors to return at all. (As noted in Section III, these and other experiments, or quasi-experiments, of type XY—which compare two or more treatments but lack a non-treatment control group—can show the <u>difference</u> in the impact of treatments X and Y but do not measure the absolute effects of either treatment.)

---

[1] Abstracts or summaries are presented by E. T. Hilton (1973) in a Battelle Technical Memorandum for all of these 12 field experiments, as well as for the quasi-experiments and other studies of program impact mentioned throughout this chapter.

Table 3. Summary of Twelve Experimental Field Trial Studies Employing
Unbiased Assignment to Treatment and/or Control Conditions
by Randomization or "Pararandom" Procedures.*

Characteristics of Study	Control & Treatment Combination
1. Individuals Assigned Randomly (or by Alternation, in E-8)	
E-7: Hong Kong Visit Types (Mitchell, 1968) Random assignment of individuals to one of two treatments (type of field worker visit) or control; cost effectiveness of treatments compared.	$C-X_1-X_2$
E-8: Hong Kong Reassurance (Chan, 1971) Unbiased assignment (by alternation) of individual IUD acceptors to treatment (reassurance visit by field worker) or control; clinic staff "blind" to treatment; cost-effectiveness considered.	$C-X$
L-6: Bogotá Pilot Study (Mail/Visits) (Simmons, 1973) Random assignment of individuals to control or to one of two treatments (mailing vs. home visits).	$C-X_1-X_2$
2. Ad Hoc Groups (Clinic Daily Contingents) Assigned Alternately	
K-4: IUD Checkups (Bang, 1970b) Unbiased group assignment (using rotation) of a given day's contingent of IUD acceptors at a Korean clinic to one of three treatments (how soon acceptor was to return for checkup); distribution of months of use among groups was roughly equal by the time final impact measures were taken; no control group.	$-X_1-X_2-X_3$
3. Random Unit Assignment (by Villages, Counties or Provinces)	
T-3: Group Meetings (Lu, Chen, & Chow, 1967) Random unit assignment of 37 Taiwan villages to either of two treatments--group meetings in every neighborhood of the village vs. in every other neighborhood; no control group.	$-X_1-X_2$
T-4: Agent Incentives (Chang, Cernada, & Sun, 1972) Random unit assignment of 10 Taiwan counties to treatment (incentive to field workers for each acceptor obtained) and 10 to control; assignment by township rejected to avoid contamination.	$C-X$
E-3: Thailand Nurse-Midwife (Rosenfield & Limcharoen, 1972). Random unit assignment of treatment (pills prescribed by auxiliary midwives) to 4 Thai provinces out of 17 provinces studied; other 13 provinces served as control.	$C-X$

*Studies are grouped on the basis of whether the treatment was assigned by
individual or by population unit, and are coded (right-hand column) to indicate
control/treatment(s) patterns--i.e., single or multiple treatment(s) $[X_1-X_2,$
etc.], and whether no-treatment control [C] was included.

Characteristics of Study	Control & Treatment Combination

4. Factorial Designs:

4a. Unit Assignment (of Villages or Townships) Randomly Within Demographic Strata

K-2: **Mothers' Clubs** (Yang, 1972)
Within two subgroups of Korean villages--higher than average or lower than average on IUD acceptance--random unit assignment of 31 villages to control and 27 to treatment (mothers' classes); the 27 "treatment" villages were assigned to one of two treatments (alternative types of educational presentation); whether the two treatments were randomly assigned could not be determined.

C-X
(randomly)
and X_1-X_2...

K-3: **Mothers' Clubs Intensity** (Yang, 1972)
Within three equal-sized subgroups of Korean townships--each group relatively homogeneous on several demographic and program indices--random unit assignment of townships to one of two treatments (differing in amount of financial support given for mothers' club) or to control; interpretation of results clouded by contamination of control groups, and by incomplete application of treatment.

C-X_1-X_2

4b. Units (Villages or Lins) Randomly Assigned Within Treatment Blocks

T-1: **Taichung City Visits/Mail** (Freedman & Takeshita, 1969)
Complex design; randomized unit assignment, within city sectors, of 2200 lins (neighborhoods) to three treatments--mailings, home visits (including or not including husband), plus a no-treatment control condition. "Density" treatment (proportion of lins receiving information treatments) was assigned by city sector, one sector to each treatment.

C-X_1-X_2-X_3
(random within 3 "density" sectors)

L-4: **Puerto Rico Message/Milieu** (Stycos, 1972; Hill, Stycos, & Back, 1959)
Random assignment of villages from an "eligible" pool of villages (those that had a meeting hall) to control or to one of nine treatments, comprising all combinations of two treatment factors: type of communication program--i.e., mailings vs. large meetings vs. small meetings; and kind of educational content presented, also with three variations.

C, and
X_1-X_9
(3 by 3 factorial)

5. Rotated/Counter-balanced Assignment of Units (Township Groups)

T-2: **Free IUD Offer** (Chen & Chow, 1973)
Treatment (offer, good for a three-month period, for a free IUD insertion) was rotated during the two-year study in turn to each of seven groups of 30 townships, with the remaining six groups of townships at each period serving as control, and thus both counter-balancing the treatment groups and providing time-series data prior to and following the treatment period for each group of townships.

C-X

Four of the experiments listed in Table 3 have a single treatment with a nontreatment control group (type CX). The Taiwan field worker incentive experiment (T-4), as described in Section III-A, considered a single incentive scheme. The Thailand midwives experiment (E-3) investigated the single treatment of allowing auxiliary midwives to prescribe contraceptives. The Hong Kong reassurance project (E-8) examined the single treatment of field worker follow-up for IUD acceptors. The Taiwan free offer study investigated the effect of giving free IUD's during a three-month period.

Comparing two or more treatments, of course, affords a better opportunity to select the better (or best) out of a variety of programs tried out. It may be that the program decision makers in the Thailand study had decided that the only treatment of interest was the one which they examined. Indeed, it may have been the only feasible alternative to the prior program. In the Hong Kong reassurance study, however, it would seem to have been reasonable to set up alternate schedules or other variations on field worker contact to discover if one or another method could have an effect. In the Taiwan field worker study (T-9), varying incentive schedules would have been of interest. It is not often that there is such a good case for a particular course of action that all other possibilities should be eliminated before they are given a chance in the field.

The most interesting and valuable type of investigation thus is, other things equal, clearly the CXY type experiment, of which Table 3 lists half a dozen examples that were reviewed for this report. The Taichung experiment (T-1) compared three treatment variations (home visits to women only, home visits to husbands and wives, and mailings) with a "control" consisting of the already on-going mass media/group meeting campaign. The two mothers' club studies from Korea (K-2, K-3) each compared two treatment variations to a control. In one study, two types of education programs were compared with having no classes at all. In the second study, a single intensity and a double intensity treatment were compared to no treatment at all. The Hong Kong field worker evaluation (E-7) compared two differently trained types of field workers to no field worker, as we described in Section III-A. The Bogotá pilot experiment (L-6) compared home visits and pamphlets with the "control" (a radio campaign). Finally, the Puerto Rico experiment (L-4) is a good example of an attempt to make program decisions on the basis of comparing many variations in treatment. A total of nine treatment variations (three types of communication channels overlapped with three types of education content) were compared to each other and to a nontreatment control group.

All of the CX and CXY types of studies mentioned above appear, on the basis of the information available, to have used adequately randomized or "pararandom" control groups. However, we should note that unit-by-unit data for assessing the consistency of the results across units sampled (see below) thus far have been obtained for only one of these 12 experimental studies. These data were obtained from Chen for the Taiwan study (T-2) further described later in this section, although they had not been presented in the original report on the study (Chen & Chow, 1973).

Ten of these 12 experimental studies utilized some form of interpersonal communication in individual or group sessions; three of them (Taichung [T-1], Bogotá [L-6], and

Puerto Rico [L-4]) employed printed media in conjunction with the personal forms of communication.[1]

2. Individual and Group Sampling

For reasons noted below, in many experiments on population programs, experimental treatments must be sampled and/or assigned to intact population units or groups (villages, lins, etc.), rather than randomized among individuals. The need for unit assignment arises because of administrative constraints, and because of the need for realistic conditions in which individuals within a neighborhood and in close contact are not forced to respond in atypical fashion by being differentially treated. For example, if different individuals in a common setting or in nearby areas realize they are receiving different program treatments, the intercommunication about these treatments will probably dilute

---

[1]None of these studies was concerned solely with the effects of mass media. This is perhaps understandable, since clean-cut experiments employing widely broadcast mass media may have difficulty providing an unbiased control group that is not self-selected. Such difficulties can be overcome, however--e.g., by giving experimental broadcasts over a number of local, short-range stations in separated localities, so that one set of localities (control group) cannot receive the broadcasts from the other localities (experimental).

any differences between treatments. Such dilution (or so-called "contamination") may result in underestimating, perhaps grossly, the size of any true effects of the programs.

This unit-assignment procedure may pose difficulties by affecting the measure of experimental error. One way of handling this situation--though it is seldom, if ever, fully satisfactory except as an adjunct to some appropriate randomization procedure (see below; also see Campbell & Stanley, 1966)--is to try to obtain comparability (elimination of bias) by use of equating or by covariance analysis, employing background or prediction variables to match the groups so as to try to assure that they are equivalent except for the effect of the experimental variable(s).

In any case, an essential condition for a rigorous experimental test (cf. Fisher, 1960, pp. 17, 19) is that the estimate of experimental error be based on the operations that actually determine experimental error. Basing degrees of freedom on the number of independent acts of randomization means, in practical terms, that spurious attribution of effects will not result from the frequent situation in which group-to-group (e.g., village-to-village) variability may grossly exceed what would result from random sampling of equivalent-sized groups.

3. Estimates of Variance with Unit-Assigned Treatments

It is important to emphasize the need for ascertaining unit-to-unit variability in comparing population programs that employ unit sampling for the experimental design. As noted above, the assignment to program treatments in experiments or controlled field studies of population programs, such as those examined in the present report, is commonly by units--lins, regions, villages, townships--rather than by individuals randomly assigned to the programs or treatments.

The most defensible analysis for a group-assignment experiment involves using groups, not individuals, as the unit of analysis for estimating chance variability or experimental error and, thus, for determining the reliability or so-called "significance" of treatment differences or program impacts (see Hovland, Lumsdaine, & Sheffield, 1949). Unit data provide considerably more stable measures than do data for single individuals, but they also involve a smaller sample size, or "N," in terms of the number of independent random assignments of population units to treatments.

It is, unhappily, a common occurrence in reports of field experiments in all areas, including instruction and education as well as studies of the impact of the various psycho-social variables, for the number of individuals and variation among them to be made the basis for estimating the stability of the findings. Instead, the unit-to-unit variability should generally be used as the measure of error, as is most appropriate in the case where the sampling or assignment to treatment was done on a unit basis rather than by individuals (see also Lumsdaine, 1963).

Of the studies we examined, there are several where either unit sampling was used or unit assignment to treatments was used. However, in only one instance--the Taiwan free offer study (T-2)--is adequate unit-by-unit data available to us. These data were obtained only by personal correspondence with one of the investigators, and apparently have not yet been published. (Attempts have been made to obtain unit-by-unit data for other studies, particularly the true experiments.) In this particular instance, the conclusions made appear to be consistent with the more detailed information, as well as with the summary tables (see Figure 2, page 382). However, it should not be assumed that this will always be the case.

The desirability of providing unit-by-unit data where assignment or sampling by population units (rather than by individuals) is employed is of particular interest in the case of randomized units in experimental comparisons. However, such unit data are also relevant in quasi-experimental and correlational studies that employ unit sampling.

4. Mixed Random/Nonrandom Complications

When studies include multiple treatment groups--some of which may be no-treatment or "as-is" control (comparison) groups--simple characterization of a study as a "randomized" or "nonrandomized" field test may give an incomplete picture of the design and of its implications for valid attribution of obtained differences in outcomes to the causal factors of difference in treatment. For example, in the Korean mothers' club study (K-2), control versus experimental groups may be randomly assigned but, as noted in Table 3, the allocation between two experimental treatments may not be random. Also, persons (or population units) may be randomly assigned to some of the experimental treatment conditions, but other treatment variations may be assigned nonrandomly (e.g., en bloc), as in the Taichung City study (T-1), described below in more detail. Thus, within a given experiment, the assurance provided by randomization may apply to some of the comparisons of differently treated groups, but not to all of the comparisons. But experience suggests that this difference may be readily overlooked or forgotten when conclusions are later drawn concerning the results.

B. *FEATURES BROUGHT OUT IN MORE COMPLEX EXPERIMENTS*

In order to clarify some important methodological points that are illustrated by their more complex designs, three of the earlier-cited experiments (Taichung [T-1], Puerto Rico [L-4], and the Taiwan free IUD offer study [T-2]) are examined at greater length below.

1. Taichung City Experiment (T-1)

This widely known study was carried out in 1963-65 by the Taiwan Provincial Health Department in collaboration with Freedman and Takeshita (1969) of the University of Michigan. It utilized a very interesting 12-group experimental design. The city was divided into three contiguous sectors, identified as being roughly equal in fertility, occupational composition, educational level, etc. In one sector, half of the neighborhoods (lins) were randomly assigned to a treatment condition employing home visits (in addition to mailings and meetings); in a second sector, one-third received this treatment, and in a third sector, one-fifth. In each sector, those neighborhoods that got home visits were then randomly divided equally into those in which the husband and wife were both contacted and those in which only the wife was contacted. The remaining neighborhoods--those which did not receive home visits--were randomly divided equally between a third and fourth treatment:

mailings only and no treatment. Posters were displayed and mass meetings were held at various public halls in all areas during the period of the campaign.

The primary measures in this study were acceptance rates of various contraceptives at the clinics. A sample of all women throughout the city was interviewed before and after the experiments about the awareness of various methods of contraception.

The main conclusions drawn by the investigators were:

- that direct personal contact definitely produced more acceptances;

- that contacting both the husband and wife, in the home visit, had no discernably greater effect than contacting only the wife;

- that use of letters did not prove effective in Taichung, since the acceptance rate in the mail-only neighborhoods was not discernibly higher than in the control neighborhoods;

- that "heavy density" areas (in which one-half of all homes were visited) showed acceptance rates distinctively higher than the areas with lighter densities of home visits; and

- that overall (averaged across groups), there was a decline in the proportion of women reporting a current pregnancy, between the before and after surveys, from 17% just before the year's program to 12% immediately after.

Strengths of the Taichung experiment were its well controlled, randomized assignment of some of the treatments, and the fact that several program variations were tried out. As pointed out earlier, a study that considers relative as well as absolute effectiveness of variations in treatment provides the most useful kind of information for program decision making, particularly when that information has as its basis a controlled experiment (randomized field trial).

The experimental design used in the Taichung study allows us to make fairly confident conclusions about the relative effect of certain treatment variations on acceptance rates, though less strong conclusions on others. The differential effects on fertility are not as clear. The impact on fertility of the total program in Taichung is the object of considerable attention by the investigators, primarily via comparing the fertility of acceptors and nonacceptors. Fertility rates are also reported for Taichung as a whole, and compared to rates for other provinces and for all of Taiwan. However, treatment-to-treatment variations in fertility are not reported, even though it appears that they might be extracted from the original data, since the samples for the before and after surveys were selected by districts (lins). The only indication of treatment variations in fertility is through translation of acceptance differentials into fertility differentials via the differential fertility of acceptors and nonacceptors. This involves a distorting selection bias of undetermined amount which could grossly overestimate the true program impact.

The conclusions regarding treatment density for home visits should be given further consideration. Since the density variations were not randomly assigned, and since each level was assigned to only one area, conclusions about the relative effectiveness of densities are less solid than those about the relative effectiveness of mailing versus home visits.

The Taichung study also provides a good illustration of one of the problems in impact assessment that random assignment of treatments does not eliminate: "contamination" or dilution effects. For example, individuals in a lin receiving no special treatment could have lived across the street from individuals in a lin receiving the "everything" treatment. Because of close neighbor interaction, the information received by the individuals in the "everything" lin might well have been transmitted to individuals in other lins and thus had an effect on behavior in those lins not receiving the "everything" treatment. If acceptance rates do not differ by considerable amounts, it may be only an indication that the "nontreatment" lin was in fact partially treated; i.e., was not a true control lin. The actual treatment effects are then underestimated.

This "dilution" hypothesis is consonant with the Taichung data in that there were greater differences in acceptance rates between "everything" and "nothing" lins in light density areas than there were in the heavy density area. This source of bias can be largely eliminated by studies which randomly assign treatments to geographic units that are more insulated against spillover or intertreatment contamination effects--e.g., geographically separated towns or villages. Under propitious conditions such an experimental arrangement does not have to be much more costly than a design that is confined to adjacent units, and may provide a much less biased (because less diluted) estimate of treatment effects. (Where concern is with the effect of radio or other broadcast programs, the assignment of treatment to well separated geographic entities is generally the only way to avoid serious dilution of treatment impacts.)

2. Puerto Rico Experiment (L-4)

This experiment was the third phase of a lengthy study, comprising Stage I (Exploration--qualitative field studies for establishing hypotheses); Stage II (Quantitative verification--surveys of a representative sample of families); and Stage III (Experimental validation--field studies to validate the importance of survey variables and to give bases for action programs).

In this 1959 study, 23 communities having at least 100 households in a one-mile radius were randomly assigned to one of nine treatment groups or to a control group with no program.[1]

Three types of education/communication programs were examined, with three of the experimental groups having small meetings, three having large meetings, and three receiving pamphlets instead of having meetings. In addition, three types of educational program content were given, one type of content to each of the experimental groups that had small meetings, large meetings or pamphlets. Type 1 programs

---

[1]However, the significance tests reported (chi-square) are based on the number of individuals in the samples, unfortunately, rather than using the number of communities (sampling units) as degrees of freedom.

stressed the importance of planning and the advantages of small families ("values"), as well as the anatomy of reproduction and the features and availability of different birth control methods ("information"). Type 2 programs stressed the need for communication and for sharing of responsibilities ("family organization") in addition to the "information" component, while Type 3 programs had all three kinds of content. No less than two villages were randomly assigned to each of the nine total possible combinations.

Interviews conducted in advance in each community were used to select couples to be included in the educational program. Eligible couples in each of four categories ("ready," "uninformed," "ineffective," and "opposed" with respect to contraception) were selected until the quota for each type of respondent was filled. For a subsample of half the respondents selected in each village, collateral interviews were conducted with "control" subjects who comprised one of three women designated as the closest friends of the experimental group wives. Only those cases sampled received pamphlets or invitations to meetings. A postinterview was conducted two months after the program and a fertility check in the form of an interview was conducted one year later.

For those who had not previously used contraception, the "values" program and combined program were slightly more effective than the "family organization" program (68%, 63%, and 46%, respectively, using contraceptives after one year). The opposite was true for those with previous contraceptive experience (78%, 75%, and 86%). The meetings and pamphlets increased slightly the number using contraceptives over the control group. At the end of one year, those without prior contraceptive history were practicing at rates of 67% (meetings), 58% (pamphlets), and 50% (control). Among those with prior contraception, the rates were 79%, 80%, and 69%, respectively.

The Puerto Rico experiment has several noteworthy features which are indicated below.

1. The universe of communities randomly allocated to treatments or control was limited to those communities which had appropriate facilities (meeting halls), so that any one of them could have been assigned to one of the group-meeting treatments. A common practice in some studies has been to increase the number of communities sampled by assigning meeting treatments to communities with the needed facilities (e.g., halls), and assigning other experimental or control treatments to communities without such facilities. Had the communities with meetings shown more contraceptive use after such a study, we would not know if this was due only to the treatment. It could well be that the communities had good facilities (halls, in this case) because of some aspect of the communities (e.g., higher educational levels, better economic situation) which made the people living there more receptive to family planning. The Puerto Rico investigators wisely avoided such a confounding of treatment and community selection by limiting the sampling to a subuniverse for which the treatment was appropriate (i.e., feasible).

2. The comparative as well as absolute merits of more than one treatment were assessed, through the use of the preferred type CXY experimental pattern.

3. Furthermore, the educational-content treatments, or program variations, were related to behavior theory, so that the results of the experiment have a bearing on theoretical knowledge relevant to future programs, as well as affording immediately practical feedback for current program decision making.

4. An attempt was made to determine the differential impact of program variations on different segments of the target group. Such information can be used to increase program effectiveness by directing suitably different programs to different groups; it can also be used to avoid costly overlap of multiple programs across the total audience.

5. The one-year fertility check provides a relatively strong index of program impact on fertility; other measures of changes in knowledge, attitude, and/or reported practice of contraception, may not give a strong indication of subsequent fertility changes.

3. Free IUD Offer

Our third detailed example is not a "true" experiment in the strictest sense, since the treatment was, although impartially, not really randomly assigned. However, the primary purpose of randomized assignment is to control for selection effects, and this study has utilized a unique rotation system over time to accomplish this.

In the Taiwan study (T-2), a free offer program was assigned on a rotating basis to seven groups of 30 townships each. These townships were usually those with low IUD acceptance rates. There was no apparent systematic bias in the manner in which they were chosen, 30 at a time, except that some attempt was made to choose noncontiguous townships in any one group of 30. The essential treatment, the offer of a free IUD insertion for a limited period of time, was limited to three months for each group of townships.

The primary measure was the number of IUD acceptors in the three-month periods before, during, and after the free offer. The acceptance rates are subject to seasonal variation, which was controlled by obtaining the ratio between acceptors in "free" areas and acceptors in "nonfree" areas for a given period of time.

Table 4 shows the number of acceptors for the periods before, during, and after the free offer for each of the seven groups. These rates are compared to the acceptances in the other six groups ("nonfree" areas) at the same period of time. This very persuasive analysis, permitted by the treatment rotation feature (which, in effect, made every treatment group its own control), provides very strong experimental evidence on treatment impacts in this unusual case, despite the absence of formal randomization.[1]

The overall results for the program are impressive. The mean ratio between acceptances in the free offer areas and acceptances in the nonfree areas doubled from .12 before the offers to .24 during the offers, and then decreased back to .12 after the offers were terminated. This effect is further substantiated by the relatively uniform pattern of change over all seven groups. Figure 2 (il-

---

[1] But it should be noted that this design is appropriate only where the impact to be assessed is, as in this case, that of a temporary (short duration) program (though not necessarily one, as in this case, whose effects are of transient duration).

Table 4. Taiwan Limited Free IUD Offer.*

Time Period in Relation to "Free" Treatment	Areas Compared	Three-month Treatment Cycles**							Total
		I	II	III	IV	V	VI	VII	
Three Months Before	Treatment Area	1,933	2,585	2,182	3,813	2,352	2,627	3,176	18,668
	Nontreatment Areas***	19,045	20,571	23,580	28,160	21,719	21,306	25,839	160,220
Three Months During	Treatment Area	4,397	7,201	6,682	6,578	4,863	4,973	5,822	40,516
	Nontreatment Areas	19,579	25,195	26,434	22,481	20,983	25,997	28,257	168,926
Three Months After	Treatment Area	1,658	3,196	1,963	3,059	2,408	2,967	2,490	17,741
	Nontreatment Areas	18,648	23,363	22,608	19,047	22,567	26,084	19,234	151,531
1st Month After	Treatment Area	595	1,038	624	924	1,119	924	883	6,107
	Nontreatment Areas	6,767	7,605	6,958	6,048	10,991	8,339	6,764	53,472
2nd Month After	Treatment Area	468	1,053	674	1,047	671	973	812	5,678
	Nontreatment Areas	4,979	7,699	7,367	6,636	5,742	8,702	6,040	47,165
3rd Month After	Treatment Area	615	1,105	665	1,088	618	1,070	795	5,956
	Nontreatment Areas	6,902	8,059	8,283	6,363	5,814	9,043	6,430	50,894

* We are grateful to H. C. Chen, Population Studies Center, University of Michigan, for providing these as yet unpublished data.

** As explained in the text, treatment was rotated such that just one of the seven groups of townships was receiving the treatment during each of the seven cycles of the experiment.

*** The nontreatment areas comprise the other six areas, which were "control" areas not receiving treatment during any particular treatment cycle.

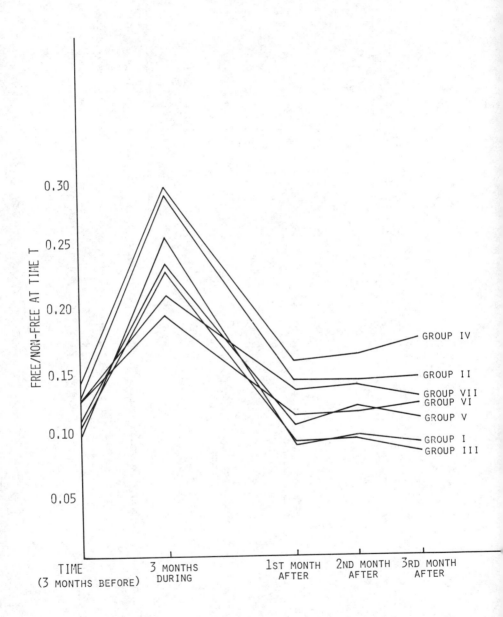

Fig. 2. Taiwan free IUD offer data, based on Table 4, plotted as ratios of acceptance rates for treatment areas to acceptance rates for nontreatment areas.

lustrates graphically the high degree of uniformity in the data.[1]

V. MEASURES OF IMPACT USED IN FIELD STUDIES

No matter how rigorous the design of a field experiment, and no matter how carefully controlled the implementation of the program or programs, little useful information will be obtained if the measures of program effect are not

---

[1]The outcomes for all seven groups, as shown in Figure 2, obviously are essentially the same, with all of the "during" values above any of the "before" or "after" values. Thus, as it turned out, the treatment effect was so highly consistent, and the differences so large, that the experiment clearly could have demonstrated the principal result with fewer groups—doubtless, with not more than three groups. Although it might have been necessary for political reasons to continue the free offer innovation in the remaining groups of townships, more could have been learned if, in the spirit of "evolutionary experimentation," the later-treated groups could have been given a variant of the initial treatment. Such a variant, for example, might have been to try a cut-rate rather than completely free offer, or, of even more interest, to see whether the markedly enhanced acceptance rate would continue unabated instead of declining if the free offer were extended over a greater number of months than the three-month initial interval.

adequate. Four levels of effects (impacts) for population programs are suggested by Reynolds (1970a). These may be summarized as:

- Changes in knowledge and attitudes--i.e., the "K" and "A" of the "KAP" surveys[1]--including interest, motivation, etc.

- Mediating-behavior outcomes, such as information-seeking activities, obtaining counseling, attending group meetings, exposure to communications, etc.

- Individual's fertility-linked behavior--trial adoption or continued use (reported or confirmed) of a particular form of contraception or other fertility-regulating procedure.

- Resulting "social indicator" effects--i.e., changes in rates of fertility or related health statistics (and, in some cases, indices of economic well-being or "quality of life," etc.). As Reynolds notes, a program may have one or more of these kinds of effects, and the effects may be positive or negative, planned or unplanned. Most population program evaluation has focused on measurement of expected and desirable effects, including attitudes toward family planning, behavior such as use of contraceptives, and derived indices such as births averted.

---

[1] Knowledge, attitude, and practice (KAP) surveys have been widely used in a number of countries, primarily to measure the current status of knowledge, attitudes, or contraceptive practice rather than the effects of programs, though changes

A problem that is a source of concern in assessing the outcomes of social programs is the tendency to assess them in terms of things that are handy to measure. In the particular case of fertility planning programs, follow-up studies on IUD's and oral contraceptives have uncovered high discontinuation rates. In Isfahan (S-9), a precampaign survey of previous family planning acceptors found that 80% of pill acceptors and 50% of IUD acceptors had dropped out of the program after two years. If acceptors continue to use the methods sporadically, then the media campaign is unlikely to have any long-term effect on fertility. Acceptor data are liable to the same response error problems as KAP surveys, since they rarely include reliability and validity checks (some exceptions are noted below). Thus, measures of program effects based on acceptance and short-term continuation rates are open to skepticism.

All of the 12 experiments listed in Table 1 measured impact on fertility-related behavior as well as on knowledge and/or attitudes. Four of the studies measured at least some index of contraceptive acceptance. The primary measure in the Taichung experiment (T-1) was acceptance rates of various contraceptives at the government family planning clinics. A before-after KAP survey was also conducted and acceptors were asked about their sources of information. The Taiwan group-meeting study (T-3) measured clinic attendance rates and related the costs of the every-other-lin treatment and those of the every-lin treatment to the

---

in KAP-type measures are obviously relevant indicators of program effects.

differential acceptance rate. A before-after KAP study was also conducted. The Taiwan field worker incentive study (T-4), the Hong Kong field worker evaluation (E-7), and the Bogotá pilot experiment (L-6) measured acceptance rates. (The Bogotá rates were so low as to render the measure practically worthless.)

Happily, a number of the studies also measured some observations of continued use as well as initial acceptance. In the case of the Korean IUD checkup study (K-4) and the Hong Kong reassurance project (E-8), continuation rates were the primary measure since only acceptors were studied. In the Korea IUD checkup study, a great effort was made to follow up acceptors who did not revisit the clinic as instructed. Thirty-nine percent of the acceptors did revisit the clinic, and constant field worker follow-up reached an additional 52% of the acceptors. The Hong Kong reassurance study related output to cost of field worker time, with the result that the increased service appeared to be too costly for the results obtained. The two studies on the Korean mothers' classes (K-2, K-3) and the Thailand midwife study (E-3) measured continuation rates for periods of up to one year. (The data on the mothers' classes intensity study are not available, but, according to the report, were collected.) Only one experiment--Puerto Rico (L-4)--recorded impact on actual fertility in the form of a fertility interview conducted one year after the experiment. The Puerto Rico study is also notable for the effort made to validate the information obtained for KAP surveys by conducting collateral interviews with close friends and/or the husband of each of the women originally interviewed.

Several quasi-experimental studies, even some with very weak designs, did include a strong effort to validate the measures of outcome or to utilize measures that were strongly related to fertility. The Dacca study (S-5) utilized independent interviews of husband and wife. The Khanna studies (S-8) included the monthly collection of demographic information—verification of all deaths, births, and in- and out-migration—as well as reported acceptance rates. (Some evidence was gathered that indicated that actual use did not correspond to reported use.) In the El Salvador study (L-2), the costs of services were the primary measure and as such were clearly unambiguous and interpretable. The S/K marketing survey (K-9) utilized field worker supervisors to validate, in person, 10% of the interviews.[1]

The studies which make the strongest attempts to measure fertility outcomes are not controlled experimental studies. This is not surprising in view of the difficulties of maintaining experimental control over a relatively long period of time, and in view of the fact that the number of

---

[1]Some studies conducted in the United States are notable for their use of multiple measures of outcome. The Chicago fertility control studies (Bogue, 1966) measured trends in new Planned Parenthood patients, contraceptive sales, follow-up interviews with acceptors, and overall birth rates. A mass media study (Udry et al., 1972) included weekly street corner interviews over a nine-month period, clinic attendance records for new patients, and records of inventory, invoice, and new prescription audits from a sample of drugstores for a one-year period.

387

units which could potentially remain uncontaminated is usually so small as to make inferences somewhat weaker than desired.

The Singur study (S-1) does make a clear attempt to measure subsequent fertility. However, it is not clear how comparable the experimental and control areas were and, as indicated in Section III the large differential in birthrates may perhaps have occurred without the experimental program. This is one case in which it would have been very useful to have had time series data on birthrates for a longer period prior to the advent of the program.

Two Taiwan studies mentioned in earlier sections have attempted to assess the impact of the Taiwan family planning program on fertility. The Taiwan area analysis of fertility (T-8) relates measures of family planning program intensity (including IUD acceptance rates) to subsequent fertility. The study of the demographic impact of the Taiwan IUD program (T-6) matched groups of acceptors and nonacceptors in 240 different categories and found that the acceptors' fertility rate fell 32% more than that of the nonacceptors.

In the Koyang traditional methods study (K-5), the age-specific fertility rates for each year of the program fell in both Koyang and Kimpo. However, the second year saw a greater drop (36% versus 16%) in Koyang than Kimpo. The report relates this change to the differential program effects measured by contraceptive users. Based on the investigators' arbitrary criterion that a program is "successful" if an additional 10% of the married women become effective users in the first year or an additional 20% in the second year, the Koyang program, with 37.9% of current users for the two years, reached that goal, where Kimpo's program did not.

A problem that is present in most of the studies examined is that of measurement definitions and measurement error. Both Reynolds (1972) and Goldstein (1973) have noted that there is a great need for consistent and standardized criteria of evaluation. For example, the term "acceptor" can refer to first acceptance of contraception, first acceptance of a particular method, or first acceptance of a particular program. In many cases, pill users who stop for three or four months and then start again are treated as new acceptors; this both <u>overestimates</u> the number of new users and <u>underestimates</u> continuation rates. Measurement error is a particular problem when the measures involve interview data on family planning knowledge, attitudes, and/or behavior. For example, interview data from the Meerut program (S-2) showed that knowledge of the condom <u>decreased</u> after the information campaign. Since the condom has many names in India and since many people are reluctant to discuss this method, the validity of response is open to considerable question. The interview for the Dominican Republic radio campaign (L-5) made an attempt to avoid large response bias by asking individuals if they could remember advertisements for fictitious products as well as real ones. Thus, the interview could identify those individuals who wished to appear knowledgeable and responded affirmatively in general, whether or not they had actually received the message; the accuracy of a particular individual's recall could also be measured in this way. In the Koyang traditional methods study (K-5), the interpretation of family size preference shifts was difficult to make. The investigators felt that ideal size values are ambiguous, so that some of the apparent shifts might not have indicated real changes, but only shifts within an acceptable range. A better measurement might be to ask for lower and upper limits rather than a single number.

The methodology used in the Honduras Barrios campaign (L-3) may have influenced the changes in knowledge and attitude that were measured. Separate samples were used for the before and after survey. The samples were, however, selected prior to the program, so that by the time the "after" sample was ready to be interviewed, several of the people in the sample had moved away. All samples were fixed in June. The sample taken in July for the "before" survey had an 88% response while the sample taken in late August ("after" survey) had a 75% response. This fact, plus some unusual results indicating that the knowledge of douche and condom decreased by significant percentages from before to after the program, makes some of the other "significant" changes open to doubt.

VI. SUMMARY AND CONCLUSIONS

A. *RESUME*

This report and the recommendations which follow derive from a survey of evaluative studies of population planning programs, including special attention to communication/education elements in such programs. One of the main purposes of this survey was to identify ways in which future research and evaluation for population programs can be improved in usefulness and efficiency.

Several dozen studies of program impact were examined, with particular attention to the incisiveness of the methodology employed. Over half the studies reviewed were conducted in Taiwan, Korea, or India; the remainder included studies in Indonesia, Pakistan, Thailand, Malaysia, and several Latin American countries. In assessing program impact, most of the studies reported behavior indicating acceptance of contraceptive methods. A smaller number presented evidence of change in fertility. In a relatively few studies, an explicit comparison was made in terms of cost in relation to program effectiveness.

About a dozen of the impact studies were able to successfully use a design employing randomized treatments in a true experimental design--common beliefs in the unfeasibility of such designs notwithstanding. Quasi-experiments of varying strength were used where true experiments providing unbiased control of extraneous nonprogram effects apparently were deemed unfeasible.

The nonexperimental studies we examined illustrate some inherent limitations and some good features found in such studies, including effective use of time series data. Such data were in some cases of considerable value in interpreting changes that took place after initiation of the experimental program. Seven of the studies surveyed that used "suspect" comparison groups were strengthened by the provision of time series data; three other studies with inadequate comparison groups would have been more convincing had time series baselines been provided. The remaining impact studies used weaker designs--e.g., one group used pre-and-post measures with no comparison to indicate what might have occurred in the absence of the program.

B. RECOMMENDATIONS

The recommendations given here deal primarily with the design and basic methods of practical evaluative studies applicable to specific programs, rather than with substantive problems for "basic" or theoretical research on the operation of underlying psychological and sociological variables.

General recommendations of interest to program administrators (Section 1) are followed by more specific recommendations dealing with "impact" evaluation (Section 2), with reporting and utilization (Section 3), and with some more technical recommendations on the design and conduct of studies for determining program impact (Section 4).[1]

---

[1] Some of these recommendations derive from Lumsdaine's earlier work on field evaluation of educational program impacts (supported in part by the Ford Foundation and the U.S. Department of Health, Education, and Welfare), as well as from the work of an American Psychological Association committee on field research methods, which he has chaired for the past several years.

1. General Recommendations

1. Activities critical to the comprehensive evaluation of programs should encompass three basic functions: evaluation of <u>needs and plans</u> for program efforts; evaluation of <u>program processes or operation</u> (sometimes referred to as program monitoring or operational feedback); and determination of the demonstrable <u>impact(s)</u> of programs on critical outcomes, as an input to major program decisions.

2. Descriptive "process" features of program operation, which experienced observers regard as generally important for programs to operate effectively, should be considered as working criteria for evaluating the current operation of an ongoing program or to assess the plans for proposed programs. (Such guidelines may be thought of as a basis for judging <u>predicted</u> impacts or effects.)

3. Actual program impact can best be assessed by adequately controlled field experiments, designed to determine the <u>demonstrable effects</u> that programs produce. Such studies should, whenever feasible, be designed to ascertain the differing effects of alternative forms of programs, as this affords a better opportunity to select the better (or best) out of a variety of programs tried out.

4. Assumptions that should be reviewed at the planning or design stage of programs include the availability of personnel and material resources necessary to physically implement the program plans once the program is put into operation.

5. A new program should generally be tried out initially only on a pilot basis with a few selected groups, so that it will be possible, before its wider application, to make changes that are pointed up by the initial evaluative

data. (Limitation of initial tryout to a few pilot groups also insures the potential availability of equivalent control groups needed to properly assess program impact.)

6. A question to be answered before a "successful" pilot program is extended, is: To what extent is the program reproducible? (For example, it is often the case that resources--money, personnel, facilities, etc.--available for pilot testing are of much higher quality than those available for a wider-scale program.)

7. Planning and initiation of evaluation activities, including design of studies and procedures for collection of data, should be initiated at the very outset of program planning, rather than being deferred until after the program is already under way.

8. In order to avoid real or apparent bias, the individuals responsible for program operation commonly should not have executive responsibility for summative evaluation studies. When outside, independent evaluators are employed, however, the indices and procedures they utilize should be made known as early as possible to program management or operation personnel, so that there may be an opportunity to correct any real or perceived unfairness in the evaluative procedures.

9. The control groups that will be needed to ascertain a program's impact should be selected at the same time as the pilot test groups so the two sets of groups will be exactly comparable and will be as representative as possible of the entire population.

2. Recommendations on Assessing Program Impact

1. A distinction should be made between interim or preliminary data on the effects that programs seem to be having (useful for "formative evaluation"—i.e., as a diagnostic basis for day-to-day or month-to-month decisions about program revisions), and data to ascertain with some precision the total impact a fully developed program will produce (so-called "summative evaluation").

2. "Hard" data are most needed for the summative evaluation that is called for at major decision points, where the total effectiveness of a program over an appreciable period of time is involved, and where information on the magnitude of impact a program has produced will provide a major input to higher-level decisions concerning a program's continuation, expansion, curtailment, or basic modification.

3. Controlled field experiments conducted under realistic conditions are the most definitive method for providing "hard" data to establish the magnitude of effects produced by any particular communication program, or to indicate the comparative effects produced by alternative programs. The experiments should be of sufficient precision to reveal any effects that are large enough to be of practical consequence.

4. While "soft" or observational, qualitative data are often cheaper and faster to obtain, it should be realized that more definitive, useful "hard" data, such as that from well-controlled field experiments, sometimes can also be obtained cheaply and expeditiously. This is especially true

if adequate preparation is done to insure the basic requirements of experimental design before implementation of the
program.

5. Greater use should be made of formative evaluation
in which not only informal observation but also "hard data"
on impacts of preliminary stages or forms of the program are
fed back into the program production and operation process,
so as to afford an empirical basis for improving the program's operation.

6. Wider use should be made of estimation and confidence limits to show the range of the probable size of
effects, rather than merely using "significance" tests,
which only show the likely existence of program effects.

3. Recommendations on Reporting and Utilization of Research

1. Evaluative research findings are more likely to be
utilized in program decisions if they go beyond the usual
summary of recommendations and explain step-by-step how they
can be translated into specific program activities. Both
research and program staff should be involved in the process
of translation.

2. Those who manage and conduct evaluative research
should obtain the active participation and involvement of
the program staff who will ultimately be responsible for
using the findings. (Policy makers who understand the objectives of evaluation are much more likely to consider
research findings when making program decisions.)

3. There is a critical need for proper understanding
and appreciation of pilot program experimentation; it is
very important to insure that the needs and capabilities of

such experimental evaluation will be clearly understood and taken adequately into account from the outset of program planning by key policy makers and program managers at all levels.

4.   Aside from other publication in technical or popular works, the procedures and results of studies of program impact should be thoroughly documented in a detailed technical report that exemplifies rigorous standards of scientific reporting and gives <u>full</u> information, to permit replication of the study or reanalysis of its data.

5.   Briefer reports and summary statements on the results of each study should always cite the basic technical report, so that the correspondence between summary or interpretative statements and underlying data is explicit and verifiable.

4.   Supplementary Technical Recommendations

1.   More attention should be given in field comparisons to use of proper randomization and to closer relation of error estimates to the actual manner of sampling.

2.   Consideration should be given to establishing a representative population of subunits (geographical radio coverage areas, towns, counties, school districts, etc.) for the experimental study of new programs before they are used nationwide over a long period of time.

3.   Care is needed to preclude contamination due to the fact that if different individuals in nearby areas realize they are receiving different program treatments, the intercommunication about these treatments will probably dilute any differences between treatments, thus underestimating the size of any true effects of the programs.

4. Accordingly, in most experiments on major programs, experimental treatments must be assigned to intact population units or groups (cities, districts, etc.) rather than randomized among _individuals_.

5. The most valid analysis for a group-assignment experiment requires using groups, _not_ individuals, as the unit of analysis for estimating chance variability or experimental error in determining the reliability or so-called "significance" of treatment differences or program impacts.

6. To support conclusions as to program effects, unit-by-unit data should be preserved and made available for review or analysis. At the very least, unit-by-unit means within each program treatment should be presented in a summary table in the published report of the study.

7. Particularly in the absence of an equivalent (random) control group, time series data are of considerable importance in interpreting changes in criterion indices that take place after the initiation of the experimental program treatment--for example, to allow for a preexperimental declining trend from which further decline (after the experimental treatment begins) is to be anticipated, _even if_ the experimental treatment were ineffective.

8. Safeguards are needed to avoid measurement error due to ambiguities (e.g., in interview data) arising from different meanings of terms used, etc., since such ambiguities can invalidate responses.

9. The basic technical report on a study should describe the procedures used and the results obtained in such a way that a technically qualified person 1) can assess the validity of the statements concerning what outcomes the program's use will achieve, and 2) could replicate the study

in substantially identical fashion. To satisfy these basic requirements, the technical report should give full details on all relevant aspects of the study, including criterion measures, characteristics of subjects, procedures, data collection, experimental design, and data obtained.

10. Complete tables of the data for each unit should also be available on request, to permit subsequent supplementary analyses of unit-by-unit variations for subcategories of the population, such as those of a given age group or parity. Supplementary data, though bulky, may be kept readily available in project files or preserved in microfilm. (The American Psychological Association has recommended that all data on group experiments and related studies be preserved for at least five years.)

11. For improving the methodology of evaluative studies, adequate resources should be directed toward the development of better methods than are now available, as well as the better application of existing methods.

12. Among the improvements in the state of the art of program evaluation on which methodological research is needed are improved theory and techniques for scaling of human values and social benefits (needed for useful cost-benefit analysis, and for weighing trade-offs between desirable and undesirable outcomes).

13. Consultants to advise on design of impact studies should have had practice in applying the most suitable statistical and other methodological expertise to practical field situations; also needed are consultants having deep familiarity with local conditions affecting the realism and validity of specific projects.

14. Experiments and studies of program effectiveness should make stronger efforts to use, as measures of outcome, the kinds of observations that can be analyzed in relation to cost-effectiveness or cost-benefit. For such an analysis, measures of input cost and output effect need to be expressed in comparable terms whenever possible. To this end there is a need to develop better ways to calculate the direct and indirect costs as well as short- and long-term benefits (social, economic, educational) of capital projects, operational programs and of R & D efforts themselves.

C. CONCLUDING REMARKS

In this chapter we have tried to describe and analyze salient features of field test methodologies used in fertility planning projects in a way that brings out their general applicability to experiments and field tests for any social-educational or medical program treatment variations or innovations. We expect the present analysis will be of special interest to those who are directly concerned with the effectiveness of population planning (fertility reduction) programs, but its main relevance for the present volume is in relation to the wider sphere of program impact determination in general. Though some aspects of practicality in implementing the field tests described here are conditioned by their locale in developing nations, the main considerations of method stressed seem generally applicable to field trials or experiments in industrialized as well as developing regions.

REFERENCES

Balakrishnan, T. R., & Matthai, R. J. India: Evaluation of a publicity program on family planning. Studies in Family Planning, June 1967, 1(21), 5-8.

Bang, S. The Koyang study: Results of two action programs. Studies in Family Planning, April 1966, 1(11), 5-12.

Bang, S. Improving access to the IUD: Experiments in Koyang, Korea. Studies in Family Planning, March 1968, 1(27), 4-11.

Bang, S. A comparative study of the effectiveness of a family planning program in rural Korea: Summary and conclusions. In Population and family planning in the Republic of Korea (Vol. I). Republic of Korea: Ministry of Health and Social Affairs, March 1970. (a)

Bang, S. Can IUD retention be improved by prompt check-up visits? In Population and family planning in the Republic of Korea (Vol. I). Republic of Korea: Ministry of Health and Social Affairs, March 1970. (b)

Bogue, D. J. United States: The Chicago fertility control studies. Studies in Family Planning, October 1966, 1(15), 1-8.

Campbell, D. T., & Stanley, J. C. Experimental and quasi-experimental designs for research. Chicago: Rand McNally, 1966.

Cernada, G. P. (Ed.). Taiwan family planning reader. Taichung, Taiwan: The Chinese Center for International Training in Family Planning, 1970.

Cernada, G. P., Chow, L. P., & Lee, T. M. The use of mailings. In G. P. Cernada (Ed.), Taiwan family planning reader. Taichung, Taiwan: The Chinese Center for International Training in Family Planning, 1970.

Cernada, G. P., & Lu, L. P. The Kaoshiung study. Studies in Family Planning, August 1972, 3(8), 198-203.

Chan, K. C. Hong Kong: Report of the IUD reassurance project. Studies in Family Planning, November 1971, 2(11), 225-233.

Chang, M. C., Cernada, G. P., & Sun, T. H. A field-worker incentive study. Studies in Family Planning, November 1972, 3(11), 270-272.

Chang, M. C., Liu, T. H., & Chow, L. P. Study by matching of the demographic impact of an IUD program. In G. P. Cernada (Ed.), Taiwan family planning reader. Taichung, Taiwan: The Chinese Center for International Training in Family Planning, 1970. Reprinted from Milbank Memorial Fund Quarterly, April 1969, 47(2).

Chen, H. C., & Chow, L. P. Strategies for the introduction of contraceptive methods: The Taiwan experience. In G. W. Duncan, E. J. Hilton, P. Kreager, & A. A. Lumsdaine (Eds.), Fertility control methods: Strategies for introduction. New York: Academic Press, 1973.

Chen, H. C., & Hermalin, A. I. Factors affecting the performance of field workers in the Taiwan IUD program. Taiwan: Taiwan Population Studies, Working Paper No. 7, 1970.

Chow, L. P., Chang, M. C., & Liu, T. H. Taiwan: Demographic impact of an IUD program. Studies in Family Planning, September 1969, 1(45), 1-6.

Clark, L. T., Udry, R. J., & Nelson, S. S. Appointment backlog frustrates ad campaign potential. Family Planning Perspectives, Winter 1973, 5(1).

Fawcett, J. T., & Somboonsuk, A. Thailand: Using family acceptors to recruit new cases. Studies in Family Planning, March 1969, 1(39), 1-4.

Fawcett, J. T., Somboonsuk, A., & Khaisang, S. Thailand: An analysis of time and distance factors at an IUD clinic in Bangkok. Studies in Family Planning, May 1967, 1(19), 8-12.

Fayyaz, Mohammad. The impact of the motivational campaign on family planning knowledge, attitudes, and practices. Lahore, Pakistan: West Pakistan Family Planning Association Report, 1971.

Finnigan, O. D., & Koo, S. D. The use of post cards in recruiting IUD dropouts to the pill. In Population and family planning in the Republic of Korea (Vol. 1). Republic of Korea: Ministry of Health and Social Affairs, March 1970.

Fisher, R. A. The design of experiments (7th ed.). New York: Hafner, 1960.

Freedman, R., & Takeshita, J. Family planning in Taiwan: An experiment in social change. Princeton: Princeton University Press, 1969.

Goldstein, H. Observations on evaluation of family planning programs. Health Services Reports, March 1973, 88(3), 213-217.

Green, L. W., Gustafson, H. C., Griffiths, W., & Yaukey, D. The Dacca family planning experiment (Pacific Health Education Report No. 3). Berkeley, California: University of California, School of Public Health, 1972.

Hermalin, A. I. Taiwan: An area analysis of the effect of acceptance on fertility. Studies in Family Planning, August 1968, 1(33), 7-11. Reprinted in G. P. Cernada (Ed.), Taiwan family planning reader. Taichung, Taiwan: The Chinese Center for International Training in Family Planning, 1970.

Hill, R., Stycos, J. M., & Back, K. W. The family and population control: A Puerto Rican experiment in social change. Chapel Hill, North Carolina: The University of North Carolina Press, 1959.

Hilton, E. T. Evaluative studies of population-program effectiveness (Technical Memorandum). Seattle: Battelle Population Study Center, 1973.

Hovland, C. I., Lumsdaine, A. A., & Sheffield, F. D. Experiments on mass communication. Princeton: Princeton University Press, 1949.

Indian Institute of Mass Communication. Report of an intensive family planning promotion campaign: An experiment and a survey in South Delhi area. In Communication and family planning. New Delhi, India: May 1967.

Kanagaratnam, K. Singapore: The national family planning program. Studies in Family Planning, 1968, 1(28), 1-11.

Karlin, B., & Ali, S. M. The use of radio in support of the family planning program in Hyderabad District of West Pakistan. Preliminary report, prepared for the Fourth Biannual Seminar on Research in Family Planning, Karachi, Pakistan, March 1968.

Keeny, S. M. (Ed.). East Asia review, 1971. Studies in Family Planning, July 1972, 3(7).

Khoon, Y. G. A proposal for evaluation of population attitude and knowledge of form III pupils in Malaysian schools. Prepared for the Workshop for Population Education Programme Development Specialists, Communication Institute, East-West Center, Honolulu, Hawaii, July 31-September 1, 1972.

Kim, T. I., Ross, J. A., & Worth, G. C. The Korean national family planning program. New York: Population Council, 1972.

Kline, D. A case study on the development of school population education: The Tjikini Foundation School in Indonesia. Cambridge, Mass.: Harvard University, Graduate School of Education, Center for Studies in Education and Development, 1972.

Kwon, E. H. Use of the agent system in Seoul. Studies in Family Planning, November 1971, 2 (11).

Kwon, E. H., Kim, T. R., et al. A study on urban population control: Sung Dong Gu action-research project on family planning and fertility: Summary and conclusions. In Population and family planning in the Republic of Korea (Vol. 1). Republic of Korea: Ministry of Health and Social Affairs, March 1970.

Lapham, R. J., & Mauldin, W. P. National family planning programs: Review and evaluation. Studies in Family Planning, March 1972, 3(3).

Lee, M. G., & Kim, Y. M. Evaluation of the study on family planning services in urban Korea. In Social evaluation of family planning programs and research activities in Korea. Seoul: Korean Sociological Association, 1972.

Lieberman, S. S., Gillespie, R., & Loghmani, M. The Isfahan communication project. Studies in Family Planning, April 1973, 4(4), 73-100.

Londoño, J. B. A cost-effect analysis of a family planning program: Findings of a quasi-experimental study. Studies in Family Planning, January 1973, 4(1), 11-15.

Lu, L. P., Chen, H. C., & Chow, L. P. An experimental study of the effect of group meetings on the acceptance of family planning in Taiwan. The Journal of Social Issues, October 1967, 23(4), 171-177.

Lumsdaine, A. A. Instruments and media of instruction. In N. L. Gage (Ed.), Handbook of research on teaching. Chicago: Rand McNally, 1963.

Lumsdaine, A. A., & Hilton, E. J. Suggestions for introducing fertility control methods. In G. W. Duncan, E. J. Hilton, P. Kreager, & A. A. Lumsdaine (Eds.), Fertility control methods: Strategies for introduction. New York: Academic Press, 1973.

Lumsdaine, A. A., Hilton, E. T., & Kincaid, D. L. Evaluation research methods. In E. M. Rogers and R. Agarwala-Rogers (Eds.), Evaluation research on family planning communication. Paris: UNESCO, in press.

Marino, A. The radio and family planning in the Dominican Republic. In J. M. Stycos (Ed.), Clinics, contraception, and communication. New York: Appleton-Century-Crofts, 1973.

Mathen, K. K. Preliminary lessons learned from the rural population control study of Singur. In C. V. Kiser (Ed.), Research in family planning. Princeton: Princeton University Press, 1962.

Mauldin, W. P., & Ross, J. A. Family planning experiments: A review of design. New York: The Population Council, 1966.

Mitchell, R. E. Hong Kong: An evaluation of field workers and decision making in family planning programs. Studies in Family Planning, May 1968, 1(30), 7-12.

Nortman, D. Population and family planning: A factbook (4th ed.). (Reports on Population/Family Planning, 2.) New York: Population Council, 1972.

Park, H. J. Use and relative effectiveness of various channels of communications in the development of the Korean family planning programme. Communications in Family Planning, Asian Population Studies Series, No. 3. United Nations ECAFE, November 1968.

Peng, J. Y. Thailand: Family growth in Pho-tharam District. Studies in Family Planning, October 1965, 1(8), 1-7.

Population Council. India: The India-Harvard-Ludhiana population study. Studies in Family Planning, July 1963, 1(1), 4-7. (a)

Population Council. India: The Singur study. Studies in Family Planning, July 1963, 1(1), 1-4. (b)

Population Council. Taiwan: Experimental series. Studies in Family Planning, August 1966, 1(13).

Raina, B. L., Blake, R. R., & Weiss, E. M. India: A study in family planning communication, Meerut District. Studies in Family Planning, June 1967, 1(21), 1-5.

Raina, B. L., et al. A study in family planning communication--Meerut District. New Delhi: Central Family Planning Institute, 1967. (a)

Raina, B. L., et al. Family planning communication action research project--Meerut District. New Delhi: Central Family Planning Institute, 1967. (b)

Reynolds, J. A framework for the design of family planning program evaluation systems. Manual No. 2 of Manuals for the evaluation of family planning and population programs. New York: Columbia University Division for Program Development and Evaluation, International Institute for the Study of Human Reproduction, 1970. (a)

Reynolds, J. Operational evaluation of family planning programs through process analysis. Manual No. 4 of Manuals for the evaluation of family planning and population programs. New York: Columbia University, Division for Program Development and Evaluation, International Institute for the Study of Human Reproduction, 1970. (b)

Reynolds, J. Evaluation of family planning program performance: A critical review. Demography, 1972, 9, 69-85. (a)

Reynolds, J. Family planning program evaluation: Status, problems, prospects. New York: Columbia University, Division for Program Development, International Institute for the Study of Human Reproduction, 1972. (b)

Rogers, E. M. Questioning some assumptions about family planning behavior, with implications for the introduction of fertility control innovations. In G. W. Duncan, E. J. Hilton, P. Kreager, & A. A. Lumsdaine (Eds.), Fertility control methods: Strategies for introduction. New York: Academic Press, 1973.

Rosenfield, A. G. The role of nursing and auxiliary personnel in family planning programmes. Australia-New Zealand Journal of Obstetrics and Gynecology, August 1972.

Rosenfield, A. G., & Limcharoen, C. Auxiliary midwife prescription of oral contraceptives: An experimental project in Thailand. American Journal of Obstetrics and Gynecology, December 1, 1972, 114(7), 942-949.

Ross, J. A., Finnigan, O. D., III, Keeny, S. M., & Cernada, G. P. Korea and Taiwan: Review of progress in 1968. Studies in Family Planning, April 1969, 1(41).

Ross, J. A., Han, D. W., Keeny, S. M., & Cernada, G. P. Korea/Taiwan 1969: Report on the national family planning programs. Studies in Family Planning, June 1970, 1(54).

S/K Marketing Research Company. A study of the effectiveness of family planning communications in the Republic of Korea. Seoul, Korea: May 1972.

San Salvador Demographic Association. Preliminary evaluation of the "PATER" campaign. Sociological Research Program, July 1970. (Translated from the Spanish)

Schultz, T. P. Effectiveness evaluation of family planning: Case study Taiwan. Santa Monica, California: The RAND Corporation, 1972.

Simmons, A. B. Information campaigns and the growth of family planning in Colombia. In J. M. Stycos (Ed.), Clinics, contraception, and communication. New York: Appleton-Century-Crofts, 1973.

Stycos, J. M. Experiments in social change: The Caribbean fertility studies. In C. V. Kiser (Ed.), Research in family planning. Princeton: Princeton University Press, 1962.

Stycos, J. M., & Marden, P. G. Honduras: Fertility and an evaluation of family planning programs. Studies in Family Planning, September 1970, 1(57), 20-24.

Stycos, J. M., & Marden, P. G. Health and family planning in a Honduran barrio. In J. M. Stycos (Ed.), Clinics, contraception, and communication. New York: Appleton-Century-Crofts, 1973.

Takeshita, J. Y. Lessons learned from family planning studies in Taiwan and Korea. In Berelson et al. (Eds.), Family planning and population programs: A review of world developments. Chicago: University of Chicago Press, 1969.

Udry, J. R., Clarke, L. T., Chase, C. L., & Levy, M. Can mass media advertising increase contraceptive use? Family Planning Perspectives, July 1972, 4(3), 37-44.

UNESCO. Report of a meeting of experts on research in family planning communication, in Davao City, Philippines, October 1972. Paris: UNESCO, May 1973. (Mimeo)

UNESCO. Meeting of experts for developing guidelines for evaluation of national family planning communication programmes, in Davao City, Philippines, April 1974. "Secretariat Working Document No. 2," prepared by E. T. Hilton, A. A. Lumsdaine, and D. L. Kincaid. Paris: UNESCO, 1974. (Mimeo)

Worth, G., Watson, W. B., Han, D. W., Finnigan, O. D., & Keeny, S. M. Korea/Taiwan 1970: Report on the national family planning programs. Studies in Family Planning, March 1971, 2(3).

Wyon, J. B., & Gordon, J. E. Khanna study: Population problems in the rural Punjab. Cambridge, Mass.: Harvard University Press, 1971.

Yang, J. M. Studies in family planning and related programs in rural Korea. In Social evaluation of family planning programs and research activities in Korea. Seoul, Korea: Korea Sociological Association, 1972.

6
Experiments and Evaluations: A Reexamination

WARD EDWARDS and MARCIA GUTTENTAG

I. INTRODUCTION

Our message is simple; we might as well start with a bald statement of it. The function of evaluation is to guide decision making. Every decision does, and should depend on the answers to two questions: what is at stake, and what are the odds of gaining or losing the stakes? Experiments ordinarily serve only one function: they help to appraise the odds. They neither define nor measure the stakes, nor do they perform aggregation over the numerous and often inconsistent stakes to be won or lost in every significant social program. Moreover, even in the task of appraising odds, they have severe limitations: they require constrained, inflexible program designs; they bias in various ways the selection of which stakes to assess; they encourage neglect of less rigorously collected data; and above all they present difficult problems of generalization.

The task of evaluation is large and complex; the tools used by evaluation researchers should be comparably numerous and complex. One of those tools should be experimentation. Seldom if ever should that tool alone determine a decision. Often, though not always, the experimental tool should be left unused, because other tools are more appropriate, or because use of this one would be actively harmful or misleading.

We sketch very briefly some other tools for evaluation research, and describe one, multi-attribute utility measurement, at some length. Our reason for giving it such extensive discussion is that we believe it can serve an integrative and organizing function. It specifies what tasks need to be done in order to perform an evaluation; suggests methods, including experimentation among others, for doing these tasks; and provides aggregation rules for putting the pieces of the evaluative process together.

We also spend an unduly large number of words spelling out our complaints about experimental approaches to evaluation research. Our only defenses against the quite just criticism that we devote much more space to experimentation in evaluation research than it deserves are that the other discussions in this volume also concentrate on experimentation, from a quite different point of view, and that we enjoy arguing with our friends.

A. A DEFINITION

It may help if we start by defining what we mean by evaluation. All evaluations involve judgments, usually comparative, about the desirability of action alternatives. Such judgments are shaped by values and by inferences about states of the world. These inferences, and perhaps the values also, are affected by relevant information of many kinds, from many sources, collected in many ways. Evaluation research, therefore, requires an intellectual framework that links <u>inferences about states of the world to the</u> <u>values of decision makers and thus leads to decisions.</u>

B. *THE CONFUSING DIVERSITY OF CURRENT EVALUATION PRACTICE*

Every program gets evaluated, many times and by many people. The word "evaluation" is often not used, but every time someone asks, "Is this program worthwhile?" and answers the question, he has performed an evaluation.

Most evaluations are informal, easy, and unambiguous. If Crunchy-Wunchy Munchies sell, while Cap'n Charlie's Chaff Crispies do not, Cap'n Charlie will either soon conclude that his Chaff Crispies program needs modifying—or go broke.

The economic criterion used in most evaluations is less appropriate to social programs than to merchandising. Yet most social programs, too, are evaluated informally, easily, and unambiguously. Few would propose discontinuing schools, or the IRS, or the use of stop signs and traffic lights.

Social programs require more serious, more elaborate evaluation if the following criteria apply. First, the net result of the program should not be transparently and obviously good or bad; the most common way in which this occurs is that the result is good for some and bad for others. Second, meaningful alternatives to the existing program should be under consideration; often, a meaningful alternative to a program is to do nothing. Third, it helps to encourage evaluation if the program is new, or newly changed, or about to be changed.

This amounts to saying no more than that a serious, elaborate evaluation should be undertaken only if a decision is needed. The function of the evaluation should be to facilitate and improve that decision.

This all seems very simple to us. Yet current work in evaluation exhibits a remarkable diversity of definitions, distinctions, methods, and aims. Two distinctions seem especially in need of discussion.

One is the distinction between pragmatic evaluation and field experiments. Pragmatic evaluation, by far the more common, is typically data-rich, inductive, and relates closely to the content of a particular program. Most pragmatic evaluations are performed by some version of what Edwards, Guttentag, and Snapper (in press) have called the baseball statistician's approach to evaluation. The name comes from the practice, familiar in baseball, of collecting as many different numbers as possible, making rather simple calculations based on them, and using the results for evaluative purposes.

The principles underlying pragmatic evaluations are usually simple and closely related to the content of the program to be evaluated. In Chapter 5 of this volume, Hilton and Lumsdaine, discussing the evaluation of population programs, distinguish between the evaluation of needs and plans, the evaluation of processes or operations, and the evaluation of the impact of the programs on critical outcomes. Hargreaves and his colleagues (1974) make a similar sort of distinction among three kinds of evaluation in a Mental Health Center context: elements of program evaluation, needs assessment and planning, and management information systems.

Often, a peer review process must be built into a pragmatic evaluation. The recent guidelines for evaluation of

Community Mental Health Centers (CMHC) presented by Hargreaves et al. (1974) provide an example of this. Their five-volume guidebook for CMHC evaluation includes a volume concerned with needs assessment evaluation, since Community Mental Health Centers are directed to serve the needs of the community. This series also presents guidelines for peer review evaluations, which are required by the enabling legislation for Community Mental Health Centers. The issue of peer review is one illustration of the broader question of whom the evaluation researcher serves, the scientist or the decision maker--a question of importance discussed later in this chapter. Suffice it to note here that in the case of Community Mental Health Centers, peer review evaluation is necessary. In many other government programs, diverse groups, each with some decision-making power, must somehow be made a part of the evaluation.

At a different level of specificity, a number of pragmatic approaches are intended solely for individual self-evaluations. One such system is Kiresuk and Sherman's (1968) goal attainment scaling, widely used by mental health therapists. This evaluation method permits each person to set his own goals, and, by periodic checks, to provide feedback for himself on the extent to which his performance meets his goals.

This scanty citation of instances of pragmatic approaches cannot do justice to their frequency or diversity. As our mention of Hargreaves et al. suggests, no sharp line separates the concept of pragmatic evaluation from the concept of a management information system--and every management has one of those, though it may not use that label for it.

In contrast to this busy practicality by which most evaluation is done is the exhortation to rigor often found in the more academic evaluation research literature. Such exhortations are produced most frequently by academics who try, sometimes successfully, to persuade a governmental organization to set up real field experiments either before a social program begins, or as part of that new program. In this literature, ongoing programs not designed as experiments are either ignored or used as a source of horrid examples. Evaluation problems are treated as though they were largely the problems of experimental research in field settings. The myriad distinctions and issues with which the pragmatic literature is concerned are not visible. For example, needs assessment is rarely mentioned; peer review not at all.

A second distinction often found in the evaluation research literature has to do with when the evaluation is done. <u>Planning</u> is an evaluative process, conducted before a program starts. Most social programs need continuous feedback to permit wise program management and adaptation, either to correct errors or to adapt to changing circumstances. The phrase <u>formative evaluation</u> was invented to describe this kind of feedback. It is often distinguished from <u>summative evaluation</u>, which is supposed to be the final verdict on program outcomes.

Why are these distinctions needed? Obviously, the decision problems faced at all three stages are essentially the same. Is this program a good idea? If so, what can we do to make it work as well as possible? If not, how can we devise something better, given our constraints?

As a program progresses, at least four kinds of changes occur. First, the values of those served by the program and those who operate the program change, both in response to experience with the program and in response to other, external causes. Second, the program evolves--changes shape and character. Third, the external societal circumstances to which the program is a response change. And fourth, knowledge of program events and consequences accumulates. All four of these kinds of changes affect the answer to the decision problem--and all four are continuous. In our view, any satisfactory general paradigm for evaluation research must be equally continuous. It should permit continuous assessment of program merit, taking into account all four kinds of changes, and should also permit exploration of the merits of alternative programs that could be had either by modifying or by scrapping the one being evaluated. We shall propose a paradigm that, we believe, can do that.

II. DECISION ANALYSIS AS A PARADIGM FOR EVALUATION RESEARCH

We aim to integrate the three main topics of evaluation--inferences about states of the world, values of decision makers, and decisions--in a quantitative and explicit manner. The collection of ideas called decision analysis (see, for example, Raiffa, 1968) does just that. So our main theme is to show how those ideas can be adapted to the needs of evaluation research and what the resulting gains can be.

Evaluation research should, we believe, provide the basis for decisions about the program and its competitors.

If it does not, then it loses its distinctive character and becomes simply research. Programs are evaluated, ordinarily, because some decision maker needs help in figuring out what to do. Sometimes he has clear-cut alternatives; occasionally, several programs simply compete for money. Perhaps the most common decision question of all is, "Should we go on doing this, or should we try something else, such as doing nothing?"

A. STAKES, AS WELL AS ODDS, CONTROL DECISIONS

Decision makers, not researchers, make decisions. While the decision maker always should be, and sometimes is, willing to consider the evidence bearing on his options and his choice among them, virtually never is he willing to delegate the task of being decisive to the research evidence, or its finder, the researcher. Nor, we believe, should he.

We do not intend to disparage the relevance of evidence, nor to assert that evidence is or should be irrelevant to most decisions (though it is to many, and should be to some). Our point is simply that the decision maker must consider values--and values are usually not explicitly spelled out by available evidence.

Every human decision does, and should, depend on the answers to two questions: what are the odds, and what's at stake? Most research evidence bears directly on the first of these two questions, and at best indirectly on the second. But the second is the more important. Moreover, for every real-world decision, the stakes are complicated, multidimensional, and high. For example, an educational program which, on the evidence, educates no one may never-theless be desirable. It may, for example, add to chil-dren's socio-emotional growth, or provide a safe place for children to go after school. Or perhaps an office-holder wants to be able to point to the program's existence to prove that he kept his campaign promises. Or all three. As citizens, we may question whether these are proper reasons for continuing an educationally useless program. As evalua-tion researchers, however, we clearly fail in understanding the decision problem unless we recognize that these value dimensions are relevant to it. If we want to help the deci-sion maker, our task is to provide him with appropriate techniques for: 1) assessing the strength and relevance of each of these reasons for continuing or not continuing the program, 2) appropriately aggregating these values, and 3) reaching a decision that takes them all into account, each to the extent that its importance justifies.

B. *INCONSISTENT VALUES HELD BY DISAGREEING GROUPS CONTROL MOST DECISIONS*

Decisions are not generally made by a single decision maker, with a single, though multidimensional, set of values. For any significant decision, a number of indi-viduals or groups are usually involved. Most organizations have identifiable decision makers. Their role in signifi-cant decisions was well summarized by Harry Truman's famous desk sign: "The buck stops here." Our point about that sign, different from Truman's, is that the buck seldom started on Truman's desk. It started elsewhere--typically, in dozens of places. Options were formulated; values and costs were assessed. Most commonly, "the buck," by which we mean the decision, never reached Truman's desk; a choice was made by some decision making group subordinate to him and presented to him, if at all, only for ratification. If it did reach him as a genuine decision problem, it was accompanied by extensive staff studies spelling out the relevant stakes and odds, and typically recommending one option over the others.

Whose values, then, are to be maximized? Occasionally, those of a single decision maker, as understood by those who serve and advise him. More often, some amalgam of the values of many different groups, all with stakes in the decision. A technology for explicating, comparing, and sometimes for reconciling and ultimately aggregating such inconsistent values of groups in conflict is clearly needed for social decision making.

Evaluation researchers can ignore this problem of group values in conflict only if they choose, and they often do, to ignore the problem of values altogether--typically by assuming some simple value as the only relevant one. Sometimes, this works well. Doctors, for example, can avoid many value problems by assuming that life is preferable to death and health to sickness. On those assumptions, value questions can be bypassed in favor of simpler questions such as whether a given procedure does in fact contribute to preservation of life or restoration of health. But we need only mention recent public discussions of euthanasia, abortion, and preservation of the lives of fetuses with severe genetic defects to illustrate that the values that should bear on medical decisions are often more complicated than that, and to suggest the danger of simplistic, ill-thought-through, unexplicated value systems. A careful study of the costs of such casual values, combined with other ingredients of seat-of-the-pants decision making, in a medical context, was done by Fryback (1974).

C. *THE DECISION-THEORETIC EVALUATION FRAMEWORK*

Figure 1 is a block diagram or flow chart indicating the processes that lead up to a decision. In this and following block diagrams, rectangles enclose operations, and circles enclose the informational inputs to or outputs from operations. Arrows indicate direction of information flow. Only one instance exists within Figure 1 (and none in the other flow charts) in which informational outputs combine without intervening operations to produce other informational outputs. The list of available acts combines with the list of states relevant to outcomes of acts to generate the table of outcomes without any intervening processing, because an outcome is, by definition, the intersection of an act and a state. In less mathematical language, an outcome is what happens if a given act is chosen and a particular state of the world turns out to obtain.

The main conclusion to which an initial look at Figure 1 must inevitably lead is that decision making, fully analyzed, is complicated. It divides into four phases. The first consists of recognition of a decision problem and definition of its nature and dimensions--the raw materials of a decision process. The second is called probability measurement in Figure 1; other names used for the same process in other contexts are diagnosis, intelligence

419

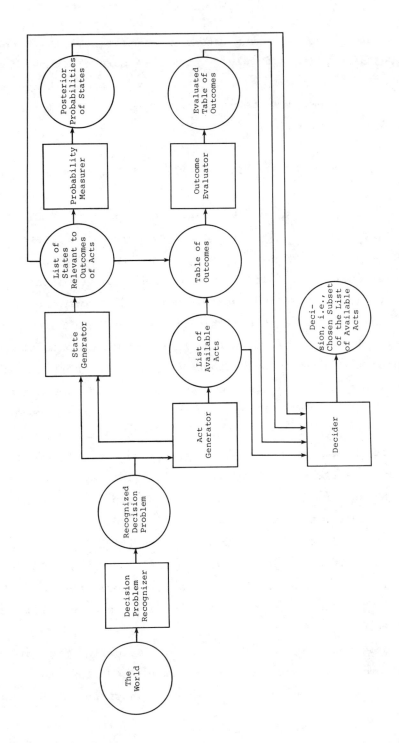

Fig. 1. *Block diagram of a decision system.*

evaluation, data gathering and interpretation, etc. It is itself a complicated process. Figure 1 indicates, in Bayesian fashion, that the output is a set of posterior probabilities of states. Less formal judgments of probability, like those contained in such intuitive processes as conventional medical diagnosis and such formal ones as the acceptance or rejection of statistical hypotheses, also fit here and can be substituted for the Bayesian version of the process.

A more detailed Bayesian version of what goes on in probability evaluation is given in Figure 2, which translates into flow diagram form some of the basic ideas of an information processing system called PIP, Probabilistic Information Processing (see Edwards et al., 1968), but applies just about equally well to any formal application of Bayesian ideas that distinguishes between priors and likelihoods.

Bayesian techniques fit into the evaluation paradigm by providing a means for revising probabilities about states of the world, given data. For expositions of the Bayesian position in statistics itself, see Edwards, Lindman, and Savage (1963) or Phillips (1973). For illustrations of how to use Bayesian inference in decision making, see Raiffa (1968), Schlaifer (1969), or any of a dozen recent texts on the subject. For an exciting example of application of Bayesian tools for evaluating alternative options in medical diagnosis, see Fryback (1974).

The essence of what these procedures have to offer evaluation researchers is flexibility. They do not rely on artificial devices such as null hypotheses. They permit, in fact encourage, quantitative combination of evidence from

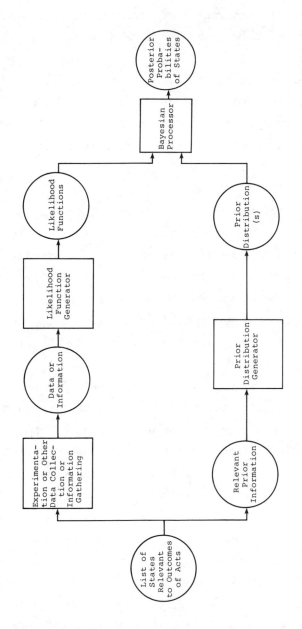

Fig. 2. Block diagram of a probability measurer.

different sources, different lines of inquiry, and different techniques of investigation. These procedures make it easy to combine judgments with experimental or other empirical data in a formally appropriate numerical way. And they combine very naturally with the value judgments that are the main topic of this paper to produce wise decisions.

The third phase of decision making, as outlined in Figure 1, is outcome evaluation. "Evaluation" here means literally that; the attachment of values, preferably in numerical form, to outcomes. And those values are not probabilities; in our preferred version of the evaluation process, values are explicit, numerical answers to the question, "Is that particular outcome good or bad, and how good or how bad?" Another way of putting the question to be answered in evaluation is: "Suppose I could know for certain that this particular act would lead to this particular outcome, and suppose I then chose this act. How attractive would that outcome be to me, or to someone, or to some collection of people?"

Note that outcomes, not acts, are evaluated. We often think of values as being attached to acts. That is in a sense appropriate, since the whole purpose of obtaining values of outcomes and probabilities of states is to permit the simple computation that associates an expected value with an act. The availability of that arithmetic means that if we know the relevant probabilities, we can immediately calculate the value of an act, given the value of its potential outcomes. In the special case of no uncertainty (i.e. some state has probability 1, or, more often, you treat it as though it had probability 1, even though you know that unlikely alternative states exist), each act has only one outcome, and so the value of the outcome is also the value of the act.

The fourth phase of decision making, as outlined in Figure 1, is actual choice among acts. It is based on the values of outcomes and the probabilities of states (or the intuitive substitutes for these numbers). In general, it is a rather straightforward process, because the major work has been done. In a pick-one-act situation, one simply picks the act with the highest value, or expected value. In a pick-several-acts situation, more complex decision rules may be used, but they are still logically simple, and have essentially the character that either the acts that have the highest values, or the acts that return the most value per unit of cost, are selected. Special situations, such as sequential decision problems, lead to still other decision rules, which are computationally more complex, but the input numbers are still the same.

Of these various processes, probability evaluation and outcome evaluation come closest to the heart of what evaluation research is typically supposed to be about. One contention of this chapter is that these two distinct operations have been mistakenly lumped together under the label "evaluation research"; that they are different; that they require quite different kinds of procedures to provide answers; and that answers to both are typically necessary for wise decision making.

D. *MULTI-ATTRIBUTE UTILITY ANALYSES*

Most outcomes have value for a number of different reasons; i.e., on a number of different dimensions. A remedial education program may contribute to the education of those receiving it. If so, the number of those people and the extent of the contribution made to each may be relevant to the value of the program. The cost of the program in money, in teaching talent, in student time, and perhaps in educational materials and facilities, is also relevant. The durability of the educational gain is relevant. The program's target population may be relevant. The generalizability of the remedial education techniques used--over students, over teachers, over settings, over cultures, etc.--may be considered relevant. The city in which the program is located may be on politically harmonious terms with the funding organization, or it may not. The program may have no educative value whatever, and may nevertheless provide employment for otherwise unemployed teachers and administrators.

All these considerations may enter into a decision about whether to continue, expand, or terminate a program--along with many others. Clearly this multiplicity of value dimensions presents a multiplicity of issues. Who determines what dimensions are relevant, and how relevant each is? How is that set of judgments made and used? How is the location of each possible outcome of each act being considered on each relevant dimension of value measured, judged, or otherwise discovered? Finally, what combination of judgmental transformation and arithmetical aggregation is used to translate all this input information into outcome evaluations?

An explicit technology, or, more precisely, several competing versions of an explicit technology, exists to answer some of these questions. Its name is multi-attribute utility measurement, and expositions of various versions of it have been presented by Raiffa (1968), Keeney (1972b), Edwards (1971), and others.

The version we present here, adapted from Edwards (1971), is oriented toward easy communication and use in environments in which time is short and decision makers are multiple and busy. Further, it is a method which is psychologically meaningful to decision makers. The judgments they are required to give are intuitively reasonable. Unpublished studies argue that the simple rating-scale procedures described below produce results essentially the same as much more complicated procedures involving imaginary lotteries.

The essence of multi-attribute utility measurement, in any of its versions, is that each outcome to be evaluated is located on each dimension of value by a procedure that may consist of experimentation, naturalistic observation, judgment, or some combination of these. These location measures are combined by means of an aggregation rule, most often simply a weighted linear combination. The weights are numbers describing the importance of each dimension of value relative to the others. In every application of multi-attribute utilities such numbers are judgmentally obtained. A flow diagram of this process is contained in Figure 3, which is an expansion of the block called "Outcome evaluation" in Figure 1.

Our implementation of Figure 3 consists of ten steps:

Step 1. Identify the person or organization whose utilities are to be maximized. If, as is often the case, several organizations have stakes and voices in the decision, they must all be identified. People who can speak for them must be identified and induced to cooperate.

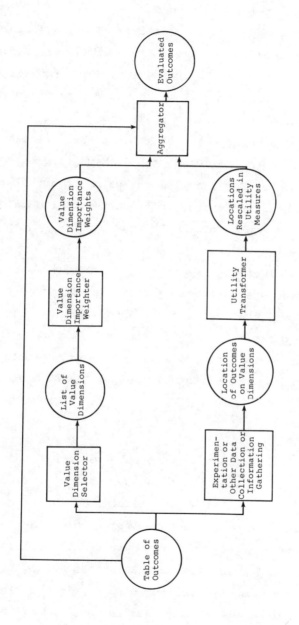

Fig. 3. Block diagram of an outcome evaluator.

Step 2. Identify the issue or issues (i.e., decisions) to which the utilities needed are relevant. The same objects or acts may have many different values, depending on context and purpose. In general, utility is a function of the evaluator, the entity being evaluated, and the purpose for which the evaluation is being made. The third argument of that function is sometimes neglected.

Step 3. Identify the entities to be evaluated. Previously, we have indicated that they are outcomes of possible actions. For example, the value of a dollar is the value of whatever you choose to buy with it; the value of an education is the value of the things that can be done with-- but not without--it.[1]

Step 4. Identify the relevant dimensions of value. The first three steps were more or less philosophical. The first answered the question: Whose utility? The second answered the question: Utility for what purpose? The third answered the question: Utility of what entities? With Step 4 we come to the first technical task: discover what

---

[1] Since it is always necessary to cut the decision tree somewhere--to stop considering outcomes as opportunities for further decisions and instead simply to treat them as outcomes with intrinsic values--the choice of what to call an outcome becomes largely one of convenience. Often, in practice, it is sufficient to treat an action itself as an outcome. This amounts to treating the action as having an inevitable outcome--that is, assuming that uncertainty about outcomes is not involved in the evaluation of that action.

dimensions of value are important to the evaluation of the entities in which we are interested.

As Raiffa (1969) has noted, goals ordinarily come in hierarchies. But it is often practical and useful to ignore their hierarchical structure, and instead to specify a simple list of goals that seem important for the purpose at hand. Goals, for this purpose, should not be stated as target numbers (e.g., reduction of drinking-driver accidents by 50%), but rather as dimensions (reduction of drinking-driver accidents).

It is important not to be too expansive at this stage. The number of relevant dimensions of value should be kept down, for reasons that will be apparent shortly. This can often be done by restating and combining goals, or by moving upward in a goal hierarchy, thereby using fewer, more general values. Even more important, it can be done by simply omitting the less important goals. There is no requirement that the list evolved in this step be complete, and much reason to hope that it won't be.

Step 5. Rank the dimensions in order of importance. This ranking job, like Step 4, can be performed either by an individual, or by representatives of conflicting values acting separately, or by those representatives acting as a group. Our preferred technique is to try group processes first, mostly to get the arguments on the table and to make it more likely that the participants will start from a common information base, and then to get separate judgments from each individual. The separate judgments will differ, of course, both here and in the following step.

Step 6. Rate dimensions in importance, preserving ratios. To do this, start by assigning the least important dimension an importance of 10. (We use 10 rather than 1 to permit subsequent judgments to be finely graded and nevertheless made in integers). Now consider the next-least-important dimension. How many times more important (if any) is it than the least important? Assign it a number that reflects that ratio. Continue on up the list, checking each set of implied ratios as each new judgment is made. Thus, if a dimension is assigned a weight of 20, while another is assigned a weight of 80, it means that the 20 dimension is one-fourth as important as the 80 dimension. And so on. By the time you get to the most important dimensions, there will be many checks to perform; typically, respondents will want to revise previous judgments to make them consistent with present ones. That's fine; they can do so. Once again, individual differences are likely to arise.

Step 7. Sum the importance weights, divide each by the sum, and multiply by 100. This is a purely computational step which converts importance weights into numbers that, mathematically, are rather like probabilities. The choice of a 0-to-100 scale is, of course, purely arbitrary.

At this step, the folly of including too many dimensions at Step 4 becomes glaringly apparent. If 100 points are to be distributed over a set of dimensions, and some dimensions are very much more important than others, then the less important dimensions will have non-trivial weights only if there aren't too many of them. As a rule of thumb, 8 dimensions is plenty, and 15 is too many. Knowing this, you will want at Step 4 to discourage respondents from being too finely analytical: rather gross dimensions will be just right. Moreover, it may occur that the list of dimensions will be revised later, and that revision, if it occurs, will typically consist of including more rather than fewer.

Step 8. Measure the location of each entity being evaluated on each dimension. The word "measure" is used rather loosely here. There are three classes of dimensions: purely subjective, partly subjective, and purely objective. The purely subjective dimensions are perhaps the easiest; you simply get an appropriate expert to estimate the position of that entity on that dimension on a 0-to-100 scale, where 0 is defined as the minimum plausible value on that dimension, and 100 is defined as the maximum plausible value.

A partly subjective dimension is one in which the units of measurement are objective, but the locations of the entities must be subjectively estimated.

A wholly objective dimension is one that can be measured rather objectively, in objective units, before the decision. For partly or wholly objective dimensions, it is necessary to have the estimators provide not only values for each entity to be evaluated, but also minimum and maximum plausible values, in the natural units of each dimension.

The final task in Step 8 is to convert measures on the partly subjective and wholly objective dimensions into the 0-to-100 scale in which 0 is minimum plausible and 100 is maximum plausible.

A linear transformation is almost always adequate for this purpose: errors produced by linear approximations to monotonic nonlinear functions are likely to be unimportant relative to test-retest unreliability, inter-respondent differences, and the like.

431

Now all entities have been located on the relevant value dimensions, and the location measures have been rescaled. In what sense, if any, are the scales comparable? The question cannot be considered separately from the question of what "importance," as it was judged at Step 6, means. Formally, judgments at Step 6 should be designed so that when the output of Step 7 (or of Step 6, which differs only by a linear transformation) is multiplied by the output of Step 8, equal numerical distances between these products on different dimensions correspond to equal changes in desirability. For example, suppose entity A has a location of 50 and entity B a location of 10 on value dimension X, while A has a locatiion of 70 and B a location of 90 on value dimension Y (only X and Y are relevant). Suppose further that dimension Y is twice as important as dimension X. Then A and B should be equivalent in value. (The relevant arithmetic is: for A, $50 + 2(70) = 190$; for B, $10 + 2(90) = 190$. Another way of writing the same arithmetic, which makes clearer what is meant by saying that equal numerical differences between these products on different dimensions correspond to equal changes in desirability, is: $(50 - 10) + 2(70 - 90) = 0$. It is important that judges understand this concept as they perform both Steps 6 and 8.

Step 9. Calculate utilities for entities. The equation is

$$U_i = \sum_j w_j u_{ij},$$

remembering that

$$\sum_j w_j = 100.$$

U_i is the aggregate utility for the ith entity; w_j is the normalized importance weight of the jth dimension of value, and u_{ij} is the rescaled position of the ith entity on the jth dimension. Thus w_j is the output of Step 7 and u_{ij} is the output of Step 8. The equation, of course, is nothing more than the formula for a weighted average.

Step 10. Decide. If a single act is to be chosen, the rule is simple: maximize U_i. If a subset of i is to be chosen, then the subset for which $\sum_i U_i$ is maximum is best.

A special case arises when one of the dimensions, such as cost, is subject to an upper bound; that is, there is a budget constraint. In that case, Steps 4 through 10 should be done ignoring the constrained dimension. Then the ratios U_i/C_i should be calculated; these are the famous benefit-to-cost ratios. Actions should be chosen in decreasing order of that ratio until the budget constraint is used up. (More complicated arithmetic is needed if programs are inter-dependent or if this rule does not come very close to exactly exhausting the budget constraint.) This is the only case in which the benefit-to-cost ratio is the appropriate figure on which to base a decision. In the absence of budget constraints, cost is just another dimension of value, to be treated on the same footing as all other dimensions of value, entering into U_i with a minus sign, like other unattractive dimensions. In effect, in the general case it is the benefit-minus-cost difference, not the benefit-over-cost ratio, that should usually control action.

An important caveat needs to be added concerning benefit-to-cost ratios. Such ratios assume that both benefits and costs are measured on a ratio scale; that is, a scale with a true zero point and ratio properties. The concepts

433

both of zero benefit and zero cost are somewhat slippery on close analysis. A not-too-bad solution to the problem is to assume that you know what zero cost means, and then attempt to find the zero point on the aggregate benefit scale. If that scale is reasonably densely populated with candidate programs, an approach to locating that zero point is to ask the decision maker, "Would you undertake this program if it had the same benefits it has now, but had zero cost?" If the answer is yes, the program is above the zero point on the benefit scale; if the answer is no, it is below the zero point.

The multi-attribute utility approach can easily be adapted to cases in which there are minimum or maximum acceptable values on a given dimension of value, by simply excluding alternatives with outcomes that transgress these limits.[1]

---

[1]_Flexibilities of the method_. Practically every technical step in the preceding list has alternatives. For example, Keeney (1972a) has proposed use of a multiplicative rather than an additive aggregation rule. Certain applications have combined multiplication and addition. The methods suggested in this chapter for obtaining location measures and importance weights have alternatives; the most common is the direct assignment of importance weights on a 0-to-100 scale.

Independence properties. Either the additive or the multiplicative version of the aggregation rule assumes value independence. Roughly, that means that the extent of your

E. *INTERPERSONAL AND INTERGROUP DISAGREEMENTS*

We distinguish between two kinds of disagreements. Disagreements at Step 8 seem to us to be essentially like disagreements among different thermometers measuring the same temperature. If they are not too large, we have little compunction about taking an average. If they are, then we

---

preference for location a_2 over location a_1 of dimension A is unaffected by the position of the entity being evaluated on dimensions B, C, D, ... Value independence is a strong assumption, not easily satisfied. Fortunately, in the presence of even modest amounts of measurement error, quite substantial amounts of deviation from value independence will make little difference to the ultimate number U_i, and even less to the rank ordering of the U_i values. (For recent discussions of the robustness of linear models, on which this assertion depends, see Dawes and Corrigan [1974].) A frequently satisfied condition that makes the assumption of value independence very unlikely to cause trouble is monotonicity; that is, the additive approximation will almost always work well if, for each dimension, either more is preferable to less or less is preferable to more throughout the range of the dimension that is involved in the evaluation, for all available values of the other dimensions. When the assumption of value independence is unacceptable even as an approximation, much more complicated models and elicitation procedures that take value dependence into account are available.

are likely to suspect that some of the thermometers are not working properly and to discard their readings. In general, we think that judgmentally determined location measures should reflect expertise, and typically we would expect different value dimensions to require different kinds of expertise and therefore different experts. In some practical contexts, we can avoid the problem of diagreement at Step 8 entirely by the simple expedient of asking only the best available expert for each dimension to make judgments about that dimension.

Disagreements at Steps 5 and 6 are another matter. These seem to us to be the essence of conflicting values, and we wish to respect them as much as possible.

One of the greatest advantages of this approach is that it permits each group, if a number of groups are relevant, to specify its own values and their ordering. It is not necessary that there be any overlap in values between groups, although such overlap is frequent. For example, in the evaluation of a Community Mental Health program, one group might be consumers, another program administrators, a third Federal staff, etc. The fact that different groups have different values will generally have two consequences. One is that more value dimensions may need to be taken into account than would be the case if the groups agreed. Unimportant dimensions can be neglected only if all major participants in the decision agree on their unimportance. The other consequence is that data must be gathered, when possible, bearing on each value dimension that anyone cares about. The same set of data can lead different groups to very different conclusions, depending on differences in weighting assigned to various value dimensions.

436

If one of the aims of the evaluation process is to resolve differences between the values of different individuals and groups, then Steps 5 and 6 can be conducted face-to-face, urging group members in free discussion to try to reach consensus about value dimensions and their ordering. In past work, we have found that this procedure can be quite useful for an agency. Individuals frequently agree more about values than they would predict. Even when they do not agree, the process of generating and rating value dimensions is often useful in providing information to members of a group about their own values.

In fact, one study (Gardiner, 1974; see also Gardiner & Edwards, 1975) shows that the multi-attribute utility measurement process can produce considerable agreement about values as compared with other value measurement methods, such as direct rating. Individuals who differ strongly about value dimensions A and B often will allow that disagreement to dominate argument or direct value assessment. But they may agree very well about dimensions C, D, E, ..., and in multi-attribute procedures this agreement about some dimensions will reduce the disagreement caused by dimensions A and B. In the Gardiner study, correlations as low as -.5 between conflicting groups were, by a multi-attribute procedure that did not include face-to-face discussion, increased to as high as .6. Presumably discussion might have produced still more agreement.

When groups clearly have different value systems, it is often useful to have each group generate its own values independently. Then information about dimensions, weights, and aggregate values can be provided to every other group.

This permits explicit, quantitative examination of differences, thus pleasantly cutting down the noise of rhetoric.

If disagreement is real and persistent, how can decisions be made? First, consensus is not a sine qua non of evaluation. If different groups have very different values, then data must be gathered to examine how contemplated actions bear on these values. This forces the evaluation researcher into multiple measurement. In addition, it means that decision makers receive research data on issues that may be foreign to their own values, but quite germane to the values of other groups, such as those affected by a program. The result of this diversity is a much greater richness of evaluation information. All concerned groups benefit.

Value conflicts should, whenever possible, lead to the time-honored processes of negotiation and compromise. Multi-attribute utility measurement, by quantifying the dimensions and amounts of disagreement, provides a starting point for such negotiations and a scale for measuring their progress. Perhaps more important, it provides an explicit language in which the discussion can be phrased.

Sometimes, however, compromise cannot be reached, and yet a decision must be made. The decision maker will, by this time, have enormous amounts of guidance about the value issues inherent in his decision. He can proceed in various ways. One, often used in bureaucracies, is to substitute his judgment for that of his subordinates. Multi-attribute utility offers another. He can weight each disagreeing subordinate individual or group, and then calculate weighted-average importance weights to use in the rest of the multi-attribute utility evaluation process.

We have already indicated how we feel about disagreements at Step 8. Whenever possible, they should be resolved by expertise, not argument.

F. THE INTEGRATION OF PLANNING AND EVALUATION

Earlier, we asserted that the planning and evaluation process could and should be integrated. What has just been described is clearly planning, although it can be done at any time before or during a program. How, then, does one proceed from planning of this kind to the evaluation process?

A matrix has geen generated as part of the multi-attribute utility planning process. All of the values that have been rank ordered and weighted for importance are in the matrix. The rows of the matrix consist of the programs, subprograms, etc.; i.e., the entities which are being evaluated. The columns are the value dimensions. In the first cell of the matrix, there is a location judgment of the extent to which program 1 is likely to contribute to value A, and so on for value B, etc., and the other programs. In the planning stage, this judgment has been made using all the available data on the program. Where programs do not exist, and are potential new options, these judgments are no more than educated guesses.

As the program proceeds, data are gathered. The standard techniques of Bayesian statistics can be used to update initial guesses as data accumulate. Thus the original evaluation structure used in planning the program can also be used to evaluate it as it proceeds and to assess its merits when it is over.

It is with respect to the individual cells of the matrix that research choices can be made about how to gather data, and whether experimental or observational methods are most germane. For example, it may be that in order to obtain data relevant to certain values, experimental methods are most appropriate. For data relevant to other values such methods may be irrelevant or impossible. It is up to the researcher to use the most appropriate methods to find data relevant to every cell in the matrix. But one fundamental tenet of the Bayesian point of view is: never throw data away, unless they are utterly irrelevant. Bayesian methods are, at least in principle, capable of combining experimental results, judgments, anecdotal observations, and everything else that bears on the question at hand. Any datum is better than none, and any two are better (or at least no worse) than only one of them. Of course data can be misleading--but in principle, this can happen only by accident. A wise evaluation researcher should never be misled by substantial additional information. Of course, in practice, attaining that standard of wisdom is sometimes quite a task!

Obviously, how seriously a datum should be taken in revising an assessment is a function of the quality of the datum. Sometimes, the preceding paragraph notwithstanding, datum B is so uninformative compared with datum A that B should not even be considered if A is available. (Technically, this implies that the likelihood for B is so flat compared with that for A that the product of the two looks essentially like the likelihood function for A alone--in which case the multiplication, though formally appropriate, is a waste of time.) But we consider such situations to be rare in evaluation research contexts.

It may be that for certain cells of the matrix it is either logically or practically impossible to obtain any data. This information must go back to the decision makers. They may then decide to delete or modify a value, or to stick with it, even though they know they will have to rely on sheer guesswork about the state of the world, since there will be no data that would permit them to revise their prior probability judgments.

It is important to note that the data needed are directly related to the values that govern the decision making process. Further, it is not the researcher, but the various decision making groups who decide what shall be studied. The multi-attribute utility matrix gives the researcher his multiple measure marching orders.

However, values (here interpreted as importance-weighted) change as a program proceeds, as circumstances change, as time passes. The weights appropriate for this year may not be appropriate next year. This suggests that two different evaluation questions, both based on the same updated location measures, can and should be asked. One is, "How does the present program measure up to the expectations we had for it when we planned it?" The other is, "Given this year's values, how does the present program look? Should it be changed? If so, how?"

It is fairly often reasonable to define a value dimension as a goal. A very abstract dimension can often be operationalized by specifying some measure or set of measures such that attainment of them constitutes success, and failure to attain them constitutes failure. Then the probability of success can be treated as the location measure, and can be updated by standard Bayesian procedures as data accumulate.

III. SOME COMMENTS AND COMPLAINTS, MOSTLY ABOUT EXPERI-MENTAL EVALUATIONS

We now turn to the alternate approaches. The baseball statistician's approach need detain us only briefly. In part this is because we like it; it provides data inputs that we can use for multi-attribute utility analysis, without excluding relevant data.

Our complaints against it, used alone, are two. First, and by far most important, is that the baseball statistician's approach has nothing explicit to say about values. It leaves assessment of value to the intuition of the decision maker. The decision maker usually responds by skimming the statistics, selecting a few that seem to him of at least some relevance to what he really cares about, and then making whatever decision he feels is best.

The big hang-up of the baseball statistician's approach, like that of the experimentalist's, is objectivity. Even fundamentally judgmental questions are approached as though one should apologize for using judgmental information. But values, as we have already insisted, are inherently judgmental. So, in spite of his thoroughness, they escape the baseball statistician's ledger, box score, environmental impact report, management information system, or whatever.

A secondary but serious complaint about the baseball statistician's approach is simply its voluminousness. It solves the data aggregation problem by not aggregating very much. The result is huge tomes or print-outs that go unread--while the decisions continue to be made by the seat-of-the-pants method.

Of course, this failure to aggregate results from failure to know how to aggregate. The problem of aggregation is always that of adding apples to oranges; one can do so only if one knows ahead of time that one wants to count fruit. Our solution to this problem, as we have already emphasized, lies in the use of multi-attribute utility, which is an explicit tool for defining not only what we want to count but also how the aggregating should be done.

A. *WHAT IS A VARIABLE IN A SOCIAL PROGRAM?*

We now turn to experimental approaches to evaluation. Experiments are supposed to be elegant. Independent variables are manipulated, according to some coherent, previously thought-through plan. Dependent variables are observed, preferably to three decimal places. Concomitant variation between independent and dependent variables is observed, and number magic is performed to permit an argument that the observed concomitant variation is no accident. Then, inferences are made. Always, these inferences assume that the experimentally studied conditions and individuals in some sense represent some larger set of conditions and individuals. Two different senses of representativeness are common. In one, the conditions have been systematically chosen and are considered to represent the dimension from which they were chosen. In the other, some "universe" of objects is supposed to exist, and the objects studied in the experiment are considered to be random samples from that universe, and so to represent it.

Beyond the assumption of representativeness, further inferences usually concern the reason for the observed concomitant variation. Naive formulations tend to say that the changes in the dependent variable(s) are caused by changes in the independent variable(s). More sophisticated writers avoid the philosophically knotty idea of "cause," and instead construct what has come to be called a model of the phenomenon under study. The model, of course, predicts the concomitant variation that was (or, occasionally, will be) observed. Models come in various sizes, flavors, and degrees of decoration with letters from the Greek alphabet, but the ones of most interest to us for the purposes of this paper are usually qualitative verbal statements about a network of relationships among the variables that collectively constitute a social phenomenon or program.

And thus science progresses. But what has that got to do with evaluation?

A little, say we. Experiments are tools for observing concomitant variation. They are inordinately costly tools, and they usually permit examination of only a few concomitant variations. To the degree that they do bear on location measures needed for a multi-attribute utility evaluation, they can be used as a data source from which can be derived numbers to go into some cells of the value-dimensions-by-programs matrix discussed above. But they will never specify what those value dimensions are, or how the utility transformation (Step 8) needed to fill in the

444

cell should be performed, or what the importance weights used in the aggregation process should be. Thus their function is in principle modest, but useful.

In practice, using experiments for evaluative purposes is more difficult than that. One major difficulty is with the notions of independent and dependent variables. The problem of defining a dependent variable is familiar to most behavioral scientists, and to some extent we have already discussed it. (Dimensions of value are dependent variables.) But evaluation research does add a new and special difficulty to the problem of defining independent variables. Typically, an evaluation experiment will compare one program with another, or with no program. But what is a program? In principle, anything you wish to label as a variable can be treated as one. But nonsense independent variables will, via any experiment, lead to nonsensical conclusions. And it certainly is nonsense to assume that some program, implemented in different ways by different people in different places, is a single entity simply because it is called by a single name and perhaps funded from a single source of money. An extreme example is the recent functional literacy evaluation conducted by UNESCO (1975). A group of five experts tried to look at the efficacy of functional literacy programs throughout the world. Of course, problems of data collection, translation, and the like arose. But the core difficulty of this global evaluation was that each country defined functional literacy in its own way, implemented it by its own procedures, and applied it to its own population. The central staff in Paris soon concluded that comparable data were pretty much impossible to obtain. "Functional literacy" is not sufficiently unitary over so wide a range of circumstances so that "functional literacy programs" can serve as a meaningful independent variable.

This issue is sometimes discussed as one of program implementation. How similar are the implementations of a program across sites? The more dissimilar implementations are, the less appropriate it is scientifically to lump them together and call them all by the same name. Unfortunately, the identification of programs with their names is so often accepted without question that implementation analyses are seldom done. In some cases in which such analyses have been done (e.g., Lukas, 1974), the results have shown that programs with the same title differ widely over sites. The topic is still in hot debate (Pettigrew, 1974).

One very common reason why programs in different places have the same name is that they are funded from a common source and administered by a common agency. And this seems entirely appropriate; parcels of money and administrative organizations do need names, and the names should reflect their unity of source when it exists. From this point of view, the variation from site to site is a laudable attempt by local program people to respond effectively to the unique characteristics of the program site, and perhaps to put into effect also their own knowledge and/or beliefs about the problem that the program addresses.

Our point, then, is not that local variation of programs with common names should be avoided; quite the contrary. Instead, our point is simply that such variations make the experimental approach to evaluation difficult to apply.

Of course, programs vary not only with location, but also with time. Programs may change daily, weekly, or monthly, in response to the desires of clients, the reactions of pupils, the boredom of teachers, etc. Moreover, programs often are ill-defined when they begin, so that many changes occur as they become defined.

We find it instructive to note what kinds of programs have been evaluated using randomized field designs. Obviously, medical programs lead the list. It is relatively easy to ensure that a vaccine remains the same from place to place and from time to time, thus keeping the error variance down. Among more behavioral programs, randomized field designs are most common in remedial education and in cash transfer programs--again, fairly narrowly defined programs in which control of treatment is reasonably straightforward. Other examples making the same point are the Negative Income Tax and Manhattan Bail experiments.

The desire of the decision maker to treat all programs covered by a given line item in a budget as one program is fully as legitimate and appropriate as is the local variation and temporal variation that makes such treatment intellectually misleading. The decision maker must decide what to do about that budget item; he cannot, if he is dealing with many hundreds of such line items, look into each in detail. Highly aggregated evaluations of internally diverse and changing programs are appropriate and necessary. Only decision-analytic techniques, we think, can provide them.

B. *HOW TO AGGREGATE THE EFFECTS OF HETEROGENEOUS PROGRAMS*

If you agree with us that the crucial issue for the evaluation of social programs is not, directly, what the results were, but rather whether these results were good or bad, an obvious approach to aggregation suggests itself. Each subprogram should be evaluated according to some appropriate form of multi-attribute utility methodology. Care should be taken to make sure that the units of utility used are reasonably comparable from program to program; this is relatively easy if the value dimensions and weights are the same, but in general it requires additional judgments relating one subprogram to another. Then the utilities of the various subprograms should simply be added to get the utility of the total program. The variability of these utilities, as well as the sum, will be of interest, for the usual reasons why variances are interesting.

C. EFFECT SIZE, VARIANCE, AND VARIABLE DEFINITION

Closely related to the question of whether or not a program can or should be treated as an independent variable is the problem of size of effect.

The idea of a "large effect" unfortunately has two different meanings, both important. One, the obvious one, is simple magnitude, in whatever units of measurement are natural to the problem. Polio vaccines reduce the incidence of polio, measured in relative frequency of cases per year. This is the sort of information needed as a basis for evaluation. Sometimes the same sort of information requires the more complicated device of a control measurement. For example, almost any program aimed at reducing robberies by juveniles that was started at the beginning of 1974 would now, one year later, be looking bad in absolute numbers, unless it was extraordinarily effective. Juvenile crimes went up markedly during 1974, presumably because of a depressed economy and greater unemployment. But a simple comparison might show, for example, that a police jurisdiction with a juvenile-robbery-prevention program experienced only half as much increase in juvenile robberies as did an otherwise comparable (note that weasel phrase!) jurisdiction without such a program. This might well be considered a large favorable effect for the program.

Implicit in the preceding paragraph is the assumption that an effect that is large in its natural units will be large in utility also. If not, somebody is in trouble! If the main and large effects of a program are, or are nearly, value-irrelevant, who installed the program, and why?

The second meaning of a "large effect" results from the fact that effects can occur by accident. For that reason, statisticians have developed methods for assessing effects relative to their variability. (Classical and Bayesian statisticians attack this problem in technically different ways, but the problem is the same, and we will not examine the technical differences here. For a discussion of them, see Edwards, Lindman, and Savage, 1963.) Strictly speaking, the word "reliable" would be preferable to the word "large" for effects that do well in such assessments. But the meaning of "large" discussed two paragraphs ago so interacts with this meaning that the same word is often used for both. In principle, procedures for assessing effects relative to their variability tell us how certain we can be that our conclusions about concomitant variation are generalizable. Unfortunately, it will virtually always be true that the larger an effect is, in the sense of the second previous paragraph, the surer we will be that our conclusions about it are generalizable, while the larger the variability of that effect, the less sure we will be of its generalizability. That is why the heterogeneity of programs given the same name can make experiments unsuccessful; not so much that the effects are either larger or smaller, but that the variability is larger.

As we have already pointed out, such problems don't matter if the effect is large enough, in the first sense of that word. Indeed, programs with really large effects need little or no evaluation. We can expect that programs presenting evaluative problems will have effects that are either small, in the first sense, or else diverse, so that their generalizability is subject to question.

In the second chapter in this volume, Gilbert, Light, and Mosteller reach the conclusion that most evaluations show, at best, small gains. They base this conclusion on a review of a large number of randomized-design evaluative experiments concerned with medical and social innovations. In their review they directly assigned utilities, on a five point scale, to the results of each innovation. They found a few large positive effects in medical studies, though even there small or even negative effects were more common.

We found especially instructive their treatment of the Negative Income Tax experiment. In that experiment, the question was whether a negative income tax would have undesirable consequences, such as an increase in unemployment. Such undesirable consequences were indeed found, but in a smaller amount than some had feared. Gilbert, Light, and Mosteller rated this as a highly favorable outcome. The same is true of the Manhattan Bail experiment; it also produced some undesirable effects, but fewer than had been feared, and Gilbert, Light, and Mosteller also rated it as having a highly favorable outcome. In fact, these were two of only three highly favorable social-experiment outcomes they discussed!

Clearly Gilbert, Light, and Mosteller are making utility judgments--and we applaud their willingness to do so. We wish we understood better the basis for their assessment of size of effect. For example, we were puzzled by their treatment of the selective or truncal vagotomy study (IV-H-3). The comparison was between a complicated, difficult, time-consuming surgical procedure and an easier one, both for the same condition. After one year, there was no difference in the clinical grading of patients who had received the two procedures. Gilbert, Light, and Mosteller rate the outcome of this experiment as zero--neither favorable nor unfavorable. If they had been using a multi-attribute utility procedure in which clinical consequences were one attribute, and cost and difficulty of the procedure were another, we can only assume that the simpler procedure would have come out way ahead of its competitor. (We apologize to Gilbert, Light, and Mosteller for using their application of simple utility measurement procedures as a basis for our advocacy of more complex ones.)

D. *WHAT CAN HAPPEN WHEN LARGE EFFECTS ARE NOT FOUND*

Unfortunately, it is often difficult to distinguish in experimental practice between the two different meanings of the words "large effect" distinguished above. If an effect is literally zero, in its natural units, no ambiguity arises. But suppose that the effect seems substantial, measured in its natural units--and its variability is also substantial, so that generalizability is uncertain. This is an obviously ambiguous situation--one which can be exploited to suit the purposes of the exploiters.

The Negative Income Tax experiment offers an interesting example. Its framers assumed that the negative income tax itself, which in effect gives money to the poor, would have a desirable effect. So the experimental evaluation was designed to examine whether or not it also had undesirable effects. Some were found, but they were smaller than expected, so the experiment was judged as favorable to the negative income tax.

Skeptics have suggested (and unpublished research also suggests) that the assumed positive effects simply were not there. The amounts of money transferred to the poor by the particular negative income tax scheme studied may well have been too small to have any substantial effects, good or bad. But the experimental evaluation procedure was not well suited to exploration of this question.

These two sorts of effects can interact. The assumption that a program, because it has good intentions, must have some positive effect, is obviously unwarranted but often made. The assumption that a negative effect, though present, was either small (in the second sense) relative to its variability, or, if reliable, in any case smaller than expected, can combine with the assumption of an unmeasured positive effect to lead to favorable-sounding conclusions from unfavorable data collected in experimental evaluations that do not respect the multidimensionality of the value problem.

The opposite effect can also occur. If a program must demonstrate favorable consequences or die, the fact of its variability from site to site and time to time may make the conclusion that it has favorable consequences impossible to demonstrate experimentally, for reasons of variability.

These possibilities suggest an interesting life cycle for social programs. Originally, their enthusiastic scientific advocates can set up studies that assume some favorable consequence, look for unfavorable side effects and fail to find them, perhaps for reasons of variability, and thus find in favor of the program. Later on, the program, now insitutionalized in many more sites and being looked at by skeptical budgetary eyes, can be required as a condition of survival to provide evidence of its favorable consequences, and may fail to do so, again perhaps for reasons of variability--or perhaps because those consequences simply don't exist and never did. We believe, though we could not prove it, that just such a life cycle has occurred fairly often in the past, and is likely to occur also in the future.

E. *CAUSAL INFERENCES*

We have often heard research-trained individuals in funding agencies say, "If you cannot answer 'why,' don't bother to ask 'what.'" Radical behaviorists typically assert that questions beginning "Why..." are really questions that should begin "What..," ill-phrased. Model-builders might disagree, asserting that "What..." refers to data while "Why..." refers to models. We think this is what those who insist on "Why..." questions in evaluation contexts really have in mind. But model-building, verbal or mathematical, is intellectually independent of experimentation, though not of data. No type of inference, except perhaps for certain specific kinds of statistical procedures, is linked in any necessary or inevitable way with experimentation.

In any case, models may or may not be needed for evaluation. Often, perhaps most often, the decision maker does not want to know, "Why does the effect occur?" but simply, "Is there an effect, and if so, what, and is that good or bad?"

This rejection, not only of causal inference, but even of model-building, is likely to seem blasphemous to scientists who regard the understanding of process as the underlying aim of all research, including evaluation research. We feel ourselves handicapped, therefore, in expressing our views to an experimentally oriented audience. We are apparently arguing against motherhood and for sin. Nevertheless, carefully chosen sinning has its merits, and certainly there are some defects in motherhood. So we shall continue to argue that simple description is often both necessary and sufficient as a basis for evaluation. When it is not, neither causal inference nor model-building is the inevitable next step.

F. *USING ALL THE DATA*

Evaluation researchers often tell decision makers that because a program has not been designed as an experiment, none of the data it has produced are relevant to decisions made about it. Similarly, evaluation researchers often tell decision makers that data on outcomes cannot be provided until after a certain amount of time has elapsed; if decisions must be made before then, too bad. While such unhelpful advice is a natural consequence of the experimental approach (carried, perhaps, to the point of tactlessness or even uselessness), it is both absurd and unnecessary.

What is needed in situations in which the data are sparse or of poor quality--that is, most social situations-- is a data-inclusive information processing system, capable of using data from experiments, from observations, from anecdotes, from judgments, and from any other available source. Such a system must of course be able to indicate explicitly with what certainty the decision maker can reach conclusions, given the data available to him. We believe that the Bayesian approach (see, for example, Edwards, Lindman, & Savage, 1963; Edwards, Phillips, Hays, & Goodman, 1968) can do all that.

Many evaluation situations, e.g., some in developing countries, are quite data-poor. In fact, one might conceive of a two-dimensional space in which evaluation problems can be located. One dimension has to do with the amount of data available, and the other with the amount of control the researcher has over the data. In our view, any evaluation technology worthy of the name should apply anywhere within this space--preferably with the same basic ideas regardless of location. Faced with the problem of what to do until the statistician comes, we insist that the evaluator should have an answer.

G. WHO DECIDES WHAT WILL BE STUDIED?

Who does the evaluation serve--the statistician or the decision maker? As we have earlier argued, evaluation research should be concerned with questions of value. Using the multi-attribute utility measurement matrix, the decision makers' values determine on what variables data should be gathered. The researcher then decides how to collect the data.

This strongly contrasts with a common experimentalist approach to evaluation. Experimentalists tend to impose their own value orientation by their choice of what is studied. An implicit value they often have is that what is studied must be objectively and, if possible, quantitatively assessed. This leads to the unidimensional values used in nearly all experimental evaluation designs. A frequently cited illustration was the sole use of cognitive outcomes in the early evaluation of Head Start programs. These happen to be the outcomes of greatest interest to the psychologists who worked on Head Start evaluations. Cognitive outcomes were only one of a number of outcomes valued by other groups, such as Head Start parents and program administrators. It is only in the most recent Head Start evaluations that social competences in children and program effects on families have been included in the evaluation design. We cite this as an illustration of what can and frequently does happen when experimentalists impose their own value orientation by choosing what will be studied in an evaluation. The ESAP study cited in Gilbert, Light, and Mosteller provides another illustration. The purposes of this program apparently were multi-dimensional. Yet the results showed improvement on only a single dimension for one group. Was this a sufficiently important outcome? How important was it within the aggregate set of goals for the program? The approach used did not address this question.

We believe that all the important goals of all the relevant decision making groups should be objects of study and data collection. Interpersonal and group disagreements about which goals are important is part of the fabric of program evaluation. The researcher cannot make critical choices of what is studied based on his own values, or even only on the basis of the values embodied in the legislation. It is clear that in the evaluation paradigm of this paper, the power of choice of the researcher is considerably diminished. He no longer decides what will be studied; only how it will be studied.

We must note the interaction of this view that the evaluation researcher should provide information relevant to all dimensions of value with the fact that he has a limited budget. Experiments are inordinately expensive. It is usually more important to provide some data about all relevant value dimensions than to provide excellent data about only a few.

Of course "some data" can be misleading, especially if they are uncontrolled, anecdotal, or casually collected. Experimental data can be misleading, too. Elsewhere we have discussed the dangers of the pseudo-experiment (Edwards, Guttentag, & Snapper, in press) in evaluation. Suffice it to say here that the greatest inferential difficulties arise when the assumptions of the experimental model are not fulfilled, yet the analytic and statistical methods of experimental research are used. Even a cursory look at much of what has been called experimentation in evaluation reveals that crucial assumptions of the experimental model are frequently unmet. Some control groups do not control. Random assignment of subjects to conditions often turns out not to have been random. We strongly agree with the argument presented in other chapters in this volume that randomization is best where possible. But we must add, "It's nice work if you can get it." Even more important, the evaluation researcher must have a conceptual framework and a statistical system that permits him to tell the truth at all times--permitting him to handle data generated from classical experiments and data that are not.

H. *THE TEMPORAL INTEGRATION OF PLANNING, EVALUATION, AND PROGRAM CHANGES*

Programs evolve and change over time, and decisions about such changes are intermittent. An overall conceptual framework for evaluation must provide information useful for these intermittent changes, and must not require that the program stand still or stay the same in order to be evaluated. We believe that the combination of the multi-attribute utility framework and Bayesian statistics fulfills the requirements and provides the needed flexibility. In Bayesian statistics, the rules for hypothesis revision are not linked to the data collection operations. Hypotheses can be revised, given the data on hand, frequently or infrequently, and at intermittent, irregular time intervals. The multi-attribute utility framework also permits decision makers to change their values when it is relevant for them to do so. They are not locked into the researcher's hypotheses.

In describing the multi-attribute utility evaluation model, we showed how planning and evaluation are integrally linked. The process is initially a planning process. Evaluation enters the picture as data is used to revise the inferences (probabilities) about states of the world in each of the cells of the matrix.

One of the endemic complaints of both evaluation researchers and policy makers is that the evaluation results are so little used in the actual decision making process. It should be clear from this presentation that because of the temporal integration of planning, evaluation, and program changes which is possible using the decision-analytic framework, the possibility of directly relevant and both useful and used evaluations is considerably greater.

IV. CONCLUSION

The conceptual structure of the evaluation research paradigm is different from that of classical research. Evaluation always involves a judgment of the worthwhileness of action alternatives on the part of decision makers. For that reason the values of decision making groups must be made explicit and must be ordered. Action alternatives related to the decision must be specified, and inferences about states of the world expressed. This conceptual structure specifies for the researcher the variables about which he must provide data, so that inferences can be revised given information. A statistical system that is data-inclusive should be used; the system should also permit intermittent and irregular revision of probabilities.

We believe that multi-attribute utilities combined with Bayesian statistical inference fully meets these requirements of evaluation research. Within this framework, the evaluation researcher can choose the methods to be used to provide data for the revision of probabilities. One of these methods may be experimentation.

ACKNOWLEDGMENTS

We have benefited greatly from the work done by Kurt Snapper in the application of the model presented to the research and programs of the Office of Child Development. The cooperation of Saul Rosoff, Acting Director of the Office of Child Development, and John Busa, of the same office, was instrumental in carrying through the planning phase to completion.

REFERENCES

Campbell, D. T., & Erlebacher, A. How regression artifacts in quasi-experimental evaluations can mistakenly make compensatory education look harmful. In Compensatory education: A national debate (Vol. 3, Disadvantaged child). New York: Brunner/Mazel, 1970.

Dawes, R. M. & Corrigan, B. Linear models in decision making. Psychological Bulletin, 1974, 81, 97-106.

Edwards, W. Social utilities. The Engineering Economist, Summer Symposium Series, 6, 1971.

Edwards, W., Guttentag, M., & Snapper, K. A decision theoretic approach to evaluation research. In E. L. Streuning & M. Guttentag, (Eds.), Handbook of evaluation research (Vol. 1). Beverly Hills, California: Sage Publications, in press.

Edwards, W., Lindman, H., & Savage, L. J. Bayesian statistical inference for psychological research. Psychological Review, 1963, 70, 193-242.

Edwards, W., Phillips, L. D., Hays, W. L., & Goodman, B. C. Probabilistic information processing systems: Design and evaluation. IEEE Transaction on Systems Science and Cybernetics, 1968, SSC-4, 248-265.

Fryback, D. G. Subjective probability estimates in a medical decision making problem. Unpublished doctoral dissertation, University of Michigan, 1974.

Hargreaves, W., Attkisson, C., McIntyre, M., Siegel, L., & Sorenson, J. (Eds.), Resource materials for community mental health programs evaluation (Vols. 1-4). San Francisco: NIMH, 1974.

Keeney, R. L. Multiplicative utility functions (Technical Report #70). Boston: Massachusetts Institute of Technology, Operations Research Center, 1972. (a)

Keeney, R. L. Utility functions for multi-attributed consequences. Management Science, 1972, 18, 276-287. (b)

Kiresuk, T., & Sherman, R. Goal attainment scaling: A general method for evaluating comprehensive community mental health programs. Community Mental Health Journal, 1968, 4(6), 443-453.

Lukas, C., & Wohlleb, C. Implementation in Head Start planned variation 1970-71. Cambridge, Mass.: The Huron Institute, 1973.

Lumsdaine, A. A., Hilton, E. T., & Kincaid, D. L. Evaluation research methods. In E. M. Rogers and R. Agarwala-Rogers (Eds.), Evaluation research on family planning communication. Paris: UNESCO, in press.

Phillips, L. D. Bayesian statistics for social scientists. New York: Cromwell, 1973.

Raiffa, H. Decision analysis: Introductory lectures on choices under certainty. Reading, Mass.: Addison-Wesley, 1968.

Raiffa, H. Preferences for multi-attribute alternatives. The RAND Corporation, Memorandum RM-5968-DOT/RC, April, 1969.

Schlaifer, R. Analysis of decisions under uncertainty. New York: McGraw-Hill, 1969.

Snapper, K. J., & O'Connor, M. Testing hypotheses about the utility of programs: Use of Bayesian techniques. Working paper. Center for Social and Evaluation Research, The University of Massachusetts, Boston, 1975.

UNESCO. Evaluation of functional literacy. (Henquet) 1975.

Weiss, C. H. Evaluation research. Englewood Cliffs, N.J.: Prentice-Hall, 1972.

Weiss, R. S., & Rein, M. The evaluation of broad-aim programs: Experimental design, its difficulties, and an alternative. Administrative Science Quarterly, 1970, 15, 97-109.

Williams, W., & Evans, J. W. The politics of evaluation: The case of Head Start. The Annals, 1969, 385, 118-132.

7

Feedback in Social Systems:
Operational and Systemic Research on Production, Maintenance, Control, and Adaptive Functions

DANIEL KATZ

I. INTRODUCTION

The major objective of this paper is to analyze types of feedback as they relate to the functioning of different forms of social structure.[1] The concept of feedback comes from cybernetics, but we will use it in a broader sense than that of thermostatic regulation. It reflects the idea of circular patterns of causality and the interdependence of social events, especially the continuing dependence of any living system on its environment. Without energic exchange with the environment, systems, including the human being, would run down. Without informative exchange, all biological or social systems would not survive for any length of time. The concept of feedback means that we select a major actor in a situation and then take his point of view in the interchange with his environment and see how his actions lead to reactions from the environment which reinforce or modify his behavior. The major actor may be an individual,

---

[1] I am indebted to Peter Rossi and Robert L. Kahn for their careful reading of this paper and their critical comments and constructive suggestions.

a group, or a social system, and the selection is in good part arbitrary, depending upon the purposes of the investigator.

The type of thinking exemplified by the concept of feedback is critical for an understanding of the functioning of social systems. It departs from the linear stimulus-response model in viewing action and reaction as a continuing circular process. Feedback is the response of others to one's own responses, which then affects the continuation or modification of one's behavior. At the phenomenal level, this is illustrated in Asch's concept of shared psychological fields (1952). At the behavioral level, social interaction can produce cycles of events, and these cycles in returning upon themselves provide social structure (Allport, 1962). These patterns are the outcome of many interacting mechanisms and represent the balance of mutually influencing processes. Thus the attitudes of friends in communication with one another move toward agreement as they modify their attitudes or change their friendship patterns (Newcomb, 1961). Biological analogies to a steady state may be misleading in that we are not dealing with the homeostasis of the body with its ability to maintain a constant temperature. The balance achieved through patterns of social interaction does move toward an equilibrium, but not necessarily the precise state which existed before. We need, then, to give more attention in the social sciences to the interacting mechanisms which account for change as well as for stability.

In the social sciences, there is growing acceptance of the inadequacies of the old linear model of the S-R type. The open system approach, though often difficult to apply, is based upon system transactions with the environment. In sociology, such writers as Parsons (1960) and Smelser (1962) have analyzed the relations between societal sub-systems; in political science, Easton (1965) and Almond (1963) have theorized about the inputs, outputs, and functions of political systems. In economics, George Katona (1960) has demonstrated the weaknesses of old economic models in not taking into account the reactive character of the consumer. Katz and Kahn (1966) have examined the functioning of organizations with respect to production and maintenance inputs. Recently, this more realistic orientation to social institutions has been paralleled by public concern for the evaluation of system functioning. The concept of public accountability has taken on new dimensions. Where once it meant an accounting of expenditures by an agency according to legal prescriptions, now it is coming to mean an assessment of the efficiency and effectiveness of an organization in attaining its objectives.

Another related development is the growth of computer technology, which makes possible the processing and analysis of huge quantities of information. Though the origin of computer technology is in the circular model of thinking in the physical sciences, its use in social systems may not prove faithful to its origins. The public pressure for accountability and the need of administrators for quantitative indicators come at a time when computing services are readily available. Hence, there is the danger that the complexities of adequate data gathering may be bypassed and any type of readily available or contrived data may be fed into the computer. The Pentagon's recent use of body count of enemy allegedly killed and wounded is a tragic example of reliance upon computer processing of the convenient rather than upon obtaining adequate and valid data about the nature and state of American involvement in southeast Asia.

The history of poor support for empirical research in the social sciences has aggravated the present problem. Social scientists, through lack of resources, in the past have been content with secondary analysis of data gathered by others for other than scientific purposes. As a result, many of them never mastered the art of careful data collection. Fortunately, we are getting a new generation of social researchers who recognize the importance of data collection and who are willing to learn and improve techniques for this purpose. In passing, I would venture the proposition that a field research project that does not devote a major part of its budget to data collection is in all probability poorly planned.

It is not enough, then, to be concerned about feedback and to believe that computer technology can solve the major problems of evaluating social systems. We need to utilize the theoretical analyses and empirical findings of the social sciences to help in the development of information systems. Setting up computer programs in a social vacuum is not the answer, though operations research people have sometimes gone on this principle. Too little attention has been given to the gathering of data, to techniques for data collection, and to the relation of kinds of data to theoretical concepts. We cannot skip this stage of development in the social sciences, no matter how advanced present computer technology seems to be.

II. TYPES OF FEEDBACK

A. *OPERATIONAL AND SYSTEMIC LEVELS OF FEEDBACK*

Let us start, then, with some analysis of types of feedback in social systems and how they relate to various aspects of system structure and function. The first distinction I would make is between the measurement of impact upon the immediate and direct target, on the one hand, and assessment of progress toward long-range goals, on the other; i.e., between operational and systemic feedback. The defining characteristics include: (1) the temporal dimension, whether immediate or delayed; (2) the amount of social space involved, whether a limited segment of the system or the whole organization and its environment; and (3) primary direct outcomes vs. secondary and tertiary effects. The first type (operational feedback) is more thermostatic in nature in that the measurement can be closely related to the operation and the organization can readily adjust to the information. If the product is not selling and warehouses become overloaded, then production can be slowed. If twenty men quit their jobs, another twenty can be hired. The comparison to the thermostat is far from exact because adjustments do not follow automatically from the information received. Another form of operational feedback is not especially informative about the production process, but is linked to organizational attempts to develop power and to control the social as well as the physical environment. Organizational behavior is not limited to turning out a product or rendering a service, but is also concerned with outstripping competition and overcoming opposition. These control and power operations can be guided by the gathering of intelligence about the strengths and weaknesses of the other side and their reaction to attempts to influence or coerce them. The use of espionage and surveillance to find out what the enemy is doing is utilized not only by the military but by industrial and government organizations as well. Moreover, it is utilized not only against another organization but by one subunit of the organization against another.

Both forms of operational research—the direct assessment of the productive process and the use of political intelligence—deal with limited, explicit objectives on the assumption that quantitative corrections will keep the operation on target. They do not inquire into the causes of malfunctioning nor into alternative procedures for improving the situation.

The other type of feedback would be systemic research about progress toward long-range goals. It comprises delayed assessment and is not built into ongoing operations. Ideally, it comprises some combination of basic and applied research as contemplated in the policy sciences. For a hypothetical example of the difference between operational feedback and systemic research, consider the case of a governmental agency concerned with public assistance to the needy. Operational feedback would give information about the number of people helped in any given week, the amount and type of assistance, and the degree of overload or underload on the personnel of the agency. Over time, we would know whether the incidence of people needing assistance showed any change. But we would have no information about the effects of such public assistance upon the recipients. If the number of needy did not decline, we would know nothing about how to reduce dependency, which is the long range objective of the program.

Management by crisis is the hallmark of systems basing their decisions on operational feedback. Changes in environmental support or demands are not anticipated and are reacted to at a heavy cost to the organization. In the crisis there is no lead time for the delayed assessment of organizational functioning. Systemic feedback has to be developed before the critical situation arises. Systemic research would have a broader and deeper scope. It would be less concerned with the specifics of the efficient functioning of a particular agency helping the needy, and more interested in the nature and causes of dependency. It would have implications more for policy than for detailed administration. Charles Moynihan has argued that "the welfare mess" could be corrected only by a new policy, namely, a guaranteed annual income, and that Congressional committees in a quandary about the problem in 1971 would have welcomed research dealing with alternatives to the old policy.

B. *SOCIAL SYSTEM FUNCTIONS*

These two types of feedback can be related to the operation of social systems with respect to their four major functions of (1) production, (2) maintenance, (3) adaptation, and (4) control. Production refers to the main throughput of the system: the work that gets done. It develops subsidiary systems for the procural of materials and the disposal of outputs. Maintenance has to do with preserving the internal structure of the system. The role arrangements comprising an organization are often taken for

471

granted as the walls of the maze, but they are human con-trivances, maintained by the expectations and habits of role incumbents. Hence, they do not automatically keep going once they have been set in motion. Organizations thus need feedback, not only about the reception of their outputs in the larger environment, but also about their effects upon their own people. It took years of industrial development before we considered the effects of conditions and types of work upon the physical health of workers. Only recently have we begun to study the impact of organizational life upon the mental health, morale, and motivation of organiza-tional members. Yet the maintenance and effective func-tioning of the organization is dependent upon what the organization does to its own people. Adaptation refers to survival and long-range adjustment. The turbulent character of the environment, in the language of Emery and Trist, calls for changes in organizational programs and procedures. Adaptation means the creative modification of organizational structure without destroying the long-range objectives of the organization. Feedback about environmental change is critical for making adjustments. Planning for types of contingencies or for development in the next decade calls for systemic feedback. Control has to do with the mana-gerial function of the use of authority to coordinate the activities of the system; the exertion of influence over the external environment; the adjudication of conflicts within the system; and the final decision-making about adaptive changes.

These four functions are often formalized in the departments or divisions in the organization. The technical processes of production are readily identified in the factory of the automobile firm, the teaching departments of a college, or the processing of claims in a government agency. The maintenance function is not as clearly demarcated. Personnel departments, staff benefits offices, and labor relations departments are often found, but they do not exhaust the maintenance processes carried on by the system. Adaptation is the work of the staff as against line officers and may be located in such units as planning sections or departments of research and development. Many organizations have no formally designated adaptive units, and people in managerial roles will also take over this function. Management as such is more formally designated, but the complicating aspect is that it cuts across all other sub-systems. Thus the head of production, the director of personnel, and the chief of planning are also part of the managerial structure. Functionally, there is a basis of separation. When the decision in the production department is based upon technical expertise, it is a production decision. When it is based upon broader considerations involving power, it is a managerial decision. The same distinction holds for the adaptive function. If there is no systemic study or technical expertise, the people in management who make decisions about system adjustments are not really functioning in an adaptive role. One criterion for a purely management role is whether an individual can be shifted from one management post to another, no matter what the throughput is. For example, if the same person can be shifted from one cabinet post to another, from Secretary of Defense to Secretary of Health, Education and Welfare, to Attorney General, then technical expertise about problems of defense, health, and justice are not viewed as being of major significance in the direction of these departments.

The types of feedback previously differentiated--systemic research and the two forms of operational feedback--are clearly related to these kinds of system functions. Operational feedback is utilized to regulate production processes in relation to the market. Information about personnel needs in similar fashion affects the recruitment, selection, and release of people in maintaining the organization. Surveillance and espionage fit the logic of the control function and have come into recent prominence as a major feedback mechanism of the political subsystem. Systemic research is especially appropriate for the adaptive function, but is not well developed for many problem areas of significance to the organization.

We shall examine in some detail the way in which types of feedback develop to meet system demands. It is important to do this because of the cues such an anlysis can provide for improving the utilization of information. Changes in feedback systems will not come about through ideal blueprints. They will come about because proposed modifications and innovations gear into present system needs.

C. *ENERGIC AND INFORMATIONAL FORMS OF FEEDBACK*

In differentiating among types of feedback we have restricted the term to information about organizational functioning and impact. The more fundamental level of feedback in any system, however, is energic--the resources it can import to energize its activities in relation to its exported energy. Information provides knowledge about the energic exchanges.

There is some similarity to the distinction at the individual level between drives and cues in the learning process. This distinction is not all-or-none in that energic feedback in itself provides information at a crude level about system functioning. If energic returns in the form of money, credit, materials, or people continue to pour in, that fact is a signal to organizational decision makers that something is being done right. The seeking of more detailed information involving a broader social space, a longer time span, and a greater depth of analysis becomes a specialized process in itself. It is our contention, however, that information gathering to provide feedback has its origin in energic feedback, that it first develops around the maintaining and increasing of energic inputs, and that it further develops around attempts to maximize the energic return to the system. Information of all sorts can be fed back to social systems in various ways, but that which affects organization decision making is that which is demonstrably related to energic input and its maximum return. Moreover, it needs to be related both in substance and in form through organizational mechanisms. This is not to argue that basic research is unrelated to organizational functioning, but that it has no direct impact upon decision making because it is rarely tied into any of the cycles of energic exchange of the functioning systems.

Let us develop the implications of this type of analysis. Social systems differ in the directness of their cycles of energic exchange with their environment. The more direct the cycle, the more quickly it will develop a simple informational feedback tied to its successes and failures in serving its public. Where cycles of energic renewal are very complex and indirect, the system will be slow in developing and utilizing informational feedback. The short feedback loops of many industrial and service organizations mean that the clients being serviced support the organization directly through purchasing the product or service. Support for educational institutions, for governmental agencies, and for public institutions does not come mainly and directly from the people receiving services, but from other sources in society. Accordingly, there is no simple feedback cycle for such organizations. But the push toward more systemic research embracing larger segments of social space encounters more barriers in private organizations than in public systems--an issue to which we shall return.

III. THE DEVELOPMENT OF FEEDBACK

A. *AROUND PRODUCTION PROBLEMS*

Our first type of feedback, operational feedback, develops around direct energic exchange as a natural extension of energic feedback from the marketplace--so many products of a given type sold, so many products of another type unsold. The questions then arise: what kinds of people responded positively, what kinds of people negatively, and what aspects of the product were appealing? Market research grew as a more elaborate form of operational feedback. It provided information about the characteristics of various subpublics and their reactions to certain products. By and large, market research, with some notable exceptions, did not move very far in the direction of systemic research concerned with long-range objectives. It remained true to its essential character of operational feedback--namely, providing some knowledge about specific operations. General principles about the behavior of people in their roles as consumers did not emerge from market research. The aggregation of such research could lead to inductive generalizations, but the difficulty of accumulating knowledge from market research was increased by the fact that it was often confused with the operations of advertising and selling.

The market research section of a typical business enterprise reports not to the industrial production department, but to the sales and advertising divisions. The questions that are raised by these divisions have to do with the reception of the sales message, not with the quality of the product; i.e., how many people are listening to our sales pitch and how well they like it, rather than what people really want in the way of a desirable product.

Market research will provide immediate feedback to the television networks about the number of people viewing a given program. But why people listen to a program and whether they are motivated to do anything about the message of the program remain largely unanswered questions. And here the networks betray their lack of research orientation, in that on the one hand they equate viewing and listening with action when they sell network time to advertisers, and on the other hand they assert a lack of relationship between viewing and action when they are questioned about the effect of TV violence on youngsters. It may seem mysterious to the outsider that managers are willing to spend money on market research and yet are not willing to try to develop basic knowledge so that every day would not have to be a new day for them. The answer is partly in the inadequate gearing of market research to organizational decision making, but also partly in the logic of the managerial function, which is to control rather than to adjust.

Another type of operational research addressed itself to technology--to the improvement of the efficiency of technical processes and to product development. Again, this was closely linked to energic transactions, specifically to minimum energy expenditure for given outputs. For some types of operations, the energic transactions were readily expressed by cost accounting. Detailed cost accounting permitted analysis of the factors involved in efficient performance. Research on technical processes went hand in hand with research on product development. An improved technical set of operations could lead to changes in the product itself. Moreover, product change could make for competitive advantage in the marketplace. For industrial enterprises, product development and improved technology went beyond operational feedback. The information sought was oriented toward improving specific operational procedures, but it involved some combination of basic and applied research, especially in firms working at the frontiers of knowledge, as in the electronics industry. The use of systemic research did not, however, extend to bringing together a knowledge of public needs with a knowledge of technology. The changes in production methods and the new products grew out of technology itself, rather than from a study of what people wanted. The assumption was that a market for a product would be there or could be created. Any thorough study of the needs and values of the public making up the market was not envisaged. Not only did this approach accord with the way organizations were set up, but it also reflected, as well as reinforced, the fact that basic research about people lagged behind basic research about things.

We can summarize the argument about production problems thus far in three propositions: 1) informational feedback develops as the natural extension of energic feedback; 2) it comes first where there is a direct relationship between the acceptability of output and the availability of input; and 3) feedback moves from operational to systemic research in the production subsystem of organizations. All three propositions assume something of a principle of least energy expenditure.

We have mentioned industrial enterprises as examples of our second proposition of information feedback coming first in organizations with direct energic transactions with their supporting publics. If we look at organizations that do not meet this criterion of the marketplace--organizations such as governmental agencies, schools, universities, prisons, and mental hospitals--we find little in the way of informational subsystems built into their structure. Universities carry on research, but not about their own operations. Their support comes from sources other than the people being serviced, and so there is no natural effective impact from those people most directly affected. During the years of increasing enrollments, universities functioned on a crisis basis even though their own demographic research centers could have furnished top administrators detailed information about population trends. Government agencies present a similar pattern. They often support research, but they do not apply it to their own operations.

Educational institutions and governmental agencies do not know what they are doing right and what they are doing wrong. To make a case for continuing public support they do keep a body count, but they have little information about what they do to those bodies or what procedures produce given effects. Passing examinations and receiving grades in courses lead to certification for degrees, but we know little about how degrees and grades relate to professional competence or citizen activism.

Direct accountability to the relevant public is another way of talking about the free market. The break from feudal traditions, in which the elite were not accountable to anyone but themselves, came first in commerce and industry. The idea spread to other fields, such as religion and politics. The Protestant Reformation has been interpreted as the growth of a free market for religious faiths. Political parties and candidates must compete for the support of the electorate. In practice, the economic market is not as free as in theory, and the extension of the market concept into noneconomic areas runs into similar problems. The check against the marketplace loses its force if monopoly prevails, whether in a one-party system or in an economic system dominated by a few giant enterprises.

The research and theorizing of George Katona (1964) has called attention to a significant pheonomenon related to the nature of the market in highly developed industrial societies. The rise in personal incomes has given large numbers of consumers a discretionary power they never had before. More than half the population of the U.S. commands incomes above the subsistence level. This means that these people have the power to buy or not to buy, and considerable power to choose what they will purchase. Consumers are not all-powerful, but they are not passive recipients manipulated at will by the producer. Thus the market, though not free in the classical textbook sense, is still a critical factor in the life and death of an economic enterprise. Many large firms have decentralized their operations to some extent in order to check the operations of component units against the marketplace (Drucker, 1946). In the large, centralized organization, the overall success or failure can be measured against trends in sales and net income. It is difficult, however, to assess the contribution of the many parts of the system to the overall figures. Decentralizing permits the yardstick of the marketplace to be applied to semi-autonomous units.

We would argue, then, that at the societal level, economic enterprises have had to gear their activities to the marketplace; that feedback around the inputs and outputs of production function has been the first to develop; and that subsequent elaboration of feedback has been geared to these basic cycles.

Decentralization to utilize the yardstick of the marketplace is recognized in theory and sometimes even in practice. The use of the marketplace concept within an organization is more neglected. A unit providing products or services within an organization generally does not have to compete with outside groups. But there are advantages to making the situation competitive. A department in an industrial enterprise, for example, could be allowed to go outside the construction unit of its own company for some building renovations. A department in a university could use its own selection and recruiting procedures for non-academic personnel instead of going through the personnel bureau of the university. There are, of course, disadvantages to this procedure, but the principle of direct accountability to the clientele being served has many useful applications in huge, complex organizations.

There is no real substitute for the direct feedback cycle in which people can respond to the programs involving them. It is like the principle of direct democracy in political groups, which necessarily assumes the less direct form of representative democracy in larger political systems. The virtues of direct democracy have been recognized by the new left, though their naive use of it takes no account of the complexities of large systems. All we want to call attention to here, however, is the advantage of introducing direct feedback cycles in certain sectors of large organizations. Doing so has the merit, moreover, of giving people at lower levels more potential involvement in the larger system through their participation in decision making about issues of importance to them.

In our third proposition, we emphasized that research about longer-range objectives supplemented operational feedback about the technological problems of production. It is only a step from testing a given product to experimentation with respect to the development of new products; from a perspective concerned with technical efficiency of ongoing operations to a consideration of how the organization will be faring during the next ten or twenty years. It is a long step, but one which many industrial enterprises take as they set up research and development units and so provide the first formal structure for the adaptive subsystem. Formal structure, though not necessarily accomplishing its objective, can provide constraints and pressures for directing the efforts of members of the substructure. As March and Simon (1958) point out, there is a selection of information reaching an organizational group with a given mission, a mutual reinforcement of similarly oriented group members, and a narrowing of the focus of attention to group goals. Thus, the setting up of an adaptive subsystem can mean more attention to environmental trends affecting the larger system and more consideration of fundamental causes. The emphasis is upon understanding and creative adaptation to environmental change. Though the adaptive subsystem may become a force in its own right, it does not follow that it will dominate the organization.

Adaptive subsystems, unlike operational feedback, need to be tied to the highest level of decision making. The cues about operational functioning can go directly to the appropriate operational level and the process can be speeded up or slowed down. Information implying changes in the system or its general policies must reach top decision makers without major transformations or blockages likely to occur if it has to pass through many subsystem levels.

B. *AROUND MAINTENANCE PROBLEMS*

The maintenance problems of attracting people to an organization, getting them to perform prescribed roles, and holding them in the system have generally received lower priority than production problems. The tasks to be performed and the procedures for efficient task performance came first. Somehow it was assumed that an adequate labor force could be recruited, and sufficient rewards and sanctions mobilized to insure acceptable role performance. With this emphasis, information was sought from operational feedback rather than systemic research. Absenteeism and turnover figures were utilized for allocating manpower, but the search for causes of absenteeism and turnover did not go wide or deep.

Early industrial psychology was more concerned with human factors as they related directly to the production process, as in time and motion studies; or indirectly, as with optimum work schedules to minimize fatigue. Departments of personnel research were added in many organizations, but more for worker selection and classification and operational feedback than for research on problems of worker satisfaction and motivation. The concern was for fitting the individual into the system, not for finding out how the system affected him. Studies of morale and of job satisfaction did develop over time, but rarely as systemic feedback for organizational decision making. These investigations were often single-shot affairs rather than recurring surveys. Often they were conducted by the Personnel Research Departments, departments generally so low in the organizational structure that the findings were not seen as of great importance or utility by top management.

Though techniques and knowledge about the integration of people into systems have been accumulating in universities and research centers, the adaptive systems of organizations give little place to research on how various kinds of social structures affect their members. Systemic rather than operational feedback about maintenance problems could be the area for significant breakthroughs in the future. This will not come about, however, as long as older types of thinking about expendability of people prevail. Organizational roles are regarded as basic, and if dropouts occur, it is easier to find replacements than to change the role requirements. Fairly recently, Rensis Likert, however, has been attacking this mode of thinking with his concept of human resources accounting (1969). He points out that the enormous investment most organizations have in their personnel never appears on the accounting ledger. As a result, personnel decisions are made without adequate attention to such cost factors. Yet the expenses of replacing managerial personnel, professional people, skilled workers, and employees with knowledge and experience about the system might be prohibitive. Hence, research about what the organization does to its own people and what changes in structure would make for greater physical and mental health and psychological satisfaction should be significant feedback for organizations in the future.

At the national or societal level, maintenance feedback is of interest with respect to alienation and anomie. In a sense, the way of life and the rewards and costs of working and living in a society comprise the energic feedback to societal members. Knowledge of how the nation is meeting problems of concern to them constitutes informational feedback for its citizenry. In large, complex societies, there is often not much of a meaningful relationship between these two forms of feedback--the energic and the informational--for many citizens. Times are good or times are bad, life is stressful or life is peaceful, but the specifics of individual existence are often not tied to explanations in the mass media which make sense to people. These explanations on the economic front deal with the business cycle, the balance of trade, the condition of the dollar in the world markets, all of which are remote from their own daily experience. Foreign policy is equally mysterious and is concerned with containing communism, the domino theory in southeast Asia, or competition or cooperation with the European community.

People thus receive information about remote rather than proximate objects and can become alienated in some ways from the national system. The alienated are the potential for mass movements, for leaders of such movements can furnish information about their problems in terms they can understand. The answers of demagogic leaders furnish no real solution but are temporarily satisfying. This basically is the thesis of Schumpeter (1947) and W. Kornhauser (1959). Schumpeter made a great deal of the tendency of mass media to deal with remote objects. Kornhauser emphasized the lack of ties between the individual and the national system as the basis for mass movements. Such alienation occurs more readily in societies weak in voluntary, intermediate organizations which can bridge the gap between primary associations and the national system.

Another factor of importance at the national level is the more pragmatic orientation of people in modern, technological societies. The traditionalism of agrarian society, which emphasized eternal verities, had built-in answers to all problems. Diasasters were the mysterious workings of Providence. But in the more practically oriented modern society, people become integrated into the national system on the basis of how they perceive their needs being met. They need energic feedback, and when there are problems, they need meaningful explanations of them. Otherwise they become alienated from existing institutions and can be recruited into new movements.

C. *RELATIONSHIP TO THE MANAGERIAL AND POLITICAL STRUCTURE*

The managerial structure refers to the hierarchical arrangements of authority for the coordination of activities, for adjudication of internal conflicts, and for final decision making about policies of all sorts. Hierarchy in social systems goes beyond arrangements for decision making in that it is generally correlated with differential rewards of pay, privilege, and prestige. Most organizations are not only collectivities of people engaged in a common enterprise, but are also subgroups defined by the hierarchical structure with conflicting interests, as in the division in the military of commissioned officers and G.I.'s, or the division in industry of salaried employees and hourly workers. The importance of including hierarchical differences of power and reward in a consideration of the development of feedback becomes clear when we ask the simple question: To what positions and people in the organization is feedback directed to affect system functioning? Information does not dictate the decisions unless it is consistent with the patterns of thought and motivation of policy makers. The type of information which is sought, the ways in which it is ignored or utilized are not determined solely by the knowledge available. The nature of the hierarchical arrangements, the interests of subgroups, the

degree and kind of participation, the existence of democratic checks and controls--in short, the power structure of
the system--are basic social realities to be considered in
the types of information gathered and utilized. The general
model assumed in dealing with organizations is that of a
collective effort to achieve goals in which mutual cooperation is the overriding consideration. Thus, one can attempt
to measure the effectiveness of the organization in achieving the common objective, and can evaluate the contributions
of the various units in the system and the procedures
employed for the shared goal. From this point of view, the
various role incumbents will be open to information which
will improve performance and will even seek such information. They will want to systematize information getting so
that they can improve what they are doing. This model,
although accepted by many organizational theorists about a
capitalist society, does not fit the social realities of
that society. Feedback which could result in increased
performance for the overall system but which could jeopardize the privileged position of certain echelons is not
going to be sought and welcomed by those echelons. Thus,
information in most systems is often used by various parts
of the management structure in the interests of their own
power position. This applies to the amount of information
which they pass down the line, the types of information they
seek for feedback, and the way they process that feedback.

If we see the managerial process in most systems as
political as well as administrative, then production and
maintenance issues are not going to be decided primarily on
the basis of a successful search for adequate and valid
information. The concern of management is to manage, to

control, to maneuver, to outwit, and to outpower the opposition. This often means exploitation of the environment with respect to production problems and exploitation of employees with respect to maintenance problems. A social scientist once asked a State Department official about the usefulness of research, and he replied that he would have no reluctance to use research findings. In fact, he went on, "I would use anything I could find that would help us prove our point." That research could be used to provide some of the answers was not in this man's frame of reference. He had the answers. All he needed were ways of getting them accepted. Research results or any other aid were useful if they could help him attain his objective.

The basic problem at the production level is one of dealing effectively with competitors in the environment. Competition can be for raw materials, for technological designs to improve efficiency, or for markets. Hence, management will seek information about sources of raw materials, technology, and the market. The critical question is: How can we effectively meet and beat competition? One way is to outcompete the rival in quality and cost of products and services; another is to outcompete him in advertising and propaganda; still another is to control competitors through price wars or other political moves.

The information required for manipulation adds to the power of the manipulator, especially as it becomes his exclusive possession. Hence, the gathering and analysis of facts loses something of its public character when the purpose is to outsmart the opposition. Companies try to keep detailed information about their production processes a secret from their competitors. Their market research is only for internal consumption. The extension of this type of dynamic is spying upon the activities of the competitor, and industrial espionage is of growing concern in certain kinds of enterprises. We shall return to its use in more purely political systems presently.

The interaction of adaptive and managerial processes is of especial significance for the development of feedback subsystems, with the control function tending to dominate the adaptive function. A number of students of organizational decision making have demonstrated that a rational model of problem solving is not the appropriate model to apply to social organizations. March and Simon (1958) have pointed out that the constraints and pressures in social structures make for piecemeal solutions, satisfying rather than optimizing; similarly, Braybrooke and Lindblom (1963) speak of disjointed incrementalism. These accounts of organizational decision making explicitly recognize the cognitive limitations of individual problem solving, and implicitly recognize the organizational constraints of a political nature. Incremental decision making, for example, makes policy makers less vulnerable to the mobilization of strong and widespread opposition. The search for optimal solutions includes possibilities of drastically restructuring the system. Again, this is threatening to the established echelons enjoying positions of power, prestige, and privilege. Hence, the first answer of the entrenched hierarchy is to ignore the problem, for it may disappear in short order. The second answer is to handle it with minimal change in the existing structure. Neither answer would be the appropriate response from an adaptive subsystem utilizing a more rational model of problem solution. But the political approach of management is to make little internal change in the organization and instead to control the environmental factors calling for change.

The first response of the automobile industry to the safety needs in cars was to attempt to silence the critics. It seemed like a stupid move for General Motors to intimidate Ralph Nader. But this is a judgment as if individuals were behaving just as individuals. The huge organization of General Motors had a tremendous investment in its plants and machinery, and the first organizational move would be to try to avoid costly changes in technology by controlling the environment. The psychology of manipulation at the organizational level is to try the least costly moves to see if they work. One manipulates and exerts power to see where the weak points of the opposition are. The test of a manipulation is whether it works, and it has to be tried to find out.

We are suggesting, then, that there is something of a built-in conflict between the managerial process and the adaptive function in nondemocratic structures. The adaptive subsystem has the function of studying environmental change and of proposing changes in the organization which would bring it into better equilibrium with its environment. The adaptive subsystem examines and considers structural modifications in the system itself. The managerial structure operates on a different set of principles, namely, to produce equilibrium by bringing the environment under control. The last changes it will consider are basic changes in the organizational structure itself. The conflict becomes a dilemma in that the organizations with the greatest resources for developing strong adaptive systems are the least motivated to do so. They are the large powerful structures and hence have a huge investment in plants, technology, and past ways of operating. Small companies can be more experimental, for it costs a large concern heavily to inaugurate the slightest change. Moreover, because of their size and power, big organizations do in fact have the potential for some control over their environment. Hence the very concerns that could afford to develop adequate adaptive subsystems are often the least inclined to do so.

This is all the more surprising in that the lessons of history are clear. Even at the level of technological change, one of the failures in the past has been the reluctance to scrap old plants and machines because of the investment in them. The Industrial Revolution came early in England, and England became the industrial and financial center of the world. Nation states late in industrialization had a hard time at first but then benefited by their ability to take advantage of new technology. The English, however, stuck by their heavy investment in older machinery and in time became a second-rate power. The history of American railroads is similar to the British experience. More recently, we have seen the American automobile industry caught up in a similar pattern. The Japanese were able to produce a low-pollution car in short order, whereas American automobile companies are still pleading for more time.

Whether we can profit from history and build adaptive systems which are fully utilized by top decision makers is an open question. It may be that Trist and Emery (1965) are right in pointing to the changing character of the social environment. Organizations once could depend upon a stable, predictable environment. It did change, of course, but the

492

changes themselves were those of degree, and were adequately handled by the assessment of trends. But according to Trist and Emery, environments have lost their placid and orderly character and have become turbulent. To the extent that the turbulence cannot be understood through research, there is no point in going beyond crisis management. It may be, however, that more systematic research will enable social systems to understand and plan for turbulent environments. Certainly the approach of one-level trend statistics is no longer going to provide the needed answers.

D. THE POLITICAL STRUCTURE AND MAINTENANCE PROBLEMS

The maintenance of a system has two aspects: to attract and keep people in the system, and to preserve the stability of role patterns. Since role arrangements are associated with differences in reward and power, there is a tendency toward secrecy in feedback about maintenance problems, especially in the early history of an organization. Knowledge may not always be synonymous with power, but communication and control in organizations go hand in hand. Information about maintenance issues is often not shared because its exclusive possession makes for greater control. Lines of cleavage and conflicts of interest within a system imply some degree of covert warfare in which information is withheld, distorted, and manipulated by competing groups. Before the advent of strong unions in American industry, more than one company used espionage among the workers to identify and remove malcontented activists.

The pressure for more public and more systemic information about maintenance issues in industry came not from information subsystems but from the power of worker organizations. Unions not only limited the power of management in manipulating workers, but also redirected the informational needs. What became important was not intelligence about particular militant employees, but about specific problems of absenteeism, safety, wasteful errors, etc. Surveys of workers' relevant perceptions, attitudes, and motivations became a fairly common means of gathering information. In many cases, moreover, such surveys of morale and motivation had the joint sponsorship of both company and union. The result was more publicly shared information. In Sweden, even data about company costs and profits are evaluated by a joint labor-management committee. Then, when a new contract is to be negotiated, both sides start from a common informational base and do not argue about basic facts concerning company earnings. The tendency toward the corruption of information into an espionage enterprise thus can be checked when there is some pluralism of power groups and some community of interest between them. In democratic political systems, the party in power is checked in its use of information by other parties, by other groups, and by traditions of public records and public accounting.

The tendency toward surveillance and secrecy is still a strong force, however, as recent history attests. Such instances of the growth of espionage as an important information subsystem reflect the complete domination, among top leaders, of systemic research of an adaptive character by the political structure. Power motives take over, and the orientation to all problems is that of manipulation and mastery. The mass media and public opinion polls are viewed not as sources of information, but as objects to be manipulated and controlled. Hence in 1972, in their distrust of anything but data from their own spies, the Nixon coterie disregarded the information from the polls about a coming overwhelming victory and took fantastic risks to assure his reelection. Much has been made of this apparent irrationality, but it is consistent with the pattern associated with the power orientation of a conspiratorial leader.

The weakness of informational systems of an espionage character is twofold. In detecting weaknesses in the opposition, they limit themselves to personal and often particularistic targets. A given character may be bought by money or lured by women. In warfare there are enemy concentrations in specified areas. Spying lends itself to tactics, not to strategy. A second limitation is the difficulty of checking information obtained in secrecy and fed back through secret channels. Science grows through the public character of its findings: one scientist can repeat the research of another and challenge it. But a closed system permits no such open checking, and necessitates the creation of multiple espionage systems. If the price of liberty is eternal vigilance, the price of monolithic power is constant surveillance. The competition between espionage systems, however, is likely to be not for the most valid adequate intelligence about the opposition, but in providing the most acceptable information to the next level in the hierarchy. These weaknesses lead to a private world for the top decision makers, in which conspiratorial secrecy replaces free interchange of information in the determination of policy.

Elected officials are not alone in converting information networks into restricted feedback operations. Communication patterns are found among the permanent civil servants in most established bureaucracies which preserve the tenure and power of the upper and middle echelons. Information which gets into the system is of a given type, it is coded in certain ways, and it filters upward in a restricted fashion. Hence, it is often difficult for an elected official to make judgments that would upset the customary types of decisions that his agency makes. This is not to argue that continuity in policy is undesirable, but to point out a built-in limitation in some feedback systems, which operates to protect the permanent bureaucracy.

We sometimes speak of organizational leaders as being captives of very restricted information systems of their own organizations. This was one of Franklin Roosevelt's concerns as President. He sought strenuously to break out of customary feedback procedures. It came as something of a shock to John Kennedy during the incident of the Bay of Pigs to find himself victimized by the military and CIA intelligence. The limited network operates in two ways. In the first place, it does not set a broad enough net in the original data it collects. In the second place, it screens at various levels in the system the information made available to higher levels. This filtering is more than condensation and reduction for purposes of economy. It is selective with respect both to what those of a higher level want to hear and what those of a lower level want them to hear. For example, highly relevant information is often available at lower levels of the system which does not reach the top decision making levels. The State Department had at lower levels knowledge that a basic factor in Vietnam was not so much the amount of fire power of the antagonists but the social structure of a semi-feudal society with the great majority of peasants exploited by a corrupt regime. There was also available detailed research of the effects of strategic bombing from studies conducted by the U.S. Air Force in Germany and Japan at the end of World War II. These two highly relevant sources of information apparently were never fed into the Joint Chiefs of Staff.

The basic reason, then, for the inadequacies of the information system built around a permanent bureaucracy is that information gathering and processing is utilized not for information but for control purposes. Bureaucrats want information which will maintain their own positions and their own way of operating.

E. *ADAPTATION PROBLEMS AND SECONDARY EFFECTS*

In our earlier discussion of the adaptive function, we suggested that systemic research in organizations first appeared as a consequence of the technological development of industrial enterprises. On the other hand, there is a built-in limitation to the full growth of systemic research in the interests of adaptation in a business structure. Private enterprise is narrowly directed at maintaining or increasing its power and profits and this naturally carries over into its research orientation. The full development of systemic feedback must come from a more broadly based set of public interests. The increasing importance of the secondary effects of organizational functioning makes salient the need for systemic research in which the frame of reference is societal.

Secondary effects can be of a positive or of a negative sort, and deal with consequences remote from the objectives of policy makers of a given organization. The interdependence of people in a society and even across societies means that a group action can set into motion a long causal chain of events. Technical innovations like the automobile or the transistor radio have had far-reaching effects in all societies in which they have been introduced—effects not necessarily intended or anticipated. R. Bauer (1966), discussing such second-order consequences of the exploration of space, goes on to say, "The Brookings report of 1961 contained two hundred pages (D. N. Michael, 1961), pages devoted almost entirely to informed speculation...changes in man's conception of himself and God; almost incredible consequences of vastly expanded communications via satellite communications systems... improved short- and long-range weather forecasting... revolutions in data processing and retrieval... stimulation of our system of higher education, or disruption of our system of higher education" (pp. 3-4).

The private organization in the past has assumed little responsibility for significant secondary effects of its operations. Even Exxon in its present public relations program tries to minimize the problem of pollution by showing that it has not appreciably damaged the environment. The fish are still there, game still exists, and the water is not all that polluted. A single corporation cannot be expected, from a realistic point of view, to take the lead in promoting public welfare. That is not the game it is set up to play. Concern about noxious secondary effects has to be a function of a higher level in the social system—a whole industry or the federal government. Control at higher levels has been far from adequate, partly because of structural weaknesses in our political system. In our representative democracy the impetus for legislation, as well as the pressures against it, too often comes from special interest groups, many of which maintain lobbies in Washington. Congressmen attempt some compromise and bargaining to accommodate the competitive pressures upon them. In this conflictual process, the well entrenched and permanent lobbies for partisan interests have an advantage over the temporary waves of public opinion concerned with some abuse of the public interest.

An aroused public opinion can have an effect, but it leads to some specific action (sometimes merely a delaying action) rather than a sustained positive program. Our political system works on the principle of checking abuses, and deals with the direct and immediate infringement of public interests. From a societal point of view, this can be too little and too late. Long-range planning and careful consideration of secondary effects of organizational and governmental activity are lacking. The checks and balances of a pluralistic system do not provide ideal machinery for long-term perspectives on public problems. One form of pluralism, the competition between public and private corporations in the same domain, is still potentially of great social utility. The Tennesee Valley Authority was an important check on monopolistic practices in the electric power field. Similar public organizations are needed in industries tending toward monopoly, and, in turn, governmental agencies could be improved if they had to compete with private enterprise. As we face the catastrophic consequences of an unplanned society, people are responding

favorably to ideas symbolizing a new approach. The concepts
of public accountability and corporate social responsibility
are receiving support even in some conservative quarters.
More specific proposals still have only minority backing,
but the significant thing is that they are being made and
are winning adherents. For example, John Gardner's Common
Cause deals with the problem of pressure groups' lobbying
for partisan interests with a citizens' lobby concerned with
public interest. Ralph Nader's many activities consider
consumer interests not only with respect to the person as a
purchaser, but also with respect to the common welfare.
Moreover, Nader (1972) has suggested institutional reforms
which would make whistle blowing not an accidental, occasional, sporadic act but a continuing activity. He has
proposed, for example, a bill of rights for employees in
both private and public enterprises so that people at all
levels could express their reservations and their views
about the policies and practices of their company or agency.
They should have the right, moreover, to give public expression to their criticisms when internal channels of communication are ineffective. Robert Townsend has elaborated a
plan for monitoring large corporations on a day-to-day
basis. His plan calls for each large corporation to finance
an internal office with a staff of scientists, engineers,
accountants, and investigators, with access to all company
records, files, and operations. The office would find
answers to questions the company itself was not asking, and
would make public reports on the company's progress, or lack
of progress, in areas of interest to the society. Thomas B.
Mechling's Public Equity Corporation is designed to facilitate suits against corporate or governmental transgressions
that inflict damages on people or the environment.

Thus, in spite of the strength of entrenched partisan interests, there are indications of an increased support for the use of research for societal improvement. Four reasons can be cited:

1. Though we have emphasized the openness of legislators and public officials to pressure groups, it is also true that this openness is often due to the need for information. Policy makers frequently face decisions without the time or staff to assemble and analyze data relevant for the task they face. Clear and appropriate information in the public interest could compete effectively in many instances with private lobbies, especially where it could open up the issues for public discussion.

2. As already suggested, almost all groups and individuals are sufficiently threatened by environmental exploitation and destruction to make their community of interest a clear, if not always compelling, consideration. If we face common and difficult problems, then we need to seek broad solutions and to utilize the resources and skills of the society in their solution.

3. The temporal frame of reference has been changing, both for the elite and for broader society. We are no longer a pioneering nation where every day is a new day. The leaders of industrial enterprises have been expanding their concepts of long-range planning. Where once thinking in terms of a five-year span was bold, today it is almost hopelessly conservative. At the individual level, people see the consequences of lack of planning in incidents and problems which affect them. Moreover, the more complex technological society requires more skill training and more education. Individuals have to defer gratification of some

of their needs until they complete their training. A longer
time perspective is the consequence. With a recognition of
the importance of long-range planning, the next logical step
is a realization of the need for facts on the basis of which
to plan. Planning commissions and bureaus have to make all
kinds of assumptions about present trends, their rate of
growth, and their interaction in the future. All of this
calls for better use of existing data and the collection of
data beyond the current sources of information.

4. A slow change has been taking place at a fundamental level in our orientation toward social science.
Robert Zajonc (1966) has pointed out that the great barrier
to the development of research in social psychology was in
the habitual cognitive barriers and compartmentalizations.
Problems concerning the relation of man to man were in the
political and social arena where the answers were to be
found in the mores and the folkways, the laws, the morals,
or the religion of a society. We still spend endless time
in discussion and debate on issues where questions of fact
are involved. A few years back, there was endless controversy over why little Johnny could not learn to read, until
it occurred to a Swedish educational psychologist to conduct
some research on the problem. A great deal of argumentation
goes on over drugs where assumptions rather than facts are
debated. Scientific research, of course, will not furnish
all the answers, but neither should its role be ignored when
factual questions are relevant to problem solution. The
first breakthrough in our traditional way of thinking came
with the development of experimental social psychology as a
basic science. A second breakthrough came in the work of
the Mayo group, in which the researchers discovered that

social givens ordinarily neglected were crucial variables in productivity (Roethlisberger and Dickson, 1939). The second development, emphasizing field research, has seen some progress, albeit slow and uneven. But we have moved ahead sufficiently that researchers can often get a hearing if they can show the potential helpfulness and appropriateness of research questions to policy issues. Senator Mondale has, in fact, proposed a Council of Social Advisers operating at the highest government level as part of his plan for a social accounting and evaluation of human services (1962).

These, then, are some of the reasons for the acceptance of concepts of program evaluation, public accountability, and planned change. Social scientists have proposed that implementations of these ideas could be furthered by the development of summary measures called social indicators. They would be comparable to GNP as the means for providing feedback on many social policy issues, just as economic indices have been used for decisions about interest rates and price and wage controls.

B. Gross (1966) has suggested a social systems accounting model for the nation-state as critical for national planning and the measurement of social change. Among its other uses would be potential answers for the dilemma between the necessity for concentrating upon a selected number of strategic variables and the need for a comprehensive overview. Social systems accounting could provide "a conceptual and informational basis for economically scanning the array of all possible kinds of relevant data and selecting those that are most relevant under specific circumstances" (p. 262).

The need for such an accounting is emphasized by Campbell and Converse (1972), who point out that "there has been very little systematic accounting of the meaning which recent social changes have had for the people of this country." Trend studies involving repeated measures of psychological characteristics of the American people are not found in the routines of government accounting and constitute a great exception in university-conducted research. There is nothing comparable to Katona's program of consumer surveys over the past 25 years in the psychological field, with the possible exception of the Michigan political behavior series.

Trend studies of motivations, satisfactions, values, feelings, aspirations, and frustrations of people could serve as important social indicators. The difficulty in launching such studies is not on the technical side--i.e., obtaining comparable samples, depth interviewing, or even ascertaining the functional equivalence of measures over time. The problem is more on the theoretical side, in that the scales often used in surveys getting at psychological factors are conceived of in purely individual terms. For example, Cantril's ingenious self-anchoring scale of happiness (1965) is so self-anchored that it lacks social reference. So, too, is the Rotter measure of the control of reinforcements (1966) and so, too, are some of the measures of alienation and anomie.

General life satisfaction, sense of personal efficacy, or distrust and alienation often show great unreliability when measured as free-floating attributes and are difficult to interpret. They do not need a self-anchoring scale as much as they need to be anchored to some stimulus situation and to some related behaviors. They do not exist in a social vacuum, and in the development of indicators we need to tie measures of psychological satisfaction or disaffection to a social context. Thus it is not enough to have a measure of alienation. We need to know what people are alienated from and what associated behaviors are related to types of alienation. Similarly, an overall measure of satisfaction with life is not as valuable as a series of measures of satisfaction with one's work, with one's community as a place to live, with one's family, etc. Such socially oriented measures can be related to objective conditions on the one hand and to related behaviors on the other.

Kenneth C. Land (1971) has argued persuasively for the use of social indicators in the framework of models of social processes and institutions, and distinguishes between models that deal with aggregate levels or amounts of various social activities and models that are concerned with the distribution of social activities among the various elements of society. An example of the first class is the stable theory of population growth; and of the second class, path models of the processes of social stratification.

Peter Rossi (1972) has made an interesting case for the use of community social indicators in which he provides a very important social referent for psychological measures. For example, he proposes such measures as perception of a locality as a collectivity by its residents, their affective involvement in this collectivity, their interest and involvement in local events, the social climate of the locality, and the residential locality as a reference group. Our suggestion is that many of the measures of psychological states should be similarly geared to a social context, whether it be the job, work place and occupation, the community, the family, the union, the political party or other voluntary grouping, or some informal network of friends.

IV. THE IMPROVEMENT OF SYSTEM FUNCTIONING THROUGH FEEDBACK

A. *DIRECT VS. INDIRECT FEEDBACK*

Two principles are in apparent contradiction in the improvement of system functioning through feedback. The first is the importance of immediate, direct feedback loops. In the political field, this is the application of direct democratic procedures. The assumption is that the people directly involved in an activity are the best source of information for correcting it. Complex, lengthy, and circuitous networks are inadequate mechanisms for correcting centralized large-scale programs. The federal program for housing administered from Washington was not able to correct abuses very obvious at the local level. There are those who argue that neighborhood schools should be run by the people in the neighborhood.

The second principle attaches more importance to feedback from basic and applied research and expert evaluation of the findings. The people in the neighborhood know their own feelings about their school, but they do not necessarily know how well the school is preparing their children for societal roles. Solutions to many problems do not come from a majority vote, but from specialized study by experts. Not all social situations are the equivalent of the political community where the majority does prevail. Moreover, local solutions based upon the direct democracy of short feedback circuits may not be real solutions. Problems of environmental pollution, for example, cannot be met at the neighborhood level.

There are many aspects of the dilemma between direct feedback loops with autonomy and decentralization, on the one hand, and centralized coordination with planning which extends our social space as well as time, and which involves research and expertise, on the other. Obviously, some utilization of both principles is necessary in a large society; however, curiously, there has been little theoretical analysis and research about the conditions under which one principle rather than the other should be applied. In practice, there is a tendency to move in one direction and then to have a reaction set in in the opposite direction. Yugoslavia, to take a conspicuous example, moved toward the centralization of functions under a federal system after World War II. Then, as the development of federal bureaucracy was not moving the nation ahead, decentralization both of an institutional sort and a geographical kind became the popular doctrine. This may be countered in the future by a swing toward federal centralization. What is needed, however, is not the corrective reaction in global fashion, but some analytic tools for separating out the functions which can be decentralized, the conditions for their decentralization, and the ways in which local functioning can relate to the larger system. The following suggestions are offered in an attempt to delineate the relevant factors and conditions.

For production problems, including the delivery of services, there is a need for direct feedback loops from clients. Where a firm must market a product or a service, the market itself may provide such feedback; people can accept or reject the offering and their response tells the company something about meeting public needs. Where the market is imperfect or absent, other forms of feedback are needed. For example, governmental agencies are not accountable in the market sense to the public they serve. This is true whether the office provides helpful services like Social Security and welfare, or whether it is an agency of constraint and regulation like the Internal Revenue Bureau or the police. Wherever a product or service is indirectly supported through governmental funds, the reactions of the people being served should be systematically surveyed. This information should not be binding upon the agency in the specific correction of its policies and procedures, but it should be weighed very carefully in making changes in procedures. In the long run, agency heads might find such systematic information more helpful than the strident complaints of the vocal individuals who can make the front pages of the newspaper or reach the ears of a Congressman.

In the private sector, when virtual monopoly occurs, the same principle should hold. Consumer reactions should be consistently assessed and seriously considered by public service commissions regulating monopolies. An alternative is to break down the monopolistic control even if it means setting up governmental enterprises to compete.

The direct feedback loop is more difficult to apply where system outcomes are of long temporal duration. The student being trained for a professional career is in a better position to evaluate that training after he has graduated and is putting that training into practice. This delays the feedback cycle, but it should nevertheless be utilized. With all the argument and discussion about educational practices, we have done little to utilize such an appropriate information source.

For maintenance problems, there is a need for direct feedback loops from lower to higher levels to supplement other information mechanisms. The personnel of the system can provide feedback of two sorts: information about production problems and information about maintenance problems (their own motivations and morale)--roughly, intelligence about the technical system and about the social system. The knowledge they can provide about maintenance problems is more valid than that about production problems because they are the best source of information about their satisfactions with specific aspects of the organization. They may or may not be expert about the production process. These two forms of knowledge are frequently confused. The lower echelons in a factory or hospital are the experts about their own adjustments to their roles, but they are not necessarily the best informants about how well the organization as a whole is doing its job. Similarly, the expert on production problems may know little about the effects of the role structure upon its incumbents. Of course the two sets of problems are related, but information about them has to be looked at separately with respect to source. The interrelationship between the two is critical for organizational improvement.

The freedom of the subunit to be guided by feedback from its own public gets us into the knotty question of

criteria for what can be decentralized. Unless local feedback is to be taken into account, it is meaningless to build
such cycles into the operation. On the other hand, if a
subunit operates completely on its own, it can disrupt the
operations of the larger system. The functional limits on
decentralization should be set by requirements for expertise
and scarce resources, not by political preferences for power
and control.

One solution to this problem of downward delegation is
to replace individual responsibility down the line with
group responsibility. Each level becomes an organizational
family, so that a work section of rank-and-file employees
takes over duties and responsibilities of the section as a
group. The limits of decision-making for the subunit are
not changed, but more freedom is allowed for the individuals
in it. With group responsibility, there can be meaningful
feedback about task accomplishment not available for the
individual fractionated task (Trist et al., 1963). Rensis
Likert (1965) has added to this conception the idea of overlapping groups, in which a representative from one level is
also part of the organizational family at the next higher
level. In this fashion Likert would insure the integration
of the group into the larger system. If the Likert plan is
followed, more participation at lower levels is insured even
with minimal downward delegation. The pragmatic outcome
should be the elimination of one or more hierarchical levels
in the system as groups become involved and want greater
responsibility.

Another means of involving lower levels is to give
local offices freedom to pursue organizational objectives
within broad policy guidelines. The coordinating top unit

does not attempt specifications for all contingencies, but just asks that the problem be solved on the basis of some set of general principles. In effect, such a policy was followed in World War II, with local rationing boards and local selective service boards operating very successfully with a fair amount of discretionary power. The delegation principle involved is similar to the old textbook notion of making policy decisions at the top and administrative decisions down the line. Its weakness is the lack of structural provisions, one of the strengths of the Likert proposal. Since policy and administrative decisions are difficult and sometimes impossible to distinguish, top echelons are willing to intervene in all decisions. Another way of reconciling the need for local feedback and the need for integration with the larger organization is to transmit the requirements of the organization as feedback to its subunits. The establishment of subunits as profit centers is a successful example of this mechanism.

B. *TASK REQUIREMENTS AS A DETERMINANT OF THE NATURE OF FEEDBACK LOOPS*

Systems vary with respect to the interdependence of their units in carrying out their major task. When all efforts must converge on a single common outcome, as with the space program's goal of getting a man on the moon, direct feedback cycles for small units with resulting flexibility of operation are not desirable. In this case, the dominant source of feedback has to be the larger structure. But some task structures do not require precise and rigorous coordination, in that there are many parallel operations and parallel outcomes which can proceed fairly independently of one another. In a university and in some government agencies, many departments are not highly interdependent. Hence there can be shorter feedback loops and a greater area of freedom for decision making within a single department. In graduate education, for example, where almost all of the training is at the departmental level, power tends to accumulate in departments. In systems with multiple outcomes based upon parallel rather than interdependent structures, it is appropriate for much of the decision making to be decentralized. There is probably much less decentralization in such systems, however, than logical analyses would suggest, because we have overgeneralized the coordination principle from industrial organizations built around convergence upon a single type of product.

Another aspect of task requirement concerns the nature of the material processed, whether objects or people. For processing objects, it is possible to develop a standard set of efficient procedures which can be imposed on all units in the structure, although individual differences among the people who must put these procedures into practice set limitations on the ideal of the "one best method."

For processing people, the same type of standardized routines will not have similar results. People are reactive; objects are not. The organizational treatment of the subject's response must be geared to that response and allow for differential behavior of people as having personalities of their own. Talcott Parsons has made this point about educational systems, in which pupils cannot be considered as objects (1960). W. McKeachie has shown that the most effective forms of teaching are those which involve considerable interaction between teacher and students and between students and their peers (1973). Such interaction allows for differential responses of teachers to the varying patterns of student reactions.

Most proposals for utilizing the reactions of people to correct the functioning of the system are limited to narrow areas. They suggest the involvement of people in the evaluation of a small segment of the organization--the segment closest to their own experience. In Likert's proposal the work group concerns itself with decisions about an assigned task. In my suggestion about systemic surveys of the clients of public agencies, the evaluation is tied to specific services and programs. Important as such direct feedback cycles are, they contain little information about the larger system or about its major objectives. Workers may come up with good suggestions about how to organize themselves about a job. But what they may care more about are the policies of the company with respect to the distribution of rewards. Similarly, people may evaluate favorably the way they are treated by a governmental agency, but they may have little sympathy for the way the government is handling the larger problem.

The improvement and creation of more direct feedback loops in social systems, though very significant, does not solve the basic problem. Some of the new left mistakenly believe that the solution is in turning all decision making over to such simple cycles, that direct democracy should replace representative governmental institutions, that town meetings or mass meetings should be the policy bodies. Another variation of the doctrine of direct democracy is to have the people most affected make the decisions. For example, welfare recipients should determine welfare policy; the students should run the schools. The critical issue is, however, that other groups in the larger system are also involved. Decisions affecting the system as a whole should not be made by one segment. Such contributions should be within a narrow and circumscribed area. Each segment should, however, also contribute to the general decision, which requires some summation of all units within the system. Aggregating the wishes of these units in a large society is what representative democracy is all about. What is important here is to reduce the indirection as much as possible in the form of direct primaries, equality of representation, and referenda on basic questions.

The other side of the coin, however, is that elections and plebiscites should not be concerned with technical issues and details of policy. The electorate should choose between general directions. Insofar as individuals have technical expertise, they should have an opportunity to make the most of it in their nonpolitical roles. As citizens, they should be asked only to make decisions about basic system goals. We are suggesting, then, that each type of participation be optimized for its own strength. This entails more use of the experience and specialized knowledge of people in the day-to-day functioning of systems, but within the system framework.

In their political roles as members of the nation state, their participation should involve choice between general programs or directions. Two opportunities for affecting national policy are available to the electorate. One is the vote with its power of veto--the rejection of an administration or a party when disaster has occurred during its regime. It has been asserted many times, and not without cause, that it is easier to predict what people will vote against than what they will vote for. The second opportunity for influencing major decisions occurs within a political party as the factions within it contend for positions on the candidate slate or for planks in the platform. In a large democracy, the political parties will continue to carry on the function of compromising group conflicts within the party itself. Hence, citizen participation, to be maximally effective, must occur within a political party. Reforms in the political system need to be made at the party level to make the parties more open and more responsive to the electorate. Party machinery is often cumbersome, and feedback restricted and indirect.

A critical issue is the divorce between the two types of participation we have discussed: involvement in the limited segment of the technical processes of the organization, and involvement in the policy decisions of the larger political system. One reason why most people are so poorly informed on public issues is the complex and distant relationship between their own daily involvement and the larger concerns of the polity. Increasing their participation in their own narrow sector of organizational life will do something to increase their interest in public policy. Studies indicate that participation begets participation. But this is not enough because of the lack of relation between the two areas.

The critical character of many of the unsolved problems confronting us in daily life can increase citizen involvement. What will help in producing citizen participation will be the existence of channels for mobilizing sentiment and for facilitating communication. We have already referred to some new organizations of this kind. Their present attempts to create local machinery to sustain and increase their activities at the community level may prove essential to their ultimate success.

C. *TYING FEEDBACK TO SYSTEM FUNCTIONING*

If one looks at the mechanics of feedback in physical systems, it is readily apparent why information mechanisms often do not work as true feedback in social systems. In physical systems, feedback is tied into the control mechanism and triggers the corrective response. Analogical thinking can be misleading, but we need to examine more carefully at what levels and to what parts of the social system different types of information should be directed. We have called attention to the fact that market research will always have the same limited character as long as it reports to the sales department of an industrial enterprise, and that personnel research will also be heavily operational in nature as long as its own departmental head reports to relatively low levels in the organization.

We would suggest a two-level reporting structure for both operational and systemic research. Operational research should be fed into the ongoing operation it deals with directly and to the level in the system above it. Thus, a market research unit should report both to the advertising or sales department and to a higher management level. The people for whom the information is most relevant should receive it, but their superordinates should also receive it. An excellent setup for an operational research

group is to have the program director of the line organization work directly with the project researcher on their
common problems. The opposite arrangement would be to have
the request for information move up the ladder to the head
of the line department, then across to the head of research,
and down the line to the project chief. Then the research
report would move up the research department, across to the
head of the line department, and down the hierarchy to the
program director. Obviously, this second arrangement does
not lead to meaningful applications of findings or even to
good research. Yet it is to be found in large-scale
organizations.

Systemic research should also be geared to two levels:
the level (or levels) for which the research is most appropriate and the top management level. If research findings
with implications for policy have to pass up the line, the
information is likely to become transformed or blocked in
the process of transmission. Direct transmission, moreover,
implies a commitment of top management to consider the
information. Obviously, top echelons in their crowded
schedules cannot be open to direct transmission of all
potentially useful research results. But the decision about
what they will consider should be made in consultation with
the research director. He should play a dual role both as a
member of management and as the head of his own research
unit. To prevent the research unit from turning heavily to
operational feedback, considerable autonomy of functioning
is needed. Hence its personnel should participate with the
director in the making of decisions. He needs some backing
from his research colleagues for his discussions with the

management group. The research unit in turn needs to sustain its own norms and values, and hence requires some power base. Nor should the research unit be heavily layered with many hierarchical levels in its structure. The research findings from a project should not have to be transmitted through many layers, but should go fairly directly to the research director.

Essentially, the research director has a difficult set of tasks, for in addition to his other duties he must help in the translation of research findings for management needs. James Coleman (1973), in his cogent analysis of research utilization, has pointed out the many gaps between the social scientist and the policy maker. It is our belief that these serious gaps can be bridged most successfully if organizations develop their own research departments with considerable autonomy and with a high position in the hierarchy. Such an arrangement gives a structural basis for breaking down the barriers of communication alluded to by Coleman. Moreover, it does this on a permanent, continuing basis. Thus learning can take place both for the research chiefs and management people in working on the same and related problems over time.

We have witnessed many attempts at fact finding that have no programmatic or institutional basis. One form that these attempts take at the governmental level is the appointment of an advisory commission to study a problem which has attracted attention. As of last May, the federal government had 1,439 such groups working for it. Last year their advice cost the government 25.2 million dollars. HEW alone employs 367 advisory committees. Often the advice of these committees is completely ignored, and sometimes it probably should be. Advisory committees and study groups have a place, but if the problems they attack are worth investigating, they should be investigated on a more continuing basis and their findings guaranteed some hearing.

The concept of program evaluation tied to research has gained wide acceptance in many government departments and agencies. In practice, however, evaluation attempts are often poorly planned and inadequately implemented. The major problem with them, moreover, is twofold: first, they are not part of the operating structure and do not constitute feedback of a continuing nature to the administrative agency; second, they are scattered and piecemeal in character and so do not build a cumulative body of knowledge. In other words, they are neither part of the system of government services nor part of the system of the social sciences. Bradley R. Schiller (1973) has reviewed the empirical studies in the field of welfare dependency, in which many research projects have been funded by federal agencies, especially by the Department of Labor. He concludes that these studies have yielded some valuable research evidence, but evidence inadequately reported in professional journals and not integrated into scientific knowledge. Moreover, the findings are at variance with many of the established policies and practices of welfare agencies. He writes: "Indeed the gap between public perspectives and welfare realities is staggering. As a consequence, it appears that many features of recent and pending welfare reform are likely to provide little satisfaction to either the dependent poor or the taxpayer." (1973, p. 28)

The hundreds of work groups and the numerous but scattered evaluation studies attest to the need for more systematic research structures. Nor am I arguing against independent research organizations outside the government working on issues of public concern. Even with the establishment of more systematic research in government, their existence would serve as a public check on government research bureaus. Moreover, they can cooperate in many areas of research with public or semipublic agencies. The major point I am making is that we still leave systemic research on social problems to chance, to stray encounters, to occasional forays rather than building it into the system. The informational search and the analysis of evaluation of information should be a part of the system itself. It is, of course, but in fragmented, partial, transitory, and strange ways. My thesis is that it has been too heavily operational and too little concerned with adaptation to environmental changes, with the effects a system has upon its own members, and with second-order consequences of system outputs.

REFERENCES

Allport, F. H.   A structuronomic conception of behavior. Journal of Abnormal and Social Psychology, 1962, 64, 3-30.

Almond, G. A.   A comparative study of interest groups and the political process. In Eckstein, H., & Apter, D. E. (Eds.), Comparative politics. Glencoe, Ill.: The Free Press, 1963.

Asch, S.   Social psychology. Englewood Cliffs, N. J.: Prentice-Hall, 1952.

Bauer, R. A.   Detection and anticipation of impact. In R. A. Bauer (Ed.), Social indicators. Cambridge, Mass.: M. I. T. Press, 1966.

Braybrooke, D., & Lindbloom, C. E. A strategy of decision. New York: The Free Press, 1963.

Campbell, A., & Converse, P. E. (Eds.). The human meaning of social change. New York: Russell Sage Foundation, 1972.

Cantril, H. The patterns of human concerns. New Brunswick: Rutgers University Press, 1965.

Coleman, J. Ten principles governing policy research. APA Monitor, February 1973, 4(2), 6.

Drucker, P. F. The concept of the corporation. New York: Mentor, 1946.

Easton, D. A systems analysis of political life. New York: John Wiley & Sons, 1965.

Emery, F. E., & Trist, E. L. The causal texture of organizational environments. Human Relations, 1965, 18, 21-32.

Gross, B. M. The state of the nation: Social systems accounting. In R. A. Bauer (Ed.), Social indicators. Cambridge, Mass.: M. I. T. Press, 1966.

Katona, G. The powerful consumer. New York: McGraw-Hill, 1960.

Katz, D., & Kahn, R. L. The social psychology of organizations. New York: John Wiley & Sons, 1966.

Kornhauser, W. The politics of mass society. New York: The Free Press, 1959.

Land, K. C. On the definition of social indicators. American Sociologist, 1971, 6, 322-325.

Likert, R. New patterns of management. New York: McGraw-Hill, 1961.

Likert, R. The human organization. New York: McGraw-Hill, 1967.

Likert, R., & Bowers, D. C. Organizational theory and human resource accounting. American Psychologist, 1969, 24, 585-592.

March, J. G., & Simon, H. A. Organizations. New York: John Wiley & Sons, 1958.

McKeachie, W. J. Interaction: Interpersonal and statistical. Invited address, Rocky Mountain Psychological Association, May 9, 1973.

Michael, D. N. Proposed studies on the implications of peaceful space activities for human affairs. Prepared for Brookings Institution, Washington, D. C., 1961.

Mondale, W. F. Social accounting, evaluation, and the future of human services. Evaluation: A Forum for Human Decision Makers, 1972, 29-34.

Nader, R., Petkas, P., & Blackwell, K. (Eds.). Whistle blowing. New York: Grossman Publishers, 1972.

Neustadt, R. E. Presidential power: The politics of leadership. New York: Wiley, 1960.

Newcomb, T. M. The acquaintance process. New York: Holt, Rinehart & Winston, 1961.

Parsons, T. Structure and process in modern societies. Glencoe, Ill.: The Free Press, 1960.

Roethlisberger, F. J., & Dickson, W. J. Management and the worker. Cambridge, Mass.: Harvard University Press, 1939.

Rossi, P. H. Community social indicators. In Campbell, A., & Converse, P. E. (Eds.), The human meaning of social change. New York: Russell Sage Foundation, 1972.

Rotter, J. B. Generalized expectancies for internal vs. external control of reinforcements. Psychological monographs, 1966, 80, (609), 1-28.

Schiller, B. R. Empirical studies of welfare dependency: A survey. The Journal of Human Resources, 1973, Supplement Vol. 8, 19-32.

Schumpeter, J. Capitalism, socialism, and democracy. New York: Harper & Bros., 1947.

Smelser, N. J. Theory of collective behavior. New York: The Free Press, 1962.

Trist, E. L., Higgin, G. W., Murray, H., & Pollock, A. B. Organizational choice. London: Tavistock Publications, 1963.

Zajonc, R. B. Social psychology: An experimental approach. Belmont, Calif.: Wadsworth, 1966.

8

Assessing Alternative Conceptions of Evaluation

ARTHUR A. LUMSDAINE and CARL A. BENNETT

I. INTRODUCTION

In this chapter we review and comment on some of the main themes highlighted by the conference and the previous chapters.[1] As we indicated in Chapter 1, there is almost universal agreement concerning the desirability and importance both of improved program evaluation and of improved utilization of evaluative results. Differences arise primarily in individual perceptions of the actions needed to improve the situation, and in conceptions concerning the role of the evaluator in effecting this improvement. Concerns expressed both in the discussions in this volume and at the conference on which the volume is based seem to fall into two major categories.

The first is the determination of program impact. Chapter 2 in particular considers the kinds of impacts produced by various specific innovations in social and/or medical areas and some basic aspects of the methodology whereby these impacts may be determined. Chapters 3, 4, and 5 con-

---

[1] Part of the work of the first author in the preparation of this chapter was aided by a grant from the Russell Sage Foundation on comparative methods for determining the impact of social programs.

tinue to address critical theoretical and technical aspects of the methods used in the design and conduct of field studies for ascertaining what impacts can be unequivocally attributed to specific program treatments and innovations.

The second category of concern is the <u>utilization of information to arrive at decisions or provide programmatic feedback</u>. Chapter 2 also deals with this problem to the extent that it assesses the importance of the innovations and the relationship of the impact produced to the "success" of a particular innovation. Chapter 6 looks more particularly at the information needs and the value structures associated with the utilization of such information for arriving at decisions. Chapter 7 examines the need for information as a part of a feedback process built into the system.

The main issues which arose at the Battelle conference, and which are reflected in papers in this volume, tended to focus not so much on the validity of different approaches within either of these two categories of concern, but rather with their relative importance for improved evaluation of social programs. For example, there seemed to be general agreement on the desirability of randomized experiments, or controlled field trials, as a means of unequivocally determining the dependence of a particular outcome on a given programmatic treatment. The concerns expressed revolve about 1) the <u>sufficiency</u> of this experimental approach, with particular empahsis on its implied ability to characterize programmatic success or failure in terms of a specific measurable impact or a commensurable combination of impacts; and 2) the <u>feasibility</u> of an experimental approach, both in terms of its technical and logistic requirements and in terms of the political and organizational environment in which it must be implemented. Gilbert, Light, and Mosteller (Chapter 2) suggest that few controversies about the effects of new programs survive a series of carefully designed randomized controlled trials, even though controversy about the policy implications may, of course, persist. On the other hand, Edwards and Guttentag (Chapter 6) stress the fact that the impacts determined from controlled field trials do not constitute the totality of information required to arrive at a policy decision. Thus, the question is not so much one of whether controlled field trials give unequivocal information as it is to what extent it is feasible to carry out experiments that yield the broad range of information required to arrive at a valid decision. (See also Section VII.)

Perhaps the overall situation is best summarized by saying that some people argue that a careful evolutionary approach based on "experimentation" will provide the information feedback necessary to insure continuing progress toward the solution of societal problems, while others feel that the more important need is to look at ways of structuring the broad spectrum of information and value judgments required to produce valid action decisions. The one approach will tend to bias the decision structure toward those impacts which can be measured. The other approach will tend to place undue dependence on opinion as opposed to fact.

II. DETERMINATION OF IMPACT

In Chapter 1 we distinguished five phases in the genesis and implementation of a program. Some of the questions which arise in examining these phases are as follows:

1. What are the goals of the program, and by what indices will one identify whether, or to what extent, they have been achieved?

2. On the basis of wisdom or hunches accumulated to date, can it be established, prior to any revision by formative evaluation, which process will attain these goals (or achieve the maximum impact) within established resources and with a minimum of adverse side effects?

3. As the program is designed and put into operation, what, in fact, are the processes that are being carried out and how do they compare with the plan of what the process should be?

4. What impacts are actually produced? The answer to this question should include both tentative or provisional evidence obtained during formative evaluation and more definitive evaluation obtained farther down the road. The concern here is not just with a time distinction but also a distinction regarding the definitiveness of the evidence. One can afford to accept tentative results early in the program, but at later major decision points, more formal evidence is needed since the consequences of making the wrong decision at such points are more far-reaching and less subject to subsequent correction.

5. What is responsible for the effects? The basis for this determination may be 1) hunches about the process and examination of output data for other more or less similar programs; 2) comparative assessment of the impact of two or more programs representing alternative plans or procedures; or 3) the scientific kind of experiment, conducted either in the laboratory or as a field study, that analyzes in finer grain the factors responsible for the effects produced. In any case, the results of the analysis feed back into step

number two and enable the modification of subsequent programs or the revision of the existing program to achieve improved performance.

An examination of the questions raised above reveals at least three classes of methodological need: 1) methods for characterizing and measuring both inputs and outputs of the program or system under consideration; 2) methods for identifying relationships between the variables measured, particularly with regard to the network of causal relationships between inputs and outputs; and 3) methods for establishing value structures and for dealing with multiple criteria and trade-offs between various outcomes.

The emphasis on the determination of impact can be justified on the basis either that 1) the goals of the program and the measurable indices of their achievement, as well as the process for achieving them, can be specified in advance based on theory or as a hypothesis to be tested; or that 2) the process for achieving success, or even the definition of "success" per se, will evolve as the program is implemented. The first, or a priori, position implies the preexistence on either a theoretical or empirical basis of a definite value structure. On the other hand, the latter position implies that the value structure, as well as the causal relationships, may be generated from the empirical evidence gained as the program unfolds.

A closely related issue seems to revolve about the desirability of a systematic evolutionary approach to innovation based on the assumption that the barriers to the unequivocal determination of specific treatment impacts, through randomized controlled field trials or other appropriate methods, can be surmounted. As noted earlier, this contrasts with an approach that emphasizes both the importance of the multivariate nature of criteria for program success and that of associated value structures, and deemphasizes the precise determination of specific impacts.

As to the validity of methods used for determining program impact, the evidence indicates that randomized controlled field trials do provide better evidence of the effect of treatment. Furthermore, the absence of randomization does generate a concern with the degree to which unascertained bias may exist, and the extent to which any estimation of treatment effects must depend on theoretical assumptions, particularly those concerning absence of selection biases and the effects of covariates likely to represent potential sources of influence.

The issues that arise at a strictly methodological or analytical level commonly reflect more important conceptual issues. Inferences from observational data, which are highly dependent on theoretical justification for assumed models, are used not because of their optimality, but because of their feasibility under circumstances where truly experimental data cannot be obtained. The balance is between the risk of misinterpreting available evidence and the risk of ignoring it. Also, the conclusions reached by Gilbert, Light, and Mosteller (Chapter 2) with respect to the importance of detecting small effects versus those reached by Edwards and Guttentag (Chapter 6) represent only one reflection of the basic issue of what routes will lead most efficiently to social progress through innovation.

III. EVALUATION AND EXPERIMENT

A. *PILOT PROGRAMS*

The relation of experimentation to evaluation is inti-
mately tied up with the question of whether a program is
implemented at the outset on a full-scale basis, or whether
it is first tried out as a pilot program. With a pilot
program, which is subject to modification and revision before wider adoption, the function of evaluation can be maximally useful for improving the program or for making decisions about its use. In addition, the control or comparison
group needed for many evaluative purposes may be rendered
unavailable if a new program is disseminated completely
instead of on a pilot basis for evaluation.[1]

Radically different departures or innovations increase
the uncertainty of attendant outcomes, unanticipated as well
as hoped for. This fact stresses the need not only for
innovations that are carefully conceived to maximize potential benefits and minimize possible adverse effects, but
also for experiments that are sensitive enough to reveal the
occurrence and extent of such good or bad effects at a
pilot-experimental stage. Further, it is important that the
experiments reveal as fully as possible what characteristics
of a program produced the good or bad effects, so that the
program can be redesigned in a way that will augment good
effects and ameliorate bad effects before it goes into full-
scale implementation.

---

[1]See also the discussion by Gilbert, Light, and Mosteller in
Sections IX and X of Chapter 2.

What can and should be done to evaluate a given program is tied closely to how, where, and when the program is introduced. For example, extensive and costly experimentation may be justified for programs that are essentially reproducible and/or exportable, and for those which are large in scale (in terms of the extent of benefits anticipated for large numbers of recipients of the program's activities or products); however, it may not be justified for limited or nonreproducible programs. Similarly, definitive ascertainment of program impacts is possible as well as defensible for pilot programs introduced selectively, so as not only to allow subsequent improvement based on initial tryout but also to preserve the opportunity for comparison with otherwise comparable control groups.

The general case for pilot-program or prototype evaluation in social innovation has been well put by Miller (1966):

> In spite of all the practical and theoretical knowledge in the automobile industry, no one of the large manufacturers ever considers putting out a radically new model without extensive road tests of a prototype model.... Similarly, one can never be certain whether a new social program actually will be a cure or whether it will have undesirable side effects. To start such a program without out some plan for evaluating it is just as inefficient as it would be to start mass production on a radically new automobile without any road tests .... It is only with the new sciences, such as those dealing with behavior, that the would-be users often are so impatient for quick results of practical value that they will not support the long program of developmental research and field-testing that often is especially needed in just these cases (pp. 114-115).

B. *EXPERIMENTATION AND INNOVATION*

It must be recognized that the connection between evaluation and experiment goes beyond the role of experimentation or controlled field trials as a definitive method of ascertaining program impact. In most instances the program being evaluated--that is, the intervention or treatment under study--is in itself necessarily an "experiment," in at least the general lay sense of an exploratory innovation. In this sense, experiment is not merely a method to use in program evaluation, but also is the essence of what is evaluated. Thus "experiment" and "evaluation" inevitably tend to go hand in hand, even in the cases where true, formal experiments have not been used to ascertain program impacts, and even though the merit-assessment or goal-assessment aspect of evaluation transcends what is experimentally tested or testable. Experimentation in this broad sense embraces creative innovation and the systematic introduction and testing of bold new approaches. It also includes the more specialized use of scientifically designed experiments, either for ascertaining the outcomes produced by such programs or for identifying the factors responsible for such outcomes. It is complemented rather than opposed by the emphasis on a value structure for dealing with multiple criteria and trade-offs between outcomes.

Why stress the need to experiment--in this sense of innovation, of trying new approaches? In relation to the case for an "experimenting society" put by Campbell (1971), we could argue that an emphasis on experimentation finds one of its sources of support in the urgency of trying fresh approaches to solving basic social problems.[1] A good many decades of failure to solve them suggest that experimentation with markedly new kinds of solutions is almost certainly going to be necessary. As long as there persist conditions involving misery and/or severe deprivation to major segments of humanity, no consistently humane philosophy can rest content with the status quo. In addition, so long as great human potentialities remain frustrated or unfulfilled, there is clearly a need for changes to improve that situation. If this is apparent to many, it is equally true but evidently less obvious that a society (or its leadership) that does not seek to foster innovation in the persistent quest for solutions to urgent imbalances of these kinds is hardly defensible in the present era. The future--as goes a contemporary catch phrase--belongs to those who prepare for it (as individuals); so also a better future (for society's members in the aggregate) may accrue to societies which actively seek it, through innovation and experiment.

C. COMPARATIVE EVALUATION AND PROGRAM EVOLUTION

Much, though not all, of the emphasis in the present volume has been on ascertaining and interpreting the effects ascribable to a particular social program, rather than on attempting comparison of alternative programs or variant treatments with each other. However, the need to ascertain comparative effects, either between available policy alternatives or between different ways of implementing a given

---

[1]See also Gilbert and Mosteller (1972).

policy, has been remarked on several times, as has the need
for "evolutionary" experimentation, or "formative" program
development based on empirical trials. The latter terminol-
ogy--"formative" evaluation--is currently applied to a quite
wide and diverse range of practices, including the informal
pretesting of reactions to a program or proposal, but it can
also comprehend major sequential try-outs to ascertain the
impacts demonstrably produced by successively modified programs in the spirit of "evolutionary experiment" suggested
by Gilbert, Light, and Mosteller (Chapter 2).

The concept of evolutionary program development can
include not only successive improvement of programs by sheer
empiricism, but also identification of those program features associated with the more successful outcomes. Features thus identified might be specific to a particular
program, or might have more general significance to a variety of kinds of social and educational programs. In either case, however, a fairly definitive pinning down of
features associated with success requires not only an evolutionary succession of revisions, but an actual comparison
of program variants randomly assigned and exemplifying alternative program features. Such experiments have seldom
been done in very large-scale social experimentation, although a number of examples of such randomized field tests
of program alternatives are reviewed by Hilton and Lumsdaine
(Chapter 5) and by Gilbert, Light, and Mosteller (Chapter 2). Also, in some instances (e.g., Section IV-D of
Chapter 2), the "things-as-they-are" control group can be
considered a genuine alternative treatment.

Comparison of experimental treatments may have some
generalizable significance outside the immediate situation,
provided the experimental conditions are defined in sufficiently generalizable or reproducible terms so that the

comparison can be replicated and is thus "exportable." When program variants compared are potentially generalizable-- i.e., not limited to the immediate program or situation under consideration--they can be regarded as contributions to general scientific knowledge about the effects of social interventions. That is, by giving us generalizable knowl- edge about what kinds of program features or variables in a social intervention represent the "active ingredients," or are demonstrably more effective than definable alternatives, these findings make at least some contribution to under- standing as well as to decisions.

IV. DECISION VS. UNDERSTANDING

There is general agreement among the writers on eval- uation and evaluative research that it is not sufficient to determine that a given program was carried out as planned without also determining its impact in terms of defined goals or outcomes. To the extent that we are concerned only with "whether" a program fulfilled a need, and not "why" it succeeded or failed, outcome evaluation may be sufficient as well as necessary. However, as we suggested in Chapter 1 (see Section II-D), to determine whether the outcome was good or bad without any investigation of the reasons for success or failure of the process is not likely to be suf- ficient for improving the process or the output of the pro- gram. To meet either of these needs requires that we be concerned with the mechanism of the process as well as its output, and with comparative as well as absolute assessment of outcomes. Key issues are 1) whether one's concept of evaluation extends to include these questions of causation, and 2) whether or not good decisions are possible in the absence of process understanding.

Program assessment can be designed either to establish detailed causal relationships or simply to ascertain prog- ress toward social objectives in terms of the outcomes pro- duced. The practical relevance of the former kind of pur- pose lies in its potential to improve the basis for planning future programs. On the other hand, the latter purpose, of describing or assessing the effectiveness of a particular program as such, is sometimes a worthwhile, even though inherently limited, objective.

Both points of view are widely represented. Some writers and practitioners seem to think of evaluation only as the process of forming a value judgment as to the overall worth of a project, usually on a one-time basis, by inde- pendent assessors, and related to some predetermined set of goals and objectives. Others would prefer to think of eval- uation as an iterative or evolutionary process designed to produce continuous improvement. Basically the latter posi- tion, known as the "evolutionary" or "formative" approach, is that of the producer rather than of the consumer: it emphasizes the place of evaluation in program development and management. Those who espouse this point of view main- tain that "the basic question is not, 'Is this program any good?' but, 'How can we improve our intervention in this field?'"[1] On the other hand, those who maintain that eval-

---

[1]This statement is from the prepared discussion by John Conrad recorded at the 1973 Battelle conference (see Fore- word).

uation is literally the placing of a "value" on a program, hold that we should not "extend the term evaluation to cover all the important research investigations which are needed to make good planning decisions."[1] The issue is whether we define evaluation as a detailed assessment of a specific program or as an inherent part of an iterative feedback process. Neither model is likely to be applicable or defensible under all circumstances.

Whether or not good decisions are possible in the absence of process understanding is a more fundamental question. The answer may depend on the relative importance of the validity of information on a particular outcome versus that of the value attached to that outcome. The answer also will depend on the extent to which applicable theory or technology is available. It will further depend on the degree to which the evaluator is to rely on externally imposed concepts of "value," and on whether he is dealing with an established product or with a social intervention.

These considerations relate directly to a distinction between the "scientist" and the "evaluator." If science is primarily concerned with moving from facts to understanding, program evaluation, in the present context at least, is mainly concerned with proceeding from facts to decisions. To the extent that understanding improves the prediction of outcomes, it also aids in the decision process. Further, understanding or theory may enable the manager to be "proactive" rather than "reactive," in that it may enable him to anticipate the kind of action needed. Evaluation in this

---

[1] Michael Scriven, at the 1973 Battelle conference.

context is a planned and conscious attempt to take actions consistent with our state of knowledge of the consequences, and to modify those actions based on the effects produced. This implies that we can distinguish the effects produced by our actions from the normal dynamic state of a typical social system.

It is difficult to visualize a one-shot process of setting goals, establishing criteria, measuring performance, and reaching a decision on the outcome. This may be feasible if we are simply monitoring input, but it is hard to visualize in terms of response and goal definition. At this state, we must postulate some type of convergence, and hence an iterative order in which we go through the process of establishing both goals and criteria. This emphasizes the need to convey to administrators and planners a clear consciousness of an evaluation process which relates hard evidence about outcomes to broad, conceptual goals and objectives. This formative process and the associated feedback mechanisms help to insure implementation, and also imply that by the time an effective evaluative process is developed, it will stand a good chance of being understood and appreciated, rather than arousing suspicion and misunderstanding.

V.   OTHER CONSIDERATIONS CONCERNING IMPLEMENTATION

A.   *ROLE OF THE EVALUATOR*

In comments made to the authors following the 1973 Battelle conference, it was pointed out that there were many different conceptions of the role of the evaluator among those present at the conference. One of the ways in which roles were differentiated included the following three categories:[1]

1. The Technician. His role is to carry out the evaluation in the exact terms proposed by the sponsor, who is responsible for goal definition, process specification, and related matters. In terms of analogy to a manufacturing process, he performs acceptance inspection based on established performance requirements.

2. The Technician/Policy Consultant. The evaluator helps the sponsor and other interested parties clarify their objectives and values, in addition to carrying out a technical role. He not only helps in designing the evaluation but also interprets value/policy implications.

3. The Advocate. His role is to represent the interests of specific groups or constituencies, including those not directly involved.

A somewhat similar formulation of the evaluator's role is implied by the four types of information feedback described by Katz (in Chapter 7 and also in personal correspondence): 1) assessment of impact upon the immediate and direct target; 2) assessment of progress towards long-range goals; 3) intelligence about secondary effects upon environment and society; and 4) evaluation of effects of organizational activity upon members of the organization.

Katz points out that the widest use of feedback has been of the first type, in which an agency or organization

---

[1]This particular formulation follows a suggestion made by Donald Warwick at the 1973 conference.

seeks some direct information about its product--e.g., the number of cars manufactured and the number sold, or the number of engineers graduated and the number placed in jobs. Similarly, the "technician" evaluator role, the first one identified above, is the one most commonly observed. In considering the dual role of the evaluator implied by the second role description, the problem is whether or not both the knowledge about value/policy implications and the objectivity required for this role can be achieved by a single evaluation. The values of the evaluator, sponsor, and others shape the questions that are asked, the data recorded, and the interpretation of the "facts." The possibility of conflict with respect to these values increases as the advocacy role becomes more permanent.

While, as pointed out in Chapter 1 (Section II-D), we are concerned with the functional role of the evaluator, we are also concerned with his relation to and responsibility for the purpose of the evaluation. At least one function of an evaluation must be to assign a "value" to the observed outcomes. The evaluator's role may extend to that of a middleman, who not only observes outcomes but feeds back information (not necessarily the same information) to both program director and program sponsor.[1] But as the level of decision becomes higher, the scope broader, and the impact

---

[1] One of the examples of this role was pointed out by Thomas Cook during the discussion of Mosteller's presentation at the 1973 Battelle conference. (See Chapter 2, Section IV-F.) Cook noted the difference between considering costs of patient care on a short-term basis versus considering them on a long-term basis.

greater, the information on which to base a decision tends
to become less complete.[1] Hence we are led to the possibility that it may be "unrealistic to expect that most evaluations can evaluate programs."[2] We may be reduced to a
series of evaluations based on program components rather
than an evaluation of the program as a whole. The difficulty, but also the importance, of obtaining optimal decisions under such conditions has been frequently noted in the
context of systems analysis.

B. USE AND MISUSE OF EVALUATIVE RESEARCH FINDINGS

We may agree that a primary purpose of conducting evaluative research is to improve program operations in order to
achieve planned objectives of the program more effectively.
But evaluative research is of little use unless the findings
are translated into specific recommendations and actions to
make programs more effective.

In practice, however, there are often serious problems
in getting the findings actually implemented. Some findings
may not be implemented because they do not provide conclusive enough evidence to support the changes that are recommended. The purpose of discussing "harder" methods of impact evaluation, such as controlled randomized field studies, is to point up ways to obtain more valid findings, and

---

[1]Robyn Dawes, at the 1973 Battelle conference, commenting on
the presentation by Edwards.

[2]Thomas Cook, at the 1973 conference.

thereby increase the confidence with which administrators may use them as a basis for program decisions.

However, other reasons why findings from evaluative research are sometimes not utilized should also be noted. Not all evaluation is conducted primarily to improve the program. Formal evaluation is usually required by both internal and external sources of program funds, and there may be a tendency to regard the research component as something which merely enhances the professional or scientific prestige of the program. Under these circumstances, results are not likely to be taken very seriously when important decisions are being made by program officials. This problem may decline, however, as the program matures and the research itself becomes more useful.

There are other functions which "evaluation" may be made to serve. Selected data can be used to show aspects of a program in a favorable light, or to cover up parts of the program which have failed by purposely avoiding objective forms of evaluative data. "Evaluation" may be desired to justify the cancellation of a project, sometimes for reasons unrelated to its effect on program objectives. If evaluative research is to be effectively used for legitimate purposes, it is imperative for those who manage and conduct the research to plan in advance how it will be possible to utilize objective findings in improving the program. Where projects are successful in getting the recommendations implemented, both the research personnel and the program personnel appear to adhere to the basic assumption that research is conducted to improve the program and to aid future planning for the benefit of the consumer of the program. Successful projects place a heavy emphasis upon translating program needs into researchable projects, and then making sure that the findings are interpreted into simple, step-by-step program changes. The researchers thus make it easier for program officials to use their findings.

VI. SOME SUGGESTED CONCLUSIONS AND RECOMMENDATIONS

Among the methodological and/or policy recommendations implied or stated at various points in this volume, several may be restated or recapitulated here.[1]

A. *MANAGEMENT AND ORGANIZATIONAL ASPECTS OF EVALUATION*

1. Planning and initiation of evaluation activities, including design of studies and procedures for collection of data, should be initiated <u>at the very outset</u> of program

---

[1]About a third of the statements in this section are taken directly from comments made, as identified in subsequent footnotes, by authors and other participants at the 1973 Battelle conference (see Preface). Another third of the statements come from the list of recommendations presented in Section VI of Chapter 5, deriving from sources there acknowledged. The remainder represent the gist of remarks made by more than one individual at various points during the conference and/or in chapters of this volume. The present limited sample of suggested conclusions and recommendations that emerged from the conference and the volume is not an attempt at a comprehensive or balanced summary that would represent a complete consensus of all the contributors.

planning, rather than being deferred until after the program is already under way.

2.   Evaluators must be called in before experimental and control groups are assigned and possibilities for scientific control are washed down the drain. Otherwise, resources are wasted.

3.   In order to avoid real or apparent bias, the individuals responsible for program operation should generally not have executive responsibility for summative evaluation studies. When outside, independent evaluators are employed, however, the indices and procedures they utilize should be made known as early as possible to program management or operation personnel, so that there may be an opportunity to correct any real or perceived unfairness in the evaluative procedures.

4.   Operational or adaptive feedback should go directly into the ongoing operation and also to the level above it in the system. Systemic or policy level feedback should go to the level or levels for which the research is most appropriate and also to the top management level. Thus a research director should play a dual role as a member of management and as the head of his own research unit.[1]

5.   The adaptive or formative evaluation function should be recognized as important at the highest organizational levels, with the director of the system reporting directly to a high-level administrator.[2]

---

[1] Daniel Katz, at the 1973 Battelle conference.

[2] Peter Rossi, at the 1973 conference.

6. Attempts should be made to educate policy makers concerning the great technical advantages of true experiments in terms of both the definitiveness of results obtainable and the feasibility of setting up such experiments, particularly when a preliminary try-out or pilot-test of a program can be conducted.

7. Decision makers should be saying, wherever possible, "I won't make a decision on such weak evidence; we've got to get more evidence." Without this emphasis, evaluators are doing evaluation a disservice in the long run, since decision makers will become satisfied with poor data and not demand good data.[1]

B.   *ASCERTAINING PROGRAM IMPACTS*

1. Every effort should be made to assess the effectiveness of programs by the use of true field experiments (randomized controlled field trials), using randomized assignment of appropriate units. The experiments should be of sufficient precision to reveal any effects that are large enough to be of practical consequence.

2. It is desirable to have experiments compare more than one treatment, not only to provide information on which to base immediate choice among alternatives that differ in effectiveness, but also to afford an accumulating basis of information for predicting the success of planned future program treatments.

3. Although it is possible to come up with ways to compensate for the problems of quasi-experiments through

---

[1]John Gilbert, at the 1973 conference.

statistical analysis techniques, these may exaggerate the effects. It is easier, less expensive, and more conclusive to randomize.[1]

4. There is a need to determine when experiments are not required--when it is possible to tolerate the uncertainty resulting from other bases for causal inference.[2]

5. Greater use should be made of formative evaluation, in which not only informal observation but also "hard data" on impacts of preliminary stages or forms of the program are fed back into the program production and operation process, so as to afford an empirical basis for improving the program's operation.

6. "Hard" data are most needed for the summative evaluation that is called for at major decision points, where the total effectiveness of a program over an appreciable period of time is involved, and where information on the magnitude of impact a program has produced will provide a major input to higher-level decisions concerning a program's continuation, expansion, curtailment, or basic modification.

7. A new program should be tried out initially only on a pilot basis, with a few selected groups, so that it will be possible, before its wider application, to make changes that are pointed up by the initial evaluative data. Limitation of initial tryout to a few pilot groups also insures the potential availability of equivalent control groups needed to properly assess program impact.

----

[1] Donald Campbell, at the 1973 conference.

[2] Thomas Cook, at the 1973 conference.

8. A period of "planned variation," in which different programs are installed in different systems to learn something about the complexities of implementation, should be followed by large-scale experiments which compare the effectiveness of programs surviving the pilot period.[1]

9. Experiments and studies of program effectiveness should make stronger efforts to use, as measures of outcome, the kinds of observations that can be analyzed in relation to cost-effectiveness or cost-benefit. For such an analysis, measures of input cost and output effect need to be expressed in comparable terms whenever possible.

10. Various descriptive "process" features of program operation, which experienced observers regard as generally important for programs to operate effectively, should be considered as working criteria both for evaluating the current operation of an ongoing program and for assessing the plans for proposed programs. Such guidelines may be thought of as a basis for judging predicted impacts or effects.

11. Wider use should be made of estimation and confidence limits to show the range of the probable size of effects, rather than merely using "significance" tests, which show only the likely existence of program effects.

C. *USE OF INFORMATION FOR DECISION MAKING*

1. Although it is difficult to separate assessment of effects from assignment of value (most evaluations are sponsored by individuals who have an interest in the result, or else they wouldn't be doing an evaluation in the first

---

[1] Frederick Mosteller, at the 1973 conference.

place), such a separation is valuable since it does not allow confounding of doubts about value-assignment with questions about the "facts" of assessment.[1]

2. Before moving from a "fact" to a value judgment about its worth, one must be sure of the "fact." In many instances, this is not done. For example, when an analysis shows no positive results, it may be claimed that "circumstantial evidence shows ...."[2]

3. Producing a good effect is not enough to justify the "goodness" of its cause (that is, the end does not justify the means). The cost of the cause might be greater than that of an alternative cause, or the cause might have other, overriding negative effects.[3]

4. Systematic schemata such as have been described by Edwards and Guttentag (Chapter 6) should be tried out and applied as a tool in decision making, particularly for high-level policy decisions and where relevant inputs can be obtained. The function of such systematic analysis is to relate the worth of outcomes, or the "stakes" involved in multiple outcomes, to the available evidence and supplementary judgments concerning the likely realization of these outcomes.

5. Inputs to such decision algorithms should include the most dependable data obtainable for each input--e.g., experimental field data for immediate program impacts--even though other inputs, such as estimates of utilities and of longer-term impacts, may necessarily be less reliable.

[1,2]Thomas Cook, at the 1973 conference

[3]Michael Scriven, at the 1973 conference

VII. SOURCES OF IDEAS

Regardless of how the place of evaluation is viewed in relation to the decision process, there seems to be a growing concern with the relationship of the evaluator or of evaluative procedures to exploration and innovation, as well as to confirmation and decision. More and more, people seem to be concerned with how we get the ideas necessary to improve our social intervention rather than with how we keep score. Three sources of ideas have been suggested:[1] theory; empirical sources, particularly exploratory data analysis; and creative people.

Some people would question whether any of these, particularly the first two, is in fact a very good source of ideas at present. One would conclude from Chapter 2 that it has been difficult to determine those innovations or interventions which will solve or ameliorate social problems. On the other hand, there is obviously much to be gained from the use of evaluative data both to confirm relationships and to explore possible hypotheses. Confirmation implies that the impacts measured can be directly (and, hopefully, unequivocally) related to hypothesized causes. To the extent that a program is successful, the model on which it is based tends to receive confirmation and moves closer to being part of the theory available for prediction and extension. Exploratory analysis implies a search for potential causes, for ideas, which may be confirmed through additional experiments or experience and which may lead to unifying theoret-

---

[1]Thomas Cook, at the 1973 conference.

ical concepts. Exploratory analysis uses models as an investigative tool in the sense that prompted Wilk and Tukey (1965) to say, in effect, that models are fine if one doesn't believe them. But regardless of the difficulties, it would seem that evaluation, and particularly evaluation based on social experiment, must be an important source of the innovative ideas relevant to answering the basic question posed by Rivlin:[1] What will happen _if_ ...?

The feasibility of conducting randomized field trials to answer this question in terms of the immediate and direct impacts of any particular program tried out experimentally is well illustrated in the case of the randomized trials described in Chapters 2 and 5 and a number of additional examples of educational programs listed in the Appendix to Chapter 3. Difficulty and cost of conducting such field trials is easily exaggerated (e.g., Chapter 6, page 444). When the question of cost is being considered it should be properly analyzed. A large part of the cost sometimes attributed to an "experiment" is the cost of developing and implementing the treatment or innovation to be tried out. While this may sometimes be very great the added cost of arranging that the conditions of its tryout permit clean-cut comparison with a control group, suitably selected, can in many cases be relatively minor.

---

[1]"The new social experiments ... grew out of the real quandaries and dilemmas of policy making. The experiments were responses to the frustration of those considering new policies who found themselves unable to answer the basic question: How do you know what will happen?" (Rivlin, 1973, p. 77)

However, the uncertainties implied by Rivlin's question transcend the more elementary issue of determining through controlled field trial what immediately demonstrable impacts have been produced by any given treatment or innovation. At least two further, more difficult questions arise, which involve predicting future outcomes rather than only measurement and attribution of presently observable ones. First, what will be the longer-term effects of this program innovation--effects that are not expected to materialize until after the point in time when decisions about continuation or alteration of the program under test must be made? Second, what are the program's critical components or aspects--those "active ingredients" of the treatment that can be specified as primarily responsible for its successes and shortcomings? Knowledge or inference as to these is clearly important as a basis for deciding what program features it is necessary to preserve in the continuation or replication of the program and what features must be modified in attempting to improve it. And, to go a step further, we should like to have as good leads as can be got from experience with the program to date as to what kind of modifications to try in its further implementation or evolution.

The explication of these latter uncertainties clearly does not flow directly from data on the direct and short-term impact of any particular treatment. However, the question of what to preserve or change may be illuminated if we have compared alternative programs or treatment variations experimentally. But in the long run we must try to go beyond ad hoc empiricism to achieve the understanding that can help us to know what changes to make and to predict both the short-term and the long-term impacts in advance. Perhaps it is in this respect that new ideas and approaches by social scientists seem most acutely needed. Innovative exploratory and supporting research to improve the state of the are must therefore be made, whenever possible, a concomitant of practical field trials that are carried out for the more immediate purpose of providing the impact data that are to be used as an input to current programmatic decisions.

This brings us to a final comment on the relationship between the quality and comprehensiveness of impact data and the role of such data in decision processes such as are considered by Edwards and Guttentag in Chapter 6. The greatest contribution of such algorithmization of the decision process may reside, first, in the way it forces explicit attention to the need for better ways to come to grips with the positive and negative values to be attached to any given program outcomes and, second, in the emphasis it will place on improving ways to integrate diverse sources of relevant information in arriving at programmatic decisions.

But we should like to emphasize that decision paradigms and utility analysis are to be viewed in perspective as complements not as substitutes for the hard data on program impact that can normally be best obtained from randomized experimental field comparisons. A disservice would be done to clear perception of the total needs of program evaluation if the argument for decision-theoretic approaches were to be regarded as weakening the case for both the feasibility and the superiority of randomized field trials for providing dependable impact data. The cogency of such data as an input to program decisions at both the policy and the operating level will increase further as better methods are developed for predicting long-term impacts from short-term data.

B
C
D 8
E 9
F 0
G 1
H 2
I 3
J 4